The Logic of International Restructuring

The world economy faces an ongoing international restructuring race between industrial complexes. An industrial complex consists of a large 'core' firm and its suppliers, workers, distributors, dealers, financiers and governments. The dynamism of the relationships between the core firm and these bargaining partners is seen as a major determinant of the international restructuring race.

In this book, Winfried Ruigrok and Rob van Tulder address many current debates on topics such as 'post-Fordism', 'globalisation' and 'lean production'. They also identify a number of rival internationalisation strategies that have been adopted by different companies. Moreover, they present an abundance of new as well as historical data on the world's one hundred largest core companies. These data show that none of the largest core firms is truly 'global' or 'borderless', and that virtually all of them in their history have benefited decisively from governmental trade or industrial policies.

The authors offer a highly interdisciplinary effort to link three previously isolated debates on industrial restructuring, globalisation and international trade policies. *The Logic of International Restructuring* is aimed at a wide academic, post-graduate and professional audience working in the areas of business, economics, organisational studies and international relations.

Dr Winfried Ruigrok and **Dr Rob van Tulder** are both working at the Rotterdam School of Management, Erasmus University, Rotterdam. Winifried Ruigrok has previously worked at the European Commission and is currently a visiting researcher at the University of Warwick. Rob van Tulder is also associated to the University of Amsterdam and is the co-author of *European Multinationals in Core Technologies* (1988).

The Logic of International Restructuring

Winfried Ruigrok and Rob van Tulder

London and New York

First published 1995
by Routledge
11 New Fetter Lane, London EC4P 4EE

Simultaneously published in the USA and Canada
by Routledge
29 West 35th Street, New York, NY 10001

© 1995 Winfried Ruigrok and Rob van Tulder

Typeset in Times by Datix International, Bungay, Suffolk
Printed and bound in Great Britain by TJ Press (Padstow), Cornwall

British Library Cataloguing in Publication Data
A catalogue record for this book is available from the British Library

Library of Congress Cataloguing in Publication Data
A catalogue record for this book has been requested

ISBN 0–415–12238–4 (hbk)
ISBN 0–415–12239–2 (pbk)

Contents

Figures and tables

FIGURES

TABLES

Preface

This book originated from a fascination with international economic and political change, but at the same time from a worry about the weak analytical or even ideological basis of leading approaches to these transformations. In this book, we discuss a variety of approaches to international restructuring. We argue that many of these claims have been put forward on a very limited empirical basis, which makes it impossible to generalise the often fancy concepts to other cases. Authors who nevertheless choose to make such generalisations risk losing their academic credibility and embarking on an ideological venture.

It has been the aim of this study to contribute to an integrated and interdisciplinary framework to analyse the dynamics of International Political Economy. We cross disciplinary boundaries, trying to do justice to 'international complexity' and to the variety of actors shaping this 'complexity'. We have obtained elements from the debates on industrial restructuring, internationalisation of production and international trade and have integrated them into one analytical framework. This framework is to serve primarily as a qualitative tool with a heuristic function, to be supported by quantitative data. It builds on an eclectic presentation of approaches from disciplines such as international relations (systems approach, regime theory, dependency approach), economics (institutional economics, transaction cost approach, industrial organisation, economic geography, regulation school, Schumpetarian economics), business administration (resource dependency approach, strategic management) and approaches coming from political sciences and sociology (neo-corporatism, government–business relations, game and bargaining theory).

Our framework has its own deficiencies, and we are keenly aware of them. Initiating such an interdisciplinary approach involves certain risks, since it is almost impossible to master all their 'ins' and 'outs'. In spite of that, we have taken up the challenge, and hope we do not provide another case of 'intellectual overstretch'. (In a follow-up study, we shall apply the framework to analyse international restructuring processes in the world car industry.)

This study – like some of its forerunners – has been supported financially by various organisations: the Forecasting and Assessment of Science and Technology (FAST/Monitor) programme of the Commission of the European Union, the Dutch Organisation for Scientific Research (NWO/ZWO), the Netherlands Organisation for Technology Assessment (NOTA), the Faculty of Political and Socio-Cultural Sciences (PSCW) of the University of Amsterdam, and the Rotterdam School of Management (RSM), Erasmus University Rotterdam.

Over the past years, a number of people have been a source of continuous support and inspiration. Observing our academic and personal struggles, Gerd Junne has never ceased to encourage us to finish this study. It is due to the interdisciplinary nature of his academic interests that we 'dared' undertake such a broad endeavour in the first place. In 1983, Gerd Junne together with Annemieke Roobeek, Guido Ruivenkamp and one of the present authors initiated an interdisciplinary study project to investigate the 'international restructuring race' (Junne, 1984a). This project has led to a number of studies. Annemieke Roobeek dealt with (amongst other things) the role of governments in a large number of OECD countries in the creation and diffusion of core technologies (Roobeek, 1987, 1990), Guido Ruivenkamp focused on the impact of biotechnology in the agro-industrial production chain (Ruivenkamp, 1989), while Rob van Tulder and Gerd Junne examined the strategies of multinationals in core technologies (1988). Looking back at the insights gained and the large number of stimulating discussions held over so many years, we regret that there are so many financial, organisational and personal obstacles to embarking on these kinds of interdisciplinary and longer-term studies.

Over the years, our students at the Rotterdam School of Management, as well as managers participating in 'executive programmes' have been a source of stimulating and critical feedback to our approach. The present book has gained a lot from their insights. During the work on this particular study we have also profited from many direct contacts in industry and industry associations, in local organisations, in national governments, trade unions and in the Commission of the European Union, as well as from the help of good friends and colleagues at various universities. In random order, the following people have been very helpful: Philie Viehoff, Toru Nagatsuka, Peter van Ostaijen, Marc Ledoux, Takayoshi Amenomori, Peter van Bergeijk, Clara Eugenia Garcia, Ben Dankbaar, Kurt Hoffman, Michael Hobday, Kevin Morgan, Hans Krikke, Peter Unterweger, John Wilson, Arthur Karl, F. Saelens, Françoise Warrant, Manuel Santiago dos Santos, Jean-Michelle Corre, Riccardo Petrella, Werner Wobbe, Jean-Cristian Remond, Frans van den Bosch, Ash Amin, Dorien Flamand, Jan-Willem van Gelder, Hans Schenk, Leo van Eerden, Tetsumo Abo, John Zysman, Roger Tooze, John Dunning, Wout Buitelaar, Dany Jacobs, Peter Katzenstein, Robert Gilpin, Walter Zegveld, Wim Hulsink, and Jan Lambooy.

Geert Baven assisted us in writing an intermediary study on the car industry for the European Commission (FAST-group). Giorgio Schutte gave us feedback on the sections dealing with trade union organisation. Special thanks go to Frédérique Sachwald and Ronen Palan who, as early readers of the manuscript, were so kind as to provide us with many detailed and insightful comments. Wil Sommeling supported us in upgrading the layout of some of the figures in this book. Brian Gross, Joost Knigge and Stefanie ten Napel acted as assistants during the final stage of the book. We are very grateful for the support and encouragement of so many people.

Amsterdam/Rotterdam, June 1995

Abbreviations and acronyms

APEC	Asia-Pacific Economic Cooperation Forum
ASEAN	Association of South East Asian Nations
BMFT	German Federal Ministry of Technology
BRITE	Basic Research in Industrial Technologies in Europe
CEO	Chief executive officer
CFDT	Confédération Française Démocratique du Travail
CFTC	Confédération Française des Travailleurs Chrétiens
CGC	Confédération Française de l'Encadrement
CGT	Confédération Générale du Travail
CIM	Computer-integrated manufacturing
DDL	Diadic division of labour
ECAT	Emergency Committee for American Trade
ERT	European Round Table of Industrialists
ESPRIT	European Strategic Programme for Research and Development in Information Technology
EUREKA	European Research Coordination Agency
EU	European Union
FAST/Monitor	Forecasting and Assessment of Science and Technology programme of the Commission of the European Union
FDI	Foreign direct investment
FIOM	Italian metalworkers' union
GATT	General Agreement on Tariffs and Trade
GEC	General Electric Company (UK)
GNP	Gross national product
IBRD	International Bank for Reconstruction and Development (World Bank)

IMF	International Monetary Fund/International Metalworkers' Federation
IMVP	International Motor Vehicle Program
JECC	Japan Electronic Computer Company
JIT	Just-in-time
LTA	Long-Term Arrangement (Regarding International Trade in Textiles)
MAP	Manufacturing automation protocol
MMC	Monopolies and Mergers Commission (UK)
MFA	Multi-Fibre Arrangement
MITI	Japanese Ministry of International Trade and Industry
MNC	Multinational corporation
MNE	Multinational enterprise
NAFTA	North American Free Trade Agreement
NASA	National Aeronautics and Space Administration (USA)
NIDL	New international division of labour
NIE	Newly-industrialised economy
NOTA	Netherlands Organisation for Technology Assessment
NWO/ZWO	Dutch Organisation for Scientific Research
OECD	Organisation for Economic Cooperation and Development
OEM	Original equipment manufacturing
OPEC	Organisation of Petroleum Exporting Countries
PSCW	Faculty of Political and Socio-Cultural Sciences, University of Amsterdam
R&D	Research and development
RACE	Research and Development in Advanced Communications in Europe
RDL	Regional division of labour
RSM	Rotterdam School of Management, Erasmus University
SCAP	Supreme Command for the Allied Powers (Japan)
SMEs	Small and medium-sized enterprises
SPC	Statistical process control
STA	Short-Term Arrangement (Regarding International Trade in Textiles)
TNC	Transnational corporation

TUC	Trades Union Congress (UK)
UAW	United Auto Workers (USA)
UN	United Nations
UNCTAD	United Nations Conference on Trade and Development
UNCTC	United Nations Centre on Transnational Corporations
VCR	Video cassette recorder
VER	Voluntary export restraint
VLSI	Very large scale integration
WTO	World Trade Organisation

JOURNALS

AT	*Automotive News*
ATB	*AT Beleidsbrief Internationaal* (Newsletter from the Dutch Ministry of Economic Affairs)
BW	*Business Week*
Econ	*The Economist*
ESB	*Economisch Statistische Berichten*
EW	*Electronics Weekly*
FEER	*Far Eastern Economic Review*
FT	*Financial Times*
IMF News	*International Meltalworkers' Federation News*
IS	*Internationale Spectator*
IST	*Issues in Science and Technology*
NYT	*New York Times*
Vk	*De Volkskrant* (Amsterdam, Dutch daily newspaper)
WSJE	*Wall Street Journal Europe*

1 Introduction:

Appraising three major debates

1.1 THE PRACTICE OF BEST-PRACTICE

The 1970s and 1980s have seen a profound restructuring of the industrialised economies. North American and European observers have long regarded restructuring as a temporary stage during which the industrialised economies had to adjust to lower growth and a changing international setting with some 'new' players, such as Japan, the Asian 'newly industrialised economies' (NIEs) and perhaps a few oil-producing countries. The economic recession of the early 1990s indicated that worldwide competition has not only intensified, but that continuing and even more painful restructuring could be ahead. After dismissing over 100,000 workers each, and after gaining record profits by the late 1980s, giant corporations such as General Motors and IBM lost billions of US dollars only a few years later. Leading and formerly capital-rich European national champions like Philips and Daimler-Benz became absorbed by laborious reorganisations trying to restore competitiveness, while Japanese banks and conglomerates were struggling with the aftermath of the 'bubble economy'. Meanwhile, South East Asian firms continued to capture market niches in spite of slack worldwide growth, while Eastern European firms had little choice but to flood the world steel and chemicals markets.

In times of growing international turbulence, people tend to feel that the world has grown more complex or less manageable than before. This feeling essentially expresses that forces have come up whose strategies and objectives are not (yet) fully understood, and that old blueprints no longer seem to serve. In such times, there is always a grateful market for those who translate the 'new complexity' into simple formulae and unambiguous recommendations. The debate on international restructuring continues to be obscured by best-practice examples of commercial success ('how did they do it?'). On the basis of isolated case studies of particular regions, national economies or individual firms, academics have alternately argued that 'flexibility', 'team concepts', 'quality control', 'clustering' of firms, 'lean enterprise', 'high-tech', 'globalisation' (the list goes on and on), have been singularly conducive to competitive advantage. As an indication of the state of confusion in Western industrialised economies, case studies have obtained such 'legitimacy' that sweeping generalisations inferred from them are eagerly accepted and seldom questioned. As an essential requirement for the successful marketing of their books, the inventors of such fashionable concepts share a highly optimistic and reassuring view on the future of industrial society. If we are to believe some of these prophets, the world is on the threshold to be fully 'interdependent', controversies of old will become obsolete, and a shining future awaits us.

This book aims to shed light on the patterns by which large, primarily manufacturing, firms are trying to manage domestic and international restructuring, and on the type of 'solutions' produced by these patterns. We shall illustrate that many (best-practice) 'solutions' stem from a specific interest. This book tries to explore and assemble the building blocks of an alternative framework of analysis based on two assumptions. Firstly, it is assumed that not just firms but a multitude of other actors as well are involved in restructuring processes. After all, goods do not descend as 'manna from heaven', but because they are produced by living people who, depending on, for instance, skill and unionisation levels, influence the organisation of production or the diffusion of new technologies. Likewise, governments provide conditions and services such as a legal and a defence system, infrastructure, etc. A second assumption in this book is that firms are not only seeking profits, but that they may also seek to influence the *rules* of the game of profit-making. For instance, a campaign to restrict foreign competition may enhance profits, even if no firm would identify such a campaign as its core business. As an organising principle, the book will be based on three major debates which took place during the 1980s and early 1990s: on industrial restructuring, on globalisation, and on international trade policies.

1.2 THREE MAJOR DEBATES

The first debate centred on the nature of industrial restructuring. Restructuring refers to changes in the way goods and services are being developed, designed, produced and distributed, i.e. to changes in companies' organisation structures and the technologies they use. Restructuring has major spatial and cross-border consequences. Restructuring is affected by policies and strategies of various stakeholders such as governments, supplying firms and workers, and in turn affects these stakeholders differently.

One of the most innovative contributions to the debate on restructuring has been made by Michael Piore and Charles Sabel (1984). Taking Alfred Marshall's industrial districts as a framework for analysis, Piore and Sabel proclaimed the rise of a second industrial divide, stating that craft and mass production could be reunited into a new synthesis, which eventually could resolve the economic crisis. Piore and Sabel argued that the rise of so-called flexible specialisation networks of interdependent smaller firms, for instance in the Italian region of Emilia Romagna or the German region of Baden-Württemberg, could serve as a best-practice model applicable to other industries and countries. Following this logic, others contended that flexible specialisation networks demanded high labour skills, leading to more worker autonomy and closer cooperation between end producers and their suppliers (Friedman, 1988: 356). In this way, flexible manufacturing would be a stage beyond standardised (Fordist) production. At the same time, two leading German researchers openly speculated about the end of the division of labour – so prominent a part of the Fordist and Taylorist production organisation (Kern and Schumann, 1984).

A second body of literature addressed, in particular, the technological aspects of industrial restructuring. The deficiencies of the traditional neo-classical approach brought economists like Richard Nelson and Sydney Winter (1982) to consider technological change as an endogenous rather than an exogenous factor of economic change. They presented what they called an 'evolutionary theory' of economic change and developed the concept of technological trajectories. Departing from a reappraisal of Schumpeter's conception of long waves of technological and economic transformation, Christopher Freeman, Giovanni Dosi, Luc Soete and others (Dosi *et al.*, 1988) argued that industrial societies are about to enter the next long wave of economic growth, better known as the fifth *Kondratieff*. The rise and decline of a Kondratieff wave is supposed to take place every half a century and heralds a phase in which economies face major structural change (cf. Freeman, 1982: 207ff). According to these evolutionary approaches, the fifth Kondratieff will lead to a renewed period of economic growth and prosperity as soon as institutional and technological change are successfully 'matched'.

A third approach, based on a multi-million dollar study by James Womack, Daniel Jones and Daniel Roos on the world car industry, has claimed that lean production 'combines the advantages of craft and mass production, while avoiding the high costs of the former and the rigidity of the latter' (1990: 13). In some respects, their type of reasoning is comparable to that of Piore and Sabel. Both analyses claim an opportunity to reintegrate craft and mass production, and both draw their arguments from a specific best-practice example. Womack *et al.* have analysed the Toyota Production System in great detail and even suggest further improvements to this system which 'can be applied equally in every industry across the globe' (1990: 8). Such conversion to lean enterprise 'will have a profound effect on human society – it will truly change the world' (1990: 8).

Many analyses of structural transformation of industry and its social and political dimensions have taken the crisis of Fordism as their starting-point. Several authors have presented their concepts as a post-Fordist organisation model. The merits of this concept will be appraised in Chapter 2.

The second major debate through the 1980s has focused on the globalisation of technology, competition and finances. The 1980s had been dominated by unprecedented flows of foreign direct investments, mergers and acquisitions and strategic alliances, as well as by ever-fiercer competition from Japanese and South East Asian firms. The former director of McKinsey Japan, Kenichi Ohmae, who became the best-known proponent of the globalisation thesis, argued that these developments would constitute a new era in international business. Companies' and customers' horizons would stretch 'beyond national borders' – they would become true global citizens. More serious authors have followed this logic. Robert Reich, the former US industrial policy advocate and Labour Secretary of the Clinton administration, has claimed that it is becoming impossible to pursue an industrial policy at a national level, because in the coming century 'there will be no national products or technologies, no national corporations, no national industries. There will no longer be national economies' (1991: 3). The globalisation discussion has also produced studies and views on the impact of new technologies and the effects of globalisation on developing economies (Ernst, 1990), and on national and supranational governments (Petrella, 1989).

The globalisation hypothesis has also been criticised, however. David Gordon (1988: 25) has argued that the current worldwide production shifts are not particularly large by historical standards. Patel and Pavitt (1991) and Pavitt (1992) have suggested that globalisation may be a partial phenomenon at most, since most firms still concentrate their basic R&D in their national bases. The myths and realities of globalisation will be discussed in Chapters 6 and 7.

The third major debate of the 1980s centred on international trade theory and policies. As the significance of firms from outside Western Europe and North America entering the international markets increased, the strategic importance of international trade, and of determining its rules, increased likewise. Taking into consideration the different mix of industrial and trade policies underlying the Japanese industrial growth, a group of US trade theorists developed their models of strategic trade policy. These models argued that, under certain conditions, national welfare could be enhanced at the expense of other economies if a government temporarily supported a domestic industry (Krugman, 1986; Brander and Spencer, 1985). It took free trade theorists until the late 1980s to collect ammunition to counter the arguments in favour of strategic trade policies (Richardson, 1989; Stegemann, 1989).

A more empirical stream of analysis has focused on the formation of trade barriers, and on the (f)actors preventing the rise of these barriers (cf. Milner, 1988; Destler and Odell, 1987). According to conventional wisdom, firms with strong international interests would tend to favour open international trade routes. One of the recurring claims has therefore been that the internationalisation and/or globalisation of firms would promote a liberal international trade regime (cf. Bhagwati, 1988: 71). The debate on international trade policy and the impact of international firms on the formation or prevention of trade barriers will be the subject of Chapter 9.

1.3 TWO MAJOR DEFICIENCIES

Examining the three major debates on restructuring, globalisation and international trade a bit closer, one may observe two striking parallels. Firstly, one finds surprisingly few cross-references from one debate to another, or from one discipline to another, even if many of the issues are clearly connected. In fact, even within one debate, the various sub-debates often appear to have coexisted without extensive cross-references. Some authors have advocated the need for an integrated model of restructuring, internationalisation and international trade policies (cf. Odell, 1990: 140).

A few attempts have been undertaken to link one or two of these debates. The analysis of restructuring, for instance, has been linked to the issue of international trade and trade policy regimes by Joyce Kolko (1990). The political debate on protectionism against Japanese products or the issue of the 'new' North–South competition has also prompted some authors to link policy and processes of restructuring. Others have tried to link the evolution of trade policies with the notion of 'globalisation' (cf. Sachwald, 1994). These attempts towards integration, however, have as yet received only scanty attention; the bulk of the three debates remains conducted in relative isolation.

Perhaps this not-so-splendid isolation could be attributed to an excessive division of labour within the (Western) academic world. The highly specialised nature of each debate implied that participants to one debate have been facing serious 'barriers to entry' to another debate. Ironically, this academic risk aversion created a vacuum and a willing audience for sweeping claims on the rise of the 'global', the 'network' or the 'post-national' firm. Unfortunately, members of the academic community sometimes forgot to put these claims to the same rigorous tests as they demanded from scholars from their own disciplines and debates.

Consider for instance what will happen if a great number of firms, regions and states start to produce goods according to one particular 'best-practice' restructuring model. Will today's competitive advantages still be feasible tomorrow? What if these strategies are copied on a worldwide scale? Will worldwide flexible specialisation advance free international trade or rather foster the rise of self-reliant economies? Will a worldwide adoption of lean production further or hinder managed trade arrangements? Conversely, which restructuring strategy is most favourable for 'globalisation'? Some reflections on these types of questions might have prevented certain academics from degenerating into missionaries.

A second parallel between the above three debates is that many new concepts have been based on a remarkably limited empirical domain. The flexible specialisation thesis has been supported by evidence from a few regions in Italy, Germany and Japan, while the concept of lean production has been derived from the Toyota Production System. The globalisation thesis has been illustrated by commercially successful and rapidly expanding firms like Ford, Sony and IBM – some of which have fallen into deep problems only a few years later. Free trade theorists have built their claims on an analysis of the short-term welfare effects of international trade, assuming that all firms and states play the game of short-term welfare optimisation.

There are obvious limitations to generalising restructuring and internationalisation concepts from one industry or country to another. Some contributors to these debates were well aware of these limitations. Piore and Sabel (1984), for instance, specified which type of state policies and industry structures were required for flexible specialisation to prosper, implying that their thesis could not be generalised to other regions or industries without certain adjustments. More often, however, proponents of a new concept seemed to lack such analytical distance. When Womack, Jones and Roos (1990) predicted that lean production would conquer the world, they deliberately ignored the fact that the 'leanest' producer, Toyota, was still a far cry from introducing lean production by the early 1990s. Rather than analysing whether Toyota may have had good reasons not to implement lean production completely, the authors argued that even Toyota had not fully understood the intricacies of lean production. Similarly, authors such as William Powell have put forward one-dimensional statements on networks which would be 'lighter on their feet than hierarchies' (1990: 303). These and many other claims referred to in this book suffer from an unhealthy mixture of analysis, description and prescription.

1.4 INDUSTRIAL COMPLEXES: CENTRES OF GRAVITY OF THE INTERNATIONAL RESTRUCTURING RACE

This book sets out to restore the organic link between the three debates referred to above, and to detach prescription from analysis. In the literature on international relations, the problem of connecting the results from one study or discipline to another, even if these are measured differently and strictly speaking not comparable, has become known as the level-of-analysis problem (Singer, 1961). Analysing international relations, one has to transcend disciplinary boundaries, given the variety of political systems, industrial trends, international organisations, and cultures.

Many connections between the areas of restructuring, internationalisation and international trade can easily be seen. The internationalisation of a firm in fact represents a specific type of restructuring, as it involves a change in the organisational structure and as it directly affects domestic workers (because domestic employment may fall) and suppliers (who may also have to set up foreign branches). Conversely, the nature of a firm's internationalisation also depends on its domestic setting. For instance, a firm that has developed a highly successful exporting strategy based on a cohesive domestic production network may feel disinclined to set up international production facilities and disturb its domestic cohesion – unless outside pressures force it to do so. Likewise, a firm's trade policy orientation is linked to its restructuring and internationalisation strategies. A company with operations spread over the world and high levels of intra-company trade will probably be more opposed to trade barriers than a purely domestic firm or one with relatively independent and autonomous operations in its major markets.

Linking these strategies and policies, we assume that there is no inherently best restructuring or internationalisation strategy and no best trade policy. Under certain market conditions or international configurations, one strategy or policy may temporarily outperform the others, and if these conditions remain stable for several decades, one strategy or policy may even obtain a 'hegemonic' status. However, as elaborated in Chapter 3, each restructuring concept incorporates a number of control dilemmas or contradictions that are very difficult to resolve for a long period of time. Eventually, therefore, once-dominant concepts and strategies may lose their appeal and fall into decay. Thus in the end, restructuring concepts, internationalisation strategies and international trade policies are the result of economic, political and social interaction, i.e. struggles and bargaining processes, and thus the object of social and political choice.

Consequently, the challenge of this book is to develop a framework which systematically analyses the actors involved and the nature of their social, political and economic struggles and bargaining processes. Chapter 4 will introduce the concept of the industrial complex to capture these actors and their interrelationships. Industrial complexes represent the centres of gravity in the international restructuring race. An industrial complex can be seen as a bargaining arena made up of six actors:

1 the *core firm*, which is the spider in the industrial web and which is best positioned to manage the dependencies in an industrial complex;
2 its *supplying firms*, which may be fully or partly owned by the core firm, or financially independent of it, and which provide the parts and components to be processed into the final product to the core firm;
3 its *dealers and distributors*, which may also be fully, partly or non-owned by the core firm and which deliver the goods to the customers;
4 its *workers*, who carry out the actual production or transformation process within the core firm, and who may or may not be represented by a labour union;
5 its *financiers*, which support the core firm financially by providing loans, purchasing shares, and which may consist of, for instance, banks, pension funds, or (in the case of Japan) large parent companies engaged in a wide horizontal range of activities;

6 its local, regional and national (and even supranational) home and host
  governments.

Thus, the analysis of international bargaining in this book goes beyond the
framework as presented by John Stopford and Susan Strange (1991) who
pictured a simpler bargaining arena made up of rival states and rival firms,
which would lead to a study of the so-called trilateral diplomacy pattern
between firms and firms, firms and governments, and governments and
governments.

   As a means of assessing the interaction between these actors, Chapter 4 will
introduce a scale of dependencies to assess the latter five actors' relationships to the core firm. This scale helps to position leading restructuring and
organisational concepts in terms of different bargaining and dependency
relationships. These different positions in fact represent rival restructuring
concepts, or what will be called 'concepts of control'. A concept of control
is the strategic perspective of a core firm in trying to forge its industrial
complex. The relevance of a concept of control is not limited to a firm's
home base: it also guides its behaviour abroad, shaping its internationalisation strategies and its international trade preferences. The main argument
of this book, therefore, is that international restructuring is best studied as
a race between industrial complexes adhering to rival concepts of control.

1.5 THE LAYOUT OF THE STUDY

This argument will be set out in the following way. Chapter 2 addresses the
topic of industrial restructuring. It would require a separate book to do full
justice to the academic discussion on this subject. Therefore, this chapter
will focus on various contributions to the concept of post-Fordism. A
prime argument in the discussion on restructuring over the 1980s has been
that industrialised societies are moving away from the Fordist organisation
of production and society to a model which is referred to as post-Fordism.
A lot of contributors have pointed at examples of emerging types of
cooperation within and between firms and governments, and regulatory
structures which would signal an evolution towards a more 'interdependent'
world. Chapter 2 will categorise the various contributions to the concept of
post-Fordism at the meta, macro, micro and meso level of analysis, and
concludes that restructuring is best studied at a meso level of analysis.

   Chapter 3 introduces the notion of a concept of control. A concept of
control incorporates a set of strategic objectives regarding (the control
over) the internal and external organisation of the firm. These concepts of
control are rival concepts in the sense that they coexist and there is no
inherently superior concept, although one concept may be hegemonic for a
period of time. In the capitalist mode of production five basic concepts of
control can be identified: flexible specialisation, industrial democracy,
macro-Fordism, micro-Fordism and Toyotism.

Chapter 4 will operationalise the meso level of analysis by developing a scale of dependencies ranging from dependent, through interdependent, to independent positions of actors in relation to each other. The position of actors in relation to each other will be analysed in terms of their impact on the bargaining relations between these actors. The pattern of bargaining relations make up the building blocks of the five rival concepts of control. Chapter 4 will discuss the bargaining relations within the supply chain, i.e. with suppliers, trade unions and dealers and/or distributors.

Chapter 5 will go on to discuss a core firm's relations outside its value chain: with financial actors and governments. In this chapter various industrial complexes and concepts of control will be positioned along the dependency scale. Chapter 5 will introduce the topic of the cohesion of complexes both at the meso and macro level of analysis. The higher the cohesion of a complex, the better it will be able to shape the bargaining rules (institutions) in a country. Chapter 5 will elaborate on the distinction between an industrial complex (meso level) and an industrial system (macro level). In case of more complexes in one country, the bargaining rules adopted in the industrial system will depend on the constituting complexes with the highest cohesion.

In the following chapters, the analytical concepts as derived from the restructuring debate will be applied and put to an initial test in the two other debates: on globalisation and on trade policy. Chapter 6 will discuss the concept of globalisation. A number of previously dominant theories on internationalisation will be evaluated to establish differences and similarities with current thinking on globalisation. Postwar theorising tended to conceive of internationalisation as a progressive evolution induced primarily by company internal strategic considerations. The rise and popularity of particular models, moreover, shows a striking parallel to the cycle of hegemonic rise and decline.

Chapter 7 considers the one hundred largest core companies of the world in order to find out to what extent the claim of a 'global' corporation can be substantiated in practice. Chapter 7 will show that globalisation is best considered as a strategy and not as an obtained reality. This chapter will further indicate that it is plausible to suggest that there is a clear link between the nature of the domestic bargaining arena (i.e. the management of dependencies in the industrial complex) and the internationalisation strategy chosen.

In Chapter 8, starting at the firm level, two internationalisation trajectories will be distinguished that ultimately lead to two rival global strategies: globalisation and glocalisation. Firms adopting a globalisation strategy strive for a worldwide intra-firm division of labour, whereas firms following a glocalisation strategy will seek a geographically concentrated inter-firm division of labour. In these trajectories various sub-trajectories can be distinguished that could lead firms to aim at a regional division of labour or primarily strive for 'screwdriver' production abroad. Parallel to these location strategies, firms will adopt rival visions towards strategic alliances. Chapter 8 will illustrate that the domestic bargaining arena ('measured' along the dependency scale) influences the choice for strategic alliances in the same way as it influences the choice for a particular internationalisation trajectory. Firms adhering to one of the rival internationalisation strategies will also advocate rival visions on how the world economy should be organised. It will be argued that the clearest differences between these two strategies will be found at the level of international trade. A strategy of globalisation, which depends on a worldwide division of labour, will generally lead to a liberal trade policy orientation. Glocalisation, on the contrary, seeks to produce within trade blocs and to become relatively immune to trade barriers.

Chapter 9 confronts the current state of international trade theory with the nature of the international trade regime. In the second half of the 1980s, the strategic trade policy models provoked much debate on the use and implications of free trade. By now, many of these claims have been withdrawn, but the strategic trade policy models did challenge the self-proclaimed universal status of free trade theory, pointing at the role and interaction of firm and government strategies. To account for the rise of managed trade through the 1980s, Chapter 9 also investigates how international trade theories explain the rise and government endorsement of rival trade policy strategies such as free trade, voluntary export restraints or anti-dumping measures. Although international trade theories have attempted to link firms' internationalisation strategies to firms' trade policy orientations, few have differentiated between internationalisation strategies and trade policy outcomes. This chapter will also give a first assessment of the link between internationalisation strategy and trade policy orientations. To facilitate this, Chapter 9 takes the same one hundred core firms as Chapter 7 and looks at how these firms progressed under specific trade regimes. It will be shown that hardly any of today's leading core firms developed under a free trade regime. This makes the argument in favour of a 'level playing field', as most free trade theorists tend to do, very controversial. This chapter further illustrates that particular trade policy theories ('best-practice' solutions) originate in a clear national background and represent a specific interest constellation.

Chapter 10 will summarise the basic argument of this study and infer the 'ultimate logic' of restructuring, internationalisation strategies and trade policy orientations. This chapter will therefore discuss the relationships between industrial complexes. Firstly, this will be done at the national level of analysis. It will be assessed what the influence of industrial complexes with various degrees of outward and inward internationalisation is on the cohesion of the national industrial system. In the case of the internationalisation of US companies, we identify a 'bargaining pendulum' in which outward-oriented internationalisation strategies also aim at influencing the domestic bargaining arena. This affects the feasibility of particular national trade or industrial policies. Secondly, Chapter 10 observes the final level of analysis at which the logic of international restructuring can be studied: the intra- and interregional level. Regional ways of dealing with restructuring processes (regional regimes) critically depend on the underlying concepts of control and are influenced in particular by the industrial complex and the industrial system with the highest degree of cohesion. Analysing this logic helps to understand the nature of the regional regimes in Europe, East and South East Asia, and North America, and their prospects in the international restructuring race.

2 The elusive concept of post-Fordism

2.1 INTRODUCTION

The term industrial restructuring does not have a well-defined meaning. It only came into frequent use from the second half of the 1970s onwards. By that time, policy-makers and staff of many national governments and international organisations (cf. UNIDO, 1979) acknowledged that what was first seen as a regular worldwide recession in fact contained major structural elements. In the early 1980s, the OECD launched the concept of 'positive adjustment policies' (OECD, 1983) to discourage 'beggar-thy-neigh-bour' policies, in which state intervention in one country rekindled industrial problems in another one.

Aiming to transcend the traditional confines of country or sectorial restructuring analyses, and looking at the economic problems that emerged over the 1970s in most industrialised economies, various scholars have argued that these economies would move away from the system of Fordism which they had known for many decades. Put simply, Fordism refers to the simultaneous growth of productivity and consumption. Fordism has two varieties: micro-Fordism, where such growth had been generated at the level of the firm, and macro-Fordism, where this simultaneous growth was realised at a societal level, also involving actors such as governments and national trade union federations. These concepts will be operationalised in detail in Chapters 3, 4 and 5.

Several authors have presented the idea of a 'post-something' as a radical breach with the old order, ranging from a 'post-industrial' (Bell, 1973) to a 'post-modern' society (Clegg, 1989). The most influential notion in this 'post-something' category has been the concept of post-Fordism. The trajectory towards post-Fordism is often presented in three steps (cf. for example, Boyer, 1989; Helling, 1991). The first step is to set out the general principles of Fordist production, based on mass production by vertically integrated firms aiming for economies of scale. This opened up the way for a substantial growth of productivity, but at the expense of an increasing level of mechanisation, which narrowed down the tasks of workers and effectively de-skilled the labour force. The second step is therefore to illustrate the problems or challenges that confronted Fordism over the 1970s and 1980s, such as declining growth and growing labour dissatisfaction. The third step is to introduce a new 'post-Fordist' model of production organisation that provides the 'solution' to these problems.[1] Although post-Fordism simply means 'something after Fordism', various authors have presented sweeping statements on the unprecedented opportunities for increasing 'cooperation' between firms or between workers and management:

- Kern and Schumann (1984) have proclaimed the possible end of the division of labour as a result of the introduction of microelectronics into the firm;
- According to Piore and Sabel, 'technological advance has ended the dominion of specialized machines over unskilled and semi-skilled workers', and the 'advent of the computer restores human control over the production process' (1984: 261);
- Alain Lipietz (1987) has interpreted wage relations within large Japanese firms, characterised by job stability and worker responsibility, as a first step towards the ultimate realisation of labour's objectives;
- An impressive body of literature, finally, has focused on the re-emergence of small artisan firms in terms of the rise of networks consisting of large and small firms looking for complementary partners with which to cooperate (Håkanson, 1989; Powell, 1990; Piore and Sabel, 1984).

The concept of post-Fordism has been elaborated at various levels of analysis. Section 2.2 will commence at the most abstract or meta level of analysis. Authors of the heterodox school have argued that the integration of microelectronics into new products and into the production process functions as a new metaparadigm of restructuring (Perez, 1983, 1985). According to this school of thought, the pervasiveness of microelectronics will largely determine the restructuring trajectory of the individual firm, of entire industries and indeed of international capitalism as a whole.

Section 2.3 will look at two important arguments at the macro level analysis. Most approaches at the macro level of analysis are rather critical about the concept of post-Fordism. Scholars of the French regulation school regard post-Fordism as the breakdown of the Fordist growth compromise between capital and labour, while authors of the 'Amsterdam School' have interpreted post-Fordism as the international triumph of the neoliberal political programme. Section 2.4 will turn to the micro level of analysis. Numerous authors have investigated changes and new relationships

---

[1] According to Richard Walker, this periodisation of capitalism suggested in regulation theory, the concept of post-Fordism and the flexible specialisation approach is 'wholly unacceptable, as capitalist history is reduced to the trilogy of a distant and poorly specified past (even a Virgilian Golden Age), a well-known Middle Age extending from once upon a time to yesterday, and a vaguely emergent present/future. This is the stuff of mythology not serious social science' (1989: 9). This criticism also applies to the 'lean production' approach of Womack, Jones and Roos (1990).

between management and labour within firms, and have heralded post-Fordism as a new stage in industrial relations. Section 2.5 will discuss some approaches that relate post-Fordism to the rise of industrial networks. Generally, these contributions have been developed at the meso level of analysis. At this level of analysis, firms and industries are understood as an integral part of their environment, one affecting the other. Section 2.6 summarises the discussion on post-Fordism and evaluates the theoretical value of this concept.

2.2 THE NEO-SCHUMPETERIAN APPROACH TO RESTRUCTURING

The heterodox school of analysis, consisting of researchers such as Carlotta Perez, Christopher Freeman, Giovanni Dosi and Luc Soete, have updated the Schumpeterian approach of economic change with regard to the notion of long waves, and specifically to the importance of technology, on both the product and process sides (cf. Freeman, 1982; Dosi *et al.*, 1988). For this reason, the heterodox school, which has also made an effort to integrate institutional aspects into economic theory, is often referred to as the neo-Schumpeterian approach.

Perez and Dosi have presented technological and economic change in terms of a shift in the dominant techno-economic paradigm. A change in the techno-economic paradigm generates a wave of new innovations and inventions. In the Schumpeterian concept of long economic waves, such a techno-economic paradigm shift would produce an upswing of economic development. As Freeman summarised:

> The expression 'techno-economic' paradigm implies a process of economic selection from the start of the technically feasible combinations of innovations, and indeed it takes a relatively long time (a decade or more) for a new paradigm to crystallise and still longer for it to diffuse right through the system. This diffusion involves a complex interplay between technological, economic and political forces.
>
> (Freeman, 1988b: 74)

Traditionally, neo-classical economists have neglected the impact of technology on economic and productivity growth. In the mid-1950s, the application of Robert Solow's growth models had already provided evidence that only a small part (around 20 per cent) of productivity growth could be attributed to a growing use of capital equipment. This finding contradicted neo-classical 'knowledge' on productivity growth. From that time onwards, attempts have been made to integrate the technology factor and the way in which firms and governments 'produce' technology, into the analysis.

Only since the beginning of the 1980s has the analysis of technological change been among the leading questions of economic and social research. Nathan Rosenberg (1982), for instance, went into the 'black box' of technology and took the process of technology diffusion and development into the economic analysis. He thereby put the emphasis on incremental innovations and processes of learning in using and designing new technologies, and assessed that these incremental innovations accounted for more than half of the increase in productivity (Rosenberg, 1982: 120ff). According to Richard Nelson and Sydney Winter (1982), a specific R&D trajectory could be accelerated and the chance of technological breakthroughs enhanced, if governments decided to concentrate their efforts on such a trajectory (Brouwer and Does de Willebois, 1990: 57).

According to Carlotta Perez (1983; 1985), the current techno-economic paradigm shift will lead to a widespread use of microelectronics in production. The microelectronics revolution has acquired a meta paradigm status, due to its pervasiveness in substituting old technologies and in changing the production process. In spite of the revolutionary character of a change of technological paradigm, the heterodox writers consider their approach evolutionary, because they emphasise the gradual adaptation of society to the new paradigm. Actors would learn and identify effective strategies, while dropping ineffective ones. This also helps to explain why new technologies do not immediately lead to economic growth, even after they have been developed and have started to diffuse. Particularly, the mismatch will have to be overcome between on the one hand, interests based on the previous techno-economic paradigm which are still represented in existing institutions, and on the other hand, the unfolding technological revolution.[2]

Due to these adjustment problems, the techno-economic paradigm shift will be experienced as one of structural crisis. During such a shift, governments would have to invest in the infrastructure to create the preconditions for rapid diffusion of the new technologies. In the 1930s, for instance, the American government invested in highways, and as a consequence provided the infrastructure for a rapid growth of the car industry, car consumption and all other services related to this 'engine' of economic growth. Likewise, in the current shift towards the microelectronics paradigm, heterodox writers have supported government interference to provide an advanced telecommunications infrastructure. Particularly with regard to linking technological change to employment creation, the heterodox approach recognises the important and positive role of state investment and regulation. Nevertheless, heterodox authors consider political intervention only capable of influencing some of the (institutional) variables within an otherwise predetermined trajectory. This is precisely what the term 'meta paradigm' aims to express. According to the heterodox approach, an imminent

---

[2] Institutions in the Fordist mode of regulation are generally concerned with demand management and income distribution (cf. Perez, 1983: 366–71). More flexible technologies may reduce the need for these two aspects. As we will argue, however, technological change *alone* can hardly explain such an institutional 'mismatch'. In Chapters 4 and 5 we will specify our definition of institutions and we will make a distinction between meso and macro institutions.

techno-economic paradigm shift will occur anyway, leaving policy-makers only room to determine whether the technological development will lead to a 'reactionary or a democratic modernisation' (Peláez and Holloway, 1991: 137).

In spite of all intelligent observations and all footnotes that provide further explanation or disclaimers, the heterodox school adopts an essentially technologically deterministic approach to restructuring (cf. Peláez and Holloway, 1991: 139). Perez reacted to this criticism, stating that the way in which the socio-institutional environment adapts to the new techno-economic paradigm can differ from country to country, while the outcome of the process will partly depend on social conflict (Perez, 1985: 446). Yet one of the major weaknesses of evolutionary approaches such as the heterodox one is that these fail to take full account of such social or political conflicts or of the underlying choices facing individual actors. The heterodox approach views restructuring first of all in terms of 'adjustment' problems. In reality, technological change is far from a socially neutral process. Some groups or interests will be better able to grab the opportunity offered by technological change than others. Technological change is therefore always subject to political bargaining and power struggles. This means that one has to analyse the position of the societal groups affected by technological change, and their industrial, social or political embeddedness.

Heterodox authors have avoided using the term post-Fordism. Nevertheless, their approach is often included in discussions on post-Fordism, because it puts the role of new technologies central to the analysis, and because it considers not just the advantages of new technologies to individual firms but also the role of the state. In Chapter 3, the significance of (control over) new technologies will return, taking into account how different interests are affected by technological changes (Bonefeld, 1991: 65).

2.3 STATE-CENTRED APPROACHES TO POST-FORDISM AND RESTRUCTURING

This section will tackle two approaches to the concept of post-Fordism at the macro level of analysis. The macro level of analysis adopts a national or international perspective and looks at the state and the role of state institutions from the point of view of capitalist accumulation as such. From this perspective, macro level approaches analyse why and how particular economic interests have succeeded in establishing specific state institutions, and assess the actual effect on society and capitalist accumulation. Two macro level approaches will be addressed: the French regulation school, and the 'Amsterdam School'.

2.3.1 The regulation school: paradigm shift in the (inter)national accumulation regime

French scholars like Michel Aglietta, Alain Lipietz and Robert Boyer have been concerned with 'understanding how the reproduction of the capital–labour relation is historically realised and regulated and how capitalism is prevented from collapsing' (Bonefeld, 1991: 37). The approach of these authors is generally referred to as the 'regulation school'. Although their analysis – like the heterodox approach – hardly constitutes one coherent school of thought, most authors share the idea that structural crises in capitalism originate from a profound disjuncture between (1) the regime of accumulation and (2) the mode of regulation (Aglietta, 1979; Wolfe, 1987: 6).

The regime of accumulation refers to the way in which the 'social product' is divided and reallocated, or in a more narrow sense: to the management of demand and supply. An accumulation regime therefore provides an organisational paradigm for both the productive and the reproductive sphere. In this sense, the analytical scope of the regulation school goes beyond that of the heterodox approach. The mode of regulation refers to the existing institutional forms (in terms of values and norms) such as wage relations, and to the particular role played by state intervention.

The regulationists do not see a particular, regular, pattern of cyclical fluctuations. They consider the periods of rise and decline of accumulation regimes more in terms of their internal contradictions. 'In this sense techniques of production are themselves viewed as social relations which cannot exist independent of the environment determined by all the forms of regulation' (Wolfe, 1987: 6). The regulationists generally make a distinction between two periods of regulation – or societal paradigms.

According to Aglietta, from the mid-nineteenth century to the First World War, extensive accumulation as pioneered in the United Kingdom still had a dominance of non-commodity relations in consumption over commodity relations. Individual contracts were pre-eminent and women and children were withdrawn from the social labour force. Bargaining between management and labour as pioneered in the United States created the basis for a regime of so-called intensive accumulation in which growing production and consumption were coupled. In terms of the innovation debate (see Dosi *et al.*, 1988), technology push and demand pull became linked. Henry Ford's experiments to couple production automation and wage increases (the 'five dollar working day') enabled workers to buy their own Model T. The change towards 'intensive' or 'Fordist' regulation at a nation-wide scale appeared first in the United States and provided the foundation for the global hegemony of the American production organisation, after the forceful annihilation of contenders that had adopted comparable modes of mass production (especially Germany, but to a certain extent also Japan).

Our basic objection to the regulationist school is not so much a conceptual as an analytical one, and concerns the mechanistic view on the change of one accumulation regime to the next one (Brenner and Glick, 1991: 75). This change is analysed in a state-centred way, understating the role of and potential rivalries between particular industries. As a result, rather arbitrary turning points had to be chosen for the change of extensive into intensive accumulation. Instead of a more detailed analysis, most emphasis is being put on more or less objective 'laws' of accumulation in capitalism (cf. the heterodox inclination to conceive of restructuring in terms of predetermined trajectories).

Regulation theorists in France were among the first to launch the concept of post-Fordism, viewing it as a breakdown of the growth compromise between capital and labour. Later on, however, some regulationists became extremely positive about the use of flexible automation and computers in production as an 'anti-Taylorist Revolution'. In line with this, some argued that 'a renewed period of capital accumulation depends upon establishing a "harmonic complementarity" or "correspondence" between the dominant technology and the social environment' (Peláez and Holloway, 1991: 139). Many regulationists – joined by politicians of the French Communist and Labour parties – would not only suggest that the move towards post-Fordism is inevitable, but also desirable (ibid: 139).

The approach of Robert Boyer (1993) illustrates a basic tendency in the more recent work of the regulationists: first identify the general principles of the 'new productive model' ('post-Fordism')[3] on the basis of the observed weaknesses of the Fordist model and then find out if these weaknesses can also be observed in other countries. If not, post-Fordism may alternatively be equated with 'Toyotism' or 'Sonyism' (for Japan), 'Volvoism' for Sweden or any other 'isms' for any other country with a different social setting.

The most outspoken and optimistic exponent of the regulationists in this respect may be Alain Lipietz. Although Lipietz is aware of the paradoxes contained in the present phase of restructuring, he did point at the wage relations inside Japanese firms as a first step towards accomplishing the historical goals of labour and of all democratic movements, i.e. 'a more and more democratic, self-managed society, a step towards humanization of mankind' (Lipietz, 1987: 18, quoted in Hübner and Mahnkopf, 1988: 71). Lipietz in this context spoke of a 'real compromise only if workers get a real benefit in return for their cooperation: for instance by more job stability, more time off and/or increased buying power' (ibid). Lipietz has

---

[3] In his extremely creative essays, Robert Boyer brings together a lot of characteristics of the new production model at various levels of analysis. To recapitulate but a few (1993: 56, 57): decentralisation of production decisions; horizontal coordination by networks and partnerships; integration of R&D, production and marketing. These principles then act as a source of 'benchmarking' in which countries – not firms – score high (Japan and to a lesser extent Germany and Sweden) or low (USA and France). The implied message: the Japanese system approaches the ideal type of production organisation most closely, even with due and explicit reference to many of its drawbacks.

therefore dubbed the era of increased cooperation between wage labour and capital 'post-Fordism' to indicate a breach with the past 'Fordist' accumulation regime in which mass production and mass consumption became coupled. Section 2.4 will look at these and other claims on the rise of new cooperative relations within firms.

2.3.2 The Amsterdam School: post-Fordism as the decline of Fordism

Around 1980, conservative governments took power in the UK and the USA from more progressive administrations. 'Reaganomics' and 'Thatcherism' implied a radical monetarist reaction to the crisis of Fordism, and in that way represented a true political paradigm shift. In these new political programmes, financial interests overshadowed those of productive capital, leading to declining state intervention, a free market ideology and a return to conservative values. Authors from the 'Amsterdam School' have dubbed this the triumph of *neo-liberalism*. According to Henk Overbeek:

> Neo-liberalism is at once directed towards disarticulating the old forma-
> tion which is in crisis, that is, towards deconstructing corporatism and
> the Keynesian welfare state, and towards the formation of a new con-
> figuration, the construction of a post-Fordist accumulation regime.
>
> (Overbeek, 1990: 180)

In the eyes of the Amsterdam School, neo-liberalism has succeeded in acquiring the status of a 'comprehensive concept of control', which turns it into the dominant political project guiding restructuring over the 1980s and the 1990s. A comprehensive concept of control 'transcends narrowly defined specific fractional interests' and captures 'a coherent set of strategies in the area of labour relations, socio-economic policies and foreign policies' (Overbeek, 1990: 26). In this way, a comprehensive concept of control presents a definition of the 'general' or 'national' interest.

However, several distinct concepts of control are competing for hegemony at the same time, even if only one particular programme can acquire hegemony for a certain period. According to the writers of the Amsterdam School, these distinct concepts of control are linked either to the concept of money capital (best approximated by banking, but also attractive to other groups and interests that benefit from a minimum of regulation) and the concept of productive capital (linked to more tangible factors of production, and best approximated by industry). Thus restructuring in capitalist societies could be understood as a result of the struggle between these two spheres of capital. Neo-liberalism would originate from circles of money capital and would represent a breakdown of the postwar compromise between money and productive capital (the 'corporate liberal' synthesis: van der Pijl, 1984: 22).

The Amsterdam School provides many interesting elements for the analysis of capitalist restructuring. It does not consider restructuring as an

'objective' or 'anonymous' process, but it emphasises diverging economic, social and political strategies and interests. The notion of a concept of control enhances our understanding of how and why specific capital groups develop political programmes and how they try to raise support from other groups. Finally, the Amsterdam School explicitly takes into consideration the internationalisation of money and productive capital. The approach therefore contributes to the understanding of long-term shifts in political orientations and 'hegemonic concepts' of thinking.

The image of productive capital as one 'ideal type', however, seems to narrow the analysis. Although the contradictions between money capital and productive capital are essential to understand the dynamism of capitalist restructuring, the authors of the Amsterdam School attach such overriding importance to these contradictions that they lose sight of developments and latent contradictions within rival spheres of productive capital. The Amsterdam School does not analyse systematically how, in periods of domination of the money capital concept, productive capital restructures itself and searches for a new concept of control. The authors accept it as a natural feature of capitalist accumulation that productive capital will regain strength after a while, and that it will develop new and more ingenious ways to exploit labour and to manipulate national and supranational governments. To analyse the roots and specificities of a potentially new concept of control originating from a particular segment of productive capital would in such a view be a useless and perhaps even dangerous exercise, countering Marxist orthodoxy in suggesting possible ways out of the current crisis. Thus, members of the Amsterdam School have tended to misinterpret interest in the restructuring of productive capital as sympathy with the strategies being studied.

To the Amsterdam School, the manufacturing firm largely figures as a 'black box'. A new productive concept of control appears as a *deus ex machina*, only accounted for by *ad hoc* arguments and anecdotal evidence. In our view, however, capitalist restructuring is better understood by putting the rivalry between different spheres of productive capital at the heart of the analysis. It should be analysed whether and how these different spheres are linked to rival views on restructuring, for instance on the organisation of production, the control over labour, as well as on the access to finance. Such an analysis would also shed a better light on what the authors believe is their ultimate motivation to analyse capitalist accumulation, namely to understand the dynamism in the class contradiction between capital and labour.

A second and related remark is that the authors of the Amsterdam School fail to explain to what extent the money capital concept has truly become the dominant ideology in *all* major industrialised countries. The 'triumph' of neo-liberalism seems to be limited largely to two formerly hegemonic countries: the United States and the United Kingdom. Savings rates in the USA (1990: 7.1 per cent) and the UK (1989: 2.4 per cent) are among the lowest in the world (Keizai Koho Center, 1991: 85). These low savings rates can only be compensated for by a high international mobility of capital. Thus, the neo-liberal policies in the USA and the UK to liberalise the international flow of capital aim to *attract* money capital from more successful economies.[4] In Germany (1990 saving rate: 13.3 per cent) and Japan (1989: 14.2 per cent), on the other hand, the relationship between industrial banks and industry provides an entirely different picture. The relative rate of internationalisation of German and Japanese banks is far lower than of UK and US banks (Bröker, 1989: 145), indicating that productive capital in two of the largest and most productive economies in the world has not declined to the same extent as in the UK or in the US. Over the 1980s, relations between money and productive capital have changed in these two countries, but the 'synthesis' between the two spheres of capital has not entirely collapsed.

Not surprisingly, attempts to apply the concept of neo-liberalism to countries such as Japan or Germany are either lacking (in the case of Japan) or have confirmed that this concept is not well applicable (in the case of Germany, cf. van der Wurff, 1992). The reason is simple: The Amsterdam School documents the dominant ideology and political strategies in two declining economies, and neo-liberalism expresses the relative decline of Fordism. The Amsterdam School relates post-Fordism to the decline of Fordism, not to the rise of a new productive concept of control. An analysis of rival spheres of productive capital will have to confirm whether or not the synthesis between money and productive capital in some economies has survived, and explain why productive capital in these economies has not fallen victim to Fordist decline.

2.3.3 Conclusion: post-Fordism and state-centred approaches

This section has discussed two state-centred or macro level approaches to the concept of post-Fordism. Both the regulation school and the Amsterdam School have analysed the concept of post-Fordism as a breakdown of the Fordist growth compromise between capital and labour, although the Amsterdam School emphasises much more the underlying conflicts between the concepts of money and productive capital. The two approaches differ somewhat in their judgement on post-Fordism. Some adherents of the regulation school hope for a renewed post-Fordist growth compromise between capital and labour, based on the introduction of new technologies into the production process, while others have looked for indications of such a compromise in Japanese firms. The Amsterdam School has taken a much more pessimistic view on post-Fordism, equating it with the neo-liberal 'counter-revolution' in the USA and the UK.

---

[4] As Annemieke Roobeek aptly suggested to us, this could be called 'restructuring by borrowing'.

Both approaches contain many elements or notions that are very useful in the analysis of restructuring. Many regulationists have searched for the shape of a new growth compromise between capital and labour, but they failed to develop a critical and integrated vision of such a compromise. The notion of a concept of control, developed by the Amsterdam School, will be borrowed yet redefined to concentrate on rival productive concepts of control (see Chapter 3). The conflict between money capital and productive capital, stressed by the Amsterdam School, will also return, looking for the different patterns of how specific spheres of productive capital forge different types of relationships with or dependencies on money capital. The words 'money' and 'productive capital' will not be adopted.

2.4 POST-FORDISM AS THE COOPERATIVE MANAGEMENT OF FIRMS

The introduction of new technologies into the production process has produced a rich harvest of claims on the new nature of work and management in industrial firms. In the first half of the 1980s, the discussion centred on the question of whether the introduction of new technologies would create employment or unemployment (Daniel, 1987: 21ff; Friedrich and Rönning, 1985). Gradually, however, the tone and the focus of the discussion shifted over the 1980s. Several authors heralded advances in computer-integrated manufacturing as a contribution to the integration of activities in one firm towards 'systemofacture' (Kaplinsky, 1985; Bessant, 1991). Other authors speculated about a 'humanisation' of labour and about the emergence of 'computer-human-integrated manufacturing' (Brödner, 1987). Leading labour sociologists even argued that the use of microelectronics in firms could lead to an end of the division of labour (Kern and Schumann, 1984) or restore the worker's position as master over his machine (Piore and Sabel, 1984).

These and other claims about the restoration of the position of the worker challenged the thesis developed by Harry Braverman (1974) who had predicted a continued dequalification of labour under Fordism. According to Kaplinsky, a post-Fordist strategy aims to enhance competitiveness through innovation, using labour as a resource, rather than the Fordist practice of aiming for price competition, perceiving labour as a cost. Table 2.1 has summarised some of the attributed differences between Fordism and post-Fordism at the firm level (1990: 11).

Richard Badham and John Mathews have made a distinction between Fordism and post-Fordism on the basis of three production characteristics: the degree of product innovation; the degree of process variability; and labour responsibility (1989: 206ff). Along these dimensions, a Fordist production strategy would imply low degrees of product innovation, low process variability and low levels of labour responsibility. The post-Fordist production paradigm would be based on high product innovations, high

Table 2.1 Attributed differences between Fordism and post-Fordism at the firm level

Fordism	Post-Fordism
Competitiveness through price	Competitiveness through innovation
Labour as a cost	Labour as a resource
Specialisation of tasks	Worker has multiple tasks
Separation of work at firm level	Integration of work at firm level
Economies of scale	Economies of scope

Source: based on Kaplinsky, 1990: 11, 12

process variability and high levels of labour responsibility. The authors also identify a third type of production strategy, neo-Fordism, which would cover all the intermediate 'shades into the Fordist region when task uncertainty and job autonomy are low, and into the post-Fordist region as task uncertainty and job autonomy increase' (ibid).

To most writers on post-Fordism at the firm level, the main attraction of the concept lies in the promise of increasing labour responsibility and more cooperative management–labour relations than under Fordism. John Mathews, who belongs to the most creative thinkers on post-Fordism, has coupled these claims directly to the idea of an 'associative democratic economy' and has elaborated the notion of 'responsibility' a bit further:

> The post-Fordist perspective focuses on the need for flexibility and a capacity for innovation in an economy geared to dynamic structural adjustment. It is distinguished from competing neo-Fordist perspectives in its insistence that flexibility and productivity are most efficiently based on the skilled input of workers taking increasing levels of responsibility for the design of their jobs, their workplaces, their products and ultimately the management of their enterprises. This approach is accommodated and facilitated by the democratization of company structures, by the development of social investment funds, by planning agreements, and the host of other innovative measures available to a movement which is convinced of their relevance and practicability, and is prepared to use its strength in the political arena to bring about such structural transformations.
>
> (Mathews, 1989: 152, 153)

The French regulationist Benjamin Coriat (1990: 282) has developed similar visions. He sees a chance to create a renewed growth regime based on 'wage democracy', coupled with quality enhancement, investments in human resources, shorter working time and the usage of robots and computer-aided automation equipment in a cooperative strategy of workers and management. In such a 'post-union' industrial regime, individual workers or enterprise unions would bargain over the content of work: law rather than unions would protect individual workers (*BW*, 8 July 1985).

In our view, the concept of post-Fordism, as elaborated at the micro level of analysis, suffers from two major weaknesses. The first concerns the possible social effects of any increased worker qualification and responsibility beyond the firm level. These benefits may be feasible for some workers, but probably only for a minority. Ironically, Fordism's inflexibility provided the basis for a modest yet unprecedented level of social solidarity. Mathews acknowledges the danger of dualisation in society – characterised by a 'social gulf between a skilled, employed elite and a mass of under-skilled, under-employed and politically alienated majority' (Mathews, 1989: 153). To overcome this risk, an 'over-arching political paradigm of solidarity' would have to be forged (ibid), yet he hardly indicates how such a 'paradigm' is to emerge or how it should function. Thus Mathews is more interested in securing the perceived benefits of post-Fordism accruing to workers in the firm, than in averting the possible negative effects associated with these benefits. Below, some of these side-effects will be mentioned.

This criticism also applies to the German labour sociologists Kern and Schumann. These authors have announced the end of the division of labour within large production firms, offering a growing potential for democracy in Germany. Kern and Schumann also pointed at the danger of a social segmentation as a result of a growing division of labour with outside firms (Kern and Schumann, 1984: 314ff). To prevent such a segmentation, the authors argue in favour of 'politicising' the emerging production concept. They acknowledge that this will not be without social conflict, yet they fail to indicate which groups will be negatively affected by the ongoing changes in production, or how to politicise the rising production concept.

The second weakness of the post-Fordist thesis at the micro level of analysis concerns the trajectory towards this vision. For lack of any 'real, existing' post-Fordism, many authors have looked in particular at Japanese firms for the shape of post-Fordism to come (Mathews, 1989: 72; 1993). Martin Kenney and Richard Florida (1988, 1993) have presented the Japanese organisation of production as a 'stage beyond mass production', and as a genuine and 'progressive' shift from Fordism to post-Fordism. They cite the well-known examples such as information sharing between workers, cooperation between different departments, a reduction of alienation of workers, the existence of multi-skilled jobs, and the high flexibility and continuous innovation of production, and interpret these elements as welcome steps towards a post-Fordist production system.

At this time, these claims cannot be evaluated. However, many authors appear to have grown so familiar with the drawbacks of Fordist production that they may have overlooked the drawbacks associated with the Japanese production organisation. Even before the effects of the 'bubble economy' became evident; for instance, only about 23 per cent of all Japanese workers enjoy a position of lifelong employment, mainly in the large core firms, and this percentage is still shrinking (Sassen, 1992; other estimates indicate figures of below 20 per cent). Traditionally, the vast majority of Japanese workers have been employed by smaller, less efficient and less profitable firms, often without secure working conditions. Authors seeking 'Japanese post-Fordism' tend to stress the harmonious nature of Japanese industrial relations, ignoring the Red Purges of the late 1940s and early 1950s, and failing to see that enterprise unions were in fact deliberately designed instruments of management to persuade workers to cooperate unconditionally (Naruse, 1991: 39).

Too many analyses of 'Japanese post-Fordism' have been based on superficial or partial observations. Admittedly, it would be too simple to count post-Fordist advocates among the ranks of those defending the Japanese management system. Yet most writers searching for emerging post-Fordist structures in Japan (1) only look at the favourable examples of labour–management relations in large firms, and fail to analyse the darker sides of the Japanese production system as indispensable elements of this system. Moreover (2) they often do not take into account the economic, political and social context of this production system.

In conclusion, researchers analysing the rise of post-Fordism at the firm level of analysis tend to take a very positive view of the effects of the introduction of new technologies and of the possibilities offered by the Japanese production system. However, these authors limit their analysis to the confines of the firm, and fail to look at the potential societal effects of the observed and acclaimed changes. In Chapter 3 it will be argued that 'Japanese post-Fordism' is mistaken for an entirely different production model, which aims to erode rather than support workers' responsibilities.

2.5 POST-FORDISM AND THE NETWORK PARADIGM

Sections 2.3 and 2.4 showed that many authors on post-Fordism have treated the firm either as a 'black box', or as a unit of analysis isolated from the rest of society. Over the 1980s, a growing number of researchers came to realise the limitations of the traditional micro and macro level approaches to restructuring. Firms are developing strategies towards other actors and are responding to pressures from their environment. A growing body of literature on restructuring and post-Fordism has therefore chosen a meso level of analysis. This choice has been reinforced by the increasing importance in all industrialised economies of small firms, both in terms of output and employment, at the expense of the large firms which were the traditional vehicles of Fordism. Examples of such meso level approaches have been the perspective on the firm as a nexus of treaties (Aoki *et al.*, 1990), as an actor searching for complementary network partners (Håkanson, 1989), as part of an industrial district (Marshall, 1961; Piore and Sabel, 1984) or as part of a cluster of firms cooperating and competing at the same time (Porter, 1990). Several researchers even speculated that this resurgence of the small firm and of new patterns of inter-firm relationships constituted the outline of a new production paradigm beyond Fordism (Piore and Sabel, 1984).

Most authors who have adopted a meso level of analysis refer to Oliver Williamson's transaction cost approach. This section will therefore first discuss the key elements of the transaction cost approach, and confront this approach with the argument that networks provide a new production paradigm. Finally, the most important of these approaches, i.e. the flexible specialisation thesis, will be discussed.

2.5.1 Transaction cost approach

The transaction cost approach has been presented by Ronald Coase (1937, 1960) and further developed by Oliver Williamson (1975, 1979). Williamson provided a rationalisation for the Fordist practice of large-scale vertically integrated production in the United States of the mid-1970s.[5] He presented a simple dichotomy between the working of markets (largely consisting of interacting smaller firms) and hierarchies (large, vertically integrated firms). He identified the conditions that lead a firm either to buy a particular product or service in the market, or to carry out the activity itself. The three characteristics favouring a 'make' decision are: a high asset specificity (high investments in capital equipment, high sunk costs, high exit barriers); a high frequency of transactions, and a high degree of uncertainty. Under this scheme, for instance, many high technology industries will be dominated by hierarchies:

- They are usually characterised by a high asset specificity, needing massive capital investments. Smaller firms as a rule cannot afford such gigantic investments.
- Being in the forefront of technological development, state-of-the-art knowledge is not readily available in the marketplace, which forces these firms to rely on in-house development and diffusion of technology.
- However, firms will never be certain whether or not they have missed a vital invention or innovation. Another source of uncertainty and drive to the formation of large hierarchies is the process of standardisation. Standards are often determined not so much by technological sophistication, but by sheer market power and by lobbying political authorities.

In 1979, Williamson substituted the somewhat rigid market/hierarchy dichotomy with a more general continuum of governance structures, or forms of economic organisation, based on the degree of autonomy of each

---

[5] Williamson's 1975 book on 'markets and hierarchies' was sponsored amongst others by the Brookings Institution and the Ford Foundation. Both institutions were actively engaged in what Kees van der Pijl (1984, see section 2.3.2) would call support for the 'corporate liberal' ideology, an effort to restore the supremacy of Fordism on a global scale.

of the parties involved. Firms would choose those governance structures which minimise transaction costs and thus increase efficiency. The transaction cost approach distinguishes itself from the neo-classical approach in at least two ways. Firstly, it is acknowledged that economic actors cannot collect all relevant information, which makes them subject to bounded rationality. Treaties between actors in markets thus can only be struck for limited periods of time, because no one can predict the outcome of the contract. Secondly, Williamson introduces the possibility of opportunistic behaviour of actors which increases the uncertainty of transactions, especially in the case of a small numbers game.

Williamson's three characteristics, however, are not the only determinants of the most appropriate form of organisation. Teece (1985, 1988) issued the notion of appropriability regimes under which firms would tend to cooperate in order to exchange information in specific technologies. Under a 'tight' appropriability regime it is extremely difficult to imitate technology, making firms more inclined to cooperate than under a 'weak' regime, in which case it is almost impossible to prevent the results of cooperation from leaking away to competitors.

2.5.2 Networks: between markets and hierarchies?

The rise of various types of inter-firm networks and 'industrial districts' has made several authors reconsider Williamson's dichotomy and rephrase it into 'make, buy, or cooperate'. In the words of Walter Powell:

> Networks are 'lighter on their feet' than hierarchies. In network modes of resource allocation, transactions occur neither through discrete exchanges nor by administrative fiat, but through networks of individuals engaged in reciprocal, preferential, mutually supportive actions . . . basic assumption of network relationships is that one party is dependent on resources controlled by another, and that there are gains to be had by the pooling of resources. . . . As networks evolve, it becomes more economically sensible to exercise voice rather than exit.
>
> (Powell, 1990: 303)

Charles Sabel *et al.* have referred to these new forms of inter-organisational production organisations as 'collaborative manufacturing' (1989), while Michael Best (1990) considers competition between networks the 'new competition'. Table 2.2 compares the basic characteristics of the network paradigm as presented by Powell (cf. Cooke and Morgan, 1991) with those of 'markets' and 'hierarchies'.

Powell argues that cooperation is the central element of the network type of organisation, exemplified by the following four features:

1 actors that engage in networking relations would be of complementary strengths;

Table 2.2   Markets, hierarchies and networks

Key features	Forms of economic organisation		
	Market	*Hierarchy*	*Network*
Normative basis	Contract – property right	Employment relationship	Complementary strength (1)
Means of communication	Prices	Routines	Relational
Methods of conflict resolution	Haggling – resort to courts for enforcement	Administrative fiat – supervision	Norm of reciprocity – reputational concern (2)
Degree of flexibility	High	Low	Medium
Amount of commitment among the parties	Low	Medium to high	Medium to high
Tone or climate	Precision and/or suspicion	Formal, bureaucratic	Open-ended, mutual benefits (3)
Actor preferences or choices	Independent	Dependent	Interdependent (4)
Strategic focus of core firms*	'Buy'	'Make'	'Cooperate'
Production concept*	Craft-oriented production/ flexible specialisation	Fordism (neo-Fordism)	Post-Fordism?

Source: Powell (1990: 300); * = our additions; the numbers in brackets (final column) refer to features mentioned in the text.

2 conflicts in the network would be resolved on the basis of reciprocity, because the actors would be concerned about their reputation in the relationship, while
3 the relationship would be open-ended and would contain mutual benefits.
4 In short, the actors would have become truly interdependent.

These claims have been based in particular on the work of Michael Piore and Charles Sabel.

2.5.3 The flexible specialisation thesis

In 1984, the US scholars Michael Piore and Charles Sable introduced their flexible specialisation thesis. This thesis presented an alternative production paradigm to traditional mass production, based on networks of small artisan firms in sectors like ceramics, knitwear, handmade cars, machinery, fashion apparel and shoe manufacturing. In their impressive study, Piore and Sabel phrased their thesis as follows:

> Flexible specialization is a strategy of permanent innovation: accommodation to ceaseless change, rather than an effort to control it. This strategy is based on flexible, multi-use equipment; skilled workers; and the creation, through politics, of an industrial community that restricts the form of competition to those favoring innovation. For these reasons, the spread of flexible specialization amounts to a revival of craft forms of production.
>
> (Piore and Sabel, 1984: 17)

The regional economy thus created represents an industrial district, a term introduced in the 1920s by Alfred Marshall (1961). The Northern Italian region of Emilia-Romagna ('Third Italy') has served as the role model for flexible specialisation. The dominance of networks of flexible specialisation in Emilia-Romagna but also in districts such as Baden-Württemberg (in southwestern Germany) would mark the temporary victory of networks of craft production ('post-Fordism') over mass production (Fordism). These flexible networks were able to produce small(er) production runs of sophisticated quality products for rapidly changing consumer preferences. The networks owed their innovative performance to extensive knowledge sharing and joint development that substituted for the cooperation within a hierarchy (i.e. a single large firm).

The ultimate test of the model of flexible specialisation, according to Piore and Sabel, will still be in the market. The authors present a historical and evolutionary view on industrial transformation, or industrial divides, in which market trends determine changes in production paradigms and in the use of certain technologies. In this view, the crisis of Fordism would result from the saturation and breakup of mass markets (1984: 184). Flexible specialisation networks would be the best fit to react to the fragmentation of core markets. The authors regard flexible specialisation as the best alternative to the American system of mass production.

The most important criticism of Piore and Sabel concerns their preoccupation with market forces, which makes them essentially 'neo-Smithian' (Amin and Robins, 1990). Piore and Sabel pay too little attention to the strategic options available to existing producers. Thus they fail 'to distinguish between extensive product differentiation by established large-scale producers and market fragmentation favouring new small-scale producers' (Cough, quoted in Elam, 1988: 12). Too often, Piore and Sabel reduce the process of industrial transformation to 'the perceived actions of "sovereign consumers"' (Elam, 1988: 13). As a consequence, they downplay the ability of firms to shape markets and they marginalise the role of politico-institutional forces, for instance in providing detailed regulations favouring or discouraging the rise of particular production models.

A second remark concerns the positive assessment of the flexible specialisation thesis regarding the high level of skilled work, high wages, and the positive role of governments in creating the small firm networks. Looking at working conditions under flexible specialisation, Badham and Mathews argue:

> in discussions of flexible specialisation ... not only is it often left unspecified how exactly flexible labour is to be defined, but it is also unclear whether it is a defining characteristic of new production processes (or paradigms), a functional requirement for the efficient operation of these processes, or an independent variable that may (post-Fordism) or may not (neo-Fordism) be combined with new production processes.
>
> (Badham and Mathews, 1989: 205)

The evolutionary perspective and the positive connotations of the flexible specialisation thesis have led to inappropriate mixtures of description and prescription. The claims derived originally from Charles Sabel's research in the Emilia-Romagna region were modest and surrounded by considerable academic specifications. Enthusiastic followers, such as Paul Hirst and Jonathan Zeitlin (1989), however, have argued 'that the model is universally applicable, since cooperative and trusting relations do not depend on small scale production, nor on any particular technology or market relation, but only on the presence of an appropriate set of norms and values' (quoted in Clarke, 1990: 76/77). Sabel himself has suggested that a 'macroregulatory' system of flexible specialisation towards an (inter)national confederation of flexible localities can be possible. These 'bonds extending beyond regional boundaries ... can become the first strands in a net of broader solidarity' (quoted in Amin and Robins, 1990: 29). However, as Amin and Robins correctly remark, 'the nature of the restructuring process is, sadly, less benign and harmonious than Sabel would have us believe' (ibid). They refer to the flexible specialisation or industrial districts thesis as the new orthodoxy:

> there is a vast alternative body of work which views contemporary transformations as a threat to localities as they become fragmented, integrated into and subjugated by international forces beyond their control, and victims of more intensified interregional competition. The new orthodoxy is, we suggest, wrong in assuming that structural change within capitalism today is about the restoration of a neo-Smithian international and national division of labour composed of a myriad of self-contained and self-regulating product-specialist localities trading each with each other on equal terms.
>
> (Amin and Robins, 1990: 29)

The flexible specialisation thesis is based on evidence of smaller firms that cooperate, that have a division of labour among them, and that are unable to control the end markets. These were therefore truly horizontal networks, consisting of firms of equal strength. However, if one firm finds a way to improve its position *vis-à-vis* the remaining firms substantially, or as soon as a large company enters the scene that is able to take over some firms or seize control over the distribution, the nature of the network will change from what one might call an egalitarian network of learning into a hierarchical network of control (see Chapter 4). To prevent the rise of such controlled networks, the Italian government has played – and according to Piore and Sabel was supposed to play – a pivotal role, not only in taking care of a research infrastructure, but also in keeping firms small and thus in keeping the network relations between the firms relatively balanced.

Recent studies indicate that the nature of the Italian networks has started to change. Based on a controlling position in the distribution chain, large firms have come to dominate the activities of smaller firms (cf. Bianchi and Gualtieri, 1990). According to local trade unions (interview with Francesco Garibaldo of FIOM (the metalworkers' union of the Italian Communist Trades Union), 23 March 1989) a segmented oligopoly is evolving in which large Italian and foreign firms have started to exploit the flexibility of the region, but now in a vertical manner. This directs the analysis back to the strategies developed by large firms to control production networks and to mould a government's regulatory policies.

In spite of this criticism, Piore and Sabel have described what will be defined below as the basic elements of an alternative concept of control of productive capital. This concept of control will be defined more precisely in section 3.9.

2.5.4 Conclusion of meso level approaches to post-Fordism and restructuring

This section has looked at three analytical approaches to restructuring and post-Fordism at the meso level of analysis. While Williamson's transaction cost approach only provides a very general perspective to study restructuring and to determine a firm's most optimal form of economic organisation, Powell has extended the options available to a firm to 'make, buy, or cooperate'. According to Powell, cooperation could take place in networks of firms of complementary strength, based on reciprocity, interdependence, and mutual benefits. Piore and Sabel's study of flexible specialisation networks in the Emilia-Romagna region probably provides the best empirical example of such supposedly 'post-Fordist' networking relations.

The preceding subsections on the network paradigm have produced three types of criticism:

1 Authors writing about the rise of a network paradigm tend to claim that the firms concerned would cooperate and act as interdependent partners, without analysing the nature of the network relations, or the possible sources of power or dynamism that lead to shifting relations in these networks;

2 Powell as well as Piore and Sabel are very positive about the emerging 'post-Fordist' working conditions in inter-firm networks. However, these authors often remain rather vague on the exact nature of these working conditions, and on the question as to whether flexible labour constitutes a prerequisite for networks to function. In addition, they often fail to consider whether such supposedly flexible labour can only be used in flexible networks;[6]

3 A final weakness of the majority of literature on network forms is that the role of political and institutional forces often receives too little attention (with the exception of Weiss, 1988, 1992; and to a minor extent Piore and Sabel, 1984). According to Powell, 'we know very little about what kinds of political and economic conditions support network forms' (1990: 326). These conditions should be brought more to the fore in the analysis of network and meso level analysis of industrial restructuring.

The meso level of analysis has nevertheless enabled us to identify two different production paradigms. Referring to Williamson's transaction cost approach, which distinguished between markets and hierarchies, and Piore and Sabel's flexible specialisation thesis, networks of small (artisan) firms and the vertically integrated large firm have emerged as two rival 'ideal types' of economic organisation. Both approaches emphasise networks as the organisation principle – be it internalised or externalised networks – but fail to operationalise these networks in a satisfactory way. The next chapters will therefore develop a framework that attempts to integrate the three categories of remarks above and provide a better understanding of the nature of networks. Before that, the discussion on the concept of post-Fordism will be concluded.

2.6 CONCLUSION: THE ELUSIVE CONCEPT OF POST-FORDISM

The concept of post-Fordism has been used to label or analyse a broad range of restructuring processes. In the preceding sections, the analytical use and validity of some leading contributions to the discussion on post-Fordism have been assessed at the meta, macro, micro and meso level of analysis. Table 2.3 provides a summary overview of this discussion. The conclusions regarding the analytical use of this concept are twofold.

1 Post-Fordism is too weak an analytical concept

Most authors writing on the concept of post-Fordism take into account only one level of analysis. They often fail to analyse either the underlying backgrounds or the effects of the changes they observe, which may lead to

---

[6] We will argue (sections 3.6 and 5.4) that 'flexible labour' and small artisan firms can also figure as the low end of an entirely different model of production organisation.

Table 2.3 Summary of approaches to post-Fordism

Level of analysis	Analytical approaches (section)	Main proponents	Argument/focus
Meta	Heterodox school (2.2)	Freeman; Perez; Nelson and Winter; Soete; Dosi	Shift in dominant techno-economic paradigm; evolutionary adaption of society
Macro	Regulationist school (2.3.1)	Aglietta; Boyer; Lipietz	Internal contradictions between accumulation regime and mode of regulation
	Amsterdam School (2.3.2)	van der Pijl; Overbeek	Retreat from interventionist to monetarist state policies: triumph of neoliberalism in USA and UK
Micro	Cooperative management of firms (2.4)	Mathews; Coriat; Kenney and Florida	Innovation and flexibility based on labour as a resource rather than as a cost
Meso	Flexible specialisation thesis (2.5.3)	Piore and Sabel; Hirst and Zeitlin	Networks of small artisan firms represent new type of division of labour; rise of industrial district (Emilia-Romagna)

quite superficial observations (Clarke, 1990: 75) or reductionist theoretical frameworks.

- At the meta level of analysis, scholars of the heterodox school have emphasised the integration of microelectronics in the production process. These authors conceive of technological change as an evolutionary and 'predetermined' process. The heterodox approach therefore underestimates the role of governments and does not explicitly address the changes in the production process.
- Theorists who addressed the post-Fordist thesis at a macro level of analysis, on the other hand, analysed post-Fordism too much in political terms or in too-general categories such as money capital versus productive capital. As a result, these authors ignored the range of developments that are currently taking place in the production process. This is a major weakness if one theorises on the outlines of any kind of 'post-Fordism'. Just like Fordism was based on technological and organisational innovations in a dominant sector of US production, any extension (neo-Fordism) or follow-up model (post-Fordism?) will also have to emerge in the sphere of industrial production.

- The concept of post-Fordism has been discussed especially at the micro level of analysis. Often these analyses went along with claims on increasing cooperation within the firm between workers and management. However, these claims tend to overlook the potential side-effects of the changes in the production organisation on third parties such as subcontractors or other competitors (i.e. at the meso level of analysis). Those authors who do recognise these side-effects do not indicate how they can be overcome at a societal or macro level. This is not merely a political problem but indeed a limitation of the analysis.
- At the meso level of analysis, the concept of post-Fordism has been least developed. The rise of inter-firm networks has been hailed by several authors as a step towards increasing 'interdependence' between companies. However, neither the working conditions within these firms, nor the institutional environment has been included in any meso level contribution to the discussion on post-Fordism.

2 *Post-Fordism is vulnerable to being used as an ideological concept*

The sweeping claims regarding the supposedly 'cooperative' and 'interdependent' nature of post-Fordism have to be rejected as unsubstantiated. Bob Jessop rightfully criticises the 'reformist misappropriation by social and political commentators on the current transition to post-Fordism' (1991: 165). The post-Fordist thesis is little more than a *post hoc* rationalisation of the internal dynamism of several individual firms. Once these cases are generalised into best-practice examples, analysis turns into ideology.

One 'trick' that many researchers writing on post-Fordism have used is to present the 'trajectory' to post-Fordism as the final stage in an inevitable restructuring process. As Clarke notes, post-Fordism 'does not depict an inevitable future, but defines a political project. Its ideological appeal lies in the fact that, lacking any significant social base, it rests its claims on its historical necessity' (Clarke, 1990: 74). The post-Fordist thesis is built on 'the assumption not that people make their own history through struggle, but that social development is subject to inescapable lines of tendency and direction established by the real world' (Peláez and Holloway, 1991: 137). As Badham and Mathews (1989) correctly note, there is no such thing as an inevitable transition to post-Fordism.

In conclusion, none of the approaches above sufficiently dealt with what can be regarded as five essential requirements of any theory of industrial, inter-firm and (inter)national political relations 'after Fordism':

1 To define post-Fordism as something entirely different from Fordism;
2 To position the rise of post-Fordism in a longer-term historical perspective;
3 To explain actual changes taking place in the organisation of production;
4 To reveal how various actors will be affected by this restructuring;

5 To include the wider social context and the (political struggle over) national regulation that hampers or supports particular trajectories of restructuring.

The discussion on post-Fordism only obscures the analysis of industrial restructuring. What is needed is a further categorisation and theoretical elaboration of the production concepts currently in use or being pioneered. Keeping in mind the remarks by Mathews (1989), such an exercise will have to pay special attention to the characteristics of the Japanese production system.

3 Rival concepts of restructuring

3.1 INTRODUCTION

One executive once stated: 'restructuring is like planting asparagus: you know you should have started three years ago'.[1] Restructuring implies handling various social and economic relationships at the same time. A change in one relationship inevitably affects the other relationships as well. Thus, restructuring decisions usually require a broad scope and a long-term perspective.

Consequently, the analysis of restructuring requires an identification of the appropriate actors and their strategies. After the discussion of leading approaches of post-Fordism and industrial restructuring in Chapter 2, this chapter generates the outlines of an alternative framework for analysing restructuring processes and the various structures and strategies of (actors within) industrial networks. The discussion in this chapter builds on approaches in the area of political economy (under the heading of institutional economics; Hodgson, 1988: 145ff), strategic management/business administration and labour sociology. Our analysis will start at the level of the firm. Business administration literature has traditionally focused on the question of how to create company internal synergies, tending to conceive of the firm's environment in simple terms such as 'customers' and 'the market'. Over the 1980s, however, the environment of a firm has been interpreted in broader terms, also to include other economic, social and political actors. This has led to the rise of an 'outside-in' perspective next to the more traditional 'inside-out' perspective (cf. Porter, 1990). This chapter tries to combine these two perspectives: starting at the firm level, the positions and strategies of actors which are in some way supporting the production process, such as supplier firms, trade unions or governments, will then be related to this core firm.

This chapter focuses on the different ways in which a firm may try to control a number of vital areas of its production process. Section 3.2 will identify five areas of strategic concern in capitalist production and consump-

[1] Derived from an Andersen Consulting advertisement, *BW*, April 1992.

tion, plus a number of control dilemmas that any firm faces in these areas. It will be shown that Fordism provided one possible yet only temporary resolution of these dilemmas. Other resolutions are conceivable and have indeed developed. Section 3.3 will look at the conditions that led to the rise of three rival concepts of control. It will be argued that post-Fordism does not represent a concept of control in itself, but is better understood as a rather odd combination of two other concepts of control. From sections 3.4 to 3.8, these rival concepts of control will be defined along with the five areas of strategic concern. In this way, it will be shown that these three concepts of control do present essentially different resolutions to the five areas of strategic concern. Section 3.9 will draw some first conclusions on the nature of the international restructuring race.

3.2 CONTROL DILEMMAS IN CAPITALIST PRODUCTION

As firms have to consider an increasing number of variables, they will have to search for ways to manage these growing uncertainties and dependencies (van den Bosch, 1989). In capitalist production and accumulation, i.e. the process of creating both internal and external synergies, one can discern five areas of strategic concern:

1 The labour process;
2 The supply of components and raw materials;
3 The distribution and consumption;
4 Core production technologies;
5 Finance.

The first three areas pertain directly to a firm's value chain, while the last two areas refer to some essential requirements over a longer period of time. Each area of strategic concern can be understood as a dependency relation, representing a control problem. The more a firm depends for these essential activities on other parties which it cannot fully control, the more it will have to take the strategies of these parties into consideration, and hence the less independent the firm is. Examples of this include specific labour inputs in quantity or in quality (1), and deliveries by subcontractors or outside suppliers (2). In the distribution and consumption area (3), it makes a huge difference to a manufacturer whether its product is sold alongside other brands or whether it controls a chain of single-franchise outlets. Production technologies (4) represent a very strategic area: product technologies may be emulated or even stolen, yet production technologies also depend upon the organisational and institutional context. Finally, if in the financial sphere (5) a firm can build on long-term and patient capital at favourable conditions, it may be better equipped to develop a long-term strategy. The role of the five control areas will be elaborated below.

The management of each firm, whether small or large, faces these areas of control and has to decide whether and to what extent it can control and/

or wants to control internal and external variables. The five control areas, however, can turn into real dilemmas if solving one problem leads to another one. Let us take the area of the labour process as an example. Harry Braverman (1974) analysed the 'degradation of work' and the destruction of crafts as the consequence of advances in production technologies under monopoly capitalism. He considered the 'Taylorist' separation of conception and execution a basic element of capitalist control. Braverman, like many others, argued that in the earlier periods of capitalism in the UK, subcontracting and outsourcing prevailed, which presented the capitalist producer with a large number of uncertainties. The industrial revolution brought labourers together in the same factory. Yet as Burawoy summarised:

> in reducing one form of uncertainty a new form was created: the uncertainty in the realization of labour power in the form of labour.
>
> (Burawoy, 1985: 27)

Thus when firms limited their dependence on subcontractors by integrating vertically, it became easier for workers to create mass unions in these large firms. In this way, one kind of uncertainty was simply replaced by another one, which increased the need for direct management control over the labour process (Braverman, 1974: 57–58). The rise of organised labour increased a firm's vulnerability to strikes. To prevent these strikes, the management had to bargain with labour unions over higher wages, which in turn helped to create mass consumption and a customer base for the mass producers. Since the 1930s this has been the basic 'productivity–wage' coupling mechanism that facilitated the virtuous growth circles of the Fordist production organisation in the United States and, with some deviations, in Western Europe.

The dynamics and ultimately the crisis of Fordism can be understood as the result of the continuing efforts to resolve one set of control problems leading to the inevitable rise of another set of control problems. In the medium run, capitalist production and accumulation can only expand after the various control dilemmas have been resolved simultaneously and in an encompassing manner. To this end, representatives of firms and banks have to formulate a coherent view on internal company structures and external preconditions for longer-term growth. This requires a comprehensive vision on how to resolve the five control dilemmas, and on the role to be played by the state, including a definition of the 'national' or 'common' interest. Such a view, therefore, can be dubbed a concept of control, following the definition provided by the Amsterdam School (section 2.3.2). In contrast to the Amsterdam School, however, this term will refer to concepts based on the organisation of the productive sphere.

As the history of Fordism suggests, no resolution of control dilemmas, and therefore no comprehensive concept of control, will function for ever. In fact, history suggests that any settlement of control problems will eventually provoke new contradictions and thus lead to new control dilemmas. One can distinguish at least three rival concepts of control contending for hegemony in modern capitalism.[2]

The first concept of control is based on (networks of) small and medium sized firms aimed at industrial craft-oriented production for small to medium scale markets. This type of industrial organisation has been called flexible specialisation (Piore and Sable, 1984; see section 2.5.3). Flexible specialisation networks may of course also succeed in producing for larger markets. This would only increase the possible hegemonic aspirations of the concept.

The second category of restructuring strategies has been aimed at creating mass production in large vertically integrated firms, on the basis of formal hierarchies producing for mass markets. This production organisation strives for 'economies of scale' and has been called Fordism (Gramsci, 1980). Its updated version could be called neo-Fordism. Under neo-Fordism, vertically integrated firms would also be able to serve medium sized (and sometimes even small sized) markets, due to the use of more flexible technologies and the introduction of less rigid organisational structures. However, the distinction between Fordism and neo-Fordism is often not very useful, particularly when looking at the European variant. In terms of the analytical framework presented by Badham and Mathews (1989; see section 2.4), a number of European firms had already shifted towards 'neo-Fordism' in the 1960s, modifying the American type of Fordism.

The third concept of control involves large vertically de-integrated firms, with more informal hierarchies producing at first for medium scale markets, but later also for mass markets. When analysing the shift in German industry from Fordism to 'automated Fordism' or 'ultra-Fordism', Dohse *et al.* (1984) labelled this concept 'Toyotism'. Toyotist firms are aimed at 'economies of scope', which implies shorter production runs than Fordist firms. Toyotism, therefore, is better equipped than Fordism to produce for smaller scale and niche markets. Others have proposed the term 'Fujitsuism' (Kenney and Florida, 1988).[3]

Sections 3.4 to 3.8 will specify the three concepts of control along the five control areas. These three concepts represent three conceivable ideal types of how – temporarily – to resolve the five basic control problems of

[2] Over the years, some varieties and mixtures of these concepts have emerged. Chapter 5 will eventually identify and define five concepts of control. Two of these, the concepts of industrial democracy and of macro-Fordism, are in fact mixtures of the other three and will not be discussed in this chapter.

[3] It has been argued for instance by Annemieke Roobeek that none of these concepts of control is very future-oriented. That has been our very argument. It is essential first to analyse the existing concepts of control before proclaiming the rise of a new and 'better' concept. At the end of the day, what is announced as a new production paradigm may be little more than a variety of one of the existing concepts of control. Awareness of the conditions required for the rise of an alternative concept of control may reduce some authors' urge to derive far-fetched conclusions or recommendations from a small group of commercially successful firms.

*Concept of
control*

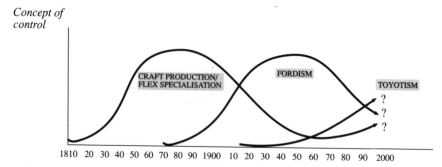

Figure 3.1 Hegemony of rival concepts of control (stylised representation)

capitalist production and accumulation. Each of these ideal types has come up in a very specific economic, social and political setting, and has flourished in a particular international context. Therefore, after it has come up, the 'purest' form of the concept of control will long be found in the country of origin. However, the principles of each of the three concepts of control are universally applicable, provided that the proper economic, social and political environment is created at the same time. The latter condition is almost impossible to realise. Thus the three concepts of control are at the same time unique in the sense that they require a specific infrastructure and governance structure to emerge, and general in their potential as a model for capitalist production and accumulation.

3.3 THE RISE OF A CONCEPT OF CONTROL: PARALLELS AND DIFFERENCES

The three concepts of control are truly rival concepts in the sense that they coexist and compete for hegemony. If one concept of control temporarily attains a hegemonic status *vis-à-vis* the other two in a particular state or trade bloc, the latter two may recede for a period of time but they will not vanish (cf. fig. 3.1). Although the three concepts of control are rival concepts, open competition between them has generally been limited. In history, the hegemony of a concept of control has been linked to the rise of particular hegemonic states (in the case of craft production and Fordism) or contending states (in the case of Toyotism and perhaps also in the case of Nazi Germany's 'variety' of Fordism).

To explain the latter observations, one has to look a bit deeper into the domestic and international setting behind the rise of the three concepts of control. In this process, one can discern parallels as well as differences. The first parallel is that a denial of access to or inadequate control over important foreign markets has spurred the three concepts of control. Secondly, being excluded from these markets, the industries concerned had to restructure, i.e. find ways to produce more efficiently for their domestic markets.

In each case, thirdly, this restructuring process was facilitated by government intervention, through direct expenditures and regulation. Fourthly, foreign firms found it very difficult to get access to and compete in the substantial domestic market of the firms pioneering the new concept. The government of the state in which a new concept of control emerged, therefore, was not able to enforce entrance to other markets, but did succeed in keeping foreign firms outside. In this way, domestic production firms could secure control over their own markets, allowing them freedom to experiment with the emerging production model and consider the control area of distribution and consumption as an integral element of the total emerging concept of control. Fifthly, both the rise of craft production and Fordism came about with large scale wars and changing positions of peripheral areas of the world economy. Below, it will be discussed whether the rise of Toyotism may lead to similar international events.

In the early nineteenth century, the Napoleonic Wars and Napoleon's Continental System effectively barred British industry from exporting to the European continent (Kennedy, 1987: 129). This blockade spurred an indigenous development in Britain that later became known as the Industrial Revolution. To compensate for the lack of external demand, and to enable Britain's war exercises, the British government stepped up expenditures for iron, steel and coal. In addition the government invested in docks, canals and railways throughout the country (Kennedy, 1987: 130). At the same time, the British government opened up new markets – primarily colonies, thus under direct control – in all other regions of the world, thereby circumventing the European Continent. Moreover, as Robert Cox pointed out, UK hegemony and the productivity rises of UK craft production have been helped by the creation of a national market, from which foreign producers were largely excluded (see also Mjøset, 1990: 4):

> Internal barriers to the movement of goods were substantially removed. So were the residual medieval guild-type restrictions on production and obstacles to the transfer of people from agricultural to industrial pursuits. Thus grew a broadly based, effective demand for the essentials of life – food and textiles for clothing. Market-oriented landowners and industrial entrepreneurs innovated production methods to meet this demand.
>
> (Cox, 1987: 57)

In the late 1920s and in the 1930s, the new techniques of Taylorism and mass production in the USA created high levels of productivity and a subsequent crisis of overproduction/underconsumption. In the 1930s, a wave of trade barriers struck the world economy, leading to a deep recession, many bankruptcies and 13 million unemployed in the USA alone. Between 1933 and 1943, the Roosevelt administration set up its New Deal institutions and invested some US\$ 15 billion (US\$ 150 billion at 1994 rates) to employ around 4.2 million people in public works, schools, airports and road construction. The National Industry Recovery Act provided for a national framework to impose shorter working hours and higher wages on all firms. Over the 1920s and 1930s, import penetration in the US market had been extremely low, providing US producers with a large home market without foreign competition (Stranger, 1990; Beniger, 1986).

However, Fordism only fully matured during the Second World War ('war-Fordism'), when the United States faced other states that had developed different varieties of mass production. Henry Ford, for one, was an admirer of mass production in Nazi Germany. The United States won the war – and concomitantly established worldwide hegemony – because US Fordism 'outproduced' its German and Japanese antagonists. Confronted with devastation in most of Europe and Japan, the Marshall Plan and 'Point Four' (a programme to spread scientific and industrial knowledge to developing countries; Lafeber, 1980: 81) had to ensure long-term US entrance to European, Japanese and developing countries' markets.

After the Second World War, Japanese manufacturers attempted to copy the American 'best-practice' system of mass production and produce large quantities of standard and cheap products. However, in the late 1950s and early 1960s Japanese companies found that it takes more than low prices to compete successfully. When Toyota and Nissan for instance tried to export cars to the United States, US car makers used their market power, lowering their prices and accepting temporary losses, to crush demand for the small Japanese cars (Friedman, 1983: 366). Thus in the postwar period, many Japanese firms experienced the situation where competition abroad was too severe to cope with on the basis of an 'inferior' variant of mass production and low wages only. Although the barriers facing Japanese producers were of a different nature from the ones facing UK producers in the early nineteenth century and US producers in the 1930s, the effect was essentially the same.

Therefore, Japanese firms were forced to produce more flexibly to meet demand in their smaller, but still sizeable, home market. In their industrial home market they were hardly confronted by foreign competition, due to an extensive system of quotas, tariffs and special technical and administrative import requirements. In fact the Japanese government had little choice but to restrict foreign producers from entering the Japanese market, because Japan's trade balance was already burdened by its high dependence on imported foodstuffs and raw materials. The Japanese Ministry of International Trade and Industry (MITI) moreover took the initiative to co-ordinate a wide range of industrial and technological development projects and stimulate inter-firm cooperation, for instance through obligatory second-sourcing to other Japanese firms.

There are also some marked differences in the rise of craft production/ flexible specialisation and Fordism on the one hand, and Toyotism on the other. It would seem that Toyotism emerged before the decaying US and

Fordist hegemony had created a vacuum for a new concept to fill.[4] There are several explanations for this paradox. Firstly, the roots of US mass production can also be traced to as early as the mid-nineteenth century (Brenner and Glick, 1991), implying that a concept of control requires a long period to fully crystallise. In the second place, the 'premature' rise of Toyotism may be due to the fact that competition between the three concepts of control has become more open after the Second World War. The very superiority of Fordism at the time left more room for rival concepts of control to (re)gain strength. Nevertheless, one could of course speculate whether the early rise of Toyotism points at a changing pattern in the rise of a new concept of control.

The second difference between the rise of craft production/flexible specialisation and Fordism on the one hand, and Toyotism on the other, is that the latter has not yet coincided with an overall wave of trade barriers or worldwide military conflicts between states and production systems. Chapter 6 will indicate how the internationalisation of Toyotism even hopes to circumvent these barriers and preclude a worldwide military conflict.

Finally, it still remains an open question whether Toyotism will become a truly hegemonic comprehensive concept of control, and whether the Japanese state will succeed in building a hegemonic position in the world on the basis of the Toyotist concept of control. Table 3.1 summarises some of the parallels in the rise of the three concepts of control.

This introductory discussion indicated that the notion of a concept of control requires a broad definition. One cannot fully understand the context or implications of any concept of control by only referring to differences in the organisation of production at the firm level. Whichever concept of control may become hegemonic at a specific time in a specific state, the explicit support by the domestic government is a *sine qua non*. The fact that the three concepts of control emerged after firms had been denied access to major markets points to the significance of controlling one's marketing and distribution.

3.4 CONTROL OVER THE LABOUR PROCESS

Having provided an initial definition of the three concepts of control and having pictured some historic circumstances behind their rise, the following sections will discuss which different resolutions these concepts offer to the five areas of strategic control identified earlier in this chapter.

The labour process constitutes the heart of production and of creating added value. Each concept of control offers markedly different mechanisms to control and secure labour's participation in capitalist production. Below, the different control mechanisms regarding labour unions, wages, worker

---

[4] Section 6.2 will discuss how the rise and fall of concepts of control coincides with hegemonic cycles.

Table 3.1   Parallels in the rise of the three basic concepts of control

Concept of control	Access to large foreign markets as takeoff of the concept	Strategic answers, government policies	Fate of peripheral countries in world economy
Craft production/ flexible specialisation	Denied due to Napoleon's Continental System	1 Napoleonic wars; 2 increasing UK state expenditures; 3 UK first 'integrated market' in the world	Colonialism
Fordism	Denied due to 1930s world recession and trade barriers	1 New Deal/National Industrial Recovery Act; 2 US trade barriers during 1920s and 1930s; 3 Second World War: USA outproduced Germany	Neo-colonialism
Toyotism	Beginning of Toyotist experiment early 1960s due to lack of marketing power. Still faces trade barriers	1 MITI guidance: weak anti-trust, enforces inter-firm cooperation; 2 closure of domestic market to outside producers; 3 1980s/1990s: internationalisation of Toyotism	Marginalisation?

skills, job security, the nature of control, and strikes will be discussed, first by stating the control mechanisms of craft production and Fordism, then by highlighting the Toyotist 'innovations'. The final subsection will present three sets of conclusions on the differences between the three concepts of control regarding control over the labour process.

3.4.1 Control over labour unions

Under craft production/flexible specialisation, labour unions tend to play a relatively marginal role. Due to the small size of firms, the basis to organise labour is often weak. In some cases, for instance when workers possess exceptional skills and large profits are being made, workers may organise and succeed in gaining improvements in working conditions and wages. Thus in the early twentieth century, highly skilled Dutch diamond workers were the first to obtain an eight-hour working day and a one-week holiday. Fordist mass production puts large numbers of workers within one company under comparable working conditions at comparable wages. This enhances workers' ability to organise and bargain with a company or even at a centralised (national) level. It is important to note that these mass labour unions often had to fight long battles with management before gaining recognition. Ford, for instance, refused to recognise the United Auto Workers until a 1941 strike forced the management to concede.

Toyotism is characterised by a decentralisation of bargaining through the establishment of enterprise unions, reducing workers' bargaining power. These unions are company sponsored and are not associated with any national federation. They include all company workers, and only company workers. In Japan, nearly one in every six executives have held a position in the enterprise union. Consequently, '(t)he union does not exist as an entity separate from, or with an adversarial relationship to, the company' (Abegglen and Stalk, 1985: 205). Such unions obviously facilitate the closure of 'constructive' deals between worker representatives and management – from the perspective of the latter.

Just as Ford had long been unwilling to accept a centralised labour union, workers will usually resist the establishment of an enterprise union as their sole representative. Analyses of Japanese trade union structures often omit the wave of union-busting, lay-offs and purges preceding the establishment of these enterprise unions in the early 1950s. In the smaller companies operating in a Toyotist context, unions will be rare. Not surprisingly, the overall membership of Japanese trade unions has steadily declined from over 55 per cent in the 1950s to only 25 per cent in 1990 (Keizai Koho Center, 1991: 72). Moreover, the production processes in Japanese firms have generally been designed in such a way that management can persuade workers and enterprise unions to cooperate unconditionally (Naruse, 1991: 39). The assembly line plays a key role in this control strategy over labour. Phenomena such as zero buffers and just-in-time delivery demand continuous allegiance from the 'favoured' workers in the large Japanese core firms.

3.4.2 Control over wages

In an economy of smaller artisan firms, wages tend to be flexible, i.e. based on demand and supply, on individual workers' qualifications and loyalty, and on the firm's performance. Legal protection of workers is often limited, to secure a 'smooth functioning' of the labour market. Under Fordism, the system of collective bargaining and the relative protection of workers by law, on the other hand, will lead more frequently to disputes between labour and management, and to a levelling of wages and income.

Toyotism implies the introduction of a hierarchy of wages, within the same firm – through the system of seniority pay – but in particular between core firms and subcontracting firms. Workers in the core firms generally enjoy relatively high wages and favourable working conditions, to assure their permanence in the production process. Workers in the smaller subcontracting firms have to work longer hours at much lower wages. A Toyotist core producer pays a large part of wages in the form of (semiannual) bonuses. In Japan these bonuses reach the equivalent of a third of total wages, while in the case of very profitable firms, bonuses may equal a full year's basic wages. Bonuses depend on a firm's performance, they allow firms to use the cash until the bonus is needed, and bonuses contrary to normal wages may be exempt from social security payment (Abegglen and

Stalk, 1985: 196). From the point of view of the national economy, bonuses lead to higher saving rates, because they are paid only twice a year.

Following the terminology of the French regulation school, craft production/flexible specialisation is characterised by partial wage relations (de Vroey, 1984). This means that there is an important role for domestic labour, such as women's labour, which is withdrawn from the social labour force. The 'reproduction' of the labour force is based on non-commodity relations, which means for instance that the unemployed and disabled are taken care of by the family or by public charity. (Neo-)Fordism is character-ised by the transformation into fully constituted wage relations. This implies that transactions in the economy are based on paid labour, i.e. that commodity relations dominate non-commodity relations. In this regime, unemployed people are taken care of by a system of social insurance, often under state control. Domestic labour has been reduced and women have – to some extent – reintegrated into the social labour force.

Toyotism to some extent reinstitutes partial wage relations. Social benefits are usually only organised for workers in the larger core firms. At a national level, the level of social security is low, which forces workers to save a high proportion of their salary for their old age (see section 3.8), increasing their dependence on the firm and enhancing solidarity at a family level. Under Toyotism, women again take care of a large part of the reproduction of labour, while unemployed and disabled workers are being 'privatised' to the family sphere. According to Christopher Deutschmann, the best way to understand the Japanese social system is 'not by considering how it provides but how it limits economic security of workers' (1987: 17). Lester Thurow contemplated: 'if each of us took care of grandmother at home, as the Japanese do, grandmother would not show up as part of the productivity problem' (1980: 79).

3.4.3 Control over worker skills

In craft production/flexible specialisation, worker skills are a firm's most important asset. A craft producer competes on quality and much less on quantity. Craft workers spend a relatively long time on one unit of output, creating an upward pressure on prices. Fordism drastically reduced the period of time spent on one unit of output, although at the expense of a lower quality, a de-skilling of the worker, and considerable worker aliena-tion (cf. Buitelaar and Vreeman, 1985).

Toyotism revolves around the dominance of the multifunctional worker. It is often claimed that the Japanese production system would have reintro-duced the multi-skilled worker (cf. Womack *et al.*, 1990: 13). This, however, is a serious misunderstanding. Workers in Toyotist core firms are a carefully selected labour aristocracy. They have undergone long and severe selection procedures, before being offered a lifetime position. Most applicants will fail during such procedures due to insufficient skills, talents, or loyalty, and will end up in lower-ranking supplier firms. The system of job rotation enables the core firms' management to keep control over essential functions in the organisation and is at least partly aimed at preventing workers from monopolising strategic information or qualifications. As Naruse argues:

> The multifunctional worker concept does not imply a skilled worker, as in the age of general machinery, before assembly-line production. .... Making a line worker multifunctional in the Toyota system means only training him in improved work methods. In other words, his work itself is essentially unskilled or semiskilled, not multiskilled, but he is required to be multifunctional so as to improve work methods and to be a leader of his work group.
>
> (Naruse, 1991: 45–46)

3.4.4 Job security

Craft production/flexible specialisation makes use of a high proportion of flexible labour with short-term contracts or contracts with an unspecified duration, leaving the employer free to decide when to dismiss a worker. Thus workers will be uncertain of their future, which depends on the firm's performance, the business cycle, and entirely personal aspects. In Fordism, the management has to ascertain a reliable work force, and labour unions will bargain for higher job security.

Toyotism is characterised by a system of restricted lifelong employment. The top management of large core firms uses lifetime employment as an instrument to 'buy' loyalty from their workers (cf. Cusumano, 1985: 140, 182).[5] The majority of workers in the lower-ranking supplying firms seldom enjoy similar provisions. However, even workers with lifelong employment will be confronted with relatively loose contracts or agreements on the nature of their work. Failing more detailed contracts, Japanese workers for instance had to bargain continuously (or reach 'mutual consent') over the exact contents of their work.

This system of restricted lifelong employment serves employers best in a less advanced economy: it will help the introduction of new technologies in the production system, since workers will not fear losing their job (Macmillan, 1984: 185). Somewhat paradoxically, however, employers may also benefit from this system in a potentially advanced economy with relatively high levels of unemployment. In such a situation, workers will highly value the long-term stability of lifelong employment, and employers may be able to play off one worker against another and create structural

---

[5] See the remarks in section 2.4, where it was indicated that at most 23 per cent of all Japanese workers enjoy lifelong employment (mainly in the large core firms) and that this share is still shrinking (Sassen, 1992). In spite of this, many Western business writers continue to celebrate lifelong employment as one of the most salient features of Japanese industrial relations (Hashimoto, 1990; Blinder, 1992).

dependencies that will be difficult to change once unemployment has largely disappeared.

3.4.5 Nature of control

In smaller firms, the owner – usually the major financier – tends to exercise a regime of direct or patronal control (Pot, 1988), accepting some responsibility in guaranteeing jobs and providing protection in return for worker loyalty and subordination, embedded in a model of 'family' relations. Under (neo-)Fordism, formal hierarchies and scale economies encourage the rise of more bureaucratic and Taylorist control mechanisms. The Toyotist labour organisation in the larger firms, involving smaller numbers of workers, represents in some respect a return to forms of patronal control – partly based on the principle of 'seniority' – but also of self-control. After all, the favoured workers would not want to risk their relatively privileged position in the core companies.

Team work is another cited characteristic of Toyotism. Team work can help to break down the traditional barriers between functional departments. Rockart and Short have referred to the establishment of such an organisational change as the 'management of interdependencies' (1989: 7ff). Imai *et al.* (1988), on the other hand, have concluded that the system of team work in fact could be better described in terms of more subtle control (or control by love):

1 A lot of attention is paid to the *selection* of the 'right' people on the project team;
2 These teams are often made to work in an *open and visible working environment*, preferably in one and the same room, to ensure that all team members get the same information and can be easily monitored;
3 Team members are encouraged 'to extract as much information as possible from the field – from customers and competitors – and more importantly, to bounce them off other members (source of *peer pressure*)' (Imai *et al.*, 1988: 549);
4 The *evaluation system* of the team looks at the group rather than at individual performance, another source of peer pressure;
5 Management, finally, establishes the *overriding values* to be shared by everyone in the organisation.

Some organisational theorists consider these teams as part of a 'concertive control' system. James Barker even draws a parallel with Weber's 'iron cage' of rational control through hierarchical and bureaucratic organisations: 'the concertive system . . . appeared to draw the iron cage tighter and to constrain the organization's members more powerfully' (1993: 408).

3.4.6 Control over strikes

Traditionally, the outbreak of strikes has been related to the size of the firm and the strength of labour unions. Thus in small craft producing firms, strikes are not very common – although, as was argued several times above, workers with special skills have always been in a much better position to bargain and, if necessary, strike to realise their demands. Generally, however, workers in craft firms will be in a in a weak position to enter into lengthy labour disputes. Under Fordism, however, strikes constitute a common phenomenon and an accepted means in workers' struggle for higher wages and/or better working conditions.

Under Toyotism, strikes in core firms will be a rare phenomenon. The Toyotist 'rules of the game' include that, in return for job security and relatively high wages, workers will not interrupt the production process. Thus Japanese workers in Toyotist core firms may show that they are on strike by wearing a black ribbon, but continuing to work. In the United States, industries and services lost fifteen times as many days due to strikes as in Japan over the 1978–87 period (Jackson, 1991: 273; in the United Kingdom this even amounted to forty times as many days).[6] The USA and the UK have been characterised by what can be referred to as micro-Fordism, in which links between productivity rises and wage increases were mostly established at the firm level. In the north-western European economies – in particular the smaller ones – corporatist bargaining structures fostered the rise of what can be called macro-Fordism (cf. Katzenstein, 1985; Mjøset, 1987).

3.4.7 Conclusions on the control over the labour process

From the six aspects of the labour process discussed above, we can derive a number of conclusions. The first set of conclusions deals with the nature of the productivity coalitions in the three concepts of control. Productivity coalitions can be regarded as the sum of the 'compromises' between management and workers, through which management secures future productivity increases, including the introduction of new technologies and automation into the production process. In principle, production coalitions are forged at a firm level but they can also be raised to a national level and become embedded in a framework of state regulation. (In Chapter 5, the term 'coalition' will be defined more precisely in terms of the relative (in/inter)dependence of two parties.)

Under craft production/flexible specialisation, explicit productivity coalitions are not very common. Weak institutional protection and vulnerability

---

[6] However, Japan lost more days in this period due to labour disputes than Germany. This is attributable mainly to the public sector, hardly to the private sector (cf. Keizai Koho Center, 1991: 70).

to the labour market cycle often suffice to enforce workers' cooperation on innovations that increase productivity. Under Fordism, workers' cooperation is sought by recognising and bargaining with mass labour unions as the key representative of all workers. Under Toyotism, finally, productivity coalitions are usually limited to the management of large firms and the enterprise unions comprising only the small group of favoured workers.

A second conclusion is that although craft production/flexible specialisation constitutes a concept of control on its own, it can also serve as the low end but as an integral part of the Toyotist concept of control. In analogy to Powell's claim on networks (cf. section 2.5.2), Toyotism does represent 'something between markets and hierarchies', yet with entirely different social implications than Powell suggested. Toyotism captures and combines many of the control mechanisms of both craft production and Fordism. While offering a minority of workers in core firms relatively favourable working conditions to gain optimal 'cooperation' and loyalty, it deliberately leaves the majority of workers exposed to uncertainty and less fortunate working conditions. Toyotism thus re-establishes productive capital's primacy over labour.

The third set of conclusions relates to the geographical division of labour. While craft production essentially leaves geographical shifts of production locations to be determined by long-term political changes and market conditions, Fordism tends to produce a gradual runaway on a national (from one domestic region to another) and even international scale, since Fordist producers will continue to look for cheaper labour and try to evade existing bargaining procedures with labour to increase their margins. Such a runaway creates leakages of purchasing power to developing and newly industrialising economies and undermines the wage–productivity coalitions in highly industrialised economies. Only a renewed productivity coalition (neo-Fordism) on a worldwide scale – including at least a part of the developing world – could perhaps close this leakage.[7] Toyotism, however, represents a major halt to the process of runaway and rather leads to a re-runaway process. Under Toyotism, the low end of the supply pyramid takes care of a much higher percentage of labour intensive work than under Fordism, which reduces the incentive for firms in industrialised economies to transplant production to low wage countries. The runaway process under Toyotism may remain limited to polluting and energy intensive industries – provided that raw materials are not readily available within the developed market itself. Ultimately, this may lead to a further marginalisation of many African and Latin American economies.

---

[7] Neo-Fordism represents the attempt to restore the Fordist compromise between management and workers at a level beyond that of the national state. The increasingly technocentric orientation of (neo-)Fordism (see section 3.7) and the challenge posed by Toyotism have been major forces behind the Triadisation of the world economy and are important barriers to establishing this compromise at an international level.

Table 3.2 Control over the labour process

Dimension of labour process	Craft production	Fordism	Toyotism
Working hours	Very long	Reduction	Long (overtime)
Labour unions	Marginal	Mass unions	Enterprise unions only in large firms
Wages	Flexible; 'partial wage relation': reproduction based on non-commodity relations	Modest levelling of wages; 'fully constituted wage relation'	Hierarchy of wages; backslide into 'partial wage relations': bonuses and overtime
Worker skills	High	Low	Multifunctional but low- or semi-skilled
Job protection	Marginal	Minimal level guaranteed by state	Only for favoured workers
Nature of control	Patronal control	Bureaucratic/ Tayloristic control	Patronal control/ self-control
Labour disputes	Marginal	Frequent	Limited, usually not affecting production as such
Nature of productivity coalition	Hardly existent	Coalition between management and mass unions	Coalition between management and favoured workers
Geographical division of labour	No runaway	Gradual national and international runaway	Re-runaway

Table 3.2 summarises the basic differences between craft production, Fordism and Toyotism in their control over the labour process.

3.5 CONTROL OVER SUPPLY

Each firm which depends on particular inputs such as raw materials or semi-finished goods will be confronted with the question of how to secure a steady flow of inputs at the lowest possible price but of sufficiently high quality. Each of the three rival concepts of control presents different solutions to this problem.

In the concept of craft production/flexible specialisation, the distinction between supplier and end producer is not as strict as in the other two concepts. While some firms may take care of the entire production chain, both making the industrial inputs, assembly and manufacturing the end product, other firms may produce only intermediary goods or finished products. Certain small firms may specialise in niches for which they produce both inputs for other firms and finished products for the market. Small firms also see their positions switch more easily from being supplier to becoming end producer and vice versa than in the other two concepts, which leads to a much more dynamic interaction pattern. This is not to state, however, that under craft production supply relations are necessarily equal. The coordination of supplies is essentially left to the market. To certify the skill levels of the workers, and thus the quality of supplies under craft production, small firms' networks have usually established training systems in which apprentices receive their training in one firm and then leave to work in another firm.

Fordism has developed an entirely different solution to the firm's vulnerability regarding price, quality and steady delivery of supplies. Henry Ford, dissatisfied with the supplies he received for assembly, decided to extend his activities to component production. At a certain moment, before the Second World War, Ford even approached a 100 per cent vertical integration level (Womack *et al.*, 1990: 58). At a theoretical level, the motives for a firm choosing hierarchies to reduce transaction costs have been elaborated by Coase (1937) and Williamson (1975, 1979, see also section 2.5.1). An end producer who produces components in-house can better control the quality and the price of these parts and guarantee their timely delivery. In this way, the management of a vertically integrated firm may include decisions on acceptable quality and price levels in its strategic planning. For some strategic components, such as computer chips in the case of IBM, or engines in the case of the large car manufacturers, it is more pressing for a firm to reduce uncertainty and produce its components in-house than for other, less strategic and technologically advanced parts.

In-house production of industrial inputs, however, also has some major disadvantages to firms. In the first place, in-house production increases the mass trade unions' bargaining power, because the unions' support base is extended to the workers in the components plants. This creates an upward pressure on wage levels for these workers, and thus on the price of the inputs. Firms' vulnerability to strikes also increases with in-house production. Thus a strategic strike in one essential component plant may thwart production in a multitude of downstream plants. A second disadvantage to in-house production of inputs is that the stock of components waiting to be used tends to be very high, partly to be prepared for strikes. This also leads to higher prices of the components, because storage space for inventories is very expensive. Thirdly, in-house production may reduce the link with technology development elsewhere. Fourthly, in-house production tends to have difficulty in supplying small series of a particular input, which reduces the end producer's flexibility.

In control strategies over supplies, Toyotism again represents 'something between markets and hierarchies'. While the typical Fordist firms' value added exceeds 30 per cent (and sometimes even 50 per cent), and the typical craft-oriented firm may score under 10 per cent, the value added of a typical Toyotist firm amounts to between 10 and 30 per cent. The Toyotist control strategy over supply can be characterised as one of vertical de-integration. Under Toyotism, most manufactured inputs are not produced by the end producer, but by strictly controlled yet formally independent supplier firms. Thus the Toyotist practice contradicts Williamson's logic that components with a high asset specificity, a high frequency of transactions and a high degree of uncertainty have to be produced in-house. Toyotism contains a number of rigorous control mechanisms to guarantee price level, quality and prompt delivery of inputs.

The role model of vertical de-integration is without doubt Toyota. The firm is an exemplar of the way Japanese end producers have organised their supply relations and designed control mechanisms to their supplying firms. Toyota developed a hierarchical supply system with a very limited number of first-tier suppliers (around 230 in 1988: see Ruigrok and van Tulder, 1991: 77). These firms in turn subcontract work to a larger number (around 5,000) of second-tier suppliers which in turn are supplied by an even larger number (around 20,000) of third- and fourth-tier suppliers. Beyond the third- and fourth-tier suppliers, household labour constitutes the most peripheral part of the supply hierarchy. Many of Toyota's suppliers are located within a range of 100 kilometres of what is actually called 'Toyota City'. The supply pyramid is translated into a profit hierarchy, in which the first-tier suppliers' profits and those of the core firm tend to converge, but in which differences increase rapidly down the pyramid. Partly due to the success of the Toyotist model, the position of the first-tier suppliers in the network has become very strong.

The pyramidal supply and profit structure is enforced by a deliberately designed one-way dependency of suppliers on the end producers, in terms of orders, access to finances, joint directorships, supply associations that certify quality control schemes, and equity relations (cf. Dore, 1987; Sayer and Walker, 1992: 213ff). As a rule, a Toyotist end producer never holds a majority of the equity shares of his supplier, but he does ensure that a majority is being controlled by the group as a whole. Suppliers' dependence on end producers is further enhanced by the latter's demand that suppliers deliver on a so-called just-in-time (JIT) basis, i.e. exactly when the end producer needs the components concerned. This forces suppliers to subordinate their production entirely to the end producer's needs – and in some cases simply shifts the burden of inventories from the final producer to the supplier. This is one of the reasons that working conditions simply *have* to deteriorate down the supply pyramid. It usually takes decades before a just-in-time system functions smoothly, because the end producer, of course, has to be absolutely sure that he can rely on his suppliers.

Toyotism therefore realises the advantages that Fordism accomplished by producing components in-house, but it does not share in the two major disadvantages associated to Fordism. Firstly, as recapitulated in section 3.4.1, labour conditions in the supplier plants under Toyotism are not being levelled automatically to those in the final assembly plant, because labour unions – if allowed – only operate at an enterprise level. This also means that the upward pressure on the price of components, and the higher vulnerability to strikes, have been removed. Secondly, the system of just-in-time production does not produce the high inventories found under Fordism.[8]

Finally, it is neither necessary nor desirable that the end producer is the *sole* buyer at all times, although this has traditionally been the case in large parts of the Toyota network. Being the sole buyer often creates a two-way dependence between the core assembler and the supplier. Moreover, if at a specific moment the end producer cannot process the suppliers' components, undercapacity and rising fixed prices will be prevented by delivering also to other clients (Junne, 1990b: 9). In this way, the supplier may also find out organisational and technological innovations being tried out in other supply networks, and channel this to its main customer.

3.6 CONTROL OVER DISTRIBUTION AND CONSUMPTION

Control over distribution and consumption is as important to a producer as control over supplies. A firm which can influence tastes, quality, size, and price of its markets reduces uncertainty and can optimise production runs and profits. In the three concepts of control, different strategies have been developed to control distribution and consumption.

Generally, craft producers have not been very successful in controlling their markets. Market power often boils down to sheer size. Craft-oriented firms have generally not been able to 'create' their own markets to the extent that Fordist or Toyotist firms have. As a consequence, craft-oriented production has been successful primarily in unpredictable markets with rapidly changing conditions or tastes, or in relatively marginal markets. In markets such as garments, ceramics, shoes, and knitwear, where fashion rules, flexible specialisation networks have been able to serve relatively large markets. Other forms of flexible specialisation have been found in such areas as the machine tool industry and specialty steel production, producing customised products for relatively small markets.

One way for smaller firms to enhance their control over larger and in particular international markets is to create their own cooperative trading organisation that handles exports to other countries. These trading organisations can also represent these firms on international trade fairs. The results with these trading organisations vary, although the results usually lag behind those realised in the agricultural sphere. This may be due to the fact that, for lack of centuries of traditions, flexible specialisation networks may

---

[8] The problem of large inventories under Fordism has also been dubbed the 'just-in-case' principle (cf. Schonberger, 1982). In spite of the 'advantages' mentioned here, there are also higher costs stemming from JIT, such as road congestion and higher risks.

be more vulnerable. Thus examples abound of large firms specialising in distribution on the basis of the smaller firms' flexibility.[9] Lacking sufficient control over distribution and consumption, the flexible specialisation concept is the least stable of the three rival concepts of control.

Fordism in principle strives for a vertical integration not only upstream – in component production – but also downstream – in distribution. Fordist producers aim to keep the maximum amount of control over their distribution channels. Before the Second World War, leading Fordist firms such as General Motors and Ford installed completely captive distribution networks and made extensive use of advanced marketing techniques. In the USA, however, the Supreme Court broke this concentration of market power and demanded that dealers could also sell other brands (Womack *et al.*, 1990: 170). After the Second World War, Fordist firms such as IBM also established fully controlled distribution channels, but added another element to the control strategy. IBM managed to strike primarily lease contracts with its customers, thus creating intimate distribution channels to its leading users. The 1980s personal computer battle between IBM, Apple and Atari showed how important sheer market power can be. IBM managed to gain the bulk of this market even though its competitors certainly did not offer technologically inferior products.

The fundamental difference between Fordist and Toyotist control strategies over distribution and consumption is that a Fordist firm produces first and sells later, whereas a Toyotist firm aims to reverse this sequence by selling first and producing afterwards. The Toyotist control strategy to distribution and consumption is derived from its higher flexibility in production, and its ability to adapt its production more easily to changing market demands. Thus it is Toyota's objective first to sell a car to a consumer, then to order the necessary components from its suppliers, then to assemble the car, and to deliver within two weeks.

Distribution and consumption are directly linked to the market, which calls for more direct forms of control if a Toyotist firm is to sell first and produce later.[10] Thus Toyotism involves the establishment of fully controlled dealership chains just like Fordism. However, *unlike* the Fordist case in the USA, Toyotist firms in Japan have been allowed to exploit single franchise dealerships. One major advantage of selling first and producing later is that the end producer prevents large and expensive stocks. Another advantage is that the end producer can react much more flexibly to changing tastes and changes in demand levels. The service to the customers

[9] This has for instance occurred in the case of the Italian flexible specialisation network producing textiles. Fiorenza Belussi (1986: 48) has documented how the Benetton family has been able to obtain its current strong position at the expense of the small fashion producing firms that were transformed into subcontractors or 'controlled firms'.

[10] Richard Samuels (1989) even goes one step further and concludes that Japanese 'consume for production' which represents a subtle difference from the western practice of 'producing for consumption'. Samuels reached this conclusion for a relatively closed market (nuclear fuel procurement), but his results hold relevance for other sectors as well.

comes at a price, however. Just as Toyotism offers the end producer higher profit margins *vis-à-vis* its suppliers, the end producer may also be able to charge higher prices *vis-à-vis* consumers. Generally, the tighter a core firm's control over its market – through an extensive network of single franchising outlets, as well as through extra services and higher quality – the higher consumer prices will be. If Toyotist firms do not control foreign markets to the extent they do at home, they usually charge lower prices abroad (cf. *Wall Street Journal*, 21 April 1987; cf. van Marion, 1992).

In the Japanese context, a specific, i.e. non-intrinsic factor to Toyotist production and distribution, greatly helped the Japanese producers to build up their concept of control. After the Second World War, the old *sogo shosha* (trading houses), linked to the important industrial groups (*keiretsu*), got reconstructed out of the remnants of smaller specialised trading companies (*senmon shosha*) into ten large trading houses. During much of the 1960s and 1970s these trading houses handled a large portion of Japan's international trade, closing the markets to unwelcome competitors. The *sogo shosha* also took care of considerable parts of domestic distribution. It is not correct, however, to characterise the *sogo shosha* as the captive marketing arm of Toyotist industrial groups (Tsurumi, 1984: 71) as they were in the pre-war *zaibatsu*. Nowadays, Toyotist core firms in Japan particularly use *sogo shosha* (sometimes more than one) when entering unknown foreign markets. Once established, however, they will gradually try to seize control over the existing import channel (cf. section 7.6).

3.7 CONTROL OVER (PRODUCTION) TECHNOLOGIES

In simple terms, production technologies are the instruments – hardware and software – which management and workers have at their disposal in the production process. One encounters markedly different corporate strategies regarding the introduction of new technologies by end producers and suppliers between the three rival concepts of control.

In craft production, the potential for anthropocentric production systems in principle is the highest of the three concepts (Lehner, 1991). In smaller firms, organisational and technological change may proceed in a more parallel way than in the other two concepts of control, and small firms may in certain cases react more flexibly to the rise of new process technologies. However, the associated financial risks will often be huge, which may prevent even flexible specialisation networks from investing in expensive process technologies. Partly therefore, small firms tend to make use of 'stand-alone' machines, but also because they generally serve smaller markets.

Fordism has traditionally opted for a technocentric orientation. In Fordist firms, production automation strategies are pursued to 'solve' organisational problems, resulting in particular from the relatively antagonistic labour relations. The Fordist rationale is to reduce the firms' dependency on (organised) labour and to reduce wage costs. Thus in Fordism, machines are developed not to complement human labour, but to substitute human labour. In this logic, automation runs counter to workers' interests. To gain acceptance for their production technology strategy, Fordist firms therefore do not speak about the 'unmanned factory', but of the 'factory of the future'.

The (neo-)Fordist technocentric obsession has led to massive investments in highly sophisticated production process technologies with often disappointing results. Leading Fordist firms such as General Motors, Ford, Kodak and General Electric have the highest density of production equipment in their factories, and have for a number of years hunted the spectre of 'computer-integrated manufacturing' (CIM). Under CIM, computers would coordinate the design, administration and manufacturing of products. To achieve the productive gains CIM was ultimately expected to yield, these firms initiated a 'manufacturing automation protocol' (MAP). MAP had to create 'open standards' in order to link computer equipment from different vendors (such as IBM and DEC). Although the MAP initiative rapidly spread to other (Fordist) user firms in Europe and Japan, it has not been very successful, partly because the initiators have tried to protect their technology (Dankbaar and van Tulder, 1989). In (neo-)Fordism, expensive automation projects therefore always face diffusion problems.

Toyotism can be typified as following an organocentric orientation regarding production technologies. In Toyotist firms, organisational change precedes the implementation of particular production technologies. Throughout the 1980s, it has proven an ineradicable misunderstanding that the performance of Japanese firms was mainly based on a widespread use of advanced production technologies. Japanese firms had made their advances in productivity, flexibility and quality long *before* the electronics technologies were widely used (Kaplinsky, 1990). Over the 1980s, Japanese firms and subcontractors did show the highest density of industrial robots, yet these were mainly standard (simple, dedicated) robots used for repetitive tasks (Edquist and Jacobson, 1988), and installed *after* the production organisation had been restructured. From then on, single purpose robots could gradually be upgraded in close interaction with operators. This also means that Toyotist firms tend to aim not for expensive state-of-the-art process technology, but for somewhat less sophisticated and less risky technological standards that leave the option of subsequent 'incremental' innovations open.

Thus under Toyotism, new process technologies can be introduced with less friction. Introduction is further facilitated by the fact that workers in the large core firm are less likely to see automation as a danger to their job, due to their lifelong employment. However, diffusion of new process technologies to users and suppliers will also create fewer problems. On the basis of their central position in the supply pyramid, Toyotist core assemblers are better able to persuade suppliers to help develop and introduce these technologies, and also take their share in the costs. Not surprisingly, therefore, Toyotist end producers have shown considerably less interest in the concept of CIM.

3.8 CONTROL OVER FINANCES

Access to and/or control over finances allows a firm to adopt a longer-term perspective and enhances its possibilities of developing independent strategies regarding the other control areas. The ideal types of the three rival concepts of control also offer markedly different patterns to obtain or control the required finances.

In craft production, the owner of the firm tends to be the major financer. In many cases, owners will not be able to finance all required investments themselves, in particular if they are operating in an innovative or highly specialised market. Thus a typical small craft-oriented firm will have to rely on banks to co-finance its investments. As a rule of thumb, banks will be cautious of financing over 50 per cent of a small craft-oriented firm's operating capital, because neither party has an interest in exceeding this level. Banks will make sure that their investments do not exceed the total value of the firm's assets, which serve as the guarantee for the outstanding loan. Of course, this percentage may rise if the owner is also willing to mortgage his personal properties. The owner of the firm, on the other hand, will have to be careful not to become too dependent on the bank, which may cast a negative verdict on the firm's prospects at a stage where it can still be sure of recovering its outstanding credits. In spite of such precautions, a relatively high proportion of craft producers go bankrupt.

The continuous financial insecurity of craft production contributes to a relatively short-term business perspective, in which survival will often be more important than strategic planning. There may be two ways of solving the craft producers' need for a stable financial base. Analogous to the distribution sphere, networks of small firms may join forces and establish cooperative banks. However, as in the distribution sphere, cooperative banks have been most successful in the agricultural sector, and much less so in manufacturing. A second and 'fatal attraction' to many small firms is to become part of a 'network of control' (see Chapter 4) and work as a supplier or subcontractor to one large customer-firm that provides financial support in return for a substantial reduction of autonomy.

In Fordism, the strategy of vertical integration has also been applied to the area of finances. Based on the rise of production and consumption, Ford and General Motors have from an early stage onwards aimed at a maximum degree of financial autonomy and self-financing of activities. A typical Fordist firm therefore owns a high percentage (between 50 and 100 per cent) of its total operating capital, which means that it wishes to occupy an independent position from banks. Nevertheless, Fordism has often been understood in terms of a (temporary) alliance between money and productive capital (cf. van der Pijl, 1984). In this alliance, banks financed corporate investments and trading. In the second place, banks helped to boost consumption, providing easy credits to consumers and financing budget deficits.

In the early days of US Fordism, this interplay of forces led to the rise of a credit economy characterised by a high level of consumption loans, state budget deficits, and low levels of household savings, each contributing to high interest rates. The rationale of this process is obviously to extend the Fordist 'growth spiral' as long as possible. However, as soon as domestic consumption approaches its limits and starts to decline – in relative or even absolute terms – firms' profits and thus their ability to self-finance their activities will come under siege. In the 1960s and 1970s, this process was in fact even enhanced by competition from non-Fordist players due to the 'import gap' referred to above. Once Fordist growth declines, the balance between money and productive capital will inevitably shift in favour of the former. Fordist banks ideally do not have direct equity links with manufacturing firms – which in the US case are banned by government – and lack a strong tradition of investment banking. Put simply, Fordist firms seeking capital in a structurally depressed economy can either turn to these banks or issue new shares. In many cases, the result will be alike: producers will be forced to shorten their time horizon and renounce longer-term strategic objectives in favour of shareholders' quarterly dividends.

Toyotism, unlike the previous concepts of control, is characterised by much closer cooperation between manufacturing firms and banks. Whereas craft production and Fordism were characterised by an uneasy relationship between money capital and productive capital, one could perhaps argue that Toyotism represents the (temporary?) triumph of productive capital over money capital. One could also speculate whether under Toyotism productive capital and money capital have finally come to terms, ultimately permitting capital's domination over other political, social and economic parties.

The Toyotist logic of outsourcing and vertical de-integration is also applied to the financial sphere. Toyotist firms generally own only a minority of their operating capital. Under Toyotism, debt–equity relations of 80 per cent are not exceptional. These debts are usually shared by several banks that each takes relatively minor participations, minimising the risks. As a rule, the bank with the closest ties to the producer concerned acts as the major financier in such deals. Large Toyotist end producers maintain close relations with at least one industrial bank, and often with several banks. The latter situation will obviously further reduce the end producers' dependency on banks.

A second characteristic of Toyotism is that financing through open securities does not play an important role. Rather, firms belonging to the same conglomerate own minority shares in many affiliated companies, both

Table 3.3   Basic differences in the financial area between the three concepts of control

	Own capital	*Household savings*	*Interest level*	*Corporate goals*
Fordism	High ($\pm$ 70%*)	Low (8%*)	High	Quarterly profit maximisation
Craft orientation	Medium ($\pm$ 50%**)	Medium (9–13%, except UK**)	medium	Both growth and profit goals
Toyotism	Low ($\pm$ 20%***)	High (19%***)	Low	Growth maximisation

Note: asterisks represent the actual levels in the USA (*); the EC (**); and in Japan (***), early to mid-1980s.

end producer and suppliers, leading to a network of cross-equity sharehold-ings, and creating a 'mutual dependency' on the 'fortunes' of the network as a whole. However, as indicated several times, these 'dependencies' and 'fortunes' are not structured evenly.

A third essential element of Toyotism is that it deliberately maintains high household savings. As was argued above, Toyotist workers have to save a high proportion of their income to support their old age, for lack of good pension schemes. This creates a reservoir of cheap domestic capital, and low interest rates. As long as this capital cannot move freely in the domestic economy, but is controlled by banks, Toyotism allows for the possibility to manage consumption, domestic investments, and, if necessary, internationalisation.

Based on these three aspects, Toyotist firms are generally able to adopt a longer-term perspective. Over the second half of the 1980s, many big Japanese Toyotist producers have even been able to reduce their ratio of debt against own capital (Itoh, 1990: 184ff), and many firms saw their deficits turn into a surplus. This only increased their bargaining position *vis-à-vis* banks, their ability to finance and thus maintain or enhance control over subcontractors or dealers, and their ability to adopt a long-term perspective to strategic investments in production equipment or inter-nationalisation activities.

Table 3.3 summarises the basic mechanisms in the control area of finances under craft production, Fordism and Toyotism.

3.9 RIVAL CONCEPTS AND THE SHAPE OF AN INTERNATIONAL RESTRUCTURING 'RACE'

This chapter identified three rival concepts of control. The concepts of craft production, Fordism and Toyotism have been introduced as simultaneously competing models of economic organisation, industrial organisation, inter-firm relations and institutional organisation. Figure 3.2 summarises the characteristics of these three concepts of control.

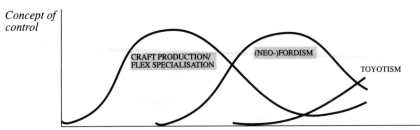

Concept of control			
	CRAFT PRODUCTION/ FLEX SPECIALISATION	(NEO-)FORDISM	TOYOTISM
Labour process	• Direct/patronal control • Extremely long working hours • National division of labour • Non-unionised/craft unions	• Bureaucratic/ Tayloristic control • Reduction of working time • international division of labour (runaway) • Mass unions	• Limited number of core workers: self-control/patronal control • Flexible/longer working time • Re-runaway • Company unions
Supply	• Flexible supply and demand networks	• Vertical integration: limit subcontracting as much as possible	• Vertical deintegration: JIT control, in vertical hierarchies and household labour
Distribution/ consumption	• Focus on fashionable goods in relatively small quantities • Limited control over (international) distribution • UK as first integrated market	• 'Creation' of mass markets through marketing techniques • Forward integration towards dealers • Most dynamic and integrated market in the United States	• 'Individualisation of consumption': mass production for 'individual needs'; marketplace as 'virtual R&D laboratory' • Integrated logistics: distribution controls production • Most dynamic and integrated market in Japan
Technologies	• Inventor is often also owner of firm; simpler technologies predominate • Greater potential for people-centred technologies • New technologies = reorganisation	• Big firms and science-based industries predominate • Technocentric: technology → reorganisation • Move towards open standards	• Technology concentrated with big conglomerates in firm laboratories • reorganisation → technology • standardisation: followers' strategy
Finances	• Owner/financier of firm together with (independent) specialised banks • Combination of market share and profit maximalisation	• Own capital financed; large number of small shareholders; commercial banks • Profit maximising as company goal	• Debt finance; industrial banks; small number of large shareholders; cross ownerships • Maximising of market share as company goal

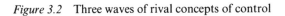

Figure 3.2   Three waves of rival concepts of control

Many researchers, as well as business and government representatives adopted the idea of an international restructuring race (Junne, 1984a). This restructuring race can be conceived of as a race between rival concepts of control. Over the 1980s, this race was run in two consecutive stages.

At first, the issue at stake was to decide which concept of control offered the 'best' solutions to the production and accumulation problems experienced by the industrialised countries. This process of comparing which concept of control will be most appropriate can be called a horizontal restructuring race. This horizontal restructuring race also involves the transition period in which business strategists (a) still attribute the failure of 'their' concept of control largely to one or two aspects that appear to function better in a rival concept of control – such as the production of new technologies (cf. Davidson, 1984; National Research Council, 1983), the introduction of new technologies into the production process, or the 'guidance' provided by government institutions – and thus (b) attempt to introduce these aspects into the ruling concept of control.

Once a significant group of strategists from certain industries, banks and government have reached a compromise on one particular concept of control, the second stage of a vertical restructuring race will commence. A vertical restructuring race centres on the question of how to resolve the inherent control dilemmas associated with the concept of control selected, but also on the transition from one concept of control to another. These dilemmas will not be resolved from one day to the next. In this stage of vertical restructuring, therefore, these strategists will experiment with new types of relationships between social actors, and thus with substantial social conflicts. In the next two chapters, the basic shape of these relationships will be defined for each of the three concepts of control.

4 The dynamism of industrial complexes I

Bargaining within the value chain

4.1 INTRODUCTION

The previous chapter identified three concepts of control and indicated their different handling of some strategic control areas. The objective of this chapter and of Chapter 5 is to elaborate the dynamism of these concepts of control at the meso level of analysis. At this level of analysis, we will get a better view of the nature of interaction within industrial networks. Sections 4.2 and 4.3 will clarify a number of methodological issues. Section 4.2 will discuss the choice of the main actors to be studied in an industrial network and defines the concept of an industrial complex. Section 4.3 will propose a scale of dependencies between (groups of) actors. This scale will be used in the rest of this book as a qualitative yardstick to assess the relative bargaining patterns within an industrial complex.

In the second half of this chapter, we will begin our analysis of the dynamism of industrial complexes by focusing on the bargaining patterns between the central actor of these networks, which will be referred to as the core firm, and the (groups of) actors engaged in the core firm's value chain. Section 4.4 will tackle a core firm's upstream bargaining relations towards suppliers. Section 4.5 will go on to analyse bargaining relations with labour. Section 4.6 will conclude the analysis of bargaining relations within the value chain by assessing the downstream relations towards distributors.

4.2 THE CHOICE OF ACTORS IN AN INDUSTRIAL COMPLEX

This section introduces the concept of an industrial complex as a specific type of network.[1] A 'network' has the following characteristics: (1) it is

---

[1] In principle, the term 'industrial complex' also pertains to 'service industries'. Over the 1980s, services contributed a growing share to developed economies' GNP, particularly in the USA, leading to claims of 'servitisation' as the new key to creating competitive advantage (cf. Vandermerwe and Rada, 1988). In reality, the distinction between industry and services (as between agriculture and industry) is becoming increasingly blurred (cf. Cohen and Zysman, 1987; van Tulder, 1992). For instance, due to outsourcing, activities such as bookkeeping or catering that were previously defined as 'industrial jobs' have been redefined as 'service jobs', without a change in the content of the work (even if the context, i.e. the

relatively stable: the actors do not meet accidentally; and the interaction is aimed (2) at the exchange of goods, capital, technology, information, skills and/or people; and (3) at the allocation of *values* (for instance on how the interaction should occur) (cf. Galtung, 1964, 1971; Wallensteen, 1973: 32).

Traditionally, industrial economics has focused on simple input–output models in which some firms act as suppliers and others as buyers of a product. These models approached an industry in terms of a value added chain, a production chain or an industrial *filière* (a concept that became popular in France in the early 1980s; cf. Groenewegen, 1989). Industrial economists primarily analysed supplier–buyer relationships in a market setting. Michael Porter has extended these models by sketching five competitive forces that determine an industry's profitability: (1) rivalry among existing competitors, (2) the bargaining power of suppliers, (3) the bargaining power of buyers, (4) the threat of new entrants, and (5) the threat of substitute products or services (Porter, 1985: 5). He regards the relative positions of suppliers and buyers in terms of bargaining relations, emphasising the importance of other than simply market-driven motives in a competition strategy.

However, Porter does not analyse all competitive forces from a bargaining perspective. He considers new entrants or substitute products/services primarily as 'factors' of competition. The same confusion between 'actors' and 'factors' appears in Porter's diamond 'model' (1990: 71), which expands the competitive advantages model from an industry to a national level. This framework distinguishes four 'attributes' of the national environment that shape the conditions for local firms to compete: (1) factor conditions, (2) demand conditions, (3) related and supporting industries, and (4) firm strategy, structure and rivalry. Compared to his earlier work, the diamond model introduces 'factor' conditions and raises the effect of the original five competitive forces to a higher level of aggregation. Porter's use of 'factors' *and* 'actors' leads to a model which is heuristically interesting, but which fails to expose the full dynamism of the network, precisely because actors are reduced to factors. In Porter's models, for instance, strategies of banks and labour unions are simply reduced to 'factor endowments' (1990: 75ff).[2]

The objective here is to formulate a more dynamic framework incorporating the bargaining perspective as a central explanatory mechanism. The third element of the definition of a network, which pointed at the allocation of values within a network, already indicated that the interaction within a network can only be fully understood if one also takes into account the power relations between the constituent parties.

---

dependency *vis-à-vis* the core firm, will have changed substantially). In general, core firms will often be manufacturing firms and less often independent service providers. To account for the growing content of industrial work in distribution activities, some have even proposed to use the term 'indistribution' as a new sector in the economy.

[2] This criticism also goes for the other approaches towards the production chain mentioned before. De Banville and Chanaron (1991) for instance criticise the *filière* approach for not taking into account how the respective stages of the *filière* are linked through financial ties.

An example of the importance of bargaining power can be read in the work of Lundvall and others, who have documented how, through the 1980s, large and technologically leading firms were able to impose the trajectory of global restructuring upon other firms. These large firms, which they labelled 'user-producers', not only produce new products and production technologies, but are also among the leading users of these technologies. This endows them with greater power and a better bargaining position than other, particularly smaller firms. In this way, these large firms have reduced the prospects for new entrants and have influenced creation of substitutes (Lundvall, 1988; Andersen and Lundvall, 1988; for related critique to Porter, see also John Dunning, 1991: 42).

Likewise, it makes sense for all big firms with large production and technological activities to position themselves in the *core* of networks of supply and distribution, and play a leading role in the creation of added value and in restructuring. A core firm tries to be such a spider of an industrial web. It can be recognised on the basis of the following characteristics:[3]

- The first characteristic of a core firm is its sheer size. A core firm has sales of at least US$1 billion. This condition serves as a *sine qua non* for the other characteristics below;
- A core firm *by definition* has a high degree of independence from other actors. A core firm is the principal actor as well as the director of the play. In certain types of networks, a core firm may have to give up its role as the sole director, yet it will always remain the leading actor, and, if given the opportunity, it will try to regain control;
- A core firm has direct access to domestic and foreign end markets and/or customers, either through subsidiary sales and service offices, or through third parties importing/distributing the core firm's product and offering service. A core firm will at all times be able to license and control the use of its own trade mark (except for criminal abuse);
- A core firm owes its relative independence (1) to its control over a series

---

[3] Throughout this study, we run the risk of reification. Reifications are a 'sin' against academic thinking and conscientious writing and suggest a simplicity which does not exist (cf. van Tulder, 1993: B15). In these types of studies, reifications are related to the level of analysis problem. For instance, it is false to suggest that a firm or government has *one* strategy since it was top management that came to this decision, after an internal and external bargaining process. One should also consider whether it was a unanimous decision, which interests or departments or persons prepared the decision and which opposed it. This problem is like the wooden Russian dolls: one always finds a new doll after opening up the previous one. Unfortunately, at the most detailed level, personal rivalries are often more important than the matter itself, and one risks losing the overall picture. Therefore, reifications can never be escaped entirely. Moreover, reifications may greatly advance the readability of a complicated analysis. The ultimate choice for a meso level of analysis also implies a choice not to deal extensively with internal organisational aspects, or to reconstruct the making of every strategy, unless the latter is essential to understanding this strategy or important conflicts.

of core technologies and other strategic competencies, particular to an industry or industrial activity; and/or (2) to its financial muscle;

- A core firm has an explicit vision of (1) the organisation and management of the value chain, including the internal labour process; and (2) the role that external actors (such as banks and governments) should play to facilitate the creation of added value and the (re)structuring of the network;
- A core firm's vision of the organisation of its industrial complex serves as an orientation point which it strives to accomplish. The logic of industrial restructuring within and between industrial complexes should be studied as an interplay between this vision and the core firm's ability to determine the rules of the game within the industrial complex;
- A core firm will often be a user-producer, meaning that it not only produces new products and product technologies, but it is also among the leading users of these technologies.

An *ascending* core firm may be recognised on the basis of the following characteristics:

- Control over relevant core technologies and other strategic competencies;
- Immature sales and services network and/or the inability to benefit fully from its own trade marks.

Conversely, a *descending* core firm may be recognised on the basis of the following characteristics:

- Gradual loss of control over relevant core technologies and other strategic competencies;
- A faltering sales and services network and/or a loss of image of its own trade marks;
- Financial difficulties that are increasingly difficult to solve;
- Defensive alliances with governments and other industry players.

An industrial complex then can be defined as a bargaining configuration organised around a core firm, consisting of (groups of) actors which are directly or indirectly engaged in the production and distribution of a given product. Chapter 7 discusses the domestic and international restructuring strategies of the world's one hundred largest core firms.

The actors most directly engaged in the production and distribution of a given product are threefold:

1 The *suppliers* or *subcontractors* which provide the components/parts to be processed in the finished product;
2 The *workers* who carry out the actual production process;
3 The *distributors* or *dealers* which deliver the goods to the customers.

However, as argued above, the strategies of (core) firms cannot be analysed satisfactorily without taking into account other environmental actors. Some have integrated these actors into the concept of a governance structure or regime (cf. Streeck, 1988; Dankbaar, 1989; Williamson, 1979; Kitschelt, 1991). A governance regime refers in particular to the institutional setting and the social relations of production.

These environmental actors arise first of all from the additional areas of strategic concern: production technologies and finances. Production technologies cannot be translated into one actor; they are produced either by the core firms themselves or by suppliers. The area of finances is represented by banks and other financial institutions. Finally, the state usually plays an important role in shaping the regulatory environment, both at a national and at an international level. In the analysis of industrial networks, the state is often not considered a separate actor but simply a 'factor' of competition. Even authors who do integrate the role of government into their analysis tend to focus on possible business responses to government regulation (cf. Rugman *et al.*, 1986: 297ff). Discussing the role of governments as a possible fifth determinant of competitive advantage, Michael Porter concluded that governments only play a partial role in influencing the preconditions for the other parts of the diamond to develop (Porter, 1990: 126ff).[4] However, if governments only play a partial role, this should be verified, not postulated. In many industrialised economies, governments have performed and continue to play a key role, for instance in promoting strategic industries. This study will integrate the role of government into the analysis of industrial complexes, and will try to identify and interpret the meaning of different types of relationships between firms and governments.

In sum, an industrial complex is made up of five types of bargaining relationships (see also Figure 4.1):

1 Relations between a core firm and its suppliers;
2 Relations between a core firm and its workers;
3 Relations between a core firm and its dealers;
4 Relations between a core firm and its financiers;
5 Relations between a core firm and its government(s).

This chapter discusses the first three relationships, i.e. a core firm's relationships within the value chain. Chapter 5 discusses the remaining two, or a core firm's relationships outside its value chain. The next two sections will indicate how these relationships will be analysed.

---

[4] In the end, however, Porter reintroduces governments for having a prominent role in influencing the other parts of the diamond. This confuses the distinction between the (four) primary determinants and the role of government as 'secondary' determinant of competitive advantage, and stems from mixing up factors and actors. Porter's plea for non-interventionism, and his choice of treating governments as a secondary force – which should leave market forces free, and which should only provide generic support to industry through education, infrastructure, and the promotion of technological innovation – primarily originates from an ideological and much less from an academic basis. For a related critique and an attempt to integrate government into Porter's competitiveness diamond, see Stopford and Strange, 1991: 8, 9.

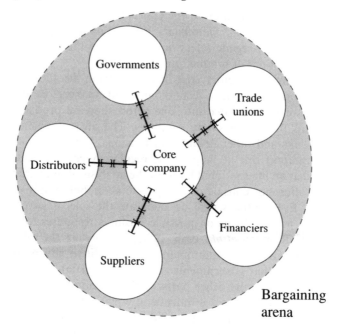

Figure 4.1 Bargaining relations within an industrial complex

4.3 THE NATURE OF BARGAINING: DEPENDENCY RELATIONS IN AN INDUSTRIAL NETWORK

The interaction within an industrial network will be analysed in terms of bargaining. Van Damme (1993) mentions four authors as providing the basic building blocks of bargaining theory (Raiffa, 1982; Fisher and Ury, 1981; Walton and McKersie, 1965; and Schelling, 1956). Raiffa formulated six 'organising questions' in the analysis of bargaining: who, why, what, where, when and how. The previous section focused on the first question, i.e. who are participating in bargaining processes. This section will take a closer look at the 'why' and 'how' questions, while the next sections will consider the remaining questions.

4.3.1 Power and dependency in political economy

A central element in the bargaining process is the concept of power. According to a traditional US definition, power represents 'the authoritative allocation of norms and values over society' (Parsons, 1957). Dahl (1957) defines power as 'actor A's ability to make B do something he would not have done otherwise'. Political scientists have also distinguished between power and influence. '(I)nfluence is applicable to a situation where A affects individual B, without B subordinating his wishes to those of A. . . .

That is to say, A has influence over B, and over the making of a decision, but it is B that has the power finally to decide' (Pateman, 1979: 69–70).

The question of how to use these concepts in analysing restructuring and corporate strategies is far from evident. According to Williamson and Ouchi, the 'distribution of power within the firms (is) endogenous and determined by the efficiency needs' (1981: 363–364). Although Williamson admits that regulation regimes are sensitive to bargaining processes and relations between business and government, he is not very impressed by the results of political scientists' research on firms' behaviour. In his view, the notion of power 'is often used in ways that are either tautological or confuse power outcomes with efficiency' (Williamson, 1990: 8). In spite of this, he added that 'delimiting the uses of power reasoning and establishing when and how the concept of power adds to rather than confuses our understanding of economic organisation would be major contributions' (Williamson, 1990: 8).

Several authors have argued in favour of introducing the role of power into economic theory. Rothschild argued that 'economics is a social science', that 'the economy is guided not only by the search for gain, but also by that for power' (1971: 7), and called upon economists to fill up this deficiency in economic theory. Mainstream economic theory seems to have made little progress in this respect.

Obviously, it is often difficult to point out exactly how and why firms are exercising power. The act of doing business does not allow businesspeople to talk openly about their strategies of playing off one supplier against another, or influencing a local government. However, this lack of reliable information may be circumvented in a similar manner as political scientists have done in analysing 'pure politics'. It is possible for instance to measure decisions to put certain issues on the agenda, or voting behaviour, even if these only show the *outcome* and not necessarily the actual process of exercising power. Likewise, one may interpret the outcome of a bargaining process between a firm and another actor as an indication that power has been exercised, even if we lack detailed information on the very 'whys' and 'hows' of this. If we define the core firm as actor A and its bargaining partner as actor B, we may assume (even without detailed information on the respective agendas of A and B) that B does not manoeuvre itself voluntarily into a position in which the core firm largely dictates to B what to do, i.e. in which B depends on A. If a bargaining process between A and B nevertheless *does* create such dependence of B on A, this can only be attributed to A occupying a stronger bargaining position than B. Such an approach implies a *post hoc* reconstruction or 'backward engineering' of A and B's initial positions.[5]

[5] The obvious criticism could read that such a *post hoc, ergo propter hoc* analysis overlooks the possibility that actors may not act rationally and may not be interested in preventing unequal dependence, or that certain dependencies can grow unintentionally, without either actor able to forecast the effects of the agreement when it was signed. The former case seems

The next step then is to assess the effects of particular deals between two actors on their respective dependence, and to rank these deals on a scale ranging from 'no effect' on either actors' dependence to 'B becoming entirely dependent on A'. One can distinguish three basic positions *vis-à-vis* the core firm: (1) independent, (2) interdependent, (3) dependent (cf. Wallensteen, 1973: 32). However, power may be used in two ways: from A to B and from B to A. Thus, even if B is more dependent on A than vice versa, B may still be able to exert some influence over A. Conversely, if B is independent of A, B may still be able to influence A. Therefore, the relative positions of actors A and B are shaped by their respective influence over each other. Figure 4.2 combines these two elements on a continuum, which shows parties' relative bargaining positions towards each other.

The upper categories in Figure 4.2 refer to the dependency relations in an industrial complex and to B's position to core actor A. The lower categories refer to the attitude or strategy of the core firm. Based on the dimensions of dependency and influence, one can distinguish six basic bargaining attitudes of a core firm *vis-à-vis* the other actors:

1 Cooperation or
2 Competition;
3 Compliance;
4 Coalition;
5 Direct control;
6 Structural control.

The next subsections will illustrate these six categories.

4.3.2 Relative independence, cooperation, competition and compliance

Adam Smith was one of the first to develop a model of (unconscious) cooperation between actors who are not only pursuing their own self-interest, but who are also independent. In Smith's terminology, actual cooperation on a societal scale would only be reached by a division of labour between specialising and competing individuals. In his time, this referred to relatively small firms (Smith, 1983: 21).

Many authors have recently highlighted the benefits of a *combination* of cooperation and competition. Best (1990: 250) has argued such a combination has been the prime factor contributing to the growth and performance of small and medium-sized enterprises in Japan and the northern Italian regions – in short to networks of flexible specialisation (cf. section 2.5.3). Porter's diamond model also emphasises the fruits of competition on the

---

quite unlikely, even if 'rationality' will often imply 'bounded rationality' (see section 2.5.1). The latter case may occur, although actors usually can be expected to make a sound assessment of the effect of a particular deal. Moreover, if an actor feels unhappy about a deal, it may still try to change it afterwards or threaten to disturb the entire bargaining process. If it does not, this either indicates its agreement to the deal or its lack of bargaining power.

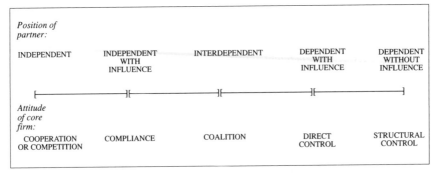

Figure 4.2 A continuum of dependency relations in an industrial complex

one hand but cooperation – through industrial clusters and other joint institutional settings – on the other (Porter, 1990). Some authors consider competition and cooperation as the 'two basic social forces whose interaction provides the dynamic of industrial change' (Cawson *et al.*, 1990: 15). Contrary to conventional wisdom, the border line between cooperation and competition may be very fluid. Cooperation will often imply 'competition by other means' (van Tulder and Junne, 1988), while other authors have launched the term of 'competitive collaboration' (Doz *et al.*, 1987).

The literature on restructuring and on the rise of 'post-Fordism' has been loaded with claims on increasing cooperation between actors (see Chapter 2). Many of these authors have built their optimism on the chances for cooperation to arise and to last on Robert Axelrod's game theoretical study on the 'evolution of cooperation' (1984). Axelrod concluded that it would pay off for actors to cooperate in a small numbers game as long as they use the principle of reciprocity or 'tit for tat'. Computer simulations showed that 'by cooperating on the first move, and then doing whatever the other player did on the previous move, TIT FOR TAT managed to do well with a wide variety of more or less sophisticated decision rules' (Axelrod, 1984: 175; original capitals). Provided the future has a 'sufficiently large shadow' (meaning that the players have a considerable chance of meeting again) such cooperation would be stable. Axelrod presented a simple evolutionary model, assuming that actors are able to learn, to stick to effective strategies and to drop ineffective strategies. He further assumed that actors pursue their own self-interest without the aid of a central authority to force them to cooperate with each other (1984: 6). Because they are supposed to be able to retaliate against the actions of other actors, and because they are free to decide whether or not to cooperate, Axelrod assumed that cooperation will eventually emerge between *independent* actors.[6]

[6] Axelrod was well aware of the limitations of his 'tit for tat' game. The game was applicable to a bipolar world (hence the small numbers game) in which actors could not defeat or escape each other. Thus they could be assumed to act 'rationally' and relatively predictably, and they had a common interest in preventing a nuclear conflict. In an infinitely more complex world economy, these assumptions would never hold.

Similarly, contract theories presuppose that contracts are settled between parties out of free will (cf. Eisenhardt, 1989: 58). Following these implicit assumptions, 'genuine' or 'voluntary cooperation' will be defined as only emerging between *independent* actors. Consequently, any claim of a 'cooperative' relationship which involves parties which are *not* independent towards each other will not be accepted as genuine cooperation and will be analysed in different terms.

As actors are shifting on the continuum towards a position of 'interdependence', they will gradually have to take into account the situation and objectives of the other party, which will make their cooperation less 'voluntary'. An interesting position is that of 'independent with influence'. In this bargaining situation, the core firm A is to some extent dependent on another actor B, without many possibilities to influence B. (See also Figure 4.3.) The definition of a core firm rules out the possibility that partner B gains control over the core firm, because that would immediately reduce A to a part of another industrial complex. With the partner relatively independent, the core actor may feel obliged to *comply* and cooperate in an 'involuntary' manner in certain areas (see the next sections for examples).

4.3.3 Interdependence and coalitions

The previous chapters have shown that many authors in some way postulated interdependence between firms or national economies without defining it properly or explaining how and why it would arise. The word 'interdependence' has been widely used but also fiercely contested. Even authors who have dug into the roots of 'interdependence' have often struggled to present a straightforward definition. Michael Best allows for the rise of what he calls 'mutual interdependence', when analysing the shift by supplier firms towards a 'product-led strategy' (1990: 274). The fact that Best adds 'mutual' to 'interdependence' suggests that in his view interdependence could also be unilateral, or unequal. Stopford and Strange (1991: 1) also use the term 'mutual interdependence', to refer to the 'interdependence' of firms and states. Rockart and Short leave room for 'large' and 'small' interdependencies (1989: 10), again without substantiating these categories.

Chapters 6 to 10 will show that the literature on internationalisation and international trade tends to use this word in a similar way. In the literature on international relations, the word 'interdependence' has given rise to much discussion. Robert Keohane and Joseph Nye, analysing American foreign policy, introduced the concept of 'asymmetrical interdependence'. As they explained:

> less dependent actors can often use the interdependent relationship as a source of power in bargaining over an issue and perhaps to affect other issues. At the other extreme from pure symmetry is pure dependence

(sometimes disguised by calling the situation interdependence); but it too is rare. Most cases lie between these two extremes.

(Keohane and Nye, 1977: 11)

Obviously, one can call two actors interdependent whenever one wishes, but it is misleading and inappropriate to refer to a relationship between two actors as 'interdependence' if one actor has more influence over the other than vice versa. To paraphrase George Orwell's words: some actors may be more interdependent than others. Most of the above observations on international economic interdependence contain interesting elements but have been formulated at such general levels of abstraction that their use and interpretation is far from self-evident. In spite of all intellectual efforts, none of the interdependency approaches have ever been elaborated into a coherent set of hypotheses (cf. Junne, 1990b: 353). Robert Gilpin therefore concluded that 'interdependence is a phenomenon to be studied, not a ready-made set of conclusions regarding the nature and dynamics of international relations' (1987: 18).

Another way to approach the meaning of 'interdependence' is by comparing it to the word 'cooperation'. Although these words are often used interchangeably, they are two different things. Genuine cooperation can only emerge between *independent* partners. Interdependent actors, however, are not independent but dependent on each other. Thus two actors will be considered interdependent if they have substantial and equal influence over each other's activities. The type of agreement concluded by two interdependent actors will be referred to as a 'coalition'. Coalition partners may have conflicting interests in some fields, but in the area where they strike a coalition their interests converge (temporarily or for a longer duration).

Coalitions may take many different shapes and may have varying backgrounds. A coalition may be struck in case of a looming conflict with a third party (Godfroij, 1981: 90).[7] A coalition may also aim to *exclude* other actors. Depending on the strategic importance of the deal, coalition partners may hold each other hostage, in which case the coalition creates considerable exit barriers to the respective partners.[8] Once these exit barriers shift in favour of one partner, however, the term coalition no longer accurately describes the relationships between the partners.

---

[7] Henk Houweling (1987: 132ff) would refer to such a situation as one of *negative* cooperation. Negative cooperation in his view is forced upon states by a hegemonic power. Positive cooperation is not induced by an external hegemonic power and aims primarily to reach a common objective a government could not achieve individually (which implies that no actor would have undertaken the activity on its own). In our terminology a situation of 'negative cooperation' would either translate into a relationship based on compliance, or, in case of a blatant power difference, even approach one of direct control.

[8] Borrowing from Max Weber's work on bureaucracies, Cawson *et al.* (1990: 6) have therefore referred to such a relationship as one based on 'social closure'.

4.3.4 Dependency, direct control and structural control

The right hand side of the scale in Figure 4.1 presents two distinct positions where an actor B is dependent on the core firm. In a situation of 'direct control', the bargaining partner depends on the core firm but it is still able to exert some influence over it. If a core firm A manages to man-oeuvre another core firm B into a dependent position, B has effectively lost its status as a core firm. The word 'direct' in direct control both refers to the way in which control is aimed to be exercised and to the time frame.

Ideally, direct control reflects a 'formal command structure' in which divisions within the core firm are told what to do by central management. Direct control strategies therefore coincide with a strategy of vertical integration. Direct control decreases uncertainty for a core firm, at least in the short run. Core firms striving for direct control often assume that once formal command structures have been established, they will yield immediate results. A weakness of direct control is that internal divisions or depart-ments, as soon as they have become part of the bureaucracy, will also become partners in the internal bargaining process, which will give them the possibility of exerting some influence on the central management's decisions.

An actor which is 'dependent with influence' but not part of a core actor's formal command structure may end the relationship, although at high costs. On the basis of this limited freedom, the actor may try to influence the core firm's behaviour. Hirschman (1970) has referred to this as the 'exit/voice' option. Helper (1990) has used this dichotomy to analyse relations between customer and supplier firms that have encountered some problems. A customer (assembler) using the 'exit' option will look for a new supplier, whereas the 'voice' option implies that the customer works together with the supplier in order to fix the problem. Likewise, a supplier which is 'dependent with influence' will first adopt the 'voice' option, since the exit option will be very costly.[9]

Once actor B's position shifts further to the right on the continuum, it will lose any room for manoeuvring. This type of relationship has been referred to by Nick Oliver and Barry Wilkinson (1988) as 'Japanisation'. In their view, Japanisation consisted of the successful management of a web of *high dependency* relationships. According to Pfeffer (1992), high dependency relations may create conflicts between actors in case of goal heterogeneity or resource scarcity (cf. also Pfeffer and Salancik, 1978). Many large Japanese manufacturers have nevertheless succeeded in making workers and suppliers highly dependent by reducing their stocks to the absolute

---

[9] In a previous study (Ruigrok and van Tulder, 1991: 11ff) we defined this type of bargaining relationship as 'coordination'. However, 'direct control' more aptly describes the strategic objectives behind this type of dependency relationship.

minimum, *without increasing uncertainty* to the core firm to unacceptable levels and while imposing goal homogeneity as defined by the core firm (Oliver and Wilkinson, 1988: 40). An assembler which manages the pattern of relationships of its entire network in such an indirect but extremely effective way exercises what will be referred to as 'structural control'.

Structural control aims to circumvent the 'exit/voice' dilemma and its related (internal) bargaining process. The structural control dimension of the dependency scale reflects what Steven Lukes has called the third dimension of power: 'A may exercise power over B by getting him to do what he does not want to do [representing the first and second dimension of power], but he also exercises power over him by influencing, shaping or determining his very wants' (1974: 23). This is the most 'subtle' way of exercising power. Traditional political science theories suppose that power only shows up in cases of actual conflict, i.e. that power will not be used unless an actual conflict arises. As Lukes put it, however, 'the most effective and insidious use of power is to prevent such conflict from arising in the first place' (ibid). A strategy of structural control then aims to establish an *in*formal command structure allowing for a long-term time frame in which the core firm's bargaining partners are facing a high level of uncertainty. Structural control is conducive to (subjective) goal homogeneity, while subduing open conflict and leaving room to forms of latent conflict at most.

In section 4.4.1, a first link will be made between these categories on the dependency scale and the concepts of control identified in Chapter 3.

4.3.5 A final note on the use of the dependency scale

The dependency scale shows two partners' relative bargaining position at a given instant. Although the scale represents the relative bargaining positions at a particular moment in time, these positions may of course shift over time. Figure 4.3 shows two lines approximating to both partners' relative influence over each other in a qualitative manner. If at a given position one line is further away from the horizontal axis than the other, this should be read as one actor occupying a better bargaining position than the other. The five positions will be briefly discussed below.

- At the left extreme of the scale ('independent'), the two actors do not interact, or only marginally, and thus do not exert any influence over each other. The distance A–a' equals the distance A–a".
- Moving to the right ('independent with influence'), the balance of influence shifts in favour of the partner. This is the only instant at which the core actor may be driven to act differently than it would have done otherwise, due to the pressure exerted by the other actor. Thus the distance B–b' is larger than the distance B–b".
- In the middle of the scale ('interdependence'), the balance of influence of

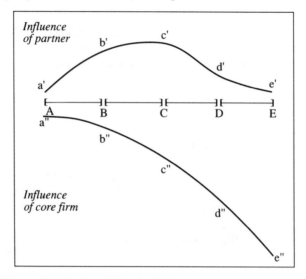

Figure 4.3 Uneven distribution of relative influence
Note: For explanation of letters see text

both partners is restored again. The distance C–c' again equals the distance C–c".

- Moving further to the right ('dependent with influence'), the core actor clearly becomes the stronger partner. The line shows that the distance D–d' is smaller than the distance D–d". Note, however, that the D position is not simply a reversal of position B. At B, the core actor may have to comply with the other actor's strategies, but it maintains its independence. At D the partner has truly come to a dependent situation.
- Finally, at the extreme right of the scale ('dependent without influence'), the partner has lost virtually every possibility of influencing the core actor's behaviour. At this position, the distance E–e" is infinitely larger than the distance E–e'.

In sum, the upper line of Figure 4.3 depicts what could be seen as an uneven distribution, whereas the lower line shows a progressively downward sloping line.

In the next sections, this scale will be used as a qualitative yardstick to assess the interaction between the various actors constituting an industrial complex. Several remarks must be made on the interpretation of the positions on this scale. Firstly, the interpretation of one particular position may shift if this actor maintains various types of deals with the core firm at the other side of the continuum. Thus a deal which suggests a considerable degree of influence yet which is embedded in an otherwise directly or structurally controlled relationship, will only marginally compensate for such high levels of control. Secondly, a position on the continuum is at the same time the outcome of previous bargaining processes and the starting-point of a future relationship/bargaining process. The scale of dependencies ranks deals between two parties according to the effect that these deals will have on the relationship and the relative power of these two parties. Thirdly, the continuum explicitly allows for the possibility that intervening variables – from outside the network – influence the bilateral dependency relationships: restructuring and the use of power do not take place in a economic or political vacuum.

Finally, it should be stated that there is no conclusive yardstick to position all dimensions of interaction on the scale. At times, positioning bargaining relationships on the dependency scale may be somewhat arbitrary, hence it will always (have to) be motivated. Some general criteria that have been used to rank bargaining relationships include: ownership structures; geographical location, degree of internationalisation; and the relative size (or power base) of the core firm *vis-à-vis* the other actor. The various additional criteria that are of relevance to one specific relation will be discussed explicitly in the following sections in order to reduce the subjective element.[10]

In the following sections, the power factor in each relationship will be discussed on a *ceteris paribus* basis, to assess the impact of one particular deal. For instance, in the assembler–supplier relationship, hypotheses will be formulated like the following: the less diversified, the more dependent a supplier is; or: the closer located to the assembler, the more dependent (for instance eligible to just-in-time); or: the more often deliveries have to take place, the more dependent the supplier will become. When taking into account one actor's entire set of relationships, the meaning of one particular deal may change.

4.4 VERTICAL RELATIONS WITH SUPPLIERS

A core firm can maintain two types of vertical relations: with dealers and with suppliers. The latter type of relationships has received widespread academic attention since the 1980s, when concepts such as outsourcing and 'lean production' became popular. The FAST-programme of the Commission of the European Communities (1988: 78) has referred to subcontracting networks as 'meta-industrial cooperation', which would also include the service sector and the use of telematics. Lynn Mytelka has quoted Japanese

---

[10] A conceivable criticism of the scale could be that a multitude of different dimensions of interaction have been ranked on only *one* dimension, which may lead one to comparing relationships of a different nature. To some readers, it may even seem as if the framework substitutes one type of reductionist thinking (based on efficiency) for another (based on dependencies). However, as stated earlier, we think that both efficiency and power considerations should be analysed to understand the dynamism of restructuring. We do not think that one way of looking excludes the other. Furthermore, we regard the scale presented here open to future elaborations and refinements, in order to elaborate the power factor in (political) economics.

sources that refer to the relations between core firms and their subcontractors as 'distributed collaboration' (1991: 3). Individual firms such as Philips have used the phrase of 'co-makership', hinting at a supposedly mutual benefit of the relationship.

This section will look at two aspects of the relations between core firms and suppliers. Firstly, a number of 'ideal type' network structures will be identified (section 4.4.1). Secondly, we shall position a number of empirical indicators of vertical relations along the continuum of dependency relations (section 4.4.1), and criticise some overly positive assessments of particular bargaining outcomes between suppliers and core firms.

4.4.1 Network topologies

This section will consider the overall topology of networks, with special attention to the relationships between suppliers and assemblers. Three ideal typical 'network topologies' can be distinguished, representing the three concepts of control (cf. section 3.2):

1 *Informal control hierarchies* represent networks of *structural control* in which one core assembler is positioned, as a monopsonist, at the apex of a hierarchical network. Ultimately all suppliers face one powerful customer. The network is *closed*: suppliers do not deliver to other complexes. These hierarchical networks are best approached by Toyotist complexes.

2 *Formal control hierarchies* represent networks of *direct control* in which the core assembler has a high level of vertical integration upstream. Thus many suppliers are part of the same firm in a formal hierarchy. Along with these direct control levels, over formal subsidiaries, the core firms in such Fordist networks tend to face major coordination problems.

3 *Egalitarian learning networks* can be positioned at the left-hand side of the scale. The interacting partners are of approximately equal strength and size, and cooperate or compete with each other on a voluntary basis. These networks are not dominated by one core firm. If one firm leaves or goes bankrupt, the network as a whole will not immediately be affected. These flexible specialisation networks can be found in some regions in Europe (cf. section 2.5.3).

Figure 4.4 positions these supply networks along our scale of dependencies. In addition, one can also identify a number of transitional networks. They include:

4 *Networks of chaos* represent the less egalitarian variety of the learning networks. Many suppliers and customers of various size interact in a relatively unstructured manner. This implies that some actors have influence over others in some areas and even large core firms have to comply from time to time with the influence of suppliers. This would make them more 'searching' than 'learning' networks (cf. Andersen and Lundvall, 1988).

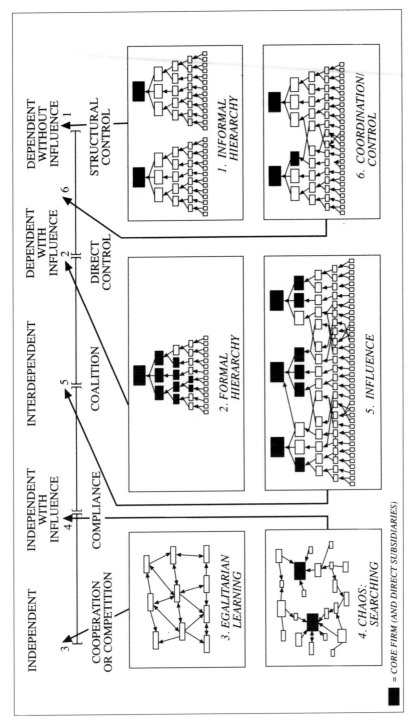

Figure 4.4 Network topologies: six ideal types of supply networks

5 *Networks of influence* involve a partial overlap of complexes, which provides leeway for suppliers to exert some influence over the strategies of the core assemblers. In these networks, the core firms are only oligopsonists or oligopolists which limits their control over the network as a whole, compared to the monopsonists of the Fordist or Toyotist networks. The higher the relative independence and the larger the size of prime suppliers, the more the core assemblers will be forced to strike coalitions with their suppliers. These types of networks have developed in Europe in particular.

6 *Networks of coordination/control*: a transitional variant between the direct and structural control networks is the case in which the first tier . supplier still maintains close ties with the core firms – delivering over half of its output to this assembler – but in which lower tier suppliers cooperate with each other to supply to these prime suppliers. This lowers the structural control of the prime suppliers.

Depending on their position within one of these networks, actors will have more or less bargaining room versus the core firm. The shape of these networks also determines the 'learning' and 'searching' potential in terms of innovation theories (cf. Rosenberg, 1982). Under certain conditions, such as a rapidly unfolding technological revolution, a core firm in a network of chaos may not be able to influence all parties active in this network, but may still benefit from the creative efforts which result from this chaos.

These six basic topologies can also be applied to the other relations, i.e. of the core firm and its dealers, with government, financial actors and the like. These topologies will not be elaborated on here, however.

4.4.2 Indicators of supply dependencies

Figure 4.5 shows the scale of dependencies, specified for a range of relationships between a core firm and its supplier firms. An example of the dynamic nature of dependency relations is the situation in which a supplier of a very strategic component [1] finds other customers for its product. Strategic components vary from industry to industry. In the car industry for instance, engines or gearboxes can be considered of high strategic importance (cf. Bongardt, 1990), whereas in the consumer electronics industry microprocessors are a strategic input to the assembler.[11] The relatively independent position of the supplier will move the initial supplier–assembler bargaining relation to the left end of the continuum. If the core firm uses the supplier as a single source of this strategic component, the supplier's influence on the core firm may even be higher than vice versa: if the

---

[11] Determining strategic inputs in the production process is gaining increasing attention, ranging from logistics departments (see Nishigushi, 1989a) to identifying strategic industries for whole national economies (see OECD, 1991).

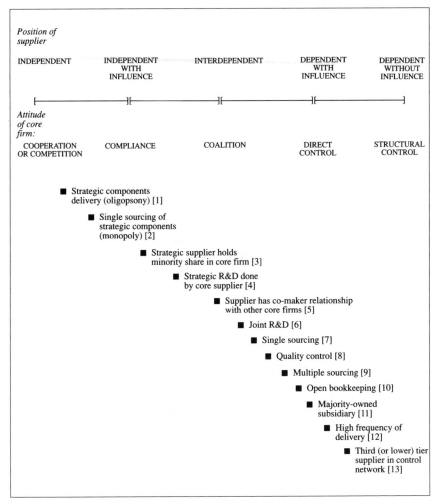

Figure 4.5 Indicators of vertical relations with subcontractors

supplier holds a monopoly [2] in the strategic component, all core firms will become partly dependent upon this one supplier. This situation will gradually change if such a strategic supplier owns a minority share [3] in the core firm. A minority share will also increase the supplier's dependence on the core firm, whose attitude then will be best characterised as compliant. If strategic component delivery is embedded in an exclusive supply relation, however, the bilateral relationship will shift more in the direction of interdependence. Towards suppliers of non-strategic products, the assembler will be in a better position to (threaten to) switch from one supplier to another, which reverses the balance in favour of the assembler, leading to a position on the right half of the scale.

A co-maker relationship [5] between an assembler and a supplier can only be labelled interdependent if this supplier is a large firm doing additional business in other areas, or doing a substantial part of its business in the same area with other important clients. A 'co-makership' relation with a supplier which for its business depends to a large extent on one single assembler, is better seen in terms of coordination or even control. In the area of R&D ventures there is an overall trend for assemblers to cooperate with their suppliers and delegate part of the design responsibility to them. If an important supplier is involved in *joint* R&D on a strategic input [4] for the assembler (engines, car electronics in the automotive industry for instance) both players will be interdependent, in which case one could talk of an R&D 'coalition'. In shared R&D projects in non-strategic areas [6], the assembler's ability to coordinate or control its suppliers' search/innovation process may be considerably larger.

More and more, assemblers look for long-term planning horizons in their relations with suppliers. One indication of this is that single-sourcing agreements [7] are becoming increasingly popular. They are substituting multiple-sourcing agreements [9] which traditionally served to play off one supplier against another, or to share the risk and have a 'spare' supplier in case of supply disruptions. Single-sourcing agreements suggest a high degree of mutual trust, yet they will often be part of a wider range of control measures.

One of these measures may be enhanced quality control [8]: the higher the level of quality control by the assembler, the more dependent the supplier will be. According to Ronald Dore who has done extensive research on Japanese restructuring strategies, 'big firms dominate their subcontractors more by tightening quality requirements than by threatening to turn to cheaper suppliers' (quoted in Sayer and Walker, 1992: 217). Programmes aimed at 'total quality control' or 'quality assurance', for instance, assume that a supplier's entire production process must be continuously monitored to sustain high levels of quality. If these quality control measures are supplemented for instance by 'quality audits', more direct forms of control are instituted upon the supplier. In such a relationship, suppliers must pass stringent audits to qualify as a component firm (and become single source, for instance). Quality audits review all business functions relevant to quality control.[12] Firms may for instance be required to adopt quality control techniques such as 'statistical process control' (SPC) and will have to keep control charts available for an examination by the assembler.

---

[12] A software firm called Applix Inc. for instance, had to field questions from ten different IBM teams during initial negotiations over the contract (*Wall Street Journal*, 10 July 1986). The same copy of the *Wall Street Journal* notes another interesting feature of the bargaining relationship between IBM and its suppliers: 'just as tradesmen to the British Royal family know they can lose the business by talking about it, most suppliers are afraid to discuss their relationship with IBM. In a practice reminiscent of Hindu wives, who never address their husbands by name, some companies forbid employees to refer to IBM except in code'. Such a mechanism could be called a 'culture of dependence': each firm is free to leave the partnership with the core company, although in reality they will seldom use the exit option – like the Hindu wife will never leave her husband.

Open-bookkeeping or open-cost accounting measures [10] imply that the supplier is required to bargain with the assembler literally with all its cards open on the table. Obviously, the assembler will not open its books to the supplier. With open bookkeeping, the price and cost structure of the component under consideration can be analysed in detail. If a supplier is assumed to have a competitive cost structure, a profit margin will be awarded on top. The price which is 'agreed upon' may also decline over time, to encourage the supplier to reduce costs on a continuous basis, and to allow the assembler to obtain most of these productivity gains. Profit margins must remain large enough, however, to allow a supplier to invest in new machinery and to fund research and development for new generations of products along directions projected by the core company.

Another powerful quality control measurement is that of 'vendor rating'. In such a relationship, the assembler regularly evaluates the suppliers, and an overall rating tells both parties how suppliers measure up against each other. Suppliers which pass the test receive a quality award. Vendor rating may occur on a monthly, quarterly, semi-annual or yearly basis, depending on the type of component and the power of the assembler. The shorter the rating period, the higher the degree of control in the relation.

A high frequency of deliveries [12] will often shift an assembler–supplier relationship to the right-hand side of the dependency scale. In some cases, subcontractors have to supply on an hourly basis, which means that the supplier's production schemes are totally subordinate to those of the assembler. In such just-in-time relationships, it makes a difference whether the assembler owns a majority share in the supplying firm. The supplier's dependency is likely to be higher if it is *not* a subsidiary of the assembler. The management of a subsidiary [11] may still be able to exert some influence over that of the parent company via other channels, such as board meetings in which it is represented or in the bargaining process over profit allocations. The legally 'independent' supplier in a high-frequency JIT relationship is literally bound to the assembler's short-term demands and if it fails to meet these demands, it may lose its business altogether.

The ultimate form of (structural) control in our model can be exercised by the core firm over actors in the low end of a hierarchical supply pyramid. No formal or direct control measures are necessary *vis-à-vis* third- or fourth-tier suppliers in a hierarchical supply network [13], because the options open to these actors are structurally limited.[13]

---

[13] In the management literature, characteristics of 'structural control' are sometimes referred to as 'secondary control'. This secondary control is most effectively practised by some large Japanese firms. Young (1992: 684) notes that 'under secondary control, individuals increase their rewards by accommodating themselves to the existing environment through an adjustment of their expectations, goals, and attitudes. Secondary control systems induce individuals to subordinate their needs to a more powerful individual or force, such as the work group or the company'. When applied to subcontracting hierarchies, the power element is even more clear, although not observable in the traditional sense of the concept (see section 4.3.1).

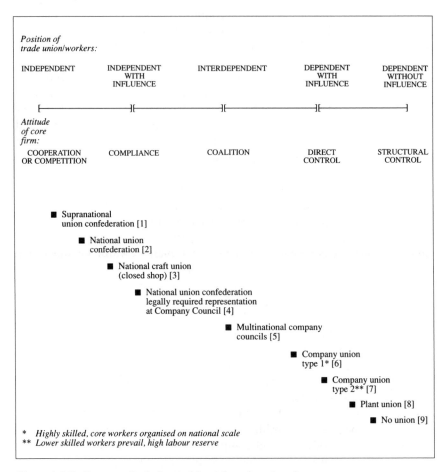

Figure 4.6 Indicators of relations with trade unions/workers

4.5 BARGAINING RELATIONS WITH TRADE UNIONS

Of all relationships within an industrial complex, those between core producers and workers have perhaps been analysed most frequently in terms of bargaining power. The bargaining power of workers depends to a large extent on whether or not they are organised in a labour union. Since the beginning of the 1980s – with some exceptions for Nordic countries such as Sweden and Norway – national union confederations represent a declining and often minor part of the working population. Overall, this has weakened the relative bargaining position of workers and strengthened the position of the management of (large) firms. Figure 4.6 summarises the relative position of trade unions towards the core firm.

In theory, a supranational confederation of unions [1] provides workers with the strongest possible bargaining position towards international firms and thus the highest degree of independence. A supranational confederation of unions transcends national boundaries as well as sectoral cleavages. In these unions, the choice to cooperate (conclude a deal for instance on working conditions and wages) or compete (organise a strike) with a particular firm is part of an independent decision-making process in which the interests of a large number of workers who do not belong to the sector or the country are taken into account. Depending on the internal decision-making procedures in such a supranational confederation, this can be a strength or a weakness of the supranational organisation. The more the internal processes represent a collective good and the more effective instruments the confederation can develop in support of their strategies, the higher the independence of the confederation versus individual core firms can become. In this case the union confederation becomes very much like an international political party.

In the history of labour relations under capitalist production systems some initiatives have been taken in order to create a supranational union confederation (Tudyka, 1974). None have succeeded. As a consequence no supranational union currently exists. There are examples of supranational categorial unions, such as the International Metalworkers' Federation in Geneva, which combine a considerable number of national union federations in the metal trades. However, the International Metalworkers' Federation never acts as a direct bargaining partner of core firms and faces great difficulty in coordinating strategies towards particular transnationals and towards national member unions (cf. note 14).

Relatively influential national union confederations [2] linking various sectoral unions can be found in European countries such as France, Sweden and the Netherlands. In the case of France, five national union confederations (CGT, CFDT, FO, CFTC, CGC) are recognised by law, each representing a different ideology. This reduces their influence, because they can be played off against one another, even though no other union confederations are allowed to enter the bargaining arena with the government and centralised employers' organisations. In Germany, the national confederation is much weaker than the unions at the state or the sectoral level. In the United States, the national union confederation (AFL-CIO) has been weaker than sectoral level unions, while national union confederations in Japan have tended to be rather weak (even after the late formation of a national union confederation, called Rengo, at the end of the 1980s). The relatively weak position of the UK union confederation (TUC), which resulted from the multitude of craft-based unions, implies that there had been no strong actor striving for officially sanctioned central negotiations over all sorts of labour-related issues. The close affiliation of the TUC with the British Labour Party further eroded the bargaining position of the confederation at a time when the Labour Party itself was marginalised due to the protracted rule of the Conservative Party in the 1980s and 1990s. Finally, in the smaller European industrial systems, the number of national union confederations tend to be more limited and their influence tends to be relatively large.

If it gets its act together, a national union confederation is able to present broader issues – even if it may be difficult to reach consensus on them – to both the organisations of employers and governments they are bargaining with. The 'natural' bargaining partners of a strong national union confederation are the national government and the employers' organisations. If a specific union (often a sectoral union) that is part of a strong and well organised national union confederation strikes a deal with an individual firm, this deal is likely to spread to other industries over the country. Often the targeted firm for a specific deal is a core firm that represents many workers. In the case where the unions are able to strike a very positive deal with this firm, the national confederation will try to proclaim this as the yardstick for other deals as well. Conversely, the core firm thus will be pressured by other national core firms (and sometimes by the government as part of its wage policy) not to come to over-generous bargaining results, for instance by agreeing upon very high wage rises. These external pressures will restrict the core firm's bargaining room, although it does not deprive it of its independence towards unions.

Workers in smaller craft-oriented firms were sometimes organised in craft unions. If these unions are brought together in a national framework, such a national craft union [3] will be fairly independent of these firms. In some industries the relative power of trade unions is illustrated by the proviso of a 'closed shop'. This implies that workers cannot work in a particular industry unless they are union members. In some industries, national craft unions even compelled firms to insist that subcontractors only use union labour. This practice was common in European artisan industries such as engineering, construction and especially in printing (Jackson, 1991: 320). The relative strength of nationally organised workers of smaller firms often results from the situation where the representation of these employers at the national level is much weaker than that of large employers.

If 'bipartite' or 'tripartite' bargaining between organisations of employers, employees and/or governments leads to the establishment of national legal 'framework agreements', there will be room for more detailed bargaining at a company level. If this framework agreement requires workers to be represented on the board of directors [4] such as in the German context, the influence of organised workers may further increase towards a situation of coalition or 'co-determination'. The significance of these co-directors (also called 'worker-directors') will increase if they are nominated by and representing a national union confederation, and if they have a true responsibility in the management of a key aspect of the firm's activities. Obviously, this form of representation is very uncommon and fiercely opposed by employers.

In the 1960s, union platforms for multinational firms were set up in order to deal with the increasing multinationalisation of (particularly US) firms. In 1966, the United Auto Workers (UAW) of the USA took the initiative to establish the first multinational company councils [5] in General Motors and Ford. The initial idea was that company councils should establish a 'countervailing force' to the growing power of transnational corporations by, in particular, working towards common expiration dates of labour contracts in all subsidiaries of that company throughout the world. 'No one would sign a contract until a satisfactory solution was negotiated for all the problems in the various plants' (International Metalworkers' Federation, 1991: 3). Before that time, international union meetings had been organised on an industry rather than on a company basis (*IMF News*, no. 6, 1991). Such meetings had increased the independence of the unions *vis-à-vis* firms and governments to such an extent that the latter did not accept these meetings as a bargaining arena.[14] In 1994, the Council of Ministers of the European Union (except for the UK: see Chapter 10) agreed to demand that firms with more than one thousand employees should institute European company councils. The function of the councils will be primarily consultative and it is generally expected that it will take way beyond the year 2000 to give the company councils real bargaining power. The latter, however, will also depend on the willingness of the national unions to give up some of their bargaining power in favour of the international union. This multifaceted interest battle within the ranks of the European trade unions to a large extent boils down to the basic question of whether the company councils should be organised on an international or supranational basis. Strategic dilemmas abound for the national unions because for the strongest unions in the meantime, the European company councils already represent a *de facto* weakening of their national bargaining position.

Usually, a core firm has to deal with one of three other types (or a

---

[14] Some of the supranational confederations actively try to support the multinational company union/council in order to increase their bargaining power with the multinationals. The International Metalworkers' Federation for instance has at the moment twenty-four world company councils in operation. In 1991 the following world company councils existed. In automobiles: General Motors/Saab, Ford, Volkswagen, Renault/Volvo, Fiat, Toyota, Nissan, Honda, Mitsubishi, Mazda, Daimler-Benz and Chrysler. In electro/electronics: General Electric, Asea-Brown Boveri (ABB), Matsushita, Siemens, Alcatel, Electrolux, Xerox and IBM. In mechanical engineering: SKF, Alfa Laval and Caterpillar. In the iron, steel and non-ferrous metals, the can industry and the aluminium industry hold world conferences every couple of years. The international exchange of information in areas such as health and safety regulations and wages via these company councils proved an effective bargaining tool. All councils, however, have remained rather weak and difficult to coordinate for three reasons: (1) language difficulties, (2) changes in members' responsibilities or (3) 'simply a lack of knowledge about developments that are taking place within the company worldwide' (IMF, 1991: 15). Coordination problems of company councils have increased because more and more firms have started to internationalise. The 1991 report of the IMF notes that 'when the IMF was limited to the ten or so companies dominating the automobile industry, things could be kept to manageable proportions' (*IMF News*, 1991: 4).

combination) of unions that are organised on a national or local basis. The first type of union is the company union which represents primarily the more highly skilled core workers [6]. Skilled workers and the company management are relatively interdependent. In the proliferation of automation, for instance, skilled workers have generally been a supportive 'layer' in the organisation (cf. Coriat, 1990). Less skilled workers may have to cope with large labour reserves, which improves the management's bargaining position. Less skilled workers can more easily be 'disposed of', and separate deals can be struck more easily with less skilled workers. Therefore, a company union 'type 2' of unskilled workers [7] will be in a weaker bargaining position than the company union 'type 1'.

As a rule, an isolated plant union [8] in a company with many plants will further erode labour's bargaining position. However, firms with dispersed international operations do run the risk that a plant union in a particular country develops into a lobbying group fighting to maintain or expand the activities performed in that plant. In this case, the plant union could form a coalition with the plant management to oppose the central board of the firm. The core firm may in this case even have an interest in having the plant union coordinated by the overall company union.

In certain cases non-unionised workers [9] may have considerable influence (such as IBM's non-unionised workforce), yet non-unionised workers will always have to manoeuvre in a bargaining arena set by the company's management. A company which prohibits unions aims to exercise structural control over its workers. The more workers find ways to organise themselves into broader and more independent organisations, both on a national and on an international scale, the better they may back their demands in the negotiating process with management.

4.6 VERTICAL RELATIONS WITH DEALERS AND DISTRIBUTORS

Marketing research has produced an impressive body of literature on power, conflict and dependency relations in marketing channels (cf. Gaski, 1984). Based on Richard Emerson's dependency theory (1962), and on the notion of 'channel control' (Stern and El-Ansary, 1988), research in marketing over the past two decades has tried to identify the determinants of channel power and has focused on the effective use of power in distribution channels, either through coercive or non-coercive influence (Butaney and Wortzel, 1988: 52; Frazier and Rody, 1991: 52).

El-Ansary and Stern (1972) consider channel power as a function of (1) the extent to which the two members in a channel depend on each other to achieve their goals and (2) the relative bases (or sources) of each channel member's power. Dependency relations in marketing channels largely depend on the dealers' and distributors' ability to develop countervailing power towards the assembler (ibid: 25). The more members of a marketing channel (i.e. dealers and distributors) are able to develop alternatives (e.g.

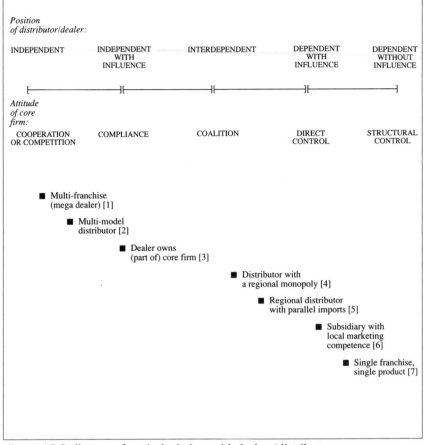

Figure 4.7 Indicators of vertical relations with dealers/distributors

market other brands, different types, and exclude competition from other dealers) the less end producers will be able to exert coercive power (Frazier and Rody, 1991: 64). Figure 4.7 summarises the relative positions of distributor and dealer versus the core firm.

Mega-dealers [1], which offer a wide range of models produced by many assemblers at the same time, are virtually independent of the end producer. A mega-dealership provides the possibility to play off one brand against another whenever this is in the dealer's interest, for instance by regulating price competition, offering discounts, or discouraging potential buyers from purchasing a particular brand. A large multi-model distributor with a local monopoly [2] can even exert some influence over assemblers. This influence will further increase if the assembler has a limited product range and/or is partly owned by the dealer [3].

If the assembler has granted one distributor in a particular region or country the sole selling rights [4], the relationship shifts into the direction of an interdependent relation: the regional distributor will depend on the assembler to supply the end products, but the assembler will also depend on the distributor to channel its products to the rest of the dealer network and to the consumers. A distributor which has been granted the right of distribution for a number of assemblers is in a better and more independent bargaining position. However, if the distributor does not have a monopoly over the region, for instance because parallel imports [5] from other regions are allowed by the assembler, its bargaining position will be weakened. An importer which is a fully-owned subsidiary of the assembler may be dependent, but may still have some influence over the assembler. The higher the percentage of parallel imports, the more the position of the distributor will erode. This will be even more so with formally 'independent' distributors.

The position of the single franchise dealers is located at the right-hand side of the scale. A local subsidiary with considerable marketing competence [6] of its own will have far more room to manoeuvre than a single franchise dealer confronted with an assembler which largely determines the marketing strategy (advertisements, layout of showrooms, etc.). Assemblers can further step up dealers' dependence by linking them to their data processing network. Again, if the dealer is not a subsidiary of the assembler, but sells only that assembler's products, the degree of structural control will be the highest.

Some assemblers insist on a contract requiring dealers to remain a single franchise or exclusive dealer. A dealer which sells only one product (one model or even one generation of a product line) has very little influence on the assembler [7]. Its influence could erode entirely if this dealer also faces direct competition either from other dealers selling the same products or from 'independents' offering maintenance activities and spare parts – threatening the dealer's final source of income.

4.7 CONCLUSION

This chapter has defined the concept of the industrial complex as a bargaining configuration consisting of a core firm and five bargaining partners, who are engaged in the production and distribution of a given product. It has developed a simple dependency scale to assess the outcomes of these five bargaining relations within an industrial complex. In the second part of this chapter, this scale has been applied to discuss and interpret a number of possible bargaining outcomes between the core firm and its bargaining partners directly involved in its value chain: suppliers, workers and dealers. The next chapter will continue this exercise by addressing the core firm's bargaining partners outside its value chain.

5 The dynamism of industrial complexes II

Bargaining outside the value chain

5.1 INTRODUCTION

Assessing bargaining relations within an industrial complex, one may observe an interesting paradox. Bargaining relations *within* the value chain, particularly between a core firm and its suppliers and dealers, have received considerable attention from authors writing on business administration and economics. Bargaining relations *outside* the value chain, however, have been ignored by these groups, and have been addressed more by political scientists, political economists and students of public administration and economic geography. Thus the former group has tended to analyse the relations between core firms and, for instance, financial actors primarily in efficiency terms, and much less so in bargaining terms.

This chapter will discuss the core firm's bargaining relations with the remaining two groups of an industrial complex. Section 5.2 will focus on the core firm's relationships with financial actors, while section 5.3 will discuss its relationships with various types of (local, regional and [supra] national) governments. Section 5.4 will aggregate the five sets of relationships to operationalise the rival concepts of control identified in Chapter 3.

5.2 RELATIONS WITH FINANCIERS

This section discusses the networking relations between core and financial firms (see also Figure 5.1). Throughout the history of modern capitalism, bank–industry relations have been the subject of intense debate about 'who owns whom' or 'who controls whom'. In the early twentieth century, Rudolf Hilferding (1910) introduced the term 'finance capital' to describe the close relationship between banks and industry, in which banks dominated industrial firms.

The core firm's bargaining attitude *vis-à-vis* financial actors is first of all shaped by the ownership structure of the core firm itself. Four (partly overlapping) ownership categories will be discussed: (a) the family-owned firm, (b) the joint-stock company, (c) the financial group, and (d) the financial holding. In the second place, the bargaining relation depends on

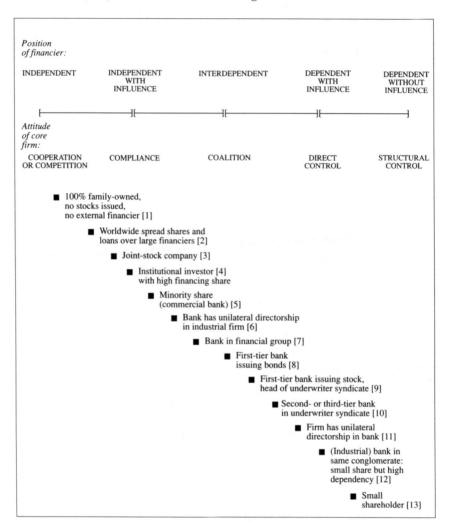

Figure 5.1 Indicators of relations with financiers

the instruments used by external actors and the inherent control mechanisms involved. In this context Paul Sweezy (1953: 161ff) distinguished between at least three control mechanisms: (1) credit relations, (2) share ownership and (3) interlocking directorates.

This section first considers the relative starting position of actors along the dependency scale (5.2.1) and then observes how some of the three control mechanisms are used by a number of external financial actors: stockholders, investment banks, commercial banks and institutional investors (5.2.2–5.2.4).

5.2.1 Ownership structures

The family owned firm [1] (see Figure 5.1) can be considered the actor that intends to remain as independent as possible from external financial influence. This applies in particular to smaller firms. In case of smaller firms managing their operations in complete financial self-reliance, one can speak of *avoidance* in the relation with financiers. This implies neither conflict nor cooperation and is linked to the left-hand side of the dependency scale. However, smaller firms also often need external funding. Since smaller firms in general are not able to issue public securities they have to bargain over external funding with a relatively limited number of banks. The smaller firm can become quite dependent on this funding source, whereas the bank will always make sure it remains relatively independent from the well-being of the small firm (see section 3.8). The bank rarely intervenes directly in the management of the business by the entrepreneur, but in case the small firm runs into difficulties the independent bank will use its influence and could even press for the firm's bankruptcy in order to save its investments. It is highly unlikely that a bank will become dependent or even interdependent on the financial well-being of individual small firms.

In order to increase their financial abilities and create scale effects, without renouncing their independence, small family-owned firms have frequently been staunch supporters of cooperatives. In many advanced industrial systems, cooperatives have been very successful as providers of capital to their small firm constituents, but also in their function as auctions and distribution centres for the products coming from (networks of) smaller firms. Bargaining in a large number of cooperatives at the moment deals with the question whether the cooperative itself should get core company status *vis-à-vis* its (previous) owners. This could change the dependency structures radically. It is not surprising therefore that these proposals come from the professional managers of the cooperative and rarely from the small companies/owners. One of the most important arguments by the managers is the alleged globalisation of markets requiring ever bigger scales of production and internationalisation (see Chapters 6 to 8).

The larger the firm, the larger the funding requirements become. The larger the funding requirements, the less likely it is that the firm will remain family owned. Family owned firms cannot use the public securities markets and thus have a more limited number of financial options open to them. The larger the firm, therefore, the higher its need for a variety of financial sources becomes. The largest variety of financial sources can be obtained by so called joint-stock companies that are able (and willing) to issue stock. Amongst the 500 largest industrial companies in the world, the overwhelming majority are joint-stock companies. This could come at a price because the firm theoretically also loses part of the control over its finances to its stockholders. Whether this really is the case will be discussed in the second section, but the starting position of the joint-stock company is one of compliance [3].

One bank holding controlling minority ownerships in a variety of industrial firms can be referred to as a financial group [7]. The membership in a financial group increases the capacity of firms to mobilise the necessary investments (Pastre, quoted in Fennema, 1982: 47), but limits the independence of the individual industrial firm. The more the bank holds a unilateral directorship in the industrial firm (i.e. without the management of the industrial firm also holding a directorship in the bank) the more the core firm will have to comply with the views of the bank. Examples of such financial groups are the Société Générale de Belgique and the Enskilda Banken in Sweden (the 'Wallenberg Consortium') that holds controlling minority stakes in firms like SKF, Ericsson, Saab, and ASEA. Both groups coordinate large parts (one-third to one-half) of the domestic economy in their respective home countries.

Although an industrial bank may not depend on the individual well-being of some of the industrial members of its group, the dominant perception will probably be one of shared interests. In a fully-fledged commercial bank holding a (controlling) minority stake in a core company, such a perception is far less likely: since industrial investments only represent a very small part of the business of the commercial bank – otherwise it would be an investment/industrial bank. As a rule, a commercial bank will therefore be less dependent *vis-à-vis* a core firm than an investment bank. Conversely, a core firm will have less bargaining power with a commercial bank which owns a minority stake in that firm than with an investment bank with the same minority stake.[1] The latter of course also depends on the distribution of other stocks as is the case in most other relationships as well.

If one only describes the starting position of industrial firms on the basis of their *official* ownership structures one could easily reach the conclusion that the competition between industrial firms is 'little more than [the] extension of conflicts among the parent banks' as William Shepherd argued

---

[1] A similar restriction to a core firm's bargaining power can be found in the case of a financial holding construction. The more a holding company is independent from the core firm (for instance because it holds a large number of other important firms) the more the ultimate independence of the industrial firm is determined by the holding. There are ample examples of companies that were sold by the holding company to a direct competitor, thereby ending their existence as a separate firm all together. The wide variety of holding constructions makes this observation only the starting position in the bargaining relations between financial and industrial actors in a holding company. The more the management of one particular firm in a holding construction is able to influence the general policy of the holding company, the more it achieves relative independence. The starting position of a firm in a financial holding group in which many other industrial firms are represented, however, remains more dependent than the starting position of a core firm without an extra layer of (financial) management beyond its own management layer. The holding construction, however, makes it very difficult to speak of a core firm. So we have left this construction out of the dependency scale.

(1989: 89). In that case the bargaining position of the core firm should be located on the left-hand side of the dependency continuum. However, the question as to who controls whom should be also linked to the issue of control mechanisms that are less formal. In the next sections, the three control mechanisms (credit relations, share ownership and interlocking directorships) as identified by Sweezy (1953) will be addressed.

5.2.2 Control mechanisms: credit relations

Credit relations, the first control mechanism, are very dependent on the relative financial muscle of the core company. Due to their enormous cash reserves, industrial firms such as Siemens in Germany, General Motors in the United States, Toyota in Japan or GEC in the United Kingdom, have sometimes been considered 'large banks with some industrial operations'.[2] By 1960, most large American (Fordist) firms did not rely on external funds (Shepherd, 1989: 82). The degree of potential self-financing increases the bargaining power of the firm's management. This does not necessarily have to lead to the actual choice for autofinance. In fact, cash-rich firms are better able to make use of various financial sources and keep their internal funds intact, because they can always choose not to enter into a credit relation. This increases their relative independence towards financiers. Regarding the choice between direct credits from banks and the issuing of stocks, cash-rich firms can also get a more rewarding access to the securities markets and do not have to rely on (a limited number of) banks. This immediately shifts their bargaining position to the right-hand side of the scale, i.e. towards control over financial actors.

The stronger the financial position of the industrial firm, the higher its ability to create a well-organised and hierarchically structured arena of credit relations with industrial banks. Strong core companies in the United States for instance maintain a list of around twenty-five first-tier banks that are allowed to issue stocks and purchase bonds for them. This can lead to an underwriter hierarchy which to some extent is even comparable to the vertical relationship between assembler and subcontractors, because these first-tier banks may in turn shift part of the financial burden to underwriters [9]. Second- or third-tier banks in such underwriter syndicates [10] have a (financial) interest in the firm, but have few possibilities to influence the strategies of the core firm directly. The difference with the vertical supply

[2] In 1992 for example, of the DM3.2 billion profits before taxes of Siemens more than half (DM1.86 billion) originated from interest payments received from its huge cash reserves. In 1993, in order to increase its control (and decrease its reliance on banks) over the investment of its almost 20 billion Deutschmarks in cash in stocks and shares, Siemens has become the first German industrial company to found its own investment company (Siemens Kapital Anlage Gesellschaft, SKAG) (*Vk*, 14/15 January 1993). Another example is the American General Electric Co., operating in a comparable business with Siemens. In 1992, $1.5 billion (or one-third of its overall profit) was earned in 'asset management' from its GE Capital subsidiary (*BW*, 8 March 1993: 36ff).

relationship is that the end producer will seldom be in a position to determine the strategies of the lower-tier banks fundamentally, since these underwriters only tend to commit a small share of their total capital to such activities.

In order to get the best short-term bid on bonds and stocks, according to bank sources, core firms dealing with underwriter syndicates in the United States often actively stimulate competition between investment banks. The more the competition between first-tier financial suppliers is enhanced, however, the more the relationship between the core firm and its suppliers can become antagonistic. This also makes it more difficult for the core firm to control (either directly or structurally) the individual strategies of the financial suppliers, because suppliers will more actively search for other customers in order not to become too dependent on this 'unreliable' company. This characteristic is one of the prime distinctive features between Fordism (antagonistic relations) and Toyotism (stable hierarchical relations).

The relationship between industry and banks in the area of bonds is generally more intense and close-knit than in the area of stocks [8]. Due to their lower risk, bonds are easier to place in larger blocks with the financial institutions (Madura, 1989: 665). The exchange of bonds between core firms and financial actors thus tends to create a more interdependent relationship. But this comes at a price for the bank, because the bank generally has to accept lower interest rates. Research on this phenomenon has revealed that 'interest rates are strongly and inversely related to the size of the borrower' (Shepherd, 1989: 88). This is due to the lower transaction costs involved in the close relation of the bank with the industrial firm, but is also due to the strong bargaining power of the client firm.

Financially weak firms on the other hand have far greater difficulty in obtaining funding on the open securities market due to the low confidence with potential stock owners. Consequently they can obtain only relatively low amounts of funds from the issuing of stocks and bonds. This limits their ability to make use of various financial sources, their ability to deal with a large number of actors and thus increases their dependence on the funding by a limited number of (investment) banks. In return, these banks will bargain for larger direct influence in the financial management of the firm. This is often symbolised by a seat of one of the bank's directors (or worse: one of the lower-ranked bank officials) on the board of the industrial firm [6].

5.2.3 Control mechanism: share ownership

The second control mechanism is share ownership which primarily relates to the joint-stock company. For this type of firm the question has been posed whether and to what extent the company is controlled by its shareholders or by its managers. The answer to this question depends on an external factor (the composition of the shareholder) and an internal factor (the composition of the management). Both aspects will be treated below.

Firstly, the influence and composition of the shareholders can be considered. In nineteenth century joint-stock companies the shareholders were considered the owners or co-owners of the company. In reality, neither large nor small shareholders can exercise their theoretical ownership role. Legally it is even the 'corporation that owns the assets and not the stockholders' (Fennema, 1982: 84). The only possibility for private shareholders to influence the company policy is via the annual stockholders' meeting. These meetings often favour the large shareholders over the smaller shareholders in various ways which will not be discussed in this context.[3] This results in a hierarchy of shareholders in which the larger shareholders are far better able to exert (some) influence over company policies. Smaller shareholders are individually perhaps more dependent upon the financial well-being of the company, but they hardly have any possibility to influence this except by selling their stock, the price of which is also beyond their influence [13].

The influence of shareholders and the dependence of the company on the trading of securities on stock exchanges is marginalised the more the company is able to get other funds *or* is able to spread its stock over a number of stable investors. The issued shares in Japanese stock markets for instance declined from around 70 per cent in 1949 to 20 per cent in 1991. Moreover, around 70 per cent of the shares in core companies on the Tokyo stock exchange is held by 'stable' shareholders that rarely trade their shares and are part of the same industrial group (Gerlach, 1992: 74/75). In addition, none of these 'insider' shareholders holds more than 5 per cent of the outstanding shares [13].

The degree of internationalisation is another factor. If a core firm has considerable control over the national market in which its stocks are traded, internationalisation of its stock may lead to some loss of control, but it will also increase the core firm's independence *vis-à-vis* national bargaining partners. In case a limited number of large foreign financiers control the core firm's shares and loans, the core firm could be manoeuvred into a compliant bargaining attitude [2]. In this case, other actors than the domestic shareholders will influence the stock prices, which will force the firm to take its international stock price more into consideration than it might have done otherwise. This may foster 'short-termism' in the management of the company's finances, lowering the possibilities for control of its financial inputs.

A group of 'outside' shareholders gaining ground are the institutional

---

[3] A strong example of the practical marginalisation of smaller shareholders could be found in Japan. According to Aron Viner (quoted in *BW*, January 1991: 38) 'individual shareholders expressing dissident views [were] often shouted down at the annual meeting of Japan's leading companies by a type of gangster (corporate meeting specialist or *sokaiya*) engaged for the purpose'.

investors, such as pension funds and insurance companies. In the United States, for instance, 50 per cent of the publicly quoted stocks are owned by institutional investors. Moreover, the number of institutional investors tends to be more limited and consequently the power of the managers handling the investment portfolio of the institutions more concentrated. A British survey of top corporate pension funds showed that around ten money managers handle 55 per cent of all the investment funds (*FT*, 30 January 1993). Individual institutional investors often have greater financial investment muscle than individual banks, and tend to opt for saver investments (such as government bonds) rather than buy shares. When institutional investors purchase shares they often prefer to invest in all core companies in the same industrial complex to spread risk. These factors make the institutional investor both more independent and potentially even more influential than most banks. As long as the whole industrial complex fares well, however, institutional investors will not use their potential influence. They tend to remain tacit investors and thus a quite stable source of external funds for the core companies. But with a declining competitiveness of the whole complex, institutional investors are bound to use their influence. Since the early 1980s this has gradually increased in the United States (Viner, 1988) [4].[4]

The second aspect of company control concerns how the composition of the company's management influences the way in which the company relates to financial markets. Directors of a firm who are 'home-bred' – i.e. after a long career in the firm itself – will tend to be very loyal to this firm. If this is the case with the majority of the members of the board of directors, they will share a common perception of the mission statement of the firm and they can be expected to be committed to limiting the firm's dependence on outside influences, including stockholders or banks. In Japanese firms, for instance, on average 90 per cent of the directors are full-time corporate employees and trained in the company (*FEER*, 15 August 1991: 38). Moreover, these directors are paid wages on the basis of seniority. There is no relationship between the value of the company on stock markets and the income they receive.

In the United States the situation is almost reversed. A considerable number of 'outside' directors appear on the boards of large firms. They have had jobs in other firms, even in completely different industries or in banks, and were often brought in for that reason. If managers coming from banks continue to hold close contact with their previous employer, the link

---

[4] Pension funds in the USA use 'indexing' as their most important fund-management technique. This implies a non-active spread of investments over shares that comprise some widely recognised stock market index. In 1993, some big pension funds, like Calpers, the second largest pension fund, started to discuss more active equity strategies. This is called 'relationship investments' and implies buying stakes in companies that are doing badly, negotiate a seat on the board and actively trying to acquire control of the company strategy formulation (*Econ.*, 30 January 1993).

could even represent an (informal) unilateral directorship of the bank in the firm [6]. 'Outside' officials are pampered by considerable wages, but moreover stimulated to identify themselves with the well-being of the company by adding bonuses to their wage in the form of company shares. The annual income of senior managers may well depend partly on the ups and downs of the company's stock. The value of the company's stock then becomes one of the most important strategic considerations for the individual directors and tends to reinforce the short-term horizon of the company's management. It also increases the (indirect) influence of other actors operating on the stock market who do not even need to have a seat on the board of such a firm.

In joint-stock companies, management on average, controls the company far more than the shareholders do (cf. Fennema, 1982). In this context John Scott prefers to speak not so much about management control but about 'control through a constellation of interests' (Scott, 1979). As such Scott emphasises especially the combination of different instruments available to management. This applies also to joint-stock companies in which the family owners still participate. When family members occupy central management positions, the control of management over the firm will be even stronger. This is the case for instance with the Agnelli family in Fiat or the Ford family in the Ford Motor Corporation. When the family relationships are embedded in a financial holding structure, the rest of the firm's management is likely to lose a considerable part of its bargaining independence over financial management as well.

5.2.4 Control mechanism: interlocking directorships

The most direct influence of financial actors over the firm's management would be by occupying a seat on the managing board of the core firm. This is the issue of interlocking directorships which has been researched in particular for the bank–industry relationship. According to Fennema (1982: 43) interlocking directorships are halfway between market and hierarchy and could imply competition and cooperation as well as control. This neatly represents major characteristics of the dependency scale but lacks a more precise positioning of the actors.

The relative position of the actors engaged in interlocking directorships depends on a number of characteristics. The most clear proposition exists when the representative of one firm sits on the board of the other firm, while no reciprocal relation exists. This is comparable to the 'open bookkeeping' practice in vertical supply relations. One firm thus has direct access to all information of the other firm, but not vice versa. This excludes competition between these actors. When both actors share directorships the relationship becomes more of a coalition. Actors move into the direction of independent positions once they are able to embed the cross directorships in a large number of other relations: for the industrial firm with more banks, for the bank with more industrial firms from the same sector. Depending on the intensity of the relationship the latter can be dubbed a financial group [7] (see Figure 5.1).

In case a bank holds a unilateral directorship in the industrial firm, this limits the industrial firm's room for manoeuvring with other banks [6]. However, considering the most relevant statistical studies, Fennema concluded in 1982 that the arcs through interlocking directorships between banks and industry 'most often run from industry to banks, and where banks hold substantial blocks of shares of industrial corporations, the majority of the accompanying interlocks are in the opposite direction' (1982: 205). In the latter case, the industrial firm enjoys more influence over the activities of the bank than vice versa [11]. A clear and direct relation between the size of the industrial firm and the nature of the relationship has also been witnessed in the area of interlocking directorships. 'Very large corporations often have a representative on the boards of the interlocking banks, while the smaller ones tend to have bankers on their own boards' (Fennema, 1982: 206). That is why the initial bargaining position of the 'average' large joint-stock company should be positioned at the right-hand side of the dependency scale [13].[5]

5.3 BARGAINING RELATIONS WITH GOVERNMENTS

The government–business nexus is the last – but certainly not the least – within an industrial complex. Over the 1980s, governments have continued to play an important role in the creation of a domestic institutional and regulatory (meso) environment of restructuring.

Studies on the bargaining relationship between governments and industry have often centred around the discussion whether states can be attributed (relative) autonomy in implementing and formulating public goals. The idea of state autonomy 'refers to the capacity of the state to act independently of social forces (particularly economic forces)' (Caporaso and Levine, 1992: 182). Marxist writers have often conceived of the state as an instrument or 'agent' of the ruling class. Poulantzas (1978) moderated this view somewhat, granting the possibility of states having some 'relative' autonomy, especially when confronted with competing interests from groups

---

[5] We have not included the role of the central bank in our discussion, since it is not in a direct bargaining relationship with the core firm. However, the position of the central bank influences the bargaining position of both banks and governments. In industrial systems with a macro-Fordist orientation, such as Germany, Switzerland and Austria, central banks tend to have an independent position. The UK, Italy, Japan, Norway and Belgium rank amongst the countries with the lowest degree of central bank independence. The latter industrial systems tend either to be dominated by core firms with a distinct control strategy, or tend to suffer from a lower cohesion (cf. Chapter 10). Alex Cukierman (1992) found that in industrialised countries, a legally independent central bank has been significantly associated with lower inflation, since central banks were able to pursue price stability even against the will of the government.

of relatively equal influence. Neo-classic writers on the contrary, have viewed states and governments largely as an anomaly to their free market ideal whose influence on economic affairs should be kept to a minimum. However, even Adam Smith – the founding father of liberal economic thought – accepted a role for government in the provision of some public goods and thus allowed for some influence of government over economic actors (see Skinner in his introduction to Smith's *The Wealth of Nations*, 1983: 77).

International comparisons of the government–industry relationship have distinguished between 'strong' and 'weak' states or 'policy networks' (cf. Katzenstein, 1978; Krasner, 1978). A strong state would have more autonomous power towards its own society and would often be able to resist pressures from particular interest groups. A weak state would contain a much less interventionist and less authoritarian government with fewer policy instruments and an inclination to leave restructuring to be determined by the operation of the market.

In the weak/strong state dichotomy, the United Kingdom and the United States would be 'weak' states, while Japan and France would belong to the category of 'strong' states. The role played by the Japanese government in general and the impact of the 'administrative guidance' by the Ministry of International Trade and Industry (MITI) in particular have led Western observers to speak of 'Japan Inc.' or of Japan as a 'developmental state'. The influence of the French government on industry by way of 'indicative planning' (national plans) or through nationalisations has also been emphasised. In 1974, Raymond Vernon even argued that European governments used 'large national enterprises as if they were agencies of the state' (Vernon, 1974: 3). This suggested that the state was the leading and most influential actor in the domestic restructuring process, which could hence be labelled 'state-led' (Zysman, 1983). At the other extreme, the lack of an explicit industrial policy would lead to primarily 'company-led' restructuring in the United States.

The strong/weak typology has a number of serious weaknesses. As Stephen Wilks and Maurice Wright (1987: 284ff) have pointed out, the direction of influence between state and industry can change over time, and it can differ from sector to sector and even from firm to firm. There are examples of large French firms dominating state bureaucracies (Thomson in electronics), or of British state intervention (in the pharmaceutical industry) that contradict the simple weak/strong state dichotomy. Likewise, the US Department of Defense has *de facto* conducted state-led industrial policies (cf. Junne, 1984b; Vogel, 1987: 99ff; see also Chapter 9). On the other hand, many (particularly Anglo-Saxon!) authors have probably misinterpreted the nature of the Japanese (and French) state bureaucracy's influence on domestic industrial restructuring (cf. Friedman, 1988; van Wolferen, 1989; Milner, 1988; see also Chapter 8).

These problems largely stem from the level and unit of analysis chosen.

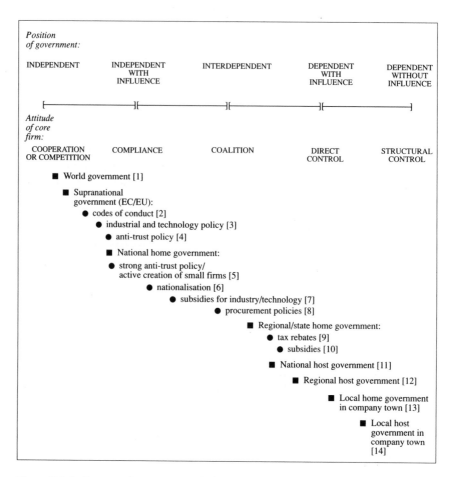

Figure 5.2 Indicators of government–industry relations

The strong/weak state dichotomy regards the national state as the 'core actor' and as a *unified* actor. In reality firms will often strike an agreement with one ministry to influence another, or team up with regional authorities to pressure national governments. While the United States lack an official industrial policy at the Federal level, for instance, individual states have often taken a much more interventionist stance. A final problem with the strong/weak state dichotomy (as well as with related theories of meso level corporatism, cf. Cawson, 1985: 10ff; Wassenberg, forthcoming) is that the position in the network as well as the origin of core firms is not taken into consideration. Subsidiaries of foreign multinationals, for instance, have a different stake in national policy networks to domestic firms.

Taking these analytical problems into account, this section will specifically address three elements of the government–industry bargaining relationship:

(1) different levels of governmental organisation (local, regional, national, section 5.3.1); (2) the 'home' versus 'host' government contrast (section 5.3.2); and (3) instruments of industrial and technology policy (section 5.3.3). Figure 5.2 gives an overview of the bargaining positions along these criteria.

5.3.1 The geographical dimension: different levels of government–industry relations

The geographical dimension of the government–business relationship resembles that of the union–industry relationship (section 4.5): the higher the level of government organisation, the more independent government will be of individual core firms. Confronted with a 'world government', individual firms would have little legitimacy demanding support against foreign competition. Although one could question the desirability of a world government, the only efforts thus far to formulate some worldwide regulations have centred on the codes of conduct for multinational behaviour. In the beginning of the 1970s, following the abuse of power by some multinational companies in a number of Third World countries, the United Nations Centre on Transnational Corporations was ordered to come up with an international code of conduct that would enable the UN and national governments to apply common rules to the 'good conduct' of internationally operating firms. A comparable discussion appeared within the OECD, while at the same time the so-called Vredeling Directive was discussed within the European Commission [2]. The latter came closest to implementation; the two former codes have never been applied.

At the other extreme of the dependence scale are the 'company towns' [13,14]. Company towns are by definition highly dependent on the operations of one particular company, which will be the main employer and which will dominate economic, social and political life in that town. Examples of company towns are Flint, completely dominated by General Motors, and Wolfsburg, dominated by Volkswagen. Some towns, like Toyota City, even adopted the name of 'their' company. A dilemma any firm dominating a company town will have to deal with is that *overt* influence on the local 'hearts' and 'minds' may easily provoke resistance from those local actors traditionally having the monopoly over these matters: local churches, teachers, the medical trades and local politicians (Stoop, 1992: 31ff). To overcome such local resistance, core firms have often felt obliged to develop some social infrastructure. Firms like Philips have subsidised local museums and have supported local sports facilities. Storper and Walker (1989) have indicated how the attempt to 'create regions' will often be an integral part of corporate strategy, and how this strategy may help to gain additional tax rebates [9] or subsidies [10] from regional (or in the US case: state) authorities.

National governments have far more policy instruments available than local or regional authorities. Local authorities do not have instruments like anti-trust policies, or coordinated procurement policies for defence contracts or large infrastructural projects for instance. National governments often have more money to spend as well. Potentially, therefore, national governments are in a better bargaining position than local/regional authorities [5–11].

5.3.2 Host or home governments: a shifting balance of power in favour of governments?

An important element in industry–government bargaining relations is the distinction between home and host governments. According to Rugman *et al.*, the very nature of the multinational enterprise (MNE) makes conflict with the host government inevitable (1986: 253, 293). These conflicts centre on the distribution of the net benefits of the multinational's operations. Multinationals have many ways at their disposal to appropriate these benefits and transfer them to other locations. Rugman *et al.* conclude that 'the potential severity and range of conflicts between MNEs and host-country governments are much greater than the possible conflicts between MNEs and their home-country governments' (1986: 279/280).

The reason is simple: host governments tend to have less bargaining power *vis-à-vis* an MNE than home governments. In Figure 5.2 this is shown by a position further to the right along the dependency scale of 'host' versus 'home' governments. In manufacturing, MNEs will often (though not necessarily) regard their home base as a constant. When setting up production abroad, an MNE has a chance to 'play-off' one government against another in an attempt to bargain for favourable conditions such as tax rebates, subsidies, infrastructure and telecommunications support. As long as they are not convinced of their ability to control the foreign authorities, MNEs will often transfer only a minor share of their activities abroad to be able to exert constant pressure on these authorities (by threatening to leave) and to put their 'loyalty' to the test. After an MNE has substantially internationalised its production, the nature of bargaining will ultimately depend on the firm's internationalisation strategy (see Chapter 6).

Over the 1980s, according to Rugman *et al.* (1986), the approach to resolving the conflict of interest between multinationals and national governments 'has moved towards negotiation and bargaining within a more rational framework' (Rugman *et al.*, 1986: 275). They even note that 'the balance of power has shifted from the MNE towards the nation state' (ibid: 254), because (1) multinationals are sometimes unable to accomplish their own internal strategic objectives in the face of government regulation, (2) they are constrained by conflicting demands of various governments and multilateral regulatory bodies, while (3) the codes of conduct and regulations adopted over the 1970s and 1980s would have restricted the ability of multinational enterprises to operate efficiently on a worldwide scale.[6]

This conclusion seems rather premature. As already noted, the implications and severity of the codes of conduct have been relatively limited. Furthermore, the authors present a very traditional and evolutionary model of a firm's internationalisation strategy (Rugman *et al.*, 1986: 90), a conception which will be challenged in Chapter 6. Rugman *et al.* postulate a 'cooperative' relationship between the MNE and the home government which would be 'potential hostages in any dispute' (1986: 276); and they do not analyse the possibilities the multinational has to bargain successfully with its 'home' government, such as the threat to withdraw activities to another country if the 'home' government does not yield.[7] This is the case in particular for large multinationals based in small home countries (see also 5.3.3).

Michael Porter (1990: 59ff; see Chapter 3) supports the idea that governments may and actually do limit a multinational's freedom of action. If multinational corporations were fully able to coordinate their activities among national subsidiaries (for instance, by expanding or reducing activities in one country at the expense or in favour of others), they could exert more influence on national governments. In reality, however, many factors work against coordination by one central management in one multinational firm. Porter notes that 'full and open coordination is the exception rather than the rule in global companies' (1990: 60). In many industries, multi-domestic companies would therefore predominate and firms would have to adjust their strategies according to the country concerned, leaving their subsidiaries relatively independent. Neither Rugman *et al.* nor Porter have closely considered the relation between the *home* government and the firm.

The relationship between governments and firms obviously depends on the industry, and on the concept of control adhered to by the core firm of an industrial complex in its home country. The next section will elaborate some instruments available to governments within a particular bargaining context.

5.3.3 Instruments of government–industry relations

There are a wide range of government policies that are the object of bargaining between core companies and governments. Some generic policies in the area of, for instance, education, taxes and investments in infrastructure

---

[6] Rugman *et al.* even argue: 'While the interests of the home governments and MNEs generally coincide, the host country–MNE relationship is often one of discord' (1986: 293).

[7] Interestingly, Chapter 2 of this volume referred to a large body of literature which argued exactly the opposite, i.e. that governments over the coming years may face *declining* intervention capabilities as a result of changing corporate strategies (cf. Petrella, 1989; Ernst, 1990). What matters here, however, is that governments have at least the legal potential to limit the extent to which multinational firms can coordinate their activities worldwide. This provides home – and host – governments with some bargaining power at least.

are highly relevant but usually benefit other complexes too. At the level of each individual complex, the government–industry relation is in particular (though not solely) shaped by bargaining over various types of industrial policy.[8]

Postwar periods in industrial and technology policy

In a broad definition, industrial policy includes 'those mechanisms used by governments to pursue structural adjustment' (Hills, 1984: 17). A traditional concern of industrial policy has been to regulate competition by controlling monopolies, restrictive practices and mergers (Harrop, 1992: 113). This area is obviously one of intense bargaining, since one actor (the government) tries to curb other actors' power. In the Anglo-Saxon economies, governments have officially tried to act as independently from core firms as possible, limiting their intervention primarily to anti-trust policies. In Italy, anti-trust policies have been combined with the active creation and sustainment of small firms [5], which further enhanced the government's independence, moving it to the left of the dependency scale. In Italy, these policies have been applied in certain artisan sectors, service industries or machine-tool producers operating in niche markets (Weiss, 1992: 95ff). The policy in Emilia-Romagna to 'remain small' was supported by a variety of positive (subsidies) and negative (regulation) measures, applied equally and without discrimination to every small firm, limiting the chances for individual firms to lobby for exemptions or specific regulations.

Governments of countries that lagged behind the United States and the UK were more inclined to use other instruments such as regional aid for depressed economic regions, expanding technical education, tax rebates for some industries or national procurement to support 'national champions' and industries considered 'strategic'. From the 1960s onwards, technology policy gradually gained ground as a tool of (sector) structural policy (Roobeek, 1990: 16ff), which led the OECD in the early 1980s to speak of a 'new interventionism' (OECD, 1983: 48). Others concluded that the continuous changes in the actors advocating new instruments had produced a body of literature which had 'neither an obvious definition nor an accepted theoretical structure' (Hesselman, 1983: 197). H.W. de Jong (1985: 195) even referred to industrial policy (in its strict definition, excluding competition policy) as an 'empty box'. De Jong argued that industrial policy in many industrial countries had not been capable of 'picking winners' or 'backing up losers' efficiently (cf. Schenk, 1987). In this section, however, the

---

[8] Good comparative studies on industrial and technology policy issues have been written by Henry Ergas (1984), Richard Nelson (1984) and Annemieke Roobeek (1990). In 1983, the United States International Trade Commission reviewed industrial policies of a series of countries, to establish to what extent these states were engaged in 'industrial targeting' to promote 'unfair' competition. These wordings aptly indicate the ideological background of many studies of industrial policy.

objective is not to find out whether or not industrial policy has been effective, but merely to interpret the outcomes of industry–government bargaining.

The remainder of this section will briefly discuss three (groups of) instruments: subsidies as part of technology policy, nationalisations and anti-trust policy. Trade policies will be discussed in Chapter 9.

Technology subsidies: the instrument of the 1980s

In the 1970s and 1980s, technology policies have primarily been implemented by national governments, although regional and local authorities have also developed a number of instruments relatively independent of their national governments. Governments' interest in high technologies has been spurred by the recognition of the strategic importance of core technologies and thus of the industries producing and developing these technologies (cf. Nelson, 1984, see section 4.2). Through the 1980s, governments have started to subsidise high-tech firms in a more direct manner [7] (see Figure 5.2).

The bargaining space of governments to formulate an independent technology policy depends to a great extent upon the concentration level of R&D expenditures. In the United States and Japan, 10 to 15 per cent of all R&D is spent by the five largest industrial firms in these countries. This has enabled the Japanese government for instance to subsidise competing consortia developing semiconductors or the fifth-generation computer, which in turn kept a considerable dynamism in the industry and enhanced the government's independence. In the 1980s, the large European countries had somewhat higher levels of R&D concentration, with the five largest firms conducting about 17–25 per cent of total R&D, whereas in smaller European countries like Sweden, Switzerland and the Netherlands, the five largest industrial firms have accounted for more than 40 per cent of private R&D expenditures (van Tulder, 1989: 22). As a result, many European governments have often merely followed the strategies of dominant firms (Rothwell and Zegveld, 1985). In many cases, therefore, subsidies are an indication of the core company's influence over the government rather than vice versa [10].[9]

Since the beginning of the 1980s, efforts to transfer instruments of technology policy to a supranational government – and thus increase the bargaining power of the government towards concentrated business – have only been undertaken in the (former) European Community [3]. At the

---

[9] There is a growing body of literature that shows that R&D statistics contain a systematic negative bias regarding the R&D efforts of smaller firms, since these firms have often no official R&D laboratories or R&D personnel (cf. Kleinknecht and Reijnen, 1991). Nevertheless, considerable innovation comes from these firms. The effectiveness of innovation policies that focus on 'official' R&D therefore is bound to remain rather limited and often represents the power of large firms to get subsidies, more than anything else.

European level, governments were faced with less dominant national champions, creating the possibility of more independent policy formulation. In 1983, the ESPRIT (European Strategic Programme for Research and Development in Information Technology) marked the beginning of a number of pre-competitive technology programmes with sweeping acronyms like RACE (Research and Development in Advanced Communications technology in Europe), BRITE (Basic Research in Industrial Technologies in Europe), EUREKA (European Research Coordination Agency) and the like.

Like the national European governments, however, the EU/EC has hardly been able to direct the large European technology companies into compliance (see Figure 5.2). In the first half of the 1980s the '1992' project had not yet been launched and the EC still acted as a 'follower' rather than as an independent authority. At its onset, the twelve companies that had lobbied for the establishment of the ESPRIT programme participated in around 70 per cent of all projects. In the late 1980s, they still participated in 66 per cent of all projects, receiving 50 per cent of all funding. These twelve firms were: GEC (UK), ICL (UK), Plessey (UK), Thomson (Fr), CIT-Alcatel (Fr), Bull (Fr), Siemens (D), AEG (D), Nixdorf (D), Olivetti (I), STET (I) and Philips (Neth.). By the early 1990s, three of these firms were taken over by other European firms, while Fujitsu acquired ICL, reducing the original group to eight.

The size of these firms is another factor that makes it difficult to steer them into compliance: the annual budget of all EC technology programmes is smaller than the R&D budgets of single large companies like Philips or Siemens, hence even a strong and independent supranational government would have been able to exert only a limited degree of influence on the R&D strategies of these large firms. For this reason, the theoretical effect of supranational industrial and technology policies has been positioned left of compliance, i.e. tending towards independence of both parties.

The limited bargaining power of the EC also comes to the fore in a survey on the motivation of Dutch firms to participate in EC technology programmes (Andersen, 1989). Only 29 per cent of the large Dutch firms (over 5,000 employees) participating in EC technology programmes stated they would *not* have conducted the research without EC funding. Of the smallest firms (< 100 employees), 73 per cent doubted they would have carried out the research without the subsidy. Thus EC technology programmes did influence the strategies of small and medium-sized enterprises (SMEs). SMEs participated in 65 per cent of all EC projects, but received only 14 per cent of all (ESPRIT) funding over the 1983–9 period (cf. van Tulder, 1990: 674ff).

Nationalisations: the case of France

In several instances after the Second World War, European governments have nationalised core companies [6] (see Figure 5.2). Stephen Wilks (1989:

191) notes in this context that 'conventional wisdom would hold that a company in need of state support would be dependent on the government and therefore relatively weak. In fact, in some cases, state dependence can perversely strengthen industrial management'. In France, nationalisations proved helpful to channel *more* public money towards the companies concerned, a transfer which otherwise would have been difficult to justify.[10] Nationalisations also created a new division of labour between major domestic companies, but they seldom gave government agencies a decisive say in company affairs. In fact, the nationalisation of particular industries has led companies to colonise agencies of the state, rather than vice versa (cf. Cawson *et al.*, 1990).[11]

Governments may constrain their policy-making options if they anticipate possible adverse reactions by their 'own' nationalised companies. A nationalised firm moreover may be an active participant in decision-making processes (Wilks, 1989: 194). Thus especially large nationalised firms [8] (see Figure 5.2) may be able to exert considerable influence over government policies and keep their government hostage, shifting the relationship towards a coalition. Finally, a major effect of state ownership is that it increases the state's relative bargaining position to other firms in the same industry, in particular to foreign companies wishing to enter the country.

Large firms which have not been nationalised but produce primarily for markets dominated by government procurement (telecom, public utilities, defence) are likely to move towards an interdependent bargaining relation with their government [8]. An important aspect here is the extent to which these producers have spread their operations. Large companies serving government procurement markets have often internationalised on the basis of a multi-domestic strategy, providing their subsidiaries with more autonomy versus their home government. As a rule, the less internationalised these firms are, the more a government will be able to

[10] The early 1980s nationalisations raised the French government's control over industry from 17.2 to 29.4 per cent of total sales. The share of employees in government service increased from 11.0 to 22.2 per cent, and control over investments rose from 43.5 to 51.1 per cent (Savary, quoted in van Tulder and Junne, 1988: 196). The nationalisation of major French electronics firms (Bull, CGE, Matra, Saint-Gobain, Thomson) brought about half of all the French electronics industry's production and well over two-thirds of all R&D in electronics under state control (Webber, Moon and Richardson, 1984).

[11] This was also due to the working of the French *Grands Corps* alumni of the elite institutions of higher education). Public authority figures, who themselves often aim for a career in a public enterprise, face great difficulty trying to influence (let alone control) senior management of nationalised companies, who are their 'superiors' in the hierarchy of the *Grands Corps* and who can have a decisive influence on their professional future (so-called *pantoufflage*) (Cawson *et al.*, 1985, quoted in van Tulder and Junne, 1988: 197).

influence their activities.[12] Smaller firms operating in the same markets will have little or no influence over their government.

Anti-trust measures

In the present international restructuring race, the traditional instrument of anti-trust policy (restricting mergers and inter-company alliances) is increasingly regarded as an obstacle to improving the 'competitiveness' of national core companies. Many national governments of industrialised economies and the European Union have relaxed the enforcement of anti-trust measures, especially in certain core technologies. At the same time, the development of new core technologies has eased the entry into a particular industry of players previously active in an entirely different industry (cf. van Tulder and Junne, 1988). In spite of a rapid concentration process that is occurring in many sectors (cf. OECD, 1992), therefore, it could be argued that a relaxation of anti-trust measures does not automatically diminish competition. Yet it does suggest that governments in this area have seen their bargaining position deteriorate.

An example of this was the Reagan Administration, which in 1982 issued new rules governing mergers, including a more permissive attitude towards market concentration as long as there were no major barriers to a new competitor that might want to enter the market (*Fortune*, 1 September 1986: 49). Another example has been the greater lenience towards domestic research consortia for basic and/or applied R&D.[13] The UK, the other traditional supporter of a strong anti-trust legislation, also changed course considerably over the 1980s. In 1983, the UK Department of Trade and Industry determined that as few mergers as possible were to be subjected to a formal investigation by the Monopolies and Mergers Commission.[14] France has never had restrictive anti-trust legislation.[15] The German Bun-

---

[12] In telecommunications for instance it has been normal practice that the (state-owned or tightly regulated) PTTs organise a small group of preferred suppliers (often selected on the basis of political motives) that are awarded procurement orders for a particular product every two or three years. The provision for foreign firms to participate in these stable (and therefore very attractive) procurement groups has always been that the subsidiary should have considerable autonomy and sufficient production facilities in the local economy. As a consequence, a telecommunications firm like Ericsson that was faced with a small national procurement market like Sweden, has had to internationalise early and leave its subsidiaries a lot of freedom to become accepted as a 'national' player in these foreign markets.

[13] Thus Mostek of United Technologies had to withdraw from a prominent chip research consortium after it was taken over by the French electronics firm Thomson.

[14] In this, the Department of Trade and Industry was in direct conflict with the Monopolies and Mergers Commission (MMC), but it had the support of the (Conservative) government and the multinationals engaged in core technology areas. One of the results was that British Telecom, the privatised telecommunications company, was allowed to buy the Canadian telecommunications firm Mitel despite objections from the MMC (FT, 28 January 1986).

[15] Historically, the French state has been an agent of concentration rather than of fighting concentration, which can be explained by the rather dispersed character of large parts of French industry. This strengthened the bargaining position of French industry considerably.

deskartellamt rejected a considerable number of proposed mergers and take-overs, but its position has come under great pressure.[16]

Supranational anti-trust enforcement could theoretically compensate for these problems [4] (see Figure 5.2). The only example existing is provided by the Directorate General for Competition Policy (DG-IV) of the European Union. Until 1977, pre-competitive alliances in research were formally illegal in the EC, as in the United States. With the launch of pre-competitive Community projects, this line was relaxed. In 1985, a number of exemption categories were granted to allow firms to create production alliances as a follow-up of the R&D cooperation programmes (van Tulder and Junne, 1988: 200). With a few exceptions, however, DG-IV has been unwilling to extend this liberalisation to the commercialisation phase. (In the case of EUREKA, which is not formally monitored by the EU, the Commission has given up this opposition.) The 1993 appointment of Karel van Miert as the new Competition Commissioner appears to point the way towards a further relaxation of anti-trust measures.

5.4 CONCLUSION: THE DYNAMISM OF INDUSTRIAL COMPLEXES AND RIVAL CONCEPTS OF CONTROL

This chapter assessed a series of outcomes of bargaining processes between core firms on the one hand and suppliers, trade unions, distributors, financiers and governments on the other. Each position on the dependency scale represents a different mode of conflict management. The relation between these modes of conflict management and the rival concepts, however, has yet to be established.

The dependency scale has made it possible to discern between a large number of different bargaining constellations. Table 5.1 summarises the indicators of the five most important bargaining constellations. If a core firm has managed to organise its relationships with all five domestic bargaining partners at one and the same position on the dependency scale, bargaining takes place on the basis of clearly recognisable patterns and well-established (implicit or explicit) rules, compliance procedures and standard operating practices. Peter Hall (1986) refers to these rules, procedures and practices as institutions. In an industrial complex characterised by high levels of cohesion, the institutional setting (i.e. the bargaining arena) of the industrial complex will be very coherent.

---

[16] The German anti-trust regulation has been somewhere in between the French and British practice, partly as a legacy of the postwar occupation that shaped the German constitution. Over the 1980s, a comparable struggle developed in Germany as in the United Kingdom, with the Federal Ministry of Economic Affairs and the Federal Ministry of Technology (BMFT) gaining the upper hand in important test cases such as the Daimler-Benz expansion. The Bundeskartellamt could not prevent Daimler-Benz from increasing its power in such areas as aircraft (take-over of MTU, Dornier) and defence electronics (take-over of AEG and MBB). In the case of the MBB take-over, the Kartellamt officially decided against the deal, but it was overruled by the other ministries (cf. Harrop, 1992, p.115).

Table 5.1 Five bargaining characteristics related to five basic positions

Position of partner-core firm towards	Independent	Independent with influence	Interdependent	Dependent with influence	Dependent without influence
Suppliers	• Division of labour • Flexible supply: high degree of substitution between suppliers • Local deliveries • Competitive and co-operative relations • No clear profit hierarchy	• Minority share holding • Supplier of strategic components, longer-term supply contracts favoured • Many single sourcing relations • Profit of supplier may surpass that of core firm	• Division of labour in which (small number of) suppliers have also relationships with other core firms • Local delivery • No clear pattern of profit distribution • Single sourcing relations	• Vertical integration • Large numbers of competing suppliers • International deliveries (global sourcing) • Antagonistic relations • Profits tend to diverge, but not in a hierarchy • Low level of black box engineering	• Vertical deintegration • Small number of prime contractors • Local deliveries • Control hierarchy with coalition between core firm and first tier suppliers • Profits: only convergence with first tier suppliers • High level of black box engineering
Distributors/dealers	• Risk of becoming dominated by distributors is high • Limited influence on ultimate price of product	• Distributors can hold shares in core firms • Core firms are confronted with many mega-dealers • Dealers can earn larger profit margins than core firms	• Converging profit margins • Important function for importers • Importers 'partners' of the core company: no large price differences around the world	• Core firm tries to own the distributors and importers • Low price at production site, higher prices abroad (due to higher transport costs)	• Control (data networks) • Single franchise dealers • Less importance for importers • Higher prices in market of production site, lower prices abroad ('export residual')
Trade unions/workers	• Loose relation with (craft oriented) unions or no unions • Nationally or internationally organised unions	• National union confederations • Representation at company council • National productivity coalitions	• (Multinational) company council, representing sectoral unions • Sectoral productivity coalitions	• Firm oriented or sectoral unions • Contrasting interests • Country by country productivity coalitions (weak coordination)	• Plant/company unions • Firm loyalty • Decentralised productivity coalitions (centrally coordinated) • Rigorous selection

Table 5.1 Continued

Position of partner-core firm towards	Independent	Independent with influence	Interdependent	Dependent with influence	Dependent without influence
Financiers	• Effort to autofinance • Family company • Distant relation with (limited number of) banks • Cooperative	• Industrial bank with unilateral directorships and considerable shareholding in core firm • Institutional investors • Commercial bank having financed large part of company's debt	• Financial group • Relationship with first-tier bank issuing bonds or first-tier bank issuing stock as head of underwriter syndicate • Coalition with bank	• Direct control over own finances • Large number of small stockholders • High degree of self-financing • Underwriter hierarchies • Adversarial relations with banks	• Collaborative relation with first-tier banks • Mutual shareholdings in other firms of the same conglomerate • High degree of self-financing without this being used
Governments	• Arms-length relations • Government support of 'keep it small' policies • Relatively strong supranational governments	• Strong national home governments, making use of a variety of instruments curbing the influence of individual firms • Nationalisations	• Strong regional/state home governments • Loose coalitions • Active procurement policies • Subsidies sustaining diversity in the industrial structure	• Ad hoc coalitions with national/Federal governments. • Adaptive/independent from local environment • Active 'creation' of local environment in company towns	• Local player status preferred • Focus primarily on local governments • Structurally dominant position • No need to control the region directly

The more all actors in an industrial complex bargain on the basis of relatively independent starting positions, the looser the institutional setting will be. In this setting, actors will try to keep their independence when dealing with other actors. This may (have to) be supported by government measures, such as strict anti-trust regulation or 'keep it small' policies. The network of small cooperating firms, however, runs the risk of becoming dominated by a strong distributor.[17] Because these actors are very independent in relation to one another, deals will be struck on a voluntary basis. Only such deals represent true cooperation, since actors can without any repercussion decide to compete. Such a combination of bargaining positions at the left-hand side of the dependency scale represents the flexible specialisation concept of control.

At the other extreme, the right-hand side of the scale, where the core firm is bargaining with dependent actors without influence, the core firm will be able to exert a high degree of structural control over the industrial complex. The remaining actors in these networks may not share the core firm's objectives at all. However, by exercising structural control, the core firm aims to prevent the outbreak of open conflict, and to curb tacit or latent conflict (cf. Bachrach and Baratz, 1969). In this way, structural control prevents goal heterogeneity leading to open conflict. Therefore, the interaction in this type of network cannot be labelled 'cooperation'. This type of industrial complex corresponds to the Toyotist concept of control. Following the general characterisation of Oliver and Wilkinson (1988), Toyotism can be described as a system of constructed (structural) dependencies within networks.

At the mid-right spot on the scale of dependencies, one can distinguish another type of control network, based on coordination or direct control. Direct control is exercised by vertically integrated and bureaucratically organised firms (cf. Chapter 4), and therefore this part of the scale of dependencies most closely represents the Fordist concept of control. In a control regime of micro-Fordism, the core firm bargains with relatively decentralised trade unions, weaker banks and without a major role of a central government. *In extremo* therefore the concept of micro-Fordism approaches (and even partly overlaps) Toyotism. In terms of bargaining theory, the difference between Toyotism and Fordism can be described as follows: under Fordism, a contract will mark the end of a bargaining process, while under Toyotism signing a contract will mark the beginning of extensive bargaining.[18]

At the centre position on the scale of dependencies a macro-Fordist regime can be situated (cf. Mjøset, 1987) in which core firms are confronted

---

[17] This happened for instance with the Swatch industry in Switzerland that saved the remnants of the previously famous Swiss watch industry. It was organised on the basis of cooperation between small companies and created a big commercial success, but primarily because the marketing was undertaken by a big multinational trading company beyond their control (Lambooy, 1991: 41).

[18] Based on a remark made by a Shell manager in Japan, February 1993.

with less dependent partners, such as national trade union federations and stronger national governments. Under such a regime, actors share the highest degree of interdependence. The core firm will be forced to strike deals with a wide variety of actors which most closely resemble a coalition. Under such circumstances it can be relatively attractive for the core firm to transfer its interest representation to a national employers' organisation that bargains with governments and trade unions in a national context. In many of the smaller industrial countries this has led to tripartite corporatist bargaining institutions.

Figure 5.3 shows the position of these four concepts of control along the scale of dependencies. The figure also shows that one set of bargaining relations along the dependency scale has not been elaborated in terms of the comprehensive concept of control in Chapter 4. This is the mid-left area where a core firm is confronted with independent actors that are able to exert considerable influence on this firm's strategies. Obviously, such a compliant attitude will be the least desirable situation for the management of a core firm of all positions distinguished on the scale. For this reason probably no comprehensive concept of control (based on a core firm's compliance with other independent actors) has emerged in the leading countries. In the 1980s, some of the smaller industrial welfare-oriented countries such as Sweden, however, came close to this position, while examples of more compliant core firms could also be found in particular sectors that have been considered 'natural monopolies' or suppliers of 'collective goods'. In many countries the telecommunications industry or the defence sector are considered to supply universal services that have to be directly and democratically controlled by the government and parliament.

The comprehensive concept of control located at the mid-left position of the bargaining scale can be labelled industrial democracy. Industrial democracy will only emerge as a result of social and political strategies developed by other actors than the core firm, such as governments or trade unions. On an international scale some rather minor attempts have been made towards formulating international codes of conduct for transnationals, while trade unions' thinking on how to enforce a compliant bargaining attitude of firms have been limited to theories of 'associative democracy' (Mathews, 1989). Thus, much further attention will be required to formulate the elements of a comprehensive concept of control centring around industrial democracy.[19]

Figure 5.3 also presents three characteristics of these five concepts of control: the basis of performance contained in this concept of control, the

---

[19] It could be argued that the former socialist countries made an effort to build an industrial democracy. However, instead of raising a system of democratic 'checks and balances' to influence core firms – while leaving these firms considerable room to develop autonomous strategies – the 'real existing' socialist system of planned economy fixed all power at the state level, also subduing for instance workers' and trade unions' interests to those of the state bureaucracy.

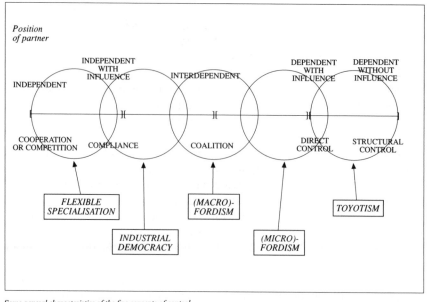

Some general characteristics of the five concepts of control

Performance based on:	Cut-throat competition and *ad hoc* cooperation focused on price and/or quality competition.	Compliance to other partners (depending on the dominant partner in the complex); cost-plus contracts.	Continuous bargaining with all partners in sectoral and national institutions: meso-corporatism.	Direct control; internal efficiency and productivity; profit maximisation.	Structural power; quality and flexibility of the supply network; cost-minus relations; market share maximisation.
Nature of core firm and customers	Polipsony. Many firms, many buyers, (closest to perfect market)	Monopsony markets; oligopoly (creating undercapacity with competitors)	Oligopoly; oligopsony	Oligopoly (striving for monopoly); polipsony	Oligopoly (creating overcapacity with competitors); polipsony
Illustrations of industries in the 1980s	Start-up industries; artisan producers for niche markets: ceramics, textiles, shoes (Italy), machine tools (Germany), service industries, software industries (USA), agricultural specialties (Netherlands); lower-tier subcontractors.	Small national(ised) producers; specialised producers in: telecommunications, defence industry, public utilities; civil industries as spinoff from defence industries; Wallenberg consortium.	Large national(ised) producers; industrial conglomerates such as IRI and ENI (Italy), or Daimler-Benz (Germany); large subcontractors: steel, tyres, semiconductors (USA, Japan), resource based industries (oil)	Mass production, vertically integrated in: cars, consumer electronics, pharmaceuticals, petrochemical industries, food industries, some retailing chains (USA)	Mass production; vertically deintegrated in: cars, consumer electronics, information technologies (vertical *keiretsu*, Japan)

Figure 5.3   Dependency relations and the position of the five concepts of control

nature of demand and supply and some illustrations of industries that have successfully developed under the guidance of these bargaining characteristics. The performance of an industrial complex – or what other authors have called the 'laws of motion' of capitalism – is clearly not determined by one single characteristic, such as high levels of productivity or profit maximising behaviour of entrepreneurs. In government procurement industries for instance, it has been more important to have stable and long-term bargaining relations with governments that are willing to buy advanced equipment at cost-plus contracts than to offer the goods at the lowest price possible.

In mass consumption industries, bargaining relations will take an entirely different shape. In these markets, high productivity levels or profit maximisation can be obtained by using the subcontractors as source of productivity, innovation or flexibility. Core firms can also maximise their profits *vis-à-vis* their competitors if they are better capable of lowering the operating margins of their suppliers. At the same time, a firm can maximise its profits if it is better capable of bargaining for lower wages with its labour unions than its direct competitors in a different institutional setting, i.e. operating in another bargaining arena.

Figure 5.3 illustrates the position of some of the leading industrial complexes as they developed after the Second World War. In some cases the relationships developed under loose networks of *ad hoc* cooperation and cut-throat competition such as the networks of small firms in Italian or Swiss craft industries. In other cases, cost-plus contracts were struck enabling firms to invest sizeable funds in innovations while still earning high profits. As the figure shows, supposedly 'best-practice' industrial settings are difficult to transplant from one setting to another, since they involve and require an elaborate set of bargaining relations.

A core firm faced with a diffuse bargaining network, in which some actors are dependent and others are more in(ter)dependent, is unlikely to resolve its control problems. To resolve all control dilemmas simultaneously (if temporarily, cf. section 3.2) a core firm needs to organise its domestic bargaining relations at the same position on the dependency scale. If a core firm succeeds in this, the industrial complex will be characterised by a high degree of cohesion. From this it follows that a core firm's bargaining relations may be structured differently to the way it aspires. A core firm can be embedded in a macro-Fordist bargaining environment, but strive for a Toyotist concept of control, because its foreign rivals compete on the basis of this concept of control. The next chapter will turn to this area of international competition, internationalisation strategies and international trade.

If a national economy contains more than one industrial complex, therefore, the distinction between the individual complex and the national industrial system becomes relevant. We define the national industrial system as the aggregate of individual industrial complexes within one national economy. The concept of a national industrial system has been used by authors like de Banville and Chanaron (1991) to analyse the car industry, and is related to the concept of national systems of innovation (Freeman, 1988a; Lundvall, 1992; Nelson, 1993). Thus the German car system consists of the Volkswagen, Ford, Opel, Mercedes and BMW complexes. These complexes may partly overlap, for instance because a leading parts supplier such as Bosch delivers to more than one core firm. It follows that in one national industrial system, different concepts of control may coexist and compete. Thus, national systems may also demonstrate low or high levels of cohesion.

After a while, bargaining patterns within a national industrial system may start to converge between individual complexes. If this happens, it is most likely to occur along the lines of the bargaining rules set by the most cohesive complex, often at the expense of the weaker complex(es). Core firms with a relatively cohesive industrial complex have usually invested a lot of money and energy in forging well-running bargaining practices. High levels of cohesion have tended to be associated with above-average profits, and have therefore tended to be perceived as 'best-practice' by other firms – correct or not. Core firms of an industrial complex with low levels of cohesion and facing competition from a complex ascribing to a different concept of control, run the risk of having to adjust to an alien philosophy of managing its dependencies. Governments also tend to favour more cohesive complexes, since these make it easier to develop the appropriate trade and industrial policies.

6   Rival views of globalisation

6.1 INTRODUCTION

In the 1980s, a new catchword entered the jargon of international business
and state policy-making: globalisation. Globalisation refers to a number of
changes in the world economy, such as the increased international mobility
of capital and the growing incidence of mergers and acquisitions and of
strategic alliances. The word indicates a growing multipolarity within the
world economy, with the East Asian economies, led by Japan, competing
vigorously and gaining market share in a range of mid and high value-
added industries. The literature on globalisation emphasises the rise of new
technologies and examines the challenges that firms are facing to integrate
these technologies into their daily activities. Others have focused on the
implications that public authorities must draw from globalisation, for
instance in the areas of competition or science and technology policy.

The term globalisation suggests a quantum leap beyond previous internationalisation stages. It is surrounded by claims of disappearing borders and
contains strong rhetorical overtones. Management gurus, journalists, government officials and even serious academics have readily adopted the word
into their vocabulary. Its popularity can be read not just by counting its
occurrence in the titles or abstracts of leading academic journals or in the
business press, but also from the fact that the top management of many
large companies have stressed the global scope of their operations.

Internationalisation is by no means a new phenomenon. For thousands
of years, people have traded goods across nations and appropriated wealth,
with or without force. In modern capitalism, internationalisation often
took shape by the conquest of colonies and the rise of mercantilism. Some
authors have explicitly used the term globalisation to refer to this
European-led campaign to gain control over other communities in the
world and integrate them into one global trading system (Modelski, 1972).
Over the centuries, the pattern of internationalisation and the words used
to signify them have changed, as old powers disintegrated and new ones
emerged with different interests and strategies. When a new state took over
the reins of colonial conquest and expansion of trade, this was often

accompanied by new theories or doctrines to account for these changes and to justify the underlying power relationships. Thus at a time when the United Provinces arose to a position of dominance in world trade, the Dutch scholar Grotius developed his legal doctrine declaring the freedom of the world oceans, meant to defy the Spanish–Portuguese division of the oceans sanctioned by the Pope. Likewise, Ricardo's theory of comparative cost advantages sustained British commercial superiority throughout the nineteenth century (see Chapter 9).

In this chapter, we shall see that even today, international economic shifts still tend to be accompanied by new concepts and theories. The way in which a lot of Japanese companies and the Japanese government have advocated globalisation as the explicit agenda for the late 1980s and 1990s is a case in point. In Toyota's 1989 annual report, for instance, Eiji Toyoda and Shoichiro Toyoda, Chairman and President of the Toyota Motor Corporation, presented their vision of the 'global village':

> This is our town. It's the global village [picture of the globe]. We live here. You do, too. We're neigbors. And since we're neighbors, we should be friends. . . . We will do our part to bring the world together by building up the global auto industry. This means that we will build major plants everywhere we can. And more, that we will do all we can to foster the development of our local parts suppliers. And of their suppliers. And of theirs. By helping in this way to create an auto industry infrastructure around the world, we will be helping to create the conditions for widespread prosperity.

Section 6.2 assesses three well-known approaches to the internationalisation process: the product life cycle model, the thesis of the new international division of labour and in particular the globalisation thesis. Each of these explanations will be related to the specific historical period and the bargaining context in which they arose. Section 6.3 focuses on the concept of globalisation and presents three specific and contrasting views of globalisation. Section 6.4 summarises the main arguments and alleged characteristics of globalisation in the academic literature. After discussing these affirmative, if diverging, views of globalisation, section 6.5 discusses some critics of the concept of globalisation. Finally, section 6.6 reviews some trends in international trade and investments since the second half of the 1980s.

6.2 HEGEMONIC CYCLES, INTERNATIONALISATION AND THEORETICAL EXPLANATIONS

Many scholars have argued that the history of modern capitalism has displayed a cyclical sequence of relatively stable periods with steady growth, followed by periods of international expansion and conflicts and culminating in periods of war. Immanuel Wallerstein has linked this pattern and the nature of internationalisation processes to the concept of the 'hegemonic cycle'. The hegemonic cycle describes the rise and decline of hegemonic states in the agro-industrial, commercial and financial areas. Wallerstein defined hegemony as 'that short interval in which there is *simultaneous* advantage in all three economic domains' (1984: 41, original emphasis). In the heyday of hegemony, the hegemon is able to dominate international trade and investment on the basis of its superiority of production. In this period:

> the products of a given core state are produced so efficiently that they are by and large competitive even in other core states, and therefore the given core state will be the primary beneficiary of a maximally free world market. Obviously, to take advantage of this productive superiority, such a state must be strong enough to prevent or minimize the erection of internal and external barriers to the free flow of the factors of production; and to preserve their advantage, once ensconced, the domin-ant economic forces find it helpful to encourage certain intellectual and cultural thrusts, movements, and ideologies.
>
> (Wallerstein, 1980: 38)

Thus during certain intervals of time, some states have been able to acquire a hegemonic position and produce more efficiently than other core states. These hegemonic states have faced the task of integrating competitors and potential contesting states, as well as peripheral regions, into an inter-national economic setting that would sustain their hegemonic position. One major element of this setting will be to liberalise international trade flows. On the basis of its productive edge and its commercial superiority, a hegemon will be interested in open trading routes. Hegemons face the continuous risk that other states resist submitting to this free trading system and maintain certain industries or develop new industrial principles that, if put to the competitive test at an infant stage, would probably perish. Therefore, other things being equal, the better a hegemon succeeds in imposing a free trade regime upon other core economies, the slower its hegemonic position will erode.[1]

As Wallerstein's quotation suggests, companies and governments of hegemonic states require theoretical constructions that legitimise their inter-national expansion and that stress the virtues of free international trade.

---

[1] The concept of hegemonic cycles is closely related to the concept of long cycles, which looks in particular at long waves in price movements and innovation clusters. In his review of the long cycles debate, Joshua Goldstein concluded that '[t]he fragmented structure of the long cycle research community has contributed to a disappointing lack of knowledge cumulation over the decades of debate on long cycles' (Goldstein, 1988: 72). Scholars of long cycles differ on essential issues such as the duration of these cycles and the clustering of innovations (upswing or downswing). Their meta level of abstraction does not allow long cycle theorists to assess the nature and implications of production and process technologies – except in an *ad hoc* manner, and not in terms of the general model – even though they would acknowledge that innovative and efficient industries are at the root of hegemony. We encountered similar problems discussing the neo-Schumpeterian approach in Chapter 2.

Thus, a theory accounting for the internationalisation of companies from the hegemonic country – through trade, direct or indirect investment, strategic alliances – will have more support in this country than in other core states. Conversely, after hegemony has started to decline and firms from other core economies in turn increase their international presence, alternative theories can be expected to come up in these rival core states which are less likely to gain the same level of support in the post-hegemonic country.

Wallerstein's understanding of historical shifts in the world economy has been criticised as too general and mechanistic. In his framework, some elements have not been elaborated very well, such as the dynamism that determines the rise and fall of hegemonic economies, the impact of inward and outward internationalisation, and the cycles of potential challenging economies. In respect of the latter, this book argues that industrial complexes can be seen as the centres of gravity of the international restructuring race.

The next three subsections consider to what extent one can link the content and popularity of particular internationalisation theories to waves of internationalisation and to the stage of the hegemonic cycle. Later in this chapter and in Chapter 7, the focus of the analysis will shift to the role of core firms and industrial complexes.

6.2.1 The rise of US hegemony and the failure of the 'one world' concept

At the start of the twentieth century, the world economy was dominated by British rather than US interests. In 1914, UK investors dominated 45 per cent of all *stock* of foreign direct investments (Dunning, 1993: 117). British internationalisation in the nineteenth and early twentieth century basically originated from flexible specialisation networks and developed into multi-domestic industries: in 1939, 94 per cent of all UK multinationals with foreign manufacturing investments first supplied the countries in which they produced by exports (Nicholas, 1986, quoted in Dunning, 1993: 58). Hence these UK firms did not establish a regional division of labour between their various international subsidiaries.

However, before the First World War, the *flow* of UK foreign direct investments had already begun to decline, and US foreign investments had started to expand. By 1901, US companies maintained around fifty overseas manufacturing operations. By 1913, this number had risen to 116, of which almost half were located in Canada and the UK (Dicken, 1986: 58). Dicken indicates that this wave of US foreign direct investments led to serious concerns in the UK, as shown by the title of a 1902 book called *The American Invaders* (ibid: 59). In this way, Britain, the declining hegemon at the time, became confronted at an early stage with competition from US companies which were moving from traditional, flexible specialis-ation types of networks to more vertically integrated and (micro-)Fordist production systems. As early as 1911 for instance, only three years after its Model T was introduced, Ford became the leading seller of cars in Great Britain. Its motive for moving to the UK was not to evade trade barriers, but to reduce shipping costs and to assemble close to existing markets.

The US drive for internationalisation soon became justified by an ideological component, the 'world order concept' (van der Pijl, 1992: 92ff). The world order concept was launched in 1900 by Woodrow Wilson, US president from 1912 to 1920. He presented a vision to include all nations of the world, both developed and developing, in one free world market. The world order concept represented perhaps the first effort to formulate a globalisation concept, yet at the time, the USA lacked the international clout over the European economies to enforce this concept. After the First World War, this globalisation *avant-la-lettre* concept served as the basis and inspiration for the establishment of the League of Nations (1919). The US government itself, however, refused to participate, and withdrew into its isolationist stance.

It took over twenty years plus the devastations of another World War before Wilson's world order concept would be relaunched. The Second World War marked the end of European economic dominance and the beginning of world supremacy of the US industrial system. By 1953, for instance, when the restoration of the European economies was well under way, the USA still accounted for 44.7 per cent of total world manufacturing output, compared to only 26 per cent for the whole of Europe (excl. the Soviet Union: Kennedy, 1987: 368). In the year 1940, the then Republican presidential candidate Wendell Willkie published a book entitled *One World*, signifying the end of US isolationism and the start of US internationalism (van der Pijl, 1992: 156). Although Willkie lost the elections, the 'one-worlders' in the Franklin D. Roosevelt administration gradually developed a policy aimed at including the entire world in a US-led liberal world economic order, after the end of the Second World War. Key elements in this policy were the United Nations and related international organisations such as the International Monetary Fund (IMF) and the International Bank for Reconstruction and Development (IBRD, also known as the World Bank).

The one-world concept represented the second US attempt to formulate a broad international economic and political order which would secure US companies' access to formerly protected European or colonial markets. The one-world concept also signified the maturation of micro-Fordism and the ability of US firms to compete successfully in any market, anywhere in the world. In the course of 1947, however, the Truman administration realised that the Soviet Union and its sphere of influence could not be included in these plans. Hence it changed its strategy to pursue 'Atlantic unity' and promote the economic reconstruction of Europe by supporting European integration. As Kees van der Pijl has argued, the Marshall Plan allowed Western European capital owners with colonial or Eastern European

Table 6.1   Growth in the volume of world trade, 1850–1971 (1913 = 100)

Year/period	Index	Year/period	Index
1850	10	1938	103
1896–1900	57	1948	103
1913	100	1953	142
1921–25	82	1963	269
1930	113	1968	407
1931–35	93	1971	520

Source: Kennedy, 1987: 414

interests to restructure these interests into a wider *Pax Americana* (van der Pijl, 1984: 161).

Apart from the objective to strengthen Western Europe and erect an anti-Soviet bloc, the US administration also aimed to secure long-term access to European markets. Bearing in mind how the prewar economic crisis had led to an escalation of trade barriers and had slowed down international trade, the General Agreement on Tariffs and Trade (GATT) had to supply free international trade as an international 'public good'. Between 1850 and 1913, world trade volumes had risen steadily (see Table 6.1). From the First World War onwards, however, trade volumes had remained relatively stable for almost forty years. GATT was to help remove tariffs and quotas as the main obstacles to free international trade. After the Second World War, the growth of world trade volumes retook its upward line. Chapter 9 discusses the neo-classical trade theory which supported international free trade.

Perhaps the most important effect of the postwar liberalisation of international trade flows was that European industries became exposed to the micro-Fordist organisation of production on which US hegemony rested. The micro-Fordist concept of control was based on the introduction of mass production techniques and on a stringent division of labour within large and vertically integrated firms, and a simultaneous increase of wages and consumption. With the liberalisation of international trade, the principles of Fordism and its regulatory setting themselves internationalised. Thus the US government attempted to lock potential contesting states into the game of international competition according to US rules.

After the Second World War, two factors diminished the US government's ability to impose (micro-)Fordism in Western Europe: the different *national* bargaining arenas, as well as the *international* bargaining context. A developed industrial economy with established bargaining patterns and institutions will always find it difficult to adopt alien principles regarding the organisation of production and the regulation of competition and society. Western European firms maintained much lower levels of vertical integration than their US counterparts, while workers' organisations had become more centralised and more powerful over the 1930s. Secondly, the perceived Soviet threat not only triggered the Marshall plan but also spurred organised labour's bargaining power. In the sphere of labour relations, this fostered the rise of centralised, rather than decentralised, bargaining between governments, labour unions and employers' federations, leading to the rise of a macro-Fordist variant of US micro-Fordism. In a macro-Fordist regime, productivity and consumption increases are coupled as well, but they are negotiated at the level of the state rather than of the individual firm or industry.

By the late 1940s, the US 'best-practice' example suggested that important advantages could be attained by creating economies of scale. The European integration process greatly helped the reconstruction of the European economies, sheltering European firms to some extent from international competition, and offering them a larger 'home' market. Similarly, the Japanese government erected high trade barriers as soon as the US-dominated Supreme Command for the Allied Powers (SCAP) had left Japanese territory. Superpower rivalry and the US fear by the late 1940s that other core economies might disintegrate, made the US administration accept that the European and Japanese states would rebuild their economies in relative isolation and at a more rapid pace than would have been possible under a true international free trade system. At the same time, by creating a macro-Fordist arena in Europe, the European economies made it easier for US companies to expand to Europe and set up direct production facilities at a later stage.

6.2.2 Hegemonic decline and the rise of US multinationals

As the European and Japanese economies adapted to Fordism, US productivity growth rates gradually diminished. US core companies tended to counter wage hikes by rising levels of automation, or to secure parts supplies by extending their direct control over suppliers (take-overs), rather than seeking to alter their external bargaining relations. As Table 6.2 shows, this led to higher capital/output ratios and a slowdown of productivity growth in the 1960s. At the societal level, the very foundation of Fordism, the combined rise of productivity and consumption, came under siege (de Vroey, 1984). Other bargaining relations also came under pressure. For instance, following a US Supreme Court of Justice verdict in the late 1940s, prohibiting exclusive car dealerships, the number of megadealers and retail chains gradually increased, undermining the Big Three's (General Motors, Ford and Chrysler) control over their domestic distribution.

The intuitive reaction of US core firms in the 1960s was to escape from their increasingly adversarial domestic bargaining arena by setting up subsidiary companies and transferring parts of their production processes abroad, in particular to Canada and the EC. In 1967, US investors held over 50 per cent of the world stock of foreign direct investments, while the British share had declined to around 15 per cent (Dunning, 1993: 17). The

Table 6.2   Productivity development in the USA, OECD, Europe and Japan

Country	Total factor productivity*			Labour productivity		
	1960–73	*1973–79*	*1979–88*	*1960–73*	*1973–79*	*1979–88*
USA	1.6	− 0.4	0.4	2.2	0.0	0.8
Japan	6.0	1.5	2.0	8.6	3.0	3.2
West Germany	2.6	1.7	1.6	5.4	3.0	2.6
France	4.0	1.7	1.6	5.4	3.0	1.6
Italy	4.6	2.2	1.0	6.3	3.0	1.6
UK	2.3	0.6	1.8	3.6	1.5	2.4
OECD Europe	3.3	1.4	1.2	5.0	2.6	2.1
OECD	2.9	0.6	0.9	4.1	1.4	1.6

* Total factor productivity growth is a weighted average of the growth in labour and capital productivity
Source: OECD, 1992: 168

rise of US multinationals meant a further internationalisation of Fordism, but at the same time the *défi américain* heralded the crisis of Fordism to come (cf. Servan-Schreiber, 1967).

Theories that tried to account for the rise of US multinationals tended to ignore the declining productivity rates and the deteriorating bargaining relations within the US industrial system. The most popular explanation was based on the 'product life cycle', which described the growth and decline of a given product. In its simplest form, it stated that a successful product goes through five stages: (1) development; (2) exploration and initiation in the market; (3) rapid growth; (4) maturation/saturation; (5) decline of demand and cutback of production capacity (Vernon, 1971: 65ff; Ansoff, 1969: 25). According to Ansoff, a product's life cycle could be extended by gaining increasing market share; by introducing improved products, creating replacement demand; and by introducing the product in markets not served previously (Ansoff, 1969: 29). After these three stages had been completed, however, the only remaining strategic option to a firm would be to diversify to different product markets (cf. Ansoff's strategy matrix, 1968: 99).

On the basis of the product life cycle, Raymond Vernon formulated an expansion and spatial growth trajectory of the firm (Figure 6.1). According to Vernon, the first three stages of the product life cycle would take place in the firm's home market. In the third stage, the firm would establish overseas sales and representative offices. In the fourth stage, when demand in the home market had gradually saturated and competition had become more intense, these overseas offices would develop into foreign production subsidiaries, producing the bulk of the good concerned. If these overseas markets were protected by high tariff barriers, this shift of production could already take place in the third stage. Certain factors could of course

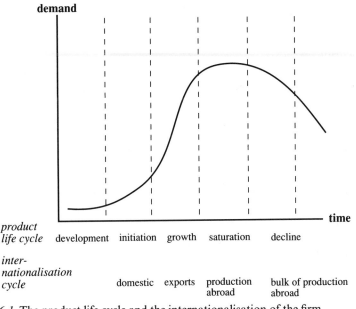

Figure 6.1 The product life cycle and the internationalisation of the firm
Source: derived from Vernon, 1971; Ansoff, 1968

speed up or slow down this process, such as the level of domestic versus foreign wage levels. However, the rationale of the product life cycle (and indeed of Fordism) was that at a certain stage production would shift to a location with lower wages.

Initially, Vernon's elaboration of the product life cycle model did have some explanatory power. Based on their still considerable technological advantages, a lot of US companies saw a gradual shift of their competitive advantages over the 1960s from process to *product* innovation. To the management of large US firms, the product life cycle model rationalised the escape from their domestic bargaining arena and signified a shift from a long-term, production-oriented outlook to a short-term, consumer-led, market-oriented focus. In the USA, the product life cycle model became the most widely accepted explanation of the rise of multinationals by the early 1970s.

Yet in spite of this acceptance, the 'model' offered little more than a one-dimensional and evolutionary international growth trajectory of a firm based on the dynamism of *one* product. The model completely disregarded a firm's domestic bargaining setting, and its impact on location decisions. Perhaps *because* of these limitations, the product life cycle model attained the status of a belief system for many US professors, managers and civil servants:

1 Its *mechanistic and stepwise approach* could easily be understood by a large audience;

2 It assumed a technological and competitive edge of the multinationalising firm *vis-à-vis* foreign competitors. The model *affirmed the superiority of US technology and production organisation* over companies from the rest of world;

3 US multinationals were presented as a *progressive force* spreading techno- logy, welfare and freedom to the rest of the world; and

4 It ignored potentially negative effects of the internationalisation of the firm, both within the company (such as increasing coordination problems as a result of internationalisation and diversification) and in the environ- ment of the firm (for instance declining workers' loyalty due to loss of employment).

The product life cycle model has become and remained a standard ingredient of textbooks on international business, trade and investments, even if it particularly served to rationalise the expansion of US multinationals, which until the early 1970s were superior *vis-à-vis* the other core economies in most industries.

6.2.3 The new international division of labour and the rise of European multinationals

When the Nixon administration ended the convertibility of gold into dollars in 1971, this manifested the collapse of the Bretton Woods system and the end of US hegemony. The first Oil Crisis in 1973 underlined that the USA was no longer able to regulate and guarantee the supply of raw materials, while the US intervention in Vietnam had developed into a disaster. These and other events signified the failure of the 'one-world' ideal underlying the postwar world economic order and the US internationalist role.

Meanwhile, the crisis of Fordism became increasingly felt in Europe too, leading to declining growth levels in total factor productivity (see Table 6.2). European firms had proved unable to emulate the US micro-Fordist example due to domestic and international circumstances, and moreover the macro-Fordist variant never yielded productivity rates comparable to US companies either. Declining productivity rates in particular prompted an internationalisation wave of European firms some five to ten years later than their US counterparts. Certain European companies already main- tained large multinational operations before the Second World War, partly as a legacy of colonialism. Oil companies such as Royal Dutch/Shell and British Petroleum, electronics firms such as Philips and food-processing companies such as Unilever are prime examples. However, the majority of the European firms, and particularly those from Germany, only started large-scale multinational production through the 1970s.

The product life cycle framework proved much less useful in analysing the internationalisation of European firms. Large European producers confronted with declining productivity growth rates and rising costs could not copy the US multinationalisation strategy of setting up production facilities in yet another industrialised area in which the Fordist crisis had made less progress. The one remaining industrialised country, Japan, had erected high barriers and had raised an industrial system that could not easily be penetrated. European – and US – multinational firms therefore spread out to South East Asian and Latin American developing countries. This runaway of European and US labour intensive industries such as textiles, shoe production and electronics assembly, followed the Fordist logic of cutting labour costs and increasing levels of automation.

The German authors Folker Fröbel, Jürgen Heinrichs and Otto Kreye (1977) analysed this development as a tendency towards a 'new international division of labour' (NIDL). On the one hand, the authors were very critical of this tendency, documenting the severe working conditions in many developing countries. On the other hand, however, they hoped that a NIDL could promote industrial independence and ultimately improve the standard of living in developing countries. In this sense, the thesis of the NIDL also presented a positive picture like the product life cycle model had done before. Perhaps due to this, and because the three authors paid most attention to German companies, the NIDL thesis never gained ground in the USA to the extent that it did in Germany and the rest of Europe. The NIDL argument may be seen as the European version of the globalisation thesis (cf. section 6.3.3). In 1986, Fröbel *et al.* published a new study on the multinationalisation of German firms, stating that their argument still held, and that large European (and American) multinationals had adopted a strategy of worldwide sourcing, leading to a search for ever cheaper labour, a flexibilisation of labour, and the development and introduction of new technologies (Fröbel *et al.*, 1986: 211). This would amount to a domination of micro-Fordist (rather than macro-Fordist) international restructuring strategies.

One of the main deficiencies of the NIDL thesis, like the product life cycle model before, was that it could not account for the wide variation of internationalisation strategies of European companies from different countries. UK multinationals have been primarily interested in North America and continental Europe to gain access to high-income markets. By the early 1990s, almost half of the UK foreign direct investments stock was located in the United States, while another 27 per cent was in Western Europe (UN, 1993: 168). Dutch and Swiss multinationals displayed a similar pattern, although these firms maintained a considerable share of their investments in continental Europe as well. Over the 1970s and 1980s, European investments into the United States – of which a large part had consisted of acquisitions – had been dominated by multinationals from these three countries (Cooke *et al.*, 1992: 66).

Many UK, Swiss and Dutch multinationals are active in the areas of (petro)chemicals, and food, beverages and tobacco (Unilever, BAT

Industries, ICI, Royal Dutch/Shell, BP, Nestlé, Ciba-Geigy). These firms often internationalised at an early stage (as a result of colonial empires and/ or relatively small home markets) and tried to become 'insiders' in other national economies. Although many of these firms had located more than half of their assets abroad, they were hardly able to establish a division of labour between their foreign locations.

This pattern differs substantially from the internationalisation of, for instance, German, French and Italian core firms, both in timing and in sectorial and geographical reach. The latter often did not commence multinationalisation until the 1960s. They focused more on the European continent, aiming to create a regional division of labour. Only since the early 1970s have German and French firms become leading investors in the United States as well. German foreign direct investments tended to be concentrated in a few sectors: pharmaceuticals/chemicals (BASF, Hoechst, Bayer), electrical engineering (Siemens) and motor vehicles (Volkswagen, Daimler-Benz). As Table 7A will show, many German, French, Italian and even Swedish multinationals still maintain most of their assets in their own industrial system. Stemming from a domestic bargaining arena that can be characterised as macro-Fordist, or in the case of Sweden even as leaning towards industrial democracy, these firms have to accommodate relatively strong bargaining partners, and therefore enjoy many less degrees of freedom to transplant activities abroad. It may even be argued that a major motive for German, French, Swedish and Italian core companies in the 1970s and 1980s to internationalise has been to reinforce their bargaining position at home.

This brief discussion suggests that there have been stark differences in the internationalisation patterns among firms from the various European national economies. The growing multipolarity of the world economy by the early 1980s created a need to account for the variety of internationalisation trajectories of firms.

6.3 THE G-WORD: HOW TO GIVE MEANING TO FANCY JARGON

By the end of the 1970s, the ongoing economic recession, continuing restructuring efforts, 'runaway' investments from the main industrialised economies, and the rise of the 'newly industrialising countries', all implied that the simple logic of the product life cycle model became increasingly criticised. In 1979, Vernon acknowledged that the product life cycle model had lost much of its explanatory power (cf. Taylor and Thrift, 1982: 22). The assumption that products are essentially independent of each other, and that every innovation would lead to an entirely new product life cycle, became increasingly difficult to hold (cf. Perez and Soete, 1988: 475). Furthermore, the difference between 'high' tech industries or products (located at the first part of the product life cycle) and 'low' tech or 'mature' industries was often very difficult to establish. Supposedly 'mature' sectors such as the car industry, for instance, have continued to serve as a testing-ground for 'new' product and process technologies.

In response, several new internationalisation models arose by the late 1970s and early 1980s that tackled internationalisation from the perspective of the *company* rather than from one product. Håkan Håkanson (1989) presented a model depicting a company's internal growth path (i.e. through the establishment of subsidiaries). Michael Taylor and Nigel Thrift complained that the business development literature had largely come up with 'static, *ahistorical* models of corporate development . . . incapable of depicting corporate development paths' (1982: 14, original italics). Instead, they argued that it was no longer possible to identify one single corporate development sequence, also in view of what they termed the emerging 'global corporation':

> The new global corporation is the result of the complex process of interlocking between the relatively autonomous development sequences of subsidiaries, branches and affiliates, especially as multinationals acquire foreign *and* domestic firms that themselves have foreign subsidiaries, branches and affiliates. Some multinationals therefore grow into quite formidably complex international economic networks.
>
> (Taylor and Thrift, 1982: 1, original emphasis)

Since the early 1980s, many scholars, academics and business people trying to understand trends in the world economy and making projections have regarded globalisation as a useful and appealing concept. These academics often originated from different national origins, which only added to the feeling that globalisation was indeed taking place. However, do all authors and observers actually interpret globalisation in the same way? In this section, we briefly address this question. One of the first to spread the G-word was Theodore Levitt, in a 1983 Harvard Business Review article. Section 6.3.1 discusses Levitt's views. Section 6.3.2 reviews some Japanese attempts to conceptualise globalisation, including Kenichi Ohmae's and those of some leading Japanese academics. Section 6.3.3 confronts these views with those of Wisse Dekker of Philips, the Dutch electronics company.

6.3.1 Globalisation I: a micro-Fordist view

Theodore Levitt, a Harvard Business School marketing professor, was one of the first to use the term 'globalisation' when referring to an alleged convergence of markets in the world. Since his work reveals a lot of the assumptions behind the literature on globalisation and its strategic implications, we shall briefly discuss his 1983 view.

Levitt identified what he called '[t]wo vectors [that] shape the world – technology and globalization' (1983: 102). Globalisation in his view would lead to 'the emergence of global markets for standardized consumer products' enabling firms to 'benefit from enormous economies of scale in production, distribution, marketing, and management' (1983: 92). In his article, Levitt stated the classical American ideal: '[T]he global corporation operates with resolute constancy – at relatively low cost – as if the entire world (or major regions of it) were a single entity; *it sells the same things in the same way everywhere*' (1983: 92/93, our emphasis).

Discussing the second vector, Levitt argued that the impact of technology would be towards a further standardisation of production, rather than towards more customised production. While acknowledging that technological development could generate flexible manufacturing systems producing smaller batches of one good with different characteristics, he downplayed the chance of technology promoting economies of scope (rather than economies of scale):

> The successful global corporation does not abjure customization or differentiation for the requirements of markets that differ in product preferences, spending patterns, shopping preferences, and institutional arrangements. But the global corporation accepts and adjusts to these differences only *reluctantly*, only after relentlessly testing their immutability, after trying in various ways to circumvent and reshape them.
>
> (Levitt, 1983: 101, our emphasis)

In the USA, Levitt's article fell on fertile ground: he voiced a strong and optimistic belief that the trend in the world market would favour a business strategy aimed at exploiting economies of scale, and thus reconfirmed the basic structures and rationale of micro-Fordism. Contrary to Vernon, Levitt stressed the rise of one world *market* rather than of one world production system. Nevertheless, his argument encouraged US core firms to assess incessantly whether their domestic bargaining arena still offered them sufficient advantages, and to keep an eye on potential low cost production bases abroad from which they could better serve the world market.

The word and principles of globalisation in this meaning have been espoused by many US managers. Ford, the US car maker, has at several points in its history tried to launch a world car. The world car concept assumed converging consumer tastes within different world regions, which would make it possible to sell one successful car all around the world. In the production area, the world car concept implied a highly extended intrafirm division of labour. Its first attempt, launched in the 1970s, failed. In the early 1990s, Ford launched a second attempt with the Mondeo model which should be marketed (although under different names) in all developed markets. Since early 1995, Ford has been trying (again) to change itself into a global car manufacturer organised by product line and not by geography with local profit centres (*FT*, 3 April 1995). The success of this so-called 'Ford 2000' programme depends, for instance, on a global free market.

Ford's management holds an optimistic view on the futher liberalisation of trade. But as Chapters 9 and 10 will show, this optimism may not be realistic.

Levitt's concept of globalisation, although in its ideals an extension of the world order and one world concept, presented a more modest version: the business-inspired, micro-Fordist formulation of globalisation lacked an elaborated political superstructure. Globalisation *á la* Levitt would probably be served by a set of multilateral organisations (such as a new World Trade Organisation), yet he only presented globalisation as an *economic* concept. Compared to the product life cycle model, moreover, the globalisation concept was more modest in its emphasis on world markets only, not on world production systems. Hence, this concept of globalisation only formulated a partial version of global (micro-)Fordism (Lipietz, 1982).

6.3.2 Globalisation II: the challenge to formulate a Toyotist variant

In Japan, the ten years following the second oil crisis (1979–81) have been a period of rapid economic expansion. From 1984 to 1990, the Japanese real gross domestic product rose between 4.1 to 6.2 per cent per year (with the exception of 1986, when the growth rate was 2.6 per cent). This growth has been spurred by what has become known as the 'bubble economy', characterised by a relative abundance of 'cheap capital', i.e. capital at very low interest rates. This led to a rapid expansion of domestic demand, translating also into rising imports and a declining trade surplus. Japanese companies over these years massively stepped up their domestic investment programmes to meet this surging demand. However, the availability of cheap capital also provoked a wave of speculative investments, leading to mounting land and real estate prices. Partly as a response to this domestic situation, and partly as a response to the erection of regional trade blocs, Japanese companies also stepped up foreign direct investments. By the end of 1991, Japanese companies had over US$231 billion of foreign direct investment stock, second only to the US-based companies (Keizai Koho Center, 1994).

Both within and outside of Japan, the Japanese internationalisation drive called for new models and concepts. Kenichi Ohmae, former managing director of McKinsey Japan, has probably become the leading prophet of globalisation in Japan. Central in Ohmae's analysis is the concept of the 'business chain'. A business chain comprises a firm's main activities such as R&D, engineering, manufacturing, marketing and sales, and services. Ohmae distinguishes five steps in the globalisation of a firm. Each of these steps involves the transfer of activities in the business chain to a foreign location (1987: 35–9):

1 *Export:* the entire range of activities is performed at home. Exports are often handled by an exclusive local distributor;

2 *Direct sales and marketing:* if the product is received favourably in the foreign market, the second step entails the establishment of an overseas sales company to provide better marketing, sales and service functions to the customers;

3 *Direct production:* the third step involves the establishment of local production activities. In this stage overseas sales and production are not yet integrated but still report individually to headquarters. In 1987, many Japanese core companies would have been somewhere between steps 2 and 3;

4 *Full autonomy:* in the fourth stage all activities of the business chain, including R&D, engineering and financing are to be transferred to the key national markets (or trade blocs). By now, the company can compete effectively with local producers on an equal footing. It can respond to local customers' needs and has become a fully-fledged insider;

5 *Global integration:* in the ultimate stage of globalisation, according to Ohmae, companies conduct their R&D and finance their cash requirements on a worldwide scale and recruit their personnel from all over the world.

Globalisation would be aimed at performing all activities in the business chain both at home and abroad. However, in this process it is deemed of vital importance to retain the corporate culture. While internationalising, Japanese firms should not undermine their domestic bargaining relations, and should work as much as possible towards similar bargaining patterns abroad:

> What is called for is what Akio Morita has termed *global localization* . . . . The real difficulty is that the challenge cannot adequately be met, cannot even be held at bay, by redrawing structural charts, no matter how complex they are. At base the question is psychological, a question of values.
>
> (Ohmae, 1990: 115, our emphasis)

Ohmae presented a vision, or a desired end result, rather than a present reality. He pictured the symbolic image of a company with its headquarters in Anchorage, Alaska, which is at equidistance of New York, Tokyo and Düsseldorf, i.e. of the three large trade blocs (Figure 6.2, 1987: 100).[2]

Ohmae's globalisation thesis served to rationalise the internationalisation of Japanese firms, just like Vernon's product life cycle model rationalised US multinationalisation. However, in the current situation of slow world-wide growth and a large number of contending states, any new entrant in the 'Big League' of international business will meet with suspicion or rivalry. Ohmae's ideology of globalisation is aimed both at a domestic and a foreign audience. Addressing such differing audiences, it required more

---

[2] Other Japanese business leaders, such as the late Soichiro Honda, presented similar visions (cf. Nonaka, 1990: 86).

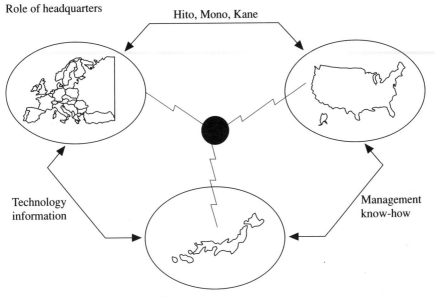

Role of headquarters

Hito, Mono, Kane

Technology
information

Management
know-how

Figure 6.2 Anchorage perspective
Source: McKinsey & Co

subtle phrasings than the product life cycle model. Japanese business people are advised to behave as 'good world citizens' and to foster good relationships with the local communities where they choose to set up operations. The Japanese government is urged to diminish its role in the domestic economy and to dismantle any remaining trade and investment barriers to foreign companies. The message to Western business people and government representatives, on the other hand, is to welcome rather than oppose the Japanese internationalisation. This ideology of globalisation can be summarised as follows:

1 It pictures a mechanistic and *evolutionary* progression of the internationalisation of Japanese firms ultimately leading to an end situation that seems desirable to both a Japanese and a Western audience, i.e. globally integrated companies producing high quality products for assertive consumers, supported but not hindered by local governments;

2 It *confirms Japanese firms' superiority*, but less explicitly than the product life cycle model confirmed US pre-eminence. The traditional export-oriented strategy is pictured merely as the first stage of a longer trajectory towards global maturity of Japanese business. The 'humble' message is that Japanese firms are determined to behave as good citizens abroad, but that it will take them some time to mature. Meanwhile Japanese firms should be excused for behaving differently, for excluding foreign staff from senior ranks, and for effectively limiting foreign companies from entering the Japanese market;

3 It appeals to *'free market' values* shared almost universally by representatives of 'big business', stressing the progressive role of multinational firms, who know best how to serve clients, and dismissing government interference;
4 It aims to *appease potential fears* held by Western business and government people in order to avert the risk of US and EU trade barriers.

Ohmae's version of globalisation is probably best known to a wider European and American audience, yet other Japanese academics have drawn essentially similar models. Noritake Kobayashi for instance presented five stages in the globalisation of a Japanese firm: '(1) management centred around the head office, (2) management delegated to overseas operating units, (3) management centring around the overseas operating units with their regional coordination, and (4) and (5) management with a global perspective and conscious integration of total system and subsystem' (Kobayashi, 1985: 231). In this view, stage 5 may be regarded as the final stage of globalisation and stage 4 as a transitional one. Many Japanese firms in this model, according to Kobayashi, would be situated somewhere between stages 3 and 5.

Another perspective on the globalisation of Japanese firms has been put forward by Masuyama (quoted in Cooke *et al.*, 1992: 76) of the Nomura Research Institute, the research unit of the Japanese finance and insurance company. Masuyama identifies eight steps in the globalisation of Japanese corporations: (1) the establishment of marketing offices; (2) raising the ratio of local production; (3) the establishment of overseas financing offices; (4) the establishment of R&D facilities; (5) the promotion of locals to managerial positions; (6) independence of management by local headquarters; (7) public offering of stock of locally incorporated companies; and (8) diversification of business.

Ikujiro Nonaka (1990: 69) provides a less conventional view on the internationalisation of Japanese firms. Nonaka rejects the product life cycle model which in his view only helps to understand the internationalisation of Western MNCs. He identifies three internationalisation models: the multinational strategy, the multidomestic strategy and the global-supplier strategy. The multinational strategy would typically have been followed by US firms, leading to highly structured MNCs with tight hierarchies. The multidomestic strategy would lead to a loose network of national subsidiaries and would have been adopted mainly by European MNCs.

> The third globalization strategy, that of global supplier, is one of export-centered global expansion and has been typically used by Japanese manufacturing firms during the post-war era. All systems such as R&D, procurement, sales and marketing, distribution, and the organizational structure are designed so as to enhance exports of products manufactured in the home country.
>
> (Nonaka, 1990: 70)

The globalisation of Japanese firms in Nonaka's view consists of four stages: (1) the creation of a global vision; (2) the integration of overseas organisations and the establishment of multiple corporate headquarters; (3) the promotion of a global hybridisation process; and (4) the globalisation of personnel administration and the cultivation of entrepreneurial middle management. According to Nonaka, one can best understand the globalisation of Japanese firms by shifting the perspective from an information processing to an information creation paradigm. In his model, regional (or what he calls 'multiple') headquarters have a function in collecting 'tacit' information, through decentralised and interdisciplinary R&D units. The 'tacit' information is only to be articulated at corporate level. Nonaka emphasises the need to establish a 'subtle balance between the headquarters' initiative and local initiative. Once that balance has been broken, not only the local subsidiary, but also the parent company may face a crisis' (1990: 90). Quoting a Sony chief of overseas sales: 'It is necessary to centralize at a certain stage of the process in order to achieve "true globalization"' (ibid).

Nonaka states that globalisation trajectories will differ according to the nationality of the company. He identifies not just differences between Japanese and Western MNCs, but also between US and European multinationals. Moreover, his classification seems to imply that globalisation could only be attained by Japanese firms, since neither American nor European firms have mastered the 'subtle balance' of headquarters control and regional initiative like the large Japanese firms.

As the various views discussed here indicate, many Japanese authors have been searching to develop an understanding of globalisation, and their search has led to very different outcomes from the Levitt interpretation. Generally, these contributions have been searching for a balance between maintaining domestic cohesion and meeting those forces and demands that made internationalisation inevitable. At home, core firms had to overcome resistance against internationalisation (and the exportation of work and orders), while sustaining the nature of their domestic bargaining arena. Interestingly, neither foreign pressure to reduce the Japanese trade surplus and establish overseas production sites, nor the need to find foreign capital outlets (to avert domestic inflation), have been elaborated in the leading Japanese literature as the major drives to internationalise.

Although Ohmae and Kobayashi have been cited most often, it is probably valid to state that no single view of globalisation has achieved a 'hegemonic' status in Japan to the extent that Levitt's view has in the USA and the product life cycle model has had in the past. One reason for this is that internationalism may build on a century's tradition in the USA, but certainly not in Japan. However, another reason is that Toyotism has not been implemented by all Japanese core firms. For instance, Sony and Honda, latecomers in their respective industries, have been unable to raise equally strong industrial complexes like established names such as Toyota,

Nissan or Hitachi, and have consequently maintained a more international outlook. The former companies have been earlier to set up foreign production, and have generally been more dependent on a favourable trade climate and a positive image of Japanese firms. This point will be further elaborated.

6.3.3 Globalisation III: a macro-Fordist view

Not just academics, but business people too have acknowledged the power of the ideology of globalisation. A leading critic has been Wisse Dekker, former president of Philips, one of the few remaining non-Japanese consumer electronics producers. Dekker (1991) also distinguishes five stages in what he calls the 'transnationalisation' of business:

1 The *local enterprise* produces and sells in one and the same country.
2 The *international enterprise* still produces entirely or predominantly in the parent country, but establishes sales representatives and possibly a distribution network abroad to initiate sales in foreign markets. International firms are characterised by a strong central organisation.
3 The *global enterprise* is transferring parts of its production process abroad – often limited to assembling – to circumvent import barriers or because of the transportation costs of a finished good. The global firm still has a strong central management.
4 The *multinational enterprise* has complete production facilities, sometimes even R&D, in a lot of countries. The multinational enterprise often has a federal structure with a good deal of power situated at the national organisations. In the countries where it is present, the multinational will behave not merely as a good citizen, but will truly be part of the national industry ('local for local').
5 The *transnational enterprise* consists of a network of organisations in which synergy plays an important role. Production in many cases is no longer 'local for local', but is situated in 'world production centres'. This means that the firm produces only in a few places for the entire world or at least for the region. Concentration of products in some world production centres will take place in particular in those production processes in which scale advantages play an important role, transportation costs are low and which serve a large and homogeneous market – e.g. by standardisation.

Thus Dekker defines globalisation as a relatively early stage in the internationalisation of a firm, with strong and centralised control. In the third stage:

> abroad may not be considered directly as 'conquered country' [in Dutch: wingewest], but the interests of the parent company are the most important. I think a number of large Japanese firms fit in nicely in this

profile and hence they are often criticised for not evolving into the next stages of the so-called globalisation process.

(Dekker, 1991: 5, our translation, original text in Dutch)

Until the 1980s, according to Dekker, Philips could be considered as a multinational firm, but since the second half of the 1980s it has been transformed into a transnational enterprise. One could argue that this fifth phase represents a company's *retreat* from a worldwide presence into large trading blocs. Companies with a macro-Fordist background, such as Philips, would therefore reserve the concept of globalisation to designate the period in which they had *their* heyday of worldwide expansion, i.e. the 1970s. To macro-Fordist firms, globalisation equals the 1970s strive to establish a new international division of labour – and the failure to do so. In the 1990s, many macro-Fordist firms have adjusted their internationalisation strategy towards establishing a regional division of labour (cf. Chapter 8).

Dekker's transnational enterprise should not be confused with Christopher Bartlett and Sumantra Goshal's 'transnational solution' (1987). In fact, their transnational solution claims to offer organisational answers to many problems that traditional multinational corporations such as Philips were facing in the mid-1980s. Chapter 8 briefly touches upon this contribution.

The models and terminology of Levitt, Ohmae and Dekker show how easily globalisation can be used to serve rhetorical objectives. Often, globalisation is advocated or rejected merely to justify a particular strategy or policy. Nevertheless, the concept has been employed not only by business strategists or politicians, but also by a variety of serious scholars. The next section will classify five leading approaches to the concept of globalisation.

6.4 GLOBALISATION: A CATEGORISATION OF APPROACHES

As one author puts it, 'jargon generally flourishes at times when concepts move more slowly than reality and leave large areas of important but intellectually unchartered lands' (Lanvin, quoted in OECD, 1992: 210). According to Stephen Cohen (1991: 1), some 670 articles were published in the year 1990 in prominent business and economics journals that had 'global' or 'globalization' in their titles, up from only fifty in 1980. Several researchers have tried to develop more clearcut and less ideological definitions of globalisation than the ones referred to in the previous section. This section will briefly categorise and discuss some important contributions.

6.4.1 The globalisation of finances

The French author Charles-Albert Michalet (1989) has defined globalisation as the deregulation of national financial markets and the subsequent internationalisation of capital flows. In the early 1980s, as productive investments were lagging in large parts of the industrialised world, a surplus of capital circulated on a national and a global scale searching for short-term, lucrative investments. This surplus of capital was the result of two worldwide economic recessions (1973–5 and 1979–82), two international oil crises (1973–4 and 1979–80), the rise of a petrodollar market, and the ensuing international debt crisis after 1982. Pressed by domestic financial circles, most Western governments decided to deregulate their national financial markets (Israelewicz, 1989). This not only increased the international mobility of capital and the volatility of international financial markets, but also precipitated the financial crises in many developing countries.

The 1980s 'casino capitalism' (Strange, 1986) or 'raider era' (Michalet, 1989) was directly related to the international crisis of Fordism. During the second half of the 1980s, mergers and acquisitions became the main form of growth of firms (De Woot *et al.*, 1990). However, mergers and acquisitions have played a much smaller role in continental Europe and Japan than in the Anglo-Saxon economies (*FT*, 24 September 1990). Mergers and acquisitions in the US economy reached a peak in value terms in 1988 (US$263.78 billion), yet the number of deals continued to rise for another two years and were still higher in 1991 than in 1988 (3,268 in 1991 compared to 2,752 in 1988). In 1993, US take-over activities nearly returned to the level of the boom years of 1988 and 1989 (*FT*, 17 February 1994).

In Europe, the year 1990 appears as the peak year of mergers and acquisitions activities (*FT,* 19 October, 1992). *In value terms, cross-border* European mergers and acquisitions declined in 1991, with take-overs taking place particularly within domestic markets by smaller companies (*FT*, 11 June 1992). In 1992, the value of cross-border mergers and acquisitions increased again, with the European Community (led by the UK) as the most popular region for take-overs by US companies (*FT*, 17 January 1993). In Japan, acquisitions have been of much smaller significance. W. Carl Kester (1991) has registered both the relative infrequency of Japanese acquisitions abroad, and the fact that only a few cases can be found of majority equity ownership of a pre-existing Japanese company leaving Japanese hands.[3]

These examples directly reflect the different regulatory and bargaining environments of these economies. The Anglo-Saxon economies are not 'more global' than others – 'more accessible' or 'less cohesive' would better

---

[3] As Kester notes, '[I]n the United States, for example, Japanese corporations executed 132 U.S. M&A transactions of all types in 1988 at a total cost of $ 12.6 billion. This compares to 389 U.S. transactions by British companies in the same year for a total of 31.7 billion' (1991: 110). Furthermore, he refers to a study which identified 'only 32 [majority acquisition] deals between 1955 and 1984 – 19 of them executed by American corporations' in Japan (1991: 137). Between 1985–9, 'American companies have purchased majority interests in 24 Japanese corporations. Eleven of these, however, were simply buy-outs of partners in Japanese joint ventures, and two were just the sale of a Japanese subsidiary by one American company to another' (1991: 137).

characterise them. In these industrial systems, capital mobility is higher than in many other economies, and restructuring through mergers and acquisitions a more frequent phenomenon. A take-over is the most basic example of a direct control strategy. Hence, the 'globalisation' of finances is linked first and foremost to the restructuring of companies with a micro-Fordist concept of control.

6.4.2 The globalisation of competition and of the firm

A second body of literature on globalisation has analysed the geographical shifts in the world economy and the changing organisation of international companies. Through the 1980s, Japan and to a lesser extent the 'Four Tigers' (South Korea, Taiwan, Hong Kong and Singapore) seemed hardly affected by the crisis of (micro- or macro-) Fordism, and developed into fierce competitors in the world market. Michael Porter (1985, 1986, 1990) looked at the effects of these changes on industries and firms, arguing that in a global industry a firm's competitive position in one country is significantly affected by its position in other countries. According to Porter, an industry can be considered 'global' if there is some competitive advantage to integrating business activities on a worldwide basis (Porter, 1986: 19).

C.K. Prahalad & Yves Doz approached the topic from the perspective of the marketing of a product or a business rather than the organisation of a firm or an entire industry. Presenting a simple 2 × 2 matrix, they stated that it is possible to map some businesses as 'global' due to advantages stemming from worldwide integration and economies of scale, and others as 'locally responsive' due to the need to adapt the business to the local market. In their view, '[t]he essence of global competition ... is the *management of international cash flows and strategic coordination*, even when global coordination across subsidiaries in terms of product flows does not take place' (1987: 40, original emphasis).

In 1992, the OECD Secretariat held the view that globalisation had only just begun. Central in the analysis of globalisation, according to the OECD, should be the changed international supply structure. Globalisation would refer 'to a set of emerging conditions in which value and wealth are increasingly being produced and distributed within world-wide corporate networks. Large multinational firms operating in concentrated supply structures are at the hub of these conditions' (OECD, 1992: 209). Robert Reich, former advocate of a US industrial policy and Labor Secretary of the Clinton Administration, has also shown himself a convert to the globalisation thesis. In his opinion, national competitiveness can no longer be defined by the strength of companies of national origin, due to the emergence of what he calls 'global webs':

The new organizational webs of high-value enterprise, which are replacing the old core pyramids of high-volume enterprise, are reaching across the globe. Thus there is coming to be no such organization as an 'American' (or British or French or Japanese or West German) corporation, nor any good called an 'American' (or British or French or Japanese or West German) product.

(Reich, 1991: 110)

Using terminology popular in the US management literature, the word 'web' implies that large firms are evolving into loosely tied and decentralised federations of business units, making products and seeking alliances both within their firm and outside, at home and abroad to serve customers' demands to their best ability.[4] Reich thus built the implicit argument that US companies adhering to micro-Fordism should relinquish their strategic outlook of direct control in favour of a shorter time horizon (as already prevailing in US financial relations, due to government-imposed regulations in the 1930s on anti-trust and on long-term credit relations between banks and industrial firms).

It is doubtful whether in the future German, French or Japanese companies will be structured as loosely as Reich wishes us to believe US firms are becoming. Companies in the former industrial systems definitely have a tradition of longer-term external ties with other firms, but the nature of these ties differs widely. As has been argued in chapters 4 and 5, a relationship which appears to the superficial observer as 'a' strategic alliance or 'a' co-makership relation, may in fact be a manifestation of a particular control strategy.

Only a few authors participating in the globalisation debate have systematically investigated inter-firm cooperative agreements on a global scale. Some early studies have looked into geographical patterns or clusters of alliances, demonstrating that the Euro-Japanese axis in the Triad was the weakest in terms of inter-firm cooperative agreements (Morris and Hergert, 1987). A few years later, Michalet suggested that inter-firm cooperative agreements would mainly appear in high technology industries (Michalet, 1989). However, as indicated in the discussion of the product life cycle model, it is often difficult to establish whether an industry should be classified high-tech or medium-tech. Others have examined cooperative agreements in one or two high-tech industries (Hagedoorn, 1990;

---

[4] In 1993, *The Economist* reported on a Booz, Allen and Hamilton study which claimed that 'today's global firms will be superseded by the "relationship-enterprise", a network of strategic alliances among big firms, spanning different industries and countries, but held together by common goals which encourage them to act almost as a single firm' (6 February 1993: p. 65). *Business Week* labelled this the 'virtual corporation': 'a temporary network of independent companies' which 'will have no hierarchy, no vertical integration' (8 February 1993: p. 37). However, in these networks, core firms will inevitably emerge that take up the role of director of the network, positioning themselves at the apex of a control network. The egalitarian 'virtual corporation' may only be an interesting model for small and entrepreneurial firms, and/or in companies the area of rapidly developing new technologies with no dominant standards.

Hagedoorn and Schakenraad, 1991), yet without looking at the relative bargaining position of each partner. Chapter 8 ranks alliances on the basis of the relative positions of the partners involved, and relates alliances to internationalisation strategies.

6.4.3 The globalisation of technology

The third category of approaches to the concept of globalisation may be considered a subgroup of the second one, emphasising the role of (information) technology in the globalisation of the firm and of competition as a whole. This category finds much support in international organisations such as the OECD, the United Nations Conference on Trade and Development (UNCTAD) and the European Commission (Forecasting and Assessment in Science and Technology programme). According to a document of the United Nations Centre on Transnational Corporations: 'Strategic alliances between firms and the pervasive use of planetary information networks are spearheading a reshuffling of comparative advantages, in which continuous innovation and flexible organization become crucial sources of profitability' (UNCTC, 1991: 1).

Documents produced by large international organisations on highly complicated issues usually build on the work of well-known scholars. Thus authors like Luc Soete (1991), François Chesnais (1988) and Dieter Ernst (1990) have had an important input to the debate of the globalisation of technology. Internationalisation and the development of new technologies are without doubt, closely related. Between 1975 and 1986, world production of technology experienced a sixfold increase and world high-technology trade underwent a ninefold expansion. Over the same period, Japan doubled its share of high-technology exports, displacing the USA as world leader (*IST*, Summer 1991: 92).

These data merely confirm that the access to and control over technology has become an important factor in international competition. However, the choice of whether to introduce new technologies, and in what manner, often depends on a core company's bargaining arena (cf. section 3.7). Section 6.6 and Chapter 7 evaluate the claims that technology has become a force of globalisation and that large companies are becoming 'global' technology companies.

6.4.4 The globalisation of regulatory capabilities

A fourth category of approaches addresses the implications of globalisation to the national state. Kenichi Ohmae has questioned the legitimacy of the state in view of the disintegration of borders. He believes that governments are not just losing their *raison d'être* but are even turning into a dangerous force fighting for their own survival:

> [Y]ou will agree that it is time to throw the bureaucrats out. . . . They miscount the trade figures and get them wrong month after month, and in the process they provide the weapons for economic war between the nations.
>
> (Ohmae, 1990: xi)

According to Ohmae, state bureaucrats are obsessed in the first place with their own survival, trying to mobilise domestic support against globalisation by producing trade statistics which necessarily distort the reality of international competition. His remarks are particularly inspired by and directed against the obsolescence and rigid structures of the Japanese state. Even before the Liberal Democratic Party (LDP) lost its power monopoly in Japanese politics, Ohmae led a grouping of people who wanted to change Japanese domestic and foreign (in particular trade) policy-making. He campaigned against the Japanese bureaucracy and the LDP, the traditional forces behind the Japanese industrialisation (*FT*, 20 and 26 November 1992). Working for a US consultancy firm, Ohmae has defended the interests of Japanese companies with a relatively international orientation, and of 'pragmatic' Western firms eager to expand their business in Japan.

Another argument within this category has taken an entirely different perspective and worries about the social and political implications of globalisation. If large economic actors are increasingly operating on a global scale, driven by the demands of international competition and by new technological developments, this may undermine the effectiveness of traditional government instruments. Globalisation could pose a threat to objectives of social, industrial, technological, or regional policies that have been decided through democratic procedures. From 1989 to 1991, the FAST-programme of the Commission of the European Communities co-ordinated a series of studies on these and other questions in the context of a project on the 'globalisation of technology and economy'. Several contributors to this project have argued that supranational authorities would be in a better bargaining position to pursue such objectives of state policy than national governments (Petrella, 1989; cf. Muldur and Colombo, 1991).

6.4.5 Globalisation as the political unification of the world

In a book which laid the foundations of his work on long cycles and superpower rivalry, George Modelski launched the concept of globalisation as early as in 1972 to refer to '[t]he process by which a number of historical world societies were brought together into one global system' (Modelski, 1972: 41). Globalisation would have started at about AD 1000, led at first by the Moslem world (1972: 42). Around AD 1500, the emerging European nation states took over the helm of the globalisation process. According to Modelski, the emergence of the nation-state was a precondition for globalisation, since it created an entity capable of organising domestic logistics and coordinating overseas naval operations – both commercial and military.

Although Modelski in his later work extensively analysed the pattern of superpower rivalry and the conquest of non-European regions (cf. Modelski, 1978), he did not elaborate the concept of globalisation itself. Some years ago, an attempt has been made to link Modelski's conceptualisation of globalisation to the analysis of contemporary international relations. As Smith (1992: 254) puts it, 'the historical process of globalization is an essential prerequisite for a notion of global politics', implying that inter-state relationships cannot be analysed without understanding the underlying processes of globalisation. According to McGrew:

> Globalization refers to the multiplicity of linkages and interconnections between the states and societies which make up the present world system. It describes the process by which events, decisions, and activities in one part of the world come to have significant consequences for individuals and communities in quite distant parts of the globe. Globalization has two distinct phenomena: scope (or stretching) and intensity (or deepening). On the one hand, it defines a set of processes which embrace most of the globe or which operate worldwide; the concept therefore has a spatial connotation. . . . On the other hand it also implies an intensification in the levels of interaction, interconnectedness or interdependence between the states and societies which constitute the world community. Accordingly, alongside the stretching goes a deepening of global processes.
>
> Far from being an abstract concept, globalization articulates one of the more familiar features of modern existence. . . . [O]f course globalization does not mean that the world is becoming more politically united, economically interdependent or culturally homogeneous. Globalization is highly uneven in its scope and highly differentiated in its consequences.
>
> (1992: 22)

McGrew distinguishes 'four fundamental processes of globalization: great power competition; technological innovation and its diffusion; the internationalization of production and exchange; and modernization' (1992: 23–4). However, this description of globalisation still leaves many questions regarding the basic dynamism and relationships between these 'four fundamental processes'. The contributors to the British Open University book *Global Politics* fail to identify the key determinants of these processes – particularly because they overstate the role of the state and because they neglect the underlying economic forces. As the above quote illustrates, McGrew, on one page, even claims that globalisation does and does not imply increasing interdependence!

If one nevertheless tries to take into account historical patterns of internationalisation and of state competition, as highlighted by Modelski and by McGrew *et al.*, one may formulate the following areas of attention:

- Globalisation implies the projection of power by a core entity to shape a global trading system or to force other geographical entities into an international division of labour controlled by this core entity;
- Globalisation does not necessarily pertain to every region of the world and may have uneven effects within the same region or state;
- Globalisation is induced and shaped by political and economic rivalry between great powers. Thus the shape of globalisation will depend on the rise and decline of great powers;
- Globalisation is no teleological concept, meaning that it incorporates no predetermined logic, such as the creation of a 'world society';
- Globalisation is also a dialectical process, stimulating forces of opposition against it;
- Globalisation therefore requires an ideological justification both *vis-à-vis* domestic and foreign parties affected by it. Today's equivalent of this ideological campaign has been provided by authors such as Kenichi Ohmae and Robert Reich.

6.5 CRITICS OF THE GLOBALISATION CONCEPT

In spite – or because? – of its vagueness and the diversity of interpretations, relatively few authors have *explicitly* disputed the globalisation claim. This section reviews the arguments of some critics.

In a vividly written article in the *New Left Review*, David Gordon (1988) challenged the 'commonplace among Left observers and activists that we have recently witnessed the emergence of a New International Division of Labour and the Globalization of Production' (1988: 24; he abbreviates these two terms as NIDL and GOP). As we have seen above, this 'common-place' is hardly limited to Left observers, although Gordon's audience is. Gordon, who has conducted extensive research into the pattern of long cycles, argues:

> that widespread perceptions about the NIDL and the GOP have been significantly distorted and that much conventional wisdom prevailing on the Left (and elsewhere) about recent changes in the global economy requires substantial revision. These changes are best understood *not* as a symptom of structural transformation but rather as a consequence of the *erosion* of the social structure of accumulation which conditioned international capitalist prosperity during the 1950s and 1960s. We are still experiencing the decay of the old order and not yet the inauguration of a new.
>
> (Gordon, 1988: 25; original emphasis)

Gordon summarises the globalisation argument as follows:

> [T]he GOP perspective places much less emphasis on the movement of production from the North to the South, and much more weight on the

concentration and centralization of capital through two related developments: first, the spreading importance of decentralized production sites
in both the advanced and developing countries; and second, the increasingly centralized control and coordination by transnational corporations
of these decentralized production units.

(Gordon, 1988: 26)

Gordon considers what he refers to as the hypotheses of the NIDL and the
GOP as related since both of them assume a transformation of the global
capitalist order. This seems like overstating the case in two respects. Firstly,
in both the NIDL and the GOP theses, the issue at stake is not so much to
change the global capitalist order, but rather to allocate business activities
over the world. Secondly, the NIDL thesis has had most support in Europe,
since it came up at a time when European multinationals, in relative terms,
were gaining ground as agents of economic and geographical shifts. The
globalisation thesis has found its support in the US and Japan, though in
very different formulations.

To test the two hypotheses, Gordon compares historical periods of
economic stagnation and instability with more recent trends. His data show
that the recent historical shift towards some developing economies and the
newly industrialised economies is not particularly large by historical standards. Between 1973 and 1984, the newly industrialised economies' share of
global industrial production increased from 7.1 per cent to 8.5 per cent.
Although substantial, during a period of stagnation and economic instability
this does not seem large enough to warrant conclusions of a fundamental
transformation (1988: 38).

Another interesting empirical study (cf. Patel and Pavitt, 1991, 1994)
addressed the hypothesis of the globalisation of technology, using data on US
patenting by 686 of the world's largest manufacturing firms. Patent statistics
are among the few that provide detailed information on firms, technological
area and geographical location – although the two researchers also list some
of the disadvantages of interpreting patent statistics as an indicator of a
firm's technological activities. The authors found that '[i]n most cases, the
technological activities of these large firms are concentrated in their home
country' (Patel and Pavitt, 1991: 1). However, the results varied widely per
country. Table 6.3 summarises some of these data at a country level.

Although international patenting has increased considerably since the
almost-stagnant 1970s, large differences exist between countries. The two
most distinct cases in Table 6.3 are the Netherlands and Japan. The high
percentage of Dutch firms can be explained by the fact that they originate
from a small economy with a few very large corporations (such as Royal
Dutch/Shell, Unilever and Philips), which may overstate the degree of
internationalisation of R&D by Dutch medium-sized enterprises (see also
section 6.6). Over the 1981–6 period, the technological activities of Japanese-
controlled large firms abroad amounted to only 0.6 per cent of their

Table 6.3 Patenting in US by nationally controlled firms from outside home country: percentage of national total (1981–6)

Country	Percentage	Country	Percentage
Japan	0.6	UK	16.7
Western Europe	8.1	Netherlands	82.0
West Germany	6.9	Switzerland	28.0
France	3.4	Sweden	11.3

Source: Patel and Pavitt, 1991: 10

activities at home (Patel and Pavitt, 1991: 10). Over the 1981–8 period, this figure had increased slightly to 0.9 per cent (Pavitt, 1992: 121). The data suggest that many firms regard technological development as a strategic asset that is best performed and secured at home. Over the 1981–6 period, the technological activities of Japanese-controlled large firms abroad in terms of patenting amount to only 0.6 per cent of their activities at home (1991: 10). Over the 1985–90 period, this figure had increased to 1.1 per cent (Patel and Pavitt, 1994).

Daniele Archibugi and Jonathan Michie (1993: 7) have confirmed these findings. Table 6.4 shows that large differences in international patenting also exist at the level of entire national industrial systems. While Japanese multinationals have been invading the patent systems of other economies, the Japanese national system itself has remained relatively sheltered from foreign patent applicants. This is partly a result of some peculiarities of the Japanese patent system, as well as linguistic and cultural barriers, all of which imply that the impediments for foreign applicants to file a patent in Japan are substantial. Japanese companies will have few incentives to alter this situation. Compared to Japan and the USA, the European national systems show a much higher degree of foreign penetration. However, the bulk of these are held by companies from other European economies. The small European countries again show the highest penetration of patents from foreign sources.[5]

6.6 TRIADISATION INSTEAD OF GLOBALISATION

Having discussed the concept of globalisation and some critiques, this section looks at some general trends in the world economy over the 1980s. Over this decade, the most important development has been the rapid

[5] Christopher Lorenz (*FT*, 15 July 1994) mentioned a forthcoming study by John Cantwell, supporting the argument that 'global R&D webs' are the exception rather than the rule. In the 1980s, according to the study, less than 9 per cent of the patents of US multinationals arose from abroad. Big American companies have only just regained the degree of internationalisation achieved in the 1920–39 period. Overall, European companies perform only 30 per cent of their 'technology activity' abroad. Only Dutch, German and Swedish companies have increased international technology activities sharply.

Table 6.4 Proportion of domestic and foreign patents

National industrial system	Percentage of patents from domestic companies	Percentage of patents from foreign companies
Japan	88.5	11.5
United States	55.1	44.9
Germany	32.6	67.4
UK	21.5	78.5
France	16.2	83.8
Switzerland	7.9	92.1
Sweden	6.9	93.1
Netherlands	5.3	94.7

Source: OECD database, MSTI, quoted in: Archibugi and Michie, 1993

increase of foreign direct investments and the fact that these investments mainly originated from and went to other industrialised countries. These investment flows have created a fundamentally different international economic setting as compared to the late 1970s. Between 1983 and 1988, foreign direct investments rose by more than 20 per cent annually, four times faster than the growth of international trade (Julius, 1990: 14). As a result, the vast majority of foreign direct investments are concentrated in the industrialised world, at the expense of investments in the less developed countries.

A 1991 report of the United Nations Centre on Transnational Corporations (UNCTC)[6] on the investment relationships between the United States, the European Community and Japan confirms these trends. According to this study, outflows of foreign direct investment grew by 28.9 per cent a year between 1983 and 1989. Over the same period, exports increased by only 9.4 per cent a year while average annual growth of the world gross domestic product amounted to 7.8 per cent. The UNCTC therefore concludes that:

> international transactions are increasingly dominated by transnational corporations. ... One implication of such a development is that the global patterns of trade, technology transfers and private financial flows could tend to converge on the foreign-direct-investment pattern, making the latter a principal force in the structuring of the world economy.
>
> (UNCTC, 1991: 82)

As Table 6.5 indicates, the growth of foreign direct investments has not been steady over the last decade. Whereas the 1980–4 annual average amounted to US$44 billion, the 1985–9 annual average grew to US$105 billion (excluding cross-border investments of US$20 billion a year among EC member states). Japanese companies registered the most spectacular

[6] The UNCTC was renamed the Transnational Corporations and Management Division in 1992.

Table 6.5   Foreign direct investment to/from the European Community, the United States and Japan, 1980–9 (billions of dollars)

Trade bloc	Stock				Flow (annual average)			
	Outward		Inward		Outward		Inward	
	1980	*1988*	*1980*	*1988*	*1980–4*	*1985–9*	*1980–4*	*1985–9*
EC excluding intra-EC FDI								
Bln $	153	332	143	239	18	39	10	19
% World total	33	34	31	23	41	37	23	19
United States								
Bln $	220	345	83	329	14	18	19	46
% World total	46	35	18	31	31	17	41	46
Japan								
Bln $	20	111	3	10	4	24	–	–
% World total	4	11	1	1	10	23	1	–
Triad								
Bln $	398	788	230	579	36	81	29	65
% World total	84	81	50	55	82	77	64	65
World, excluding intra-EC FDI								
Bln $	474	974	464	1059	44	105	45	100
EC including intra-EC FDI								
Bln $	203	492	188	399	22	59	15	40
% World total	39	44	37	34	47	47	30	33

Source: UNCTC, 1991: 32

Notes: FDI = foreign direct investments. The data on outward stock for Japan for 1988 include reinvested profits. The data on intra-EC represent UNCTC estimates based on national sources. The data for the EC do not include Ireland, Greece and Luxemburg.

growth rates. Japanese foreign direct investments increased sixfold during the 1980s. Japanese firms already spend more on foreign direct investments than their US counterparts. Firms' investments are concentrated within the Triad, i.e. the United States, the European Community and Japan. During the 1980s, the Triad accounted for around four-fifths of all international capital flows. The developing countries' share in worldwide capital inflows between these two periods fell from 25 per cent to 19 per cent, in spite of a near doubling of average annual flows to the developing countries between 1980–4 and 1985–9 (UNCTC, 1991: 10).

A 1992 update report still showed a continuation of this trend (*FT*, 15 July 1992), yet the UNCTAD World Investment Report 1993 signalled that FDI flows to developed countries had started to decline in the early 1990s, while those to developing countries in Asia, Latin America and the Caribbean had increased. Nevertheless, more than 90 per cent of the world's largest transnational corporations would still be headquartered in the developed countries (UNCTAD, 1993: 1/2).

Other data make the dominance of the Triad regions appear even more impressive. According to Kenichi Ohmae, 85–90 per cent of all high-value-added, high-tech manufactured goods are produced and consumed in North America, Western Europe and Japan, with the East Asian newly industrialising economies probably taking the bulk of the remainder. Ohmae also claims that 85 per cent of all registered patents were filed in five countries: Japan, the USA, West Germany, France and Great Britain (1987: 95). Mark Dodgson (1993: 115) reports that the vast majority (over 85 per cent) of inter-firm cooperative agreements has taken place amongst the Triad.

In conclusion, what is often referred to as 'globalisation' is perhaps better described as 'Triadisation'. The 1980s internationalisation of trade and investments was largely limited to the United States, the European Community and Japan as well as East and South East Asia. Although these three regions are the dominant economic powers of the world in the late twentieth century, other regions on the globe have been excluded from this supposedly 'global' restructuring process. It is worthwile recalling that in 1987 the Triad population accounted for only around 15 per cent of the total world's population (World Bank, 1989: 214–15)!

7 The myth of the 'global' corporation

7.1 INTRODUCTION

When in 1990 the two largest Dutch banks (ABN and Amro Bank) announced their merger, chairman of the management board Jan Nelissen claimed that ABN-Amro was becoming a 'global player'. The merger was to create the world's sixteenth largest bank with a 1992 capital of US$9.4 billion in equity and reserves and an ECU200 billion turnover (*The Economist*, 1994: 51). ABN-Amro offices were to be found in almost every major city in the world. At the time, Nelissen particularly meant to emphasise ABN-Amro's US position. ABN-Amro had managed to become one of the largest foreign banks in the USA, where it realised around 20 per cent of its 1993 business and revenues.[1] Only three years later, however, Jan Kalff, the new chairman of the ABN-Amro board, regretted that the image of the bank as a 'global player' had ever been made, since it conveyed a wrong impression of ABN-Amro's actual international position. The bank still is a European player at most, with solid Dutch roots: all members of the board of directors are Dutch, and the bulk of its turnover is obtained in Europe. Then what made Nelissen decide to drop the G-word? The answer is as banal as it is revealing to the 1990s newspeak of international business: the very morning of the press conference, Nelissen had read a *Financial Times* article about a firm which wanted to become a 'global player'. The word had such appeal to him that he dropped it casually during the press meeting – and ABN-Amro had jumped on to the globalisation bandwagon.

Quite a few managers have added to this conceptual confusion. Take the Swedish/Swiss firm ASEA Brown Boveri (ABB). Created as a 1988 merger between Swedish and Swiss power equipment makers Asea and Brown Boveri, it has a strong international outlook, selling most of its products

---

[1] In 1942, ABN had set up a US office to escape from the Nazi-German invasion of the Netherlands. Based in Chicago, Illinois, it gradually expanded its US operations, aided by regulations designed to curb concentration tendencies in the Illinois and US banking industry. These regulations *inter alia* allowed only banks headquartered in Illinois or foreign banks to take over other Illinois banks (Vk, 5 November 1993; NRC Handelsblad, 27 July 1994).

abroad. Business magazines have pictured Percy Barnevik, ABB's CEO, as the ultimate manager of the 'global' firm. Barnevik would do most of his business from an aeroplane: the Anchorage perspective (see section 6.3.2) in its most appealing form. In (again) the *Financial Times*, Barnevik stated that ABB 'prides itself on being *multi-domestic*' while it would 'strive to develop a *global* culture for all members of our *multinational* teams' (*FT*, 17 January 1994; our emphasis).

Why did Barnevik need so many words – with so many meanings? Just as a telecommunications company, ABB is producing expensive public goods and is dealing with strong bargaining partners (governments or large client firms) that historically have tended to buy from their 'national champions'. Such bargaining partners have led ABB to comply with demands on, for instance, suppliers or production locations. ABB's business portfolio allows only very limited possibilities to develop an international division of labour. To label ABB the ultimate global corporation, therefore, is the ultimate fallacy.

These two examples suggest that even large core firms may not have unlimited degrees of freedom in formulating their internationalisation strategies – in spite of their claims. This chapter aims to transcend globalisation rhetorics, and assesses the realised internationalisation strategies of the world's largest firms.

7.2 DIFFERENT RANKINGS OF INTERNATIONALISATION

To assess the internationalisation strategies of the world's largest firms, Table 7A shows the 100 largest non-financial firms in the world, based on *Fortune*'s Global 500 published in 1993 (see pages 170–3). The Fortune Global 500 ranks companies according to total sales, indicating the size of their operations and their apparent commercial success.

A number of alternative rankings, using different measures, have been considered as an approximation of the relative size of firms. *Business Week* publishes its annual ranking of the world's largest 1,000 companies based on market value, defined as a company's share price multiplied by the number of shares. One glance at the eighth column of Table 7A reveals the problem associated with such a ranking: it overrates the importance of firms with high equity/assets ratios, while it underrates the position of firms that have managed to minimise their dependence on external capital. For instance, in the 1993 Business Week Global 1000, General Motors ranks 33 and Ford ranks 46. Both corporations in this ranking are 'smaller' than for instance Coca Cola (*Business Week*, 1993: 14; *Fortune*, 1993: 106) or Merck, the US pharmaceuticals company (*Business Week*, 1993: 18; *Fortune*, 1993: 142). In terms of financial bargaining relations (see Chapter 5): firms that have successfully followed a direct control strategy, i.e. that have a high degree of auto-financing, will be ranked lower. The Business Week Global 1000 is therefore useful as a list for investors, not as a basis to assess the internationalisation strategy of a firm.[2]

Another well-known list is the UNCTAD World Investment Report 1993, which includes a ranking of the 100 largest non-financial transnational corporations in the world by total foreign assets (UNCTAD, 1993: 26). Its main disadvantage is that it overrates the degree of internationalisation of large companies: relatively small foreign investments by a big company will yield a high absolute ranking yet tell little of their relative importance to the company. This produces a different ranking, although around 60 per cent of the firms in the UNCTAD ranking are at the same time amongst Fortune's Top 100.

Only the first five columns of Table 7A have actually been taken from the Fortune list. From different sources, data have been added regarding the nature of the core firm's business, and regarding the degree of internationalisation in terms of assets, sales, employment, shares and management approach (in particular composition of the management board and nationality of the management of foreign subsidaries).

The 100 firms listed are core firms, according to our definition in Chapter 3, yet they need not be a core firm in every area of their business. For instance, Bosch is a white good end producer as well as the leading supplier to the car industry. General Electric (USA) makes electronic end products as well as plastic grains used as inputs in various chemical production processes. Furthermore, Table 7A excludes some of the world's largest combined industrial/services conglomerates, such as American Telegraph and Telephone (AT&T), British Telecom (BT) and Nippon Telegraph and Telephone (NTT). However, their internationalisation degree is still limited. Until the mid-1980s, telecom companies were only oriented to their respective national markets. Deregulation and privatisation policies have opened up competition between many telecom giants, but transforming from a domestic into an international player is a slow process. Finally, the table includes some well-known industrial and trading conglomerates such as IRI and Samsung, whereas member companies of Japanese industrial conglomerates are listed on an individual basis. For instance, the table mentions three members of the Mitsubishi industrial grouping (Mitsubishi Electric, Mitsubishi Motor and Mitsubishi Heavy Industries). In 1988, Mitsubishi's total group sales amounted to US$287.8 billion, compared to US$121 billion for General Motors and US$92.4 billion for Ford (Dodwell, 1990).[3] Hence, Table 7A overrates the weight of firms aiming for direct control or coalition strategies, while it underrates the weight of companies striving for structural control.

[2] As Chapter 5 indicated, around 70 per cent of the shares in core companies on the Tokyo stock exchange are held by 'stable' shareholders that rarely trade their shares and that are part of the broader industrial group. Gerlach therefore concludes 'that stock prices often do not accurately reflect the market value of the firm' (Gerlach, 1992: 74, 75).
[3] In 1988, total Mitsubishi group sales amounted to ¥36,833 billion. According to 1988 exchange rates, US$1 = ¥ 128 (Dodwell, 1990: 38; Keizai Koho Center, 1994: 50).

Peter Drucker has stated that '[t]he Fortune 500 is over' (*Fortune*, 20 April 1992: 38), meaning that big is no longer beautiful, and hinting at the rise of network structures. Looking at absolute employment levels, the importance of the Fortune 500 core firms appears to have declined: over the 1990–4 period, the number of people on their payroll decreased from 16.2 million to 11.8 million. However, the picture is more diffuse, both across sectors and national industrial systems. Schenk *et al.* (1994) found that over the 1978–90 period, sales by the one hundred largest European manufacturing companies as a percentage of European Union GNP increased from 18.1 per cent to 19.5 per cent, while their share of employees (as a percentage of total employment in manufacturing) increased from 25.1 per cent to 28.2 per cent. In Japan, sales of the largest one hundred manufacturing firms as a percentage of GNP have risen from 22.1 per cent to 29.7 per cent, while their share of employment has risen from 17.4 per cent to 22.4 per cent. The United States is the only country where sales by the one hundred largest manufacturing firms as a percentage of total GNP dropped from 29.1 per cent to 24 per cent over the 1978–90 period. However, employment by these firms as a percentage of total domestic employment remained almost stable (43.3 per cent and 42.3 per cent respectively). Only in Japan does the manufacturing core firms' percentage of total sales exceed the percentage of total employment. This is in line with our argument that Toyotism is the dominant concept of control in Japan, leading to large core firms that are in control of distribution but which are also at the apex of a supply network which handles most of the production.

Others, moreover, have pointed at the influence of core firms on *indirect* employment levels. According to UNCTAD (1994) estimates, the 37,000 'transnationals' in the world directly employ around 73 million people, i.e. 20 per cent of employment in the industrialised countries. In addition, their impact on indirect employment is about as large, bringing the total number of workers in some way dependent on 'transnational' firms to at least 40 per cent of total employment in the industrial countries. Because of these huge numbers, large core firms play a leading role in bargaining with labour over pay and other working conditions both in their own industries and in other industries. There is also a dire need for new statistical techniques or instruments to assess the influence of 'transnationals' on indirect employment (cf. Cohen and Zysman, 1987), and to cope with the paradox that core firms with a Toyotist concept of control have increased their structural influence over the economy, because they have lowered their number of directly employed workers. Thus, Peter Drucker's criticism of the old dictum 'big is beautiful' should not lead to the assertion that the days of the Fortune 500 are over, but perhaps to the new adage: *the core has more in store*.

7.3 THE INTERNATIONALISATION OF FUNCTIONAL AREAS OF MANAGEMENT

We have seen that at the level of the firm (or in terms of our framework: the micro level of analysis), many globalisation claims have been put forward. Sometimes, these claims were well elaborated, yet at times they were confusing or even incorrect. The simple question which emerges is therefore: to what extent do claims of a globalisation of large companies and claims of a declining significance to large companies of national borders really hold? This section addresses this question in the following manner. In business administration, a distinction is usually made between five functional areas of management: sales, production, finance, R&D and personnel (human resources) management. Below, we shall discuss the actual internationalisation of these functional areas of management of the largest one hundred firms in the world (see Table 7A).

Overall, large core firms have made most progress internationalising their *sales* (cf. 11th column). Over forty firms listed realise half or more of their sales in foreign markets. Many food and consumer products companies, chemical, oil and computer companies register most over their sales abroad. Some firms, such as ABB, Nestlé and Philips even sell over 90 per cent abroad.

To many firms, however, sales abroad primarily mean exports – the dominant mode of internationalisation. The internationalisation of production has been much less impressive. Only eighteen companies maintain the majority of their *assets* abroad, and only nineteen maintain at least half of their *workers* abroad. UNCTAD estimates support this internationalisation hierarchy of sales and production: the top one hundred firms, in terms of assets abroad, on average have 48.4 per cent of their sales abroad, but only 37.8 per cent of their assets abroad (UNCTAD, 1993: 28).

The internationalisation of *shares* is dwarfed by the internationalisation of sales, assets and workers. This suggests that core firms still regard control over their financial resources of utmost strategic importance, which can only be warranted at home. Table 7A contradicts other findings suggesting an increasing globalisation of corporate finances. For instance, in a sample of the largest US manufacturing companies, Raghunathan (quoted in UNCTAD, 1993: 140) found that 50 per cent had listed shares on stock exchanges outside the United States. Table 7A puts these findings in a more accurate perspective: many core firms may have listed some shares at foreign stock exchanges, yet only a few of them maintain over 10 per cent of their shares abroad.

Table 7A indicates that many German companies have a large percentage of shares abroad. However, this is largely limited to other German-speaking neighbour countries. These listings in neighbouring countries are partly inspired by tax reasons, and partly the result of the fact that industrial districts and national industrial systems often do not overlap. For instance, the industrial district around Munich does not end at the South German border, but also includes parts of Austria and Switzerland. In fact, German companies originate from an industrial system in which stock exchanges and shareholdings play a relatively minor role. Only in 1993, for instance, did Daimler-Benz, Europe's largest industrial conglomerate, obtain a full listing at the New York Stock Exchange. At the time, it was the first German company to take this decision, yet this had probably more to do with its changing relationship with Deutsche Bank, its longtime shareholder, than with a supposed 'globalisation' of the Daimler-Benz industrial complex.

Most Japanese and South Korean firms have a very small proportion of their shares listed abroad, usually only in a few countries. In general, however, listings on foreign stock exchanges tend to be limited to those of the USA, Japan, the UK, Germany, France, Austria and Switzerland (the latter two probably for tax reasons). At most, some firms maintain a presence at some stock markets spread over the Triad region. At times, companies have also withdrawn from foreign stock exchanges. In 1990, for instance, General Motors left the Tokyo stock exchange. In the 1990–5 period the total number of foreign listings on the Tokyo stock exchange declined from 127 to 82. Core companies like Ford, General Electric (USA), Allied Signal, Hewlett-Packard and Philips followed GM's example (Vk, 27 March 1995). Table 7A therefore even overestimates the, already low, number of firms listed at the same time in three of the world's most important regions, because it still includes the 1993 listings of a number of the above-mentioned firms on the Tokyo stock exchange that later decided to retreat.

The international composition of the management board in many cases still seems to be at the 'infant stage'. The following picture emerges:

- Of the thirty US core firms listed in Table 7A, only five (Philip Morris, Du Pont, Chrysler, Johnson & Johnson and United Technologies) had a foreigner as a member of their executive board. Regarding the composition of management boards, US core companies are hardly more internationalised than their often criticised Japanese rivals. A study by management consultants Booz, Allen and Hamilton confirms this picture: in 1991, only 2 per cent of the board members of big American companies were foreigners (*The Economist*, 6 February 1993: 65).
- Of the twenty Japanese companies, only two (Sony and Mazda) had foreigners on the executive board. Mazda was forced to accept three Ford directors on its board, as part of a management reshuffle under the Ford–Mazda partnership. Sony has been the only Japanese company to voluntarily accept a foreigner among its highest ranks. Sony is also more international in the areas of sales and production abroad. Sony was a late entrant in the Japanese consumer electronics industry, and it did not expand as part of one of the established industrial groupings. These

origins had two dramatic effects. Firstly, unlike most of its Japanese competitors, Sony faced an underdeveloped supply structure of its own, forcing it more often to make use of suppliers belonging to other *keiretsu*. Secondly, it faced an almost impenetrable home market due to the structural control of competing *keiretsu* over their distribution channels. Thus, Sony effectively had to overcome problems associated to its domestic bargaining arena which were similar to the ones foreign companies trying to export to Japan encountered. It did not succeed entirely in doing so: Sony's decision to internationalise was partly an *escape* from its own bargaining arena. Due to its relatively weak control over its home base, Sony is becoming an increasingly international company, as shown by the composition of its management board. (For similar reasons, Honda and Canon might also decide to allow a foreigner on their respective boards of directors at some point in the future.)

- Of the fifteen German firms, only four (Metallgesellschaft, Preussag, Volkswagen, Krupp) had (either one or two) foreigners on their management board. Volkswagen's decision to bring in former GM procurement vice-president José Ignacio López de Arriortúa as a member of the VW Vorstand has led to one of Europe's most serious industrial espionage cases.
- Of the eight French firms, only one (Alcatel Alsthom) had a foreigner on its top board. Alcatel Alsthom, created after a series of mergers and acquisitions between Alcatel (France), Alsthom Atlantique (France), ITT/Bell Telephone Company (US/Belgium) and STET-Italtel (Italy) moreover relocated its headquarters to The Hague (the Netherlands) – primarily for tax reasons.
- Of the four Italian firms, two (Fiat and Ferruzi) had a foreign representation on their executive board. The fact that Fiat's board includes five out of eleven foreigners is remarkable, but must be understood as an attempt to expand into new geographical, particularly Eastern European markets (both in sales and production), in the face of its overwhelming concentration of production in Italy and its dominance of the national market. However, Fiat's internationalisation of production in Eastern Europe is aimed primarily at exploiting the cheap labour available in Russia and Poland.
- Some firms maintained a predominantly binational composition of the management board (Royal Dutch/Shell, Unilever and ABB), due to an earlier merger of activities. Generally, firms with a relatively international top management board originate from small industrial systems or from the UK (see section 7.4).

Having discussed four functional areas of management, it is useful to refer to section 6.5, which showed that, with the exception of some companies originating from small industrial systems, most firms have also kept the fifth functional area of management, i.e. research and development, solidly under domestic control. On the basis of such overwhelming evidence at the firm level, it would be an understatement to conclude that national borders matter.

Conclusion 1

Of the largest one hundred core firms in the world, not one is truly 'global', 'footloose' or 'borderless'. There is however a hierarchy in the internationalisation of functional areas of management: around forty firms generate at least half of their sales abroad; less than twenty maintain at least half of their production facilities abroad; with very few exceptions, executive boards and management styles remain solidly national in their outlook; with even fewer exceptions, R&D remains firmly under domestic control; and most companies appear to think of a globalisation of corporate finances as too uncertain.

Other studies provide ample evidence to support this conclusion. Yao-Su Hu (1992) found that, with few exceptions, 'multinational', 'transnational' or 'global' companies are merely national entities with foreign operations: virtually all large companies still consider their home base as their main source of international competitive advantage. A 1990 INSEAD enquiry among top managers of two hundred large European firms on the geographical scope of their firms' planned activities for the next five years showed that these firms had planned to perform 93 per cent of their entire production within Europe, to buy 80 per cent of their inputs from European sources and to sell 83 per cent of their output to European clients. These *planned* activities were hardly more 'global' than the *accomplished* activities over 1990 (De Meyer and Ferdows, 1991: 6)! As the INSEAD enquiry showed, European managers tend to limit their perspective primarily to the European region. Allen Morrison, David Ricks and Kendall Roth have found that US managers often adopted a similar regional perspective:

> Increasingly, regionalization is being viewed by managers as a stepping-stone to more effective global competition ... regional strategies are increasingly providing the primary determinant of competitive advantage .... Instead of globalization managers are finding that regional competitive pressures are taking on an ever-greater importance by introducing a set of distinct opportunities and threats.[4]
>
> (Morrison *et al.*, 1992: 24)

Chapter 8 offers a framework of analysis to account for this shift towards *regionalisation* rather than globalisation.

---

[4] Morrison, Ricks and Roth list a number of factors that help to account for such a regional perspective: industry standards remain diverse; customers continue to demand locally differentiated products; being an insider remains critically important; and global organisations are difficult to manage and often circumvent subsidiary competencies, leading to internal tensions. The first three aspects reflect the fact that the national or regional embeddedness of the firm is vital in the process of creating competitive advantages.

7.4 THE INTERNATIONALISATION OF FIRMS FROM SMALL INDUSTRIAL SYSTEMS

In every functional area of management, companies originating from small industrial systems have shown the highest degrees of internationalisation. Yet could these companies be called footloose? Swiss industrial companies such as Nestlé and Ciba-Geigy have been frontrunners on the internationalisation track. In the 1970s, 83 per cent of the employees of the five largest Swiss companies already worked outside their home base (Niehans, 1977: 6). The Swiss home market makes up less than 5 per cent of the sales of these companies. Other small industrial systems with highly internationalised firms include Sweden (Electrolux, Volvo and ABB) and the Netherlands (Shell, Unilever and Philips). Only for these firms do the percentages of foreign sales and foreign assets tend to converge at very high levels.

A first reason for these firms to internationalise has been their small home markets. Many of these companies are active in the field of consumer products (food, electronics, healthcare, cars, oil products). Small home markets forced core firms to search for international outlets early in their corporate history. This relatively early internationalisation made it very difficult to establish a high degree of control over marketing channels even at home. Less control over marketing at home has reinforced the internationalisation track.[5]

A second reason to internationalise has been that smaller national industrial systems generally also imply a more narrow supply base. Firms such as Philips and Volvo did not have enough sophisticated domestic suppliers, and had to rely more on foreign suppliers. This reliance on foreign suppliers (which are often part of competing industrial complexes) drove many core firms from smaller countries to move part of their production operations abroad. Conversely, the possibility of purchasing inputs from advanced foreign suppliers reduced the need to try and increase the level of their home suppliers (reinforcing their international orientation, etc.).

In response to their relatively weak domestic supply base, many core firms in small industrial systems in the past opted for high levels of vertical integration and/or have relied on a more advanced international division of labour. This triggered a bargaining dynamic in the area of labour relations, which has been a third factor spurring core firms from small industrial systems to internationalise. The high concentration of power with a small number of core firms also created the breeding ground for large trade unions organised on a sectorial and national basis. In many small industrial systems, one could observe a relatively early unionisation and high levels of membership. The concentration of employment in a few core firms and the

---

[5] This lack of control over domestic markets was illustrated by Procter & Gamble's Spring 1994 attack on Unilever's new detergent (Omo Power, called Persil Power in the UK). Procter & Gamble launched this attack in Unilever's very home market, where Unilever had developed the new washing powder: the Netherlands.

early formation of trade unions increased electoral support of Left Wing parties and their participation in national governments, and encouraged centralised collective bargaining.[6] In countries such as the Netherlands, Austria, Switzerland, the Nordic countries and Belgium, this bargaining dynamism ultimately forged a coalition-oriented domestic bargaining arena, in which core firms gradually saw much of their initial bargaining position evaporate (cf. Katzenstein, 1985).

While this coalition-oriented bargaining arena spurred large companies to escape from this setting by moving abroad, many of them at the same time tried to replicate important features of macro-Fordism abroad. This gave rise to a multi-domestic strategy (see Chapter 8). For instance, Volvo set up production in Belgium and the Netherlands, while Philips in the 1970s became the prototype of the multi-domestic firm (with a high degree of autonomy to local subsidiaries in order to have sufficient freedom of manoevre in every foreign bargaining arena).

In spite of these factors spurring the internationalisation of core firms from small industrial systems, many of them still remain remarkably national in at least three respects. Firstly, they do not distinguish themselves in terms of listings on foreign stock exchanges. In fact, the domestic financial embeddedness, and particularly the role of domestic banks, has played a vital role in their internationalisation process. The internationalisation of most large Swedish firms, for instance, is backed by only two leading industrial banks: Handelsbanken and the Skandinaviska Enskilda Banken, the latter better known as the 'Wallenberg group'. Both banks have tried to keep the share of equity as a percentage of assets as low as possible, thus limiting the influence of (foreign) shareholders on the company's policy. In particular, the policy of the Wallenberg group has been in favour of – controlled – internationalisation of core firms. Firms that belong to the Wallenberg group like SKF, Atlas Copco, Alfa-Laval, ASEA, Electrolux, Saab-Scania, Ericsson and Stora were assessed to account for 25 per cent of the Swedish industrial work-force at the end of the 1980s, but for more than 70 per cent of all employees of Swedish firms abroad (Sölvell *et al.*, 1991: 40).

Secondly, in spite of the high degree of internationalisation of R&D in comparative terms, most large core firms from small industrial systems still conduct the majority of their R&D at home. Most Swiss companies still perform around two-thirds of their R&D in Switzerland, giving Switzerland a high R&D figure as a percentage of GDP. The same goes for Swedish multinationals. It has been estimated that not more than 25 per cent of all

---

[6] This point has been elaborated in literature on collective bargaining and in neo-corporatism approaches (see for instance Cameron, 1978; Braun, 1988; van Tulder, 1989). The fact that core firms originating from small industrial systems generally have less control over supply and distribution has had an interesting side-effect: the largest core firms in the small industrial systems on average employ considerably fewer workers than the five largest firms in larger countries, including Japan (van Tulder, 1989: 22).

R&D of the twenty leading Swedish multinationals is carried out by foreign R&D units (Sölvell *et al.*, 1991: 202). Even firms like Tetra Pak or Ikea, which (primarily for tax reasons) moved their headquarters abroad, source large parts of their products with Swedish suppliers, while keeping most of their R&D expenditures in Sweden (ibid: 210). The only exception to this seems to be Philips. In 1939, with the war imminent, Philips faced nationalisation of its American possessions unless these were relatively independent from their European parent operating under Nazi-German rule. The legal construction that was chosen granted the North American Philips Corporation relative autonomy. The construction was maintained for half a century, until the direct ties between parent and subsidiary were re-established. Thus Philips performs a large proportion of its R&D in the USA more because of historical particularities than as a result of deliberate strategy. Anyway, its US R&D activities are still dwarfed by its famous Eindhoven 'Natlab' headquarter laboratories.

Thirdly, as discussed above, even the most internationalised companies from small industrial systems tend to have only a few non-nationals on their top management board. Exceptions to this rule are such firms as ABB, Unilever, and Royal Dutch/Shell – the creation of cross-national takeovers and/or mergers. By 1994, only Philips had a really internationalised top management board. However, the decision to open up the formerly all-Dutch board was not taken until 1990, when heavy losses had endangered the very survival of the company.

Conclusion 2

The world's most internationalised companies tend to originate from small industrial systems. However, even their internationalisation is largely limited to sales and production abroad.

7.5 THE OIL INDUSTRY: DOMINATED BY GLOBAL PLAYERS?

To many people, the oil business would seem indisputably dominated by global companies. After all, oil companies are always searching and drilling for oil all over the world, dealing with foreign governments and local financial institutions, and shipping oil from one part of the world to another, where they may refine it and transport it further on to end users. To what extent is this image of 'global companies' dominating the oil industry tenable?

The oil industry is (next to motor vehicles and electronics) one of the most capital intensive industries. Both the capital intensity and the relative concentration in the industry create big entry and exit barriers. The six biggest companies, the so-called 'oil majors', operate on a worldwide scale and are involved in all stages of oil production – exploration, transportation, refining and marketing. Furthermore, they are active in petrochemical production. The group of six oil majors is made up of four American firms

(Exxon, Texaco, Mobil and Chevron) and two European companies (Royal Dutch/Shell and British Petroleum). From the beginning, the two European oil majors had a very international outlook – although limited to their oil-rich colonies. Only at a later stage did they begin setting up production in their home markets and increasing their levels of vertical integration. The latter (direct control) strategy helped them to be more flexible and search for suitable sites outside their protected markets.

The American oil majors could grow exploiting domestic oil fields. They only began to internationalise refinery activities after the Second World War, particularly to Europe. Today, Texaco and Chevron are still less internationalised than Royal Dutch/Shell and British Petroleum on the one hand, and Exxon and Mobil on the other, measured in terms of assets and workers abroad, and in terms of management styles. Sheltered from foreign competition (see also Chapter 9), other large players like Amoco (number 46 on the Fortune ranking) could develop, relatively independent from the oil majors. Specialising in one part of the oil business, such as refining, they initially did not strive for high degrees of vertical integration like the oil majors. The size of their home market still enabled American 'independents' to reach scale economies, but their lower levels of vertical integration implied that they did not attain firm control over their domestic bargaining arena, while their internationalisation levels trailed those of the oil majors. In Europe, 'independents' remained much smaller, which forced them to operate on a national or a regional scale at most. In the 1980s, many of these European producers were acquired by larger companies (cf. Molle, 1993).

The very domination of the oil majors, and the strategic importance that oil has taken in the modern world, provoked two alternative responses. Firstly, the French, Italian and Spanish governments created large state-owned oil complexes: in France CFP (including refinery subsidiaries Total and Elf), ENI in Italy, and INI in Spain. Due to the significant role of the national governments and their more limited degree of vertical integration, these complexes have been much less internationalised than the oil majors, although a company like Total has an increasing part of its sales spread over one region – Europe – and even acquired a resource base (Molle, 1994: 48). In Japan, the first oil crisis (1973–5) accentuated the vulnerability of all core firms to an interruption of oil supplies. Hence, the industrial conglomerates and the national government embarked upon a policy to regain control over domestic refinery and distribution, centring around firms such as Nippon Oil (number 62) and Idemitsu Kosan (number 83). As a result, the combined market share of the six oil majors between 1978 and 1988 shrank from an all-dominance of 64.1 per cent to 25.2 per cent (Keizai Koho Center, 1990: 65). In South Korea, Ssanyong (number 87) and Sunkyong (number 89) have also acquired a strong position.

The second response, developed by governments of some producer countries, was to take over parts of the oil drilling and processing facilities by instituting state-owned companies: PDVSA (Venezuela, number 56), Petrobas (Brazil, number 89) and PEMEX (Mexico, number 57). These companies reached sufficient turnover to make them the only Fortune 100 companies from developing countries (if one counts Mexico as a developing and South Korea as a developed economy). However, they operate on a much smaller scale and at considerably lower levels of efficiency, witnessing the enormous gap in sales per employee and assets per worker compared to the oil majors. At the same time, these three companies have by far the highest equity/asset ratio of all top-100 firms. Industrial complexes in the developing world are extremely dependent upon equity-funded capital provided via the national equity markets. Consequently, the internationalisation of these companies has been lowest of all the petroleum companies (including specialised refining firms).

Rather than seeing oil companies as global players, one could observe five broad groups of dominant players:

- Exxon, Mobil, Royal Dutch/Shell, British Petroleum: the largest players, with high levels of vertical integration and a very international and potentially global outlook;
- Texaco, Chevron: the remaining two oil majors, with high levels of vertical integration, yet more focused on US and European markets and a less international outlook;
- Amoco and other independent oil companies in developed economies (such as Atlantic Richfield, number 67; Nippon Oil, number 62; Idemitsu Kosan, number 83; Sangyong, number 87): specialised players, in marketing (and sometimes even production) mainly oriented to one world region;
- CPF, IRI, ENI, Petrofina (number 70) and Statoil (Norway, number 107): continental European 'national oil champions': in marketing (and sometimes production) mainly oriented to a single world region;
- PEMEX, PDVSA, Petrobas and other state oil companies in developing economies: state-owned, generally short of capital, least internationalised players.

Conclusion 3

The very domination of the oil majors, and the strategic importance of the oil industry to make other industries run, has led to government policies in Europe, Japan and developing economies that may actually have brought about a declining globalisation of companies in the world oil industry.

7.6 THE INTERNATIONALISATION OF NON-CORE ACTORS OF AN INDUSTRIAL COMPLEX

The central argument of this book is that neither individual firms, nor states, but industrial complexes constitute the centres of gravity of the international restructuring race. The above sections have indicated that the central actors or core firms of these complexes tend to be entities with clear national origins and with varying yet relatively limited degrees of international activities. Having made these observations, what can be said of the other constituents of the industrial complex, i.e. the core firms' bargaining partners?

Both trade unions and national governments have frequently expressed their fear of industries becoming footloose or borderless. The reason for this is that their relative bargaining power tends to decrease as the internationalisation of core firms increases. In spite of the efforts to establish international labour federations, trade unions have remained primarily national actors (cf. section 4.5).

The same goes for governments. Only European governments have managed to achieve some degree of 'internationalisation' in the European Union. However, both in terms of budget allocation, in terms of the size of national versus European bureaucracies, and in terms of constituency and legitimacy, even governments of EU member states have literally remained 'national'. Some governments, however, have maintained a relatively strong bargaining position. Between 1965 and 1985, the number of state-owned core firms in the top 200 non-US manufacturing firms increased from 10 to around 20 per cent. In the past, one of the motives for governments to nationalise core firms was to preserve domestic employment. Hence, governments have often tried to divert core firms from internationalising their production, and as a result, the internationalisation of state-owned corporations (with the exception of the oil industry) has remained limited (Dunning, 1993: 51).

With regard to the other actors in the industrial complex, the picture is less clear. Many suppliers can be counted among the largest firms in the world: we estimate that between 10 to 20 per cent of the Fortune 500 companies conduct the majority of their business as suppliers of core firms. Suppliers generally have a lower degree of internationalisation than core firms. For instance, international trade as well as foreign direct investment volumes in the car components sector clearly trails those of finished cars. Even the largest suppliers tend to follow rather than dictate the international investment decisions of large core companies.

The role of distributors is primarily to reach and service local markets. Service providers are generally less internationalised than industrial firms, although in this field there are obviously huge differences: while wholesale trading is among the most internationalised service sectors, transportation and retail trading are among the least internationalised (cf. Dunning, 1993: 48). An example of the former category is Japan's general trading companies (*sogo shosha*). Total 1992 sales of the largest nine *sogo shosha* amounted to over ¥111 trillion (US$878 billion). Over 41 per cent of sales were realised abroad (via exports from Japan and offshore trade). As Table 7.1 indicates, each large *shosha* is affiliated to an industrial conglomerate (*keiretsu*). Abroad, these trading houses act as the ears and eyes of the industrial core firms within the *keiretsu*. At home they act both as financers

Table 7.1 Japanese general trading companies and their industrial conglomerates

General trading company (sales – billion yen)	Keiretsu	*Nature of* keiretsu	*Other* keiretsu member companies	*Internationalisation pattern* sogo shosha (*1992 shares of total sales*)
Itochu ((¥18,529)	DKB	Organises several sub-groups, including prewar Furukawa and Kawasaki *zaibatsu*; strong in electrical and transport industries, construction; relatively little cross-shareholdings between sub-groups	Kawasaki, Fujitsu, Isuzu, [Hitachi, Shimizu Corp. (construction)]	Japan's largest *shosha* maintains strong position in domestic (50.7%) and offshore trade (27.1%); weaker in imports into Japan (10.1%)
Marubeni (¥16,863)	Fuji	Prewar Yasuda *zaibatsu* is nucleus of Fuji group, also more independent member companies; strong in construction.	Yasuda Trust and Bank, Oki, Canon, NKK Corp. (steel) [Hitachi, Nissan]	Japan's second *shosha* has average internationalisation profile
Sumitomo (¥16,530)	Sumitomo	Continuation of prewar Sumitomo *zaibatsu*: broad scope of industries; strong in electrical industries; high internal cohesion	Mazda, NEC, Asahi Breweries, many huge Sumitomo companies	Apex of strong domestic retail network; strong position in exports from Japan (17.3%); weaker in offshore trade
Mitsui (¥15,495)	Mitsui	Continuation of prewar Mitsui *zaibatsu*: broad scope of industries, yet rather weak in heavy industries	Toray Industries, Fuji Photo, many Mitsui companies	Apex of strong domestic retail network; average internationalisation profile
Mitsubishi (¥14,996)	Mitsubishi	Continuation of prewar Mitsubishi *zaibatsu*: broad scope of industries; strong in heavy industry and food and beverages; very close mutual ties	Asahi Glass, Kirin Breweries, many huge Mitsubishi companies	Apex of strong domestic retail network; strong position in imports into Japan (19.9%) and exports from Japan (16.8%); weaker in offshore trade
Nissho Iwai (¥10,149)	Sanwa	'Bank group': loosely knit group of companies, strong in chemicals and construction	Daihatsu, Kobe Steel	Relatively strong in imports into Japan (23.6%) and in offshore trade (28.2%)
Tomen (¥7,066)	Tokai	'Bank group': aggressive but still less powerful grouping of companies in Tokai region	Suzuki, Daido Steel [Toyota]	Strong in offshore trade (32.3%); weak in exports from Japan (9.7%)
Nichimen (¥6,053)	Sanwa	See Nissho Iwai	See Nissho Iwai	Second Sanwa *shosha* is strong in offshore trade (40.5%)
Kanematsu (¥5,540)	DKB	See Itochu	See Itochu	Second DKB *shosha* specialises in imports into Japan (43.4%)

Note: 1992 sales in billions of ¥ (official 1992 exchange rate: US$1 = ¥126.65)
dotted line indicates division between six largest and next three *sogo shosha*;
[ ] indicates company participating in *keiretsu* presidential meetings but with relatively independent position
Sources: Dodwell, 1990; Keizai Koho Center, 1994; Gerlach, 1992; Miyashita and Russell, 1994

and insurers to smaller companies, while at the same time checking them from expanding abroad independently. In spite of their relatively high degree of internationalisation, Table 7.1 shows that the *shosha* tend to act as an extension of their industrial group. They appear to do so along the following principles:

- The stronger the *keiretsu* cohesion, the higher the trading company's domestic sales and the higher its share of import/export activities. This can be read in the case of the Sumitomo, Mitsui and Mitsubishi *shosha*, each of which belong to a *keiretsu* which is essentially a continuation of a prewar *zaibatsu*. These three *shosha* are situated at the apex of an extensive domestic retail network;
- Conversely, lower levels of cohesion and control within the group translate into lower shares of import/export trade and sometimes even of domestic sales. Fortune 100 companies such as Toyota, Hitachi and Nissan only maintain weak affiliations to industrial groupings and have each established their own distribution channels. As a result, the *shosha* may engage relatively more in offshore trade;
- The more electronics, machinery and transportation equipment industries dominate the group profile, the more the *shosha* will engage in import/export activities; conversely, the more important domestic activities such as construction or food and beverages become, the higher the *shosha*'s share of domestic sales.

Obviously, these principles may contradict each other. Mitsui *shosha* is one of the Mitsui *keiretsu* nucleus companies, yet its weaker position in machinery and electronics implies that it is not particularly strong in import/export trade, leading to an average internationalisation profile. Between 1989, at the height of the 'bubble economy', and 1992, in the economic downturn, total sales of the *sogo shosha* decreased from ¥130 billion to ¥111.2 billion, with the sharpest decline in the categories of exports from and imports into Japan. While this fall seems to reflect the Japanese economic recession, it is not clear yet to what extent it also points to a more general decline of the role of the *sogo shosha*.

American wholesale trading companies are also relatively internationalised firms, with 23 per cent of their sales abroad (Dunning, 1993: 48). American and European trading companies generally have a higher degree of independence *vis-à-vis* industrial core firms. A relatively new phenomenon has been the emergence of large marketing-service firms like Saatchi and Saatchi. Some of these, headquartered in the UK or the USA, command an international network of offices in fifty countries (Dicken, 1992: 356). However, the difficulties Saatchi and Saatchi faced in the mid-1990s illustrate the relative instability of many international service companies.

Finally, financiers, such as banks and securities firms, have tended to follow (and facilitate) rather than to precede the internationalisation of industrial firms, but at a considerably lower level of internationalisation. A

1993 Arthur Andersen Consulting enquiry among 400 top managers of large European banks showed that their prime focus was Europe (*Vk*, 5 November 1993). The most international banks and service firms can be found in the United States, but their ratio of foreign to total sales still trails that of many manufacturing companies. Japanese and German financial actors have a considerably lower dispersion of activities worldwide – the corollary of the fact that German and Japanese core firms generally have a lower degree of internationalisation as compared to British, American and even French firms. While Japanese and German banks on average had about twenty-six foreign operations, UK banks on average had fifty-one, US banks had fifty-nine, and French banks even had seventy-six operations (Dicken, 1992: 370). The penetration of foreign banks in Japan is particularly low: while Japanese banks accounted for 12.1 per cent of assets and 16.0 per cent of lending in the US banking system, foreign banks accounted for less than 2 per cent of all bank deposits in Japan (Bergsten and Noland, 1993: 170).

Conclusion 4

There is a hierarchy in the internationalisation of the constituents of an industrial complex. On average, core firms have the highest degree of internationalisation, followed at distance by trading houses and financiers. Governments and trade unions trail far behind. This implies that core firms are more mobile than their bargaining partners, and that in principle they have the possibility of shifting parts of production abroad. Ultimately, this enhances the core firms' bargaining position.

7.7 CONCLUSIONS

This chapter assessed the internationalisation strategies of the world's one hundred largest core companies (measured by total sales) and concluded that not one of these can be dubbed truly 'global', 'footloose' or 'borderless'. The argument of the globalisation of the firm thus is unfounded and untenable.

Former US president the late John F. Kennedy once stated: 'the great enemy of truth is very often not the lie – deliberate, contrived and dishonest – but the myth – persistent, persuasive and unrealistic' (quoted in Lang and Hines, 1993: 149). The persistence of the globalisation myth seems to be based on a lack of information and confusion about international restructuring.

However, the persistence of the globalisation myth can also be attributed to its positive, if conflicting, connotations. Globalisation promises a better tomorrow. It suggests harmony, 'interdependence', and it appeals to the hope that old rivalries be overcome between people irrespective of race, colour, creed, background, etc. After all, the 'globe' concerns every human being: we are equally dependent on its fortunes, particularly in an era of increasing environmental problems.

At the same time, the word globalisation conveys an impression of strength, of healthy and vigorously expanding firms and economies, heading towards greater efficiency and increasing wealth. Such are powerful images to mobilise support in various kinds of domestic bargaining arenas where some parties are struggling to maintain whatever influence they have over core firms trying to escape from this arena. Domestic bargaining patterns effectively function as sunk costs in the process of international strategy formation of a given core firm. This chapter has indicated that, without exception, a domestic bargaining arena imposes huge social, political and financial constraints, thus setting the outer margins of a core firm's internationalisation strategy. Thus far, no core firm has managed to overcome its dependence on its home base. Globalisation remains a myth – but one which performs a function.

Conclusion 5

The nature of a firm's domestic bargaining arena is at the root of its internationalisation strategy. Hence a company's internationalisation strategy can only be understood as a direct extension of the nature of the bargaining relations within its domestic industrial complex.

The following notes and sources refer to Table 7A, pp. 170–3.

Notes:
* Estimate. † Refers to type of business along the dependency scale (see Conclusion 5): 1 Many suppliers and polipsony structures; 2 Tendency towards oligopolistic supply (chance of undercapacity) and monopsonic markets; 3–4 Oligopoly on supply side, gradual shift from oligopoly to polipsony on demand side; 5 Oligopolistic (tendency towards excess capacity) and polipsonic markets. ‡ Excludes shares in other European countries (implying the ultimate degree of internationalisation will be larger). § Internationalisation of stock is comprised of three figures: 1 Number of stock exchanges abroad in which company shares are noted – indicated by the number of countries (more than one stock exchange/bourse in one country thus accounts for only one); 2 If available estimated internationalisation degree of shares (indicated by percentage); 3 Regional spread of stock, indicated by: r Stock only in one Triad region; b Stock traded in two of the Triad regions; t Stock traded in three of the Triad regions; d Shares in developing countries. ¶ Estimate based on value of overseas sales minus exports. [b] Estimate based on capital investments in region (indication of flow figures) and/or the value of overseas production. ** 1991. Low: Less than 10%. High: Greater than 80%.

Sources:
BW, 14 May 1990; Fortune (1993); UN (1993); Stopford (1992); Standard and Poor's database (internationalisation of shares); Dodwell (1991); Hast *et al.* (1991, 1992); Mirabile (1990); Derdak (1988); Capital, 7/95:44; annual reports; own observations; direct communication with corporations.

Table 7A Fortune 100 companies (1993): nature of business, relative dependency position (1992) and degree of internationalisation (1990)

Ranking	Company	Sales ($bn)	Employment (1000)	Sales per employee (US$1000)	Nature of business (1-5),† 1960-92 period	State owned	Equity % asset	Assets (%)	Sales (%)	Workers (%)	Shares (1993)§	Management approach
1	General Motors	133	750	177	Auto, div. (2 + 4)	—	3	29	31	33	6b	Mostly American, locals in foreign operations
2	Exxon	104	95	1090	Oil (4)	—	39	59	78	63	8t	Board all-American
3	Ford Motor	101	325	311	Auto (3-4)	—	8	32+	48	51	8t	American board, increasingly international
4	Royal Dutch/ Shell	99	127	709	Oil (3)	—	53	<65+	<44	72	8b	Primarily Dutch/British board (including regional directors); of 15 directors in 1993 one German and one Indian director
5	Toyota	79	108	731	Auto (5)	—	50*	23*	40	11	0	Entirely Japanese management
6	IRI	68	400	170	Metal/div. (2-3)	Yes	Low*	Low*	16	17	0	Entirely Italian management
7	IBM	65	308	211	Computers (4)	—	32	52	61	45	10t	Relies on locals to manage non-US operations; increasing number of foreigners in top ranks
8	Daimler-Benz	63	377	167	Div. (2 + 3)	Partly	21	17b	57	19	6b 25%	No foreigners on board; many foreign operations run by locals
9	General Electric	62	268	231	Div. (2 + 3 + 4)	—	12	10*	14	21b	3t	Solidly American at all levels
10	Hitachi	62	332	187	Elect. (2 + 5)	—	38	Low*	23	7b	6t	Solidly Japanese at all top management levels
11	BP	59	98	602	Oil (2-3)	Past	28	53	73	74	8t	Board all-British
12	Matsushita	58	252	230	Tel. + electr. (2 + 5)	—	40	13b	45	32	4t	Solidly Japanese, some units run by locals
13	Mobil	57	64	890	Oil (4)	—	42	55b	77	40	8t	Board all-American
14	Volkswagen	57	274	208	Auto (2-3)	Partly	17	44b	60	35	2r 27%	Solidly German, limited number of foreigners in top management positions
15	Siemens	51	413	123	Div. (2 + 3)	—	28	29b	30	38	7r 44%	Some business groups managed from outside Germany by non-Germans; none on board
16	Nissan	50	144	347	Auto (5)	—	24	20	47	23	2b 2.9%	Board all-Japanese; foreign plants sometimes run by locals
17	Philip Morris	50	161	310	Food, div. (4)	—	25	27	35	39	9t	Board all-American except one Venezuelan, majority of foreign operations run by locals
18	Samsung	50	189	265	Divers. (2 + 5)	—	14	Low*	59		0*	Solidly Korean
19	Fiat	48	286	168	Auto, div. (4)	—	20	29*	44+	22	2b	Five of 11 on board are non-Italian
20	Unilever	44	283	155	Food (4)	—	29	High*	42+	86	27% 9b	Five nationalities on board (mostly European); very international orientation in management
21	ENI	40	124	323	Oil (2-3)	Yes	20	11	37	17	Low*	Board all-Italian
22	Elf Aquitaine	40	88	455	Oil (2-3)	1994	35	40	43	37	Low*	Board all-French
23	Nestlé	39	218	179	Food (4)	—	29	95	98	96	9t	CEO German; 5 out of 10 general managers are Swiss
24	Chevron	39	49	796	Oil (3)-4	—	40	24	25	20	4b	Board all-American
25	Toshiba	38	173	219	Electr. (2 + 5)	—	20	17	31	17	7b*	Board all-Japanese
26	Du Pont	37	125	296	Chem./mat. (4)	—	30	38	46	25	0	Board all-American except for one Canadian; all VPs American except for one Japanese; some foreign subsidiaries run by locals
27	Texaco	37	38	692	Oil (3)4	—	38	38	43	n.a.	6b	Board all-American, foreign operations run by Americans

Table 7A Continued

Ranking	Company	Sales ($bn)	Employment (1000)	Sales per employee (US$1000)	Nature of business, (1–5), 1960–92 period	Ownership State owned	Ownership Equity % asset	Assets (%)	Sales (%)	Workers (%)	Shares (1993)§	Management approach
28	Chrysler	37	128	289	Auto (2–4)	—	19	12	28	27	10t	One non-American on board
29	Renault	34	147	231	Auto (2–3)	1946	26	31	40	27	0	Solidly French
30	Honda	33	91	330	Auto (4–5)	—	35	37	60	29	5t 7%	Non-Japanese run offshore plants, none on board of directors
31	Philips	33	252	131	Telecomm., defence, electr. (2–4)	—	19	76	94	80	9t 46%	Solidly Dutch until 1991, then majority of board internationals
32	Sony	32	126	254	Electr. (4–5)	—	32	49	61	55	8t 14%	Only major Japanese manufacturer with a foreigner on board of directors
33	ABB	31	213	146	Pub. util. and equipment (2–3)	—	15	89	96	93	7b 50%	Headquarters moved to Switzerland; most important markets represented on board (Switzerland, Germany, Sweden)
34	Alcatel Alsthom	31	203	153	Div. (2–3)	−1987	20	40	50	55	6b	French dominated management approach (three non-French members on board of directors)
35	Boeing	30	143	210	Aerospace (2)	—	44	n.a.	58	n.a.	6t	Board all-American
36	Procter & Gamble	30	106	283	Soaps, cosm. (4)	—	38	35	40	49	7t	Solidly American, Europeans head European branches
37	Hoechst	30	178	169	Chem., pharm. (3–4)	—	32	14*	75	48	9t 42%	Board all-German, most foreign operations run by locals
38	Peugeot	29	151	192	Auto (4)	—	41	21[b]	54	20	1r	Solidly French
39	BASF	29	123	236	Chem. materials (3–4)	—	37	30[b]	66	34	2b 23%	Board all-German, foreign operations run by locals
40	NEC	28	141	199	Div. (2 + 5)	—	20	n.a.*	23	13	5t	Solidly Japanese
41	Daewoo	28	79	354	Div. (2 + 5)	—	13	Low*	65	n.a.	0	Solidly Korean
42	Fujitsu	28	162	173	Comp. (2 + 5)	—	29	n.a.	24	n.a.	2b	Solidly Japanese
43	Bayer	27	156	173	Pharm., chem. (3–4)	—	40	56	78	47	12t 48%	Board all-German, 6 of 25 BUs run by locals
44	Mitsubishi Electric	27	108	250	Electr. (2 + 5)	—	23	23	23	11	2b	Solidly Japanese
45	Total	26	51	510	Oil (3)	5.4%	35	n.a.	71	52	3b 40%	Board all-French
46	Amoco	26	47	553	Oil (4)	—	46	33	30	19	3b	Board and heads of foreign operations are all-American
47	Mitsubishi Motors	26	45	578	Auto (2)	—	17	12[b]	45	n.a.	10%	Solidly Japanese
48	Nippon Steel	24	52	462	Metals (2)	—	23	1	17	> 5	0	Solidly Japanese
49	Mitsubishi Heavy Industries	23	66	349	Machines (2 + 5)	—	26	n.a.	23	n.a.	0	Solidly Japanese
50	Thyssen	23	147	157	Metals (2 + 3)	—	21	Low*	49*	8	4r 10%	Board all-German; Nedstaal (Netherlands) is only subsidiary run by local
51	Pepsico	22	371	59	Food/beverages (4)	—	26	42	21	22	4t	Board all-American

Table 7A Continued

Ranking	Company	Sales ($bn)	Employment (1000)	Sales per employee (US$1000)	Nature of business (1-5) 1960-92 period	Ownership		Degree of internationalisation/activities abroad (1990) in:				Management approach
						State owned	Equity % asset	Assets (%)	Sales (%)	Workers (%)	Shares (1993)§	
52	Bosch	22	170	129	Div. (2 + 3)	–	31	31	51+	35	0	Board all-German
53	United Technologies	22	178	124	Defence (2)	–	21	28	36	44	7b	One non-American on board
54	INI	22	140	157	Ind. eq. (2–3)	Yes	19	Low*	30	n.a.	8t	Board all-Spanish
55	ICI	22	114	193	Chem. (4)	–	36	51	77	59	16%	40% of top 170 executives are non-British; top ranks include four other nationalities
56	PDVSA	21	55	420	Oil (2–3)	Yes	68	Low*	95	8	0	Board all-Venezuelan
57	PEMEX	21	125	168	Oil (2–3)	Yes	73	Low*	n.a.	n.a.	0**	Solidly Mexican
58	Conagra	21	81	259	Food (4)	–	23	n.a.	55	n.a.	0**	Board all-American
59	Mazda	21	56	375	Auto (2 + 5)	–	26	18	63	n.a.	25%	Three directors delegated on Mazda board by Ford Motor
60	BMW	21	74	284	Auto (2–3)	–	24	19b	62	16	2r	Board all-German
61	Eastman Kodak	21	133	158	Sc. photo (2–3)	–	28	27*	44	40*	0	Board and all officers American
62	Nippon Oil	20	11	1818	Oil (2–3)	–	21	Low*	9*	Low*	1d 6.6%	Solidly Japanese
63	Dow Chemical	19	61	311	Chem. (4)	66%	32	45	51	46*	10t	Board all-American
64	Repsol	19	20	950	Oil (2–3)	–	36	<10b	24	Low	4t	All Spanish
65	Mannesmann	18	137	131	Industrial equipment(2–3)	–	28	32	61	27	5r	Board all-German
66	Xerox	18	99	189	Sc./photo (2–3)	–	12	25	33	55	6b	Major ventures with Rank Fuji and Fujitsu shaped top management thinking
67	Atlantic Richfield	18	27	667	Oil (3–4)	–	28	21	21	n.a.	3b	Board all-American
68	British Aerospace	18	103	174	Aerospace (2–3)	Part	16	18b	65	5	0	One non-British board member (USA)
69	McDonnell Douglas	18	87	207	Aerospace (2–3)	–	22	Low*	21	n.a.	3b	Board all-American
70	Petrofina	18	16	1125	Oil (2)	–	34	76	>60	73	7b	Board all-Belgium
71	Hewlett-Packard	16	93	172	Computers (4)	–	55	46	55	38	6t	Board all-American
72	Usinor-Sacilor	16	89	180	Metals (2–3)	Yes	22	26	42	32	0%	Board all-French
73	Metallgesellschaft	16	63	254	Metals (2–3)	–	10	n.a.	61	17*	0	2 non-Germans on board of 20
74	USX	16	46	348	Oil (2–3)	–	22	25	5	Low*	3b	Board all-American
75	Ferruzzi	16	52	308	Food (3–4)	–	2	44	57	50	0**	2 non-Italians on board of 19
76	Ciba-Geigy	16	91	176	Pharm. (4)	–	59	56	98	73	0	4 of 15 on board are non-Swiss
77	Rhône-Poulenc	16	83	193	Chemicals (4)	1982–1993	23	61	79	55	2b	Solidly French though international takeover strategy results in foreigners in charge of units
78	Viag	16	85	188	Metals (3)	1986/8	17	>19§	40	19§	25%*	Board all-German

Table 7.4 Continued

Ranking	Company	Sales ($bn)	Employment (1000)	Sales per employee (US$1000)	Nature of business, 1960–92 period (1–5)†	Ownership: State owned	Ownership: Equity % asset	Internationalisation: Assets (%)	Internationalisation: Sales (%)	Internationalisation: Workers (%)	Internationalisation: Shares (1993)§	Management approach	Ranking
79	RJR Nabisco	16	64	250	Tobacco/food (1 + 4)	–	26	12	23	Low*	1r	Board all-American	79
80	BTR	16	135	119	Industrial equipment (2–3)	–	20	26	67	64	n.a.	8 Britons, 3 Americans, 2 Australians on board	80
81	Ruhrkohle	16	118	136	Mining (2–4)	–	6	n.a.*	n.a.	n.a.	0	Board all-German	81
82	Preussag	16	74	216	Metals (3)	–	22	Low*	48	13	1r	One non-German (French) on board	82
83	Idemitsu Kosan	16	5	3200	Oil (3)	–	3	n.a.*	Low*	n.a.	0	Solidly Japanese	83
84	Canon	15	67	224	Computers (5)	–	33	25	71	44	4t 14%	Board all-Japanese	84
85	Volvo	15	60	250	Auto/div. (2–3)	–	22	54	87	29	9t 10%	Solidly Swedish (after failed merger with Renault)	85
86	Friedrich Krupp	15	91	165	Industrial equipment (2–3)	–	12	12	50	19	25%‡	8 Germans, 2 Iranians on board 25% of shares owned by National Iranian Steel Company	86
87	Ssangyong	15	24	625	Oil (2–3)	–	29	Low*	n.a.	n.a.	0	Solidly Korean	87
88	NKK	15	44	341	Metals (2–3)	–	15	Low*	14	Low*	1d	All managing directors and presidents are Japanese	88
89	Petrobras	15	56	268	Oil (2–3)	Yes	61	0	0	0	0	Solidly Brazilian	89
90	Sunkyong	15	22	682	Oil (2–3)	– 1982–86	25	n.a.	63	n.a.	0**	Solidly Korean	90
91	Saint-Gobain	14	100	144	Materials (2–3)	–	34	56	61	66	0	Solidly French	91
92	Electrolux	14	119	118	Electr. (2–3)	–	19	67	86	82	5b	Board all-Swedish	92
93	Digital Equipment	14	114	123	Computers (3–4)	–	44	44	55	78	4b	Board all-American	93
94	Grand Metropolitan	14	102	137	Food (3–4)	–	40	59	60	n.a.	2b	9 Britons, 1 German, 1 American on board	94
95	Minnesota Mining	14	87	161	Materials/mining	–	55	43	49	44	5t	Board all-American	95
96	Bridgestone	14	86	163	Rubber/plastics (4)	–	25	40	58	64	2b	Board all-Japanese	96
97	Johnson & Johnson	14	85	165	Pharm. (4)	–	44	46	52	52	2r	15 Americans, 1 Briton on board	97
98	Sumitomo Metal Ind.	14	31	452	Metals (2)	–	22	n.a.	28	22b	1b**	Solidly Japanese	98
99	Tenneco	14	79	177	Ind. equip. (1 + 3)	–	8	27	32	n.a.	6b	Board all-American	99
100	Internat'l Paper	14	73	192	Paper (2–3)	–	38	31	30	n.a.	4b	Board all-American	100

(Notes and sources for this Table may be found on page 169.)

8 Rival internationalisation strategies

8.1 INTRODUCTION

The meaning of the word globalisation depends on the firm or on the industrial system. Just as a political party carefully weighs its programme and its propaganda to mobilise support and to attract voters, company views or symbols can rarely be taken literally. They are often aimed at mobilising employees and at influencing a particular bargaining arena. A striking example of different uses of company symbols can be seen driving from Schiphol Airport to Amsterdam, the Dutch capital. Just off the highway, two of the world's largest core firms are situated directly opposite each other. On one side of the street, Big Blue (IBM) has its offices. On the opposite side of the street, one can find Nissan's European headquarters. IBM has traditionally been an example of a Fordist firm, trying to establish direct control over its bargaining partners, with a high degree of vertical integration and a company internal and international division of labour. IBM has always advocated free trade, as signified by former CEO John Aker's slogan 'peace through trade'. To underline its worldwide standardised procedures and its global ambitions, the company only waves its blue and white IBM flag in the Dutch coastal winds, as it does anywhere else in the world.

Nissan, on the other side, has built a vertically de-integrated production system at home and strives for structural control over its bargaining partners (in particular suppliers and workers), although it has been less successful in this than longstanding rival Toyota. In Amsterdam, opposite IBM, Nissan needs *four* flags to communicate its identity. Next to its own logo, it waves the Amsterdam, Dutch, and European Union flags. These flags reflect Nissan's awareness of its bargaining partners – which it tries to get under structural control. In other countries, of course, Nissan waves different flags next to its Nissan flag.

The preceding chapters argued that domestic bargaining arenas exert a decisive influence on a company's internationalisation strategy. This chapter looks at how a core firm extends the logic of its domestic bargaining relations abroad. The internationalisation process of core firms basically consists of a combination of three sorts of activities: imports/exports, foreign (direct or indirect) investments, and (horizontal) strategic alliances with other firms. Section 8.2 develops a framework to identify rival corporate internationalisation strategies, based on contrasting foreign investment motives which lead to different location decisions. Section 8.3 discusses (international) strategic alliances from the perspective of the strength of both partners and positions them along the dependency scale. Section 8.4 then considers how a core firm's concept of control and its domestic bargaining patterns translate into an internationalisation strategy. Section 8.5 assesses the implications of rival internationalisation strategies for the dependency links between the industrialised world regions and the less developed world regions. This final section identifies four interpretations of the globalisation concept. These different interpretations largely depend on a core firm's industrial home base.

8.2 AN ANALYTICAL FRAMEWORK OF INTERNATIONALISATION STRATEGIES

The discussion on globalisation has been obscured by best-practice cases and wishful thinking on the one hand and outright rejections that international competition has undergone serious changes on the other hand. This has led to rather simplistic debates on questions such as 'globalisation – yes or no?' In reality, international competition and internationalisation strategies change constantly, but that does not necessarily imply that companies, competition or technologies become more 'global'. Therefore, globalisation is best interpreted as a strategic objective rather than as an accomplished reality. Put differently, a firm may hope to realise 'globalisation' yet fail.

This section depicts the elements of a globalisation strategy as well as its trajectory, including the effects on the firm's domestic and international environment. Section 8.2.1 introduces the building blocks for the analysis of internationalisation strategies. Section 8.2.2 then presents two rival 'global' trajectories – each originating from different bargaining settings, and each advocating fundamentally different views on how to (re-)shape a host bargaining arena.

8.2.1 The management of prescription

A substantial portion of the management literature on internationalisation strategies has a markedly prescriptive bias, focusing on such issues as the firm's 'strategic fit' or the 'best' organisation to compete successfully at a global level. Authors in this tradition champion today's 'successful' strategies of one or two firms, often ignoring how these strategies have emerged from a unique domestic bargaining context. A case in point is the discussion on how to mould a giant international firm into a flexible organisation.

Tom Peters argued against the old multi-domestic matrix structure and in favour of a new type of '"multi-domestic" corporation' (1992: 46) pioneered by . . . none other than ABB? Christopher Bartlett and Sumantra Goshal (1987), analysing how nine (non-manufacturing) companies have tried to overcome their size-related problems, went as far as to contend that:

> relations based on dependence or independence . . . moved to relations based on formidable levels of explicit, genuine interdependence. In essence, they made integration and collaboration self-enforcing by making it necessary for each group to cooperate in order to achieve its own interests.
>
> (Bartlett and Goshal, 1987: 47–8)

In 1989, Bartlett and Goshal promoted this 'transnational solution' as the one panacea to cure all international restructuring problems. It requires a lot of headquarter activity to manoeuvre employees and business units into such new patterns of interaction, hence to characterise 'transnationalisation' as 'explicit, genuine interdependence' is quite misleading. In fact, a large part of the management literature has focused more on how headquarters can maintain rather than delegate control over the firm's operations – both internally and externally. As Morrison, Ricks and Roth put it:

> The notion of global strategy has had considerable appeal for corporate managers largely because such strategies are best managed through tight central control. These strategies . . . let corporate managers ultimately determine what is produced and where it is produced. In other words, the center would continue to dominate the periphery. The global 'solution' was also a concrete step – and concrete steps were called for in an era of cutthroat international competition.
>
> (Morrison *et al.*, 1992: 21)

Michael Porter (1986) offers a less biased starting-point to define the strategy of globalisation, by distinguishing two key dimensions in a firm's internationalisation strategy: the configuration of its activities – or the location in the world where an activity is performed – and the coordination of these activities. Activities range from R&D through production to marketing and services, i.e. they comprise the company's value chain. Configuration options in this framework range from concentrated to dispersed, coordination options range from low to high levels of coordination (Porter, 1986: 23–9). Combined, these two dimensions lead to a simple figure (Figure 8.1).

In this framework, export-based strategies imply that marketing abroad is handled by local agents or by relatively independent representative offices. In multi-domestic industries, competition in one country is essentially independent of competition in other countries. In multi-domestic industries, firms' competitive advantages are largely specific to the country, and international strategies in fact are a series of *domestic* strategies (Porter,

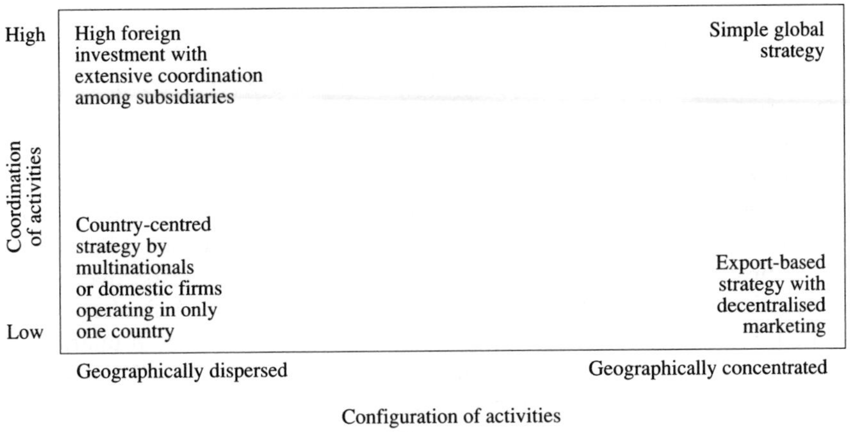

High	High foreign investment with extensive coordination among subsidiaries	Simple global strategy
Coordination of activities		
	Country-centred strategy by multinationals or domestic firms operating in only	Export-based strategy with decentralised marketing
Low	one country	
	Geographically dispersed	Geographically concentrated

Configuration of activities

Figure 8.1 Types of internationalisation strategies according to Michael Porter
Source: Porter, 1986: 28

1986: 18). High levels of coordination would automatically produce a global strategy. Porter identifies two extremes: a simple global strategy (based on a concentration of activities) and one of high foreign investments with extensive coordination among subsidiaries. A 'simple global strategy' would differ from an 'export-oriented strategy' in that the latter presupposes decentralised marketing, i.e. not directly controlled by the exporting firms, hence with low levels of coordination. Toyota in the mid-1980s would have been a company with a simple global strategy. According to Porter (1986: 23), a global strategy can be aimed at:

- Capturing economies of scale by concentrating specific activities in the value chain in sites with the strongest perceived country-specific advantages; and/or
- Reaping benefits of the increased coordination and control of geographically dispersed activities.

Just like many of his colleagues, however, Porter could not escape the traps of prescription entirely. A year before, he had listed fifteen criteria to identify a 'good global competitor' (1985). When Lance Eliot Brouthers and Steve Werner (1990) applied these criteria to the Japanese industry, they found that Japanese companies only met three of his fifteen criteria, and failed on at least nine. As Brouthers and Werner put it, Japanese companies 'can be considered good competitors only in the sense that they tend to be credible and viable, have realistic assumptions and knowledge of costs'. However, they fail to meet Porter's criteria on the following items: 'Japanese corporations tend to: (1) have no clear self-perceived weaknesses, (2) not play by American rules [i.e. market share instead of profitability], (3) not have a strategy that is inherently limiting or improves industry structure, (4) have high exit barriers, (5) have goals that are irreconcilable with an

American firm's goals, (6) have high strategic stakes, (7) view return on investment, profitability and cash generation differently, (8) have a long term horizon, and (9) be risk averse' (Brouthers and Werner, 1990: 9). Does this make them 'bad global competitors'?

Porter's definition of a 'good global competitor' seemed geared to US businesses in the first place. Moreover, neither the coordination nor the dispersion dimensions have been elaborated very well in the framework. Porter simply assumes that a firm in principle can move freely in Figure 8.1, adjusting configuration and coordination levels – irrespective of its production organisation or domestic bargaining relations. A final criticism is that Porter tends to regard internationalisation strategies primarily in terms of *expansion*. For some companies, however, the 1980s Triadisation strategy (see section 6.6) consisted of a decision to *withdraw* activities from sites outside the major trade blocs. Internationalisation works both ways: a company may 'run away' from its home industrial system, but it may also 're-runaway' back to its home bargaining arena (cf. Junne, 1987). A firm may even display a combination of both strategies.

8.2.2 Rival global trajectories

Is it possible to avoid the pitfall of prescription when analysing internationalisation strategies? Definitely – as long as one is willing to accept that one internationalisation strategy is not inherently superior to another. This subsection presents a framework to assess large core firms' internationalisation strategies. It identifies two rival global strategies as the ultimate terms of reference, which lend their names to two alternative corporate growth and retreat trajectories.

The first strategy of globalisation aims at a worldwide intra-firm division of labour. In this strategy, activities are established in many sites spread over the world, based on an area's comparative advantages. A company striving for globalisation aims to secure the supply of strategic inputs by direct control (vertical integration). Thus labour-intensive production of components will be situated in low-wage areas, while the production of high-technology and high-value-added parts or services requires a developed and highly skilled environment. A globalisation strategy thus is a logical extension of the micro-Fordist concept of control, and promotes the international division of labour as well as the growth of international trade.

The alternative 'global' strategy has been dubbed global localisation or glocalisation.[1] The objective of glocalisation is to establish a geographically concentrated inter-firm division of labour in the three major trading blocs. Glocalisation is ultimately linked to the Toyotist concept of control. Manu-

[1] The word glocalisation is not an amalgamation of gobal localisation we have invented. We first encountered it in a document of the Japan Machinery Exporters' Association: *Responding to the Need of Europeanization: Radical Measures* (Tokyo, July 1989). See also Watanabe, 1993: 231.

facturers striving for glocalisation try to build their competitive advantage on a combination of vertical de-integration of production to local suppliers and subcontractors, and structural control over local suppliers, dealers, workers and governments. As glocalisation aims to establish production within the major markets, international trade may gradually decline.

The glocalisation strategy should not be confused with the Akio Morita and Kenichi Ohmae interpretation (see also 6.3.2). Glocalisation pertains to a company's attempt to become accepted as a 'local citizen' in a different trade bloc, while transferring as little control as possible over its areas of strategic concern. Glocalisation is first of all a political and only in the second place a business location strategy: a company following a strategy of glocalisation will localise activities abroad (1) only if the company otherwise risks being treated as an 'outsider', or being hit by trade or investment barriers and thus losing market share, and (2) to the extent that the company can exert more control over its host governments than vice versa.

These two rival trajectories imply that, in spite of what many textbooks lead their students to believe, internalisation is not the only motive for internationalisation. Internalisation is the process of creating internal markets within a core firm to exploit market imperfections, or in other words: a strategy of vertical integration. Buckley and Casson (1976, 1991: 109–10) are perhaps the best-known proponents of the internalisation hypothesis (see also Rugman *et al.*, 1986: 104ff.). Buckley and Casson studied the internationalisation of 434 firms, of which 264 were American, over the 1967–72 period, and found evidence to support the internalisation hypothesis. These results tell us a lot about the dominant internationalisation trajectory of the early 1970s, which was the heyday of micro-Fordist internationalisation, but nothing about the 1990s. With the relative decline of micro-Fordism over the 1980s, the internalisation motive may also have declined.[2]

Buckley and Casson also found evidence to support the hypothesis that the 'nationality of the firm is a very significant influence on the behaviour of an MNE' (1991: 101). We argue that 'nationality' is better read as 'industrial complex' or 'industrial system'. For instance, since the growth and retreat trajectories are based on a core firm's bargaining relations and *not* on the nationality of a firm, not all Japanese companies necessarily strive for glocalisation: Honda and Sony are among the exceptions indicated in Chapter 7. Similarly, companies going for glocalisation need not be exclusively Japanese. If other firms managed to replicate the Toyotist example of vertical de-integration and structural control over the supply structure, they might also enter the glocalisation trajectory.

Table 8.1 summarises three main characteristics of both strategies at the

---

[2] Dunning (1993: 472–3) tries to sustain the internalisation hypothesis by speaking about 'quasi-internalisation' when referring to the Japanese *keiretsu* which he defines as '*de facto* . . . close economic linkages between firms, even if there is no formal hierarchical (ownership) relationship between them'.

Table 8.1 Comparison between globalisation and glocalisation at the core firm level

Internal firm organisation	Globalisation	Glocalisation
Organisation of value chain	Worldwide *intra*-firm division of labour	Geographically concentrated *inter*-firm division of labour
Locational strategy of activities based on	Comparative advantages and economies of scale: progression of international division of labour	Introduction of integrated supply, production and distribution chain in depressed regions of major international trade blocs
Production focus	Production for world markets and standard tastes; major research facilities spread around the world	Production for local/ regional markets, more allowances to local tastes; basic research concentrated at home, applied research spread

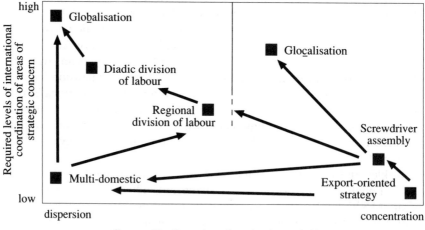

Figure 8.2 Rival internationalisation trajectories: possible upward shifts
Note: Approximate position along both dimensions

level of the core firm. Figure 8.2 subsequently depicts the globalisation and glocalisation strategies as the ultimate terms of their respective internationalisation trajectories, and indicates the possible upward shifts along both trajectories. Whereas in Figure 8.1 'activities' refer to the core company's value chain, Figure 8.2 takes a meso level approach and views 'activities' in terms of a core firm's five areas of strategic concern (see section 3.2). 'Coordination' in Figure 8.2 should not be confused with 'control'. Whereas coordination refers to the effort required to manage a company's *internal* (both domestic and overseas) activities, the word 'control' refers to the power exerted by the core firm over its *external* bargaining partners.

The emerging vertical line in the centre of Figure 8.2 indicates that a core company tries to sustain the logic of its production organisation as much as possible. For instance, a core firm with a domestic concentration of production and structural control over domestic bargaining partners will try to extend this logic when going abroad. Most changes in internationalisation trajectories therefore occur along the dimension of coordination. A shift from concentrated to dispersed activities is possible, but only at relatively low levels of coordination. As coordination levels rise, it becomes increasingly difficult for a core firm to accomplish a shift from dispersed to concentrated activities. Depending on political requirements – such as local content regulations – or feelings of animosity in a host country, a core firm may be unable to extend the bargaining logic of its domestic industrial complex to the full. The company would then revert to company tactics, but not alter its ultimate strategic preference.

Figure 8.2 distinguishes seven strategies: export-oriented strategy, multi-domestic strategy, screwdriver assembly, regional division of labour, diadic division of labour, globalisation and glocalisation. For most companies and industries, the export-oriented strategy is the logical start of their internationalisation process. An export strategy may be aimed at specific market niches, but it may also be the outlet of huge domestic production volumes. Many small and medium-sized enterprises may be able to supply some foreign clients, but may lack the size or managerial skills, the capital requirements, or the access to or knowledge of other clients to expand their presence through some sort of local production. A company may also be restricted to its domestic industrial complex in compliance with strong bargaining partners, or conversely, to sustain a very cohesive domestic industrial complex. Export-oriented core firms can opt to shift from concentration to dispersion, or continue a relatively concentrated production – depending on their organisation of production.

The multi-domestic strategy has been the traditional multinational company's expansion track, setting up foreign production on a country-by-country basis. A multi-domestic firm is well-equipped to serve local and relatively small markets, but suffers from a weakly developed international division of labour. Furthermore, the multi-domestic firm is often confronted with local bargaining partners that can exert considerable influence over it. (Concrete examples of firms are mentioned in section 8.4.)

Over the 1980s, an alternative to the multi-domestic expansion trajectory became popular, i.e. screwdriver assembly. Screwdriver assembly aims to circumvent existing trade barriers by setting up local facilities with the objective of having the locally assembled products accepted as exempt from import duties. The practice of establishing screwdriver assembly facilities has been known for decades. In particular, governments of less developed economies have ordained restrictions on the import of finished goods, to encourage domestic production and industrial activity. As a result, over the years many Western core firms have established small-scale operations in various developing countries.

After 1980, Japanese car and electronics manufacturers also stepped up the establishment of screwdriver facilities. However, they did not only locate these sites in developing countries, but primarily in the European Community and the United States (see Table 6.5). Because screwdriver assembly uses parts imported from the firm's domestic industrial complex, it increases international trade flows in the short run – albeit by aggravating the exporting country's trade surplus. When located in a developing economy, screwdriver assembly is usually the end stage of internationalisation, due to the relatively weak bargaining position of the host government. In developed regions a screwdriver strategy may evolve into a multi-domestic strategy, a regional division of labour strategy or a strategy of glocalisation – for instance if the host government(s) require a minimum 'local content'.

A core firm with a strategy to exploit a 'Regional division of labour' (RDL) concentrates most of its production and markets in one trade bloc, while the 'Diadic division of labour' (DDL) strategy aims to raise a division of labour in two regions. The latter strategy will lead to relatively autonomous operations in both trade blocs. Often, the RDL strategy's objective is to obtain higher levels of coordination at declining levels of dispersion. Core firms aiming for an RDL or a DDL seek the support of trade barriers or industrial policies. An RDL or a DDL strategy is only viable if the region(s) provide(s) a large and innovative market(s), hence only firms with a home base in one of the three large trade blocs may develop such a strategy.

A core firm with an RDL or a DDL strategy seeks to exploit comparative advantages within that region. A regional or diadic division of labour may even contribute to the rise of developmental areas, i.e. relatively low-wage regions close to and linked to one specific trading bloc. Examples of this are the incorporation of Mexico in the North American Free Trade Agreement, and the association of the Eastern European and possibly North African countries with the European Union. The internationalisation strategies are illustrated and elaborated below in sections 8.4 and 8.5.

8.3 STRATEGIC ALLIANCES: THE LINK BETWEEN INDUSTRIAL COMPLEXES

Since the early 1980s, the number of horizontal alliances has grown rapidly, both on a domestic and on an international scale. Although inter-firm alliances have been a known form of international competition for decades, in the 1980s they gained widespread attention as a complement or even substitute to foreign direct investments (Hagedoorn and Schakenraad, 1991; Hergert and Morris, 1988). Strategic alliances are usually though not exclusively concluded between two partners. They can be conceptualised in two ways. Firstly, they can be assessed on the basis of the relative positions of the two partners compared to other core firms. Secondly, the dependency scale enables us to position the most important categories of alliances in terms of the relative bargaining power of the two partners.

8.3.1 Horizontal alliances and the relative strength of the partners

Dominant analyses of strategic alliances have stressed the partners' rational optimisation of costs and benefits on the basis of escalating R&D costs, rapidly shortening product life cycles, the necessity of mastering increased complexity in the production process and the convergence of new technologies – such as microelectronics, biotechnology and new materials. These explanations contain much validity, but in the end they suggest 'objective' and 'inevitable' trends to which firms have to adapt. The bulk of the literature on strategic alliances tends to overlook the power relations between the partners (*ex post* as well as *ex ante*).

Several authors have tried to fill this gap. For instance, firms may enter an alliance as a pre-emptive strike in order to lock-out competitors from gaining access to the knowledge of the particular partner. Strategic alliances may constitute quasi cartels aimed at raising entry barriers to newcomers (Contractor and Lorange, 1988; Porter and Fuller, 1986; Wassenberg, 1990). Yves Doz, Gary Hamel and C.K. Prahalad warned that through partnerships firms may lose more than they gain, and that managers tend to recognise this 'creeping encroachment' too late (Doz *et al.*, 1987: 21). One explanation for such an imbalance arising is that large (multi-divisional) core firms hardly act as cohesive actors: competing groups or divisions within one firm may strike separate deals that could eventually destabilise the partnership. Another explanation is that although strategic alliances are concluded between core firms, they affect the entire complexes of both core firms. Creeping encroachment can result from reactions of other bargaining partners within these complexes (for this 'trilateral diplomacy' logic, see Stopford and Strange, 1991). If these reactions are not taken into account beforehand, they may seriously affect or even undermine the intended effects of the alliance.

Strategic alliances between firms (or rather between industrial complexes) are therefore far from static. After a deal has been concluded, partners rarely stop trying to dominate each other, which led Cawson *et al.* (1990) to compare partnerships with hostile brothers. Many partnerships contain a mutual incentive to cheat, creating an atmosphere of mutual mistrust (Buckley and Casson, 1988: 48ff.). Partly as a result, the majority of joint ventures in the 1980s failed (cf. Harrigan, 1988). Such mistrust is nurtured

Table 8.2   The relative strength of partners in strategic alliances

Towards: → *Initiative of:* ↓	'Strong'	'Weak'
'Strong'	(I) • Alliance based on complementarity • Offensive strategy • Not very common	(II) • 'Colonisation' • Often first phase in take-over • Stronger parties' objective: gain market entrance
'Weak'	(III) • Licensing • Second sourcing • OEM agreement • Risk of becoming 'colonised' or 'cannon fodder'	(IV) • Defensive strategy • Alliance against a 'common enemy' • Risk of low partner loyalty

by conflicting aims of both partners. A joint venture will not always be the best form to cope with conflicting interests. In this context Doz *et al.* (1987) have been particularly critical of the alliance strategies of Japanese firms which have usually only been marginally interested in cooperating with equal international partners. In the computer industry, for instance, they observed that Japanese firms used their European partners as 'cannon fodder' in the battle over market dominance with the American computer firms. This points again to the relative bargaining power of each actor (Root, 1988: 76), something which is rarely done in the statistical studies on alliances that gained much popularity in the 1980s (cf. Hagedoorn and Schakenraad, 1991).

Studies on strategic alliances often assume that two partners are complementary, independent and of equal relative strength (in terms of the cohesion of their complex, size, financial power, etc.). However, the majority of the alliances are likely to be concluded between unequal partners, or between partners that are relatively weak in the same area. Table 8.2 summarises the implications of the relative strength of alliance partners for the nature of the strategic alliance. An alliance between two strong partners (I) could be an offensive strategy towards other firms (cf. van Tulder and Junne, 1988: 231). This has not been a dominant type of partnership, however. The management of strong firms generally prefer a going-it-alone strategy to keep control over their technology. Alliances often reflect a relative weakness of one of the parties. An unequal partnership may also be motivated by political objectives (for instance, to gain access to a closed market, or to avert trade frictions).

If one of two partners is weak (II and III), this partner runs the risk of becoming 'colonised' by the stronger partner. In this case, the alliance could be the first step in a take-over strategy. If the initiative for the alliance comes from the weaker partner (III), the potential partner will be in a strong bargaining position and will probably not settle for an equal deal. Often such alliances are limited to licensing agreements, 'original equipment manufacturing' (OEM) deals or agreements in which the weaker firm serves as a second source for a specific product. In such relationships, trust levels tend to remain modest and the conflict potential tends to remain high.

A strategic alliance between weak partners (IV) is often part of a defensive strategy against a 'common enemy'. Such alliances tend to be unstable. The individual firms generally have little loyalty towards each other, and when one partner gets a chance to shift to another partner and gain short-term benefits, it will often do so. Thus the successful management of alliances between weak partners hinges on the effective elimination of exit options. 'Weak–weak' alliances may work if concluded between domestic parties and monitored by a strong government as a joint effort to stem the advance of foreign competitors. The VLSI project of the Japanese government in semiconductors at the end of the 1970s was a case in point (cf. Fransman, 1990).

Former Philips President Cor van der Klugt used to quote Bismarck, who said 'der Starke ist am mächtigsten alleine' (the strong one is the most powerful on his own). In spite of this, Philips entered hundreds of alliances throughout the 1980s. Some of these alliances were very successful, but many were not. A few examples may illustrate the bargaining dynamism of alliances.

- In 1983, the Philips telecom division entered into an alliance with US telecommunications giant AT&T – at the latter's initiative. In terms of Table 8.2, this was a type II partnership. At the same time, Philips was involved in talks on establishing the ESPRIT project (type IV). The ATT–Philips strong–weak alliance was so attractive to Philips that the ESPRIT talks on the weak–weak partnership with other European firms were stalled for some time. Ultimately, however, Philips proved unable to maintain its position in the alliance with AT&T and its telecom division was subsequently taken over by AT&T. At that time, AT&T had struck many other alliances with weaker partners (such as Olivetti), revealing its ultimate strategic intent to remain the dominant partner in any alliance and leaving open the possibility of taking over its initial partner.
- One of the best illustrations of the problems associated with a weak–weak alliance (type IV) was the UNIDATA project (1972–5) – initiated (and terminated) long before the European Commission had even thought of the ESPRIT project. In this project, Philips, Siemens and Bull, three weak computer producers, tried to develop their own mainframe computer. The 'common enemy' was American monopolist IBM. UNIDATA failed, however, for lack of loyalty of its partners. Despite fierce anti-American rhetoric, the French government at the time supported Bull

blowing up the project and entering into an alliance with American partner Honeywell. UNIDATA's failure prompted Philips to withdraw from the mainframe computer market altogether, while Siemens later became an OEM producer for Fujitsu mainframe computers. Bull never became a strong computer maker.

■ Another weak–weak alliance (type IV) was the mega-chip partnership between Siemens and Philips (1984–9). Partly due to Siemens's 1985 decision to ally with the much stronger chip maker Toshiba, and its apparent low loyalty to Philips, the mega-chip project became disrupted and was finally dissolved.

■ Did Philips only make bad deals? Certainly not. Its type I alliance with arch-rival Sony on the joint development and introduction of the compact disc in the early 1980s was an outright success. In this partnership, Philips brought in its technological know-how, while Sony provided its commercialisation and marketing expertise. The common standard that was developed was open to be used by other companies and subsequently became the industry standard.

8.3.2 Indicators of alliance dependencies

This section positions horizontal relations between core firms along the dependency scale (see Figure 8.3). Some indicators have been derived from John Hagedoorn (1990: 18), who studied international inter-firm 'cooperation' and technology transfer along a comparable scale, especially with regard to innovation-motivated alliances. Hagedoorn had built on the work of Farok Contractor and Peter Lorange (1988: 6), who positioned cooperative arrangements along a scale of organisational *dependence*. Hagedoorn rephrased this into a scale of organisational *inter*dependence, giving up the vital distinction between these two words and the analytical power of his scale. In a later work, Peter Lorange and J. Roos even followed this rephrasing (1992: 4). Hagedoorn also included customer–supplier relations. These vertical relationships, however, have already been discussed in section 4.4.

In one-directional technology and patents flow [1], large partners will keep or experience the highest degree of independence. One major reason for a firm to source technology to another firm is to try to make the other firm adopt its standard and in this way set a *de facto* standard in some product area. Technology sourcing agreements often pertain to a different region of the world where the first source has no major presence. The first source that uses this strategy may lack the size and power to penetrate this region on its own, or may be faced with an impenetrable industrial system. In case of a stronger and larger partner, in the longer run the smaller firm runs the risk of its partner gaining more profits from the licensed or second-sourced product/technology. This might even result in the stronger partner completely taking over the initial market in much the same fashion as was noted with the flexibly specialised firms that become dominated by

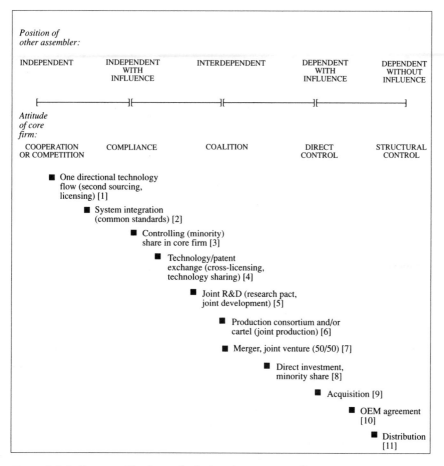

Figure 8.3 Indicators of horizontal relations between core firms

their distributor (Table 5.1). This happened for instance with the second sourcing alliances in the first three generations of microprocessors. The technologically leading, but small and not internationalised, American companies were outmanoeuvred by their large Japanese second source (van Tulder and van Empel, 1984: 31ff). In the short run, however, one-directional technology and patent flows can be profitable to both parties and based on real complementary strengths (Table 8.2).

The same may go for partners agreeing on joint standards [2], creating possibilities of system integration. These types of agreements are dominant in industrial systems consisting of many smaller firms. In the case of smaller biotechnology start-up firms in the United States, for instance, Bruce Kogut, Weijan Shan and Gordon Walker (1990) observed a high density of one-directional technology agreements aimed at spreading technology through patents and standards. They found that the nature and number of a firm's alliances was better explained by the position of the small firm in the industrial system than by its individual characteristics.

As these joint standards relate to a strategic part of their business, the partners will become more interdependent.[3] A two-directional exchange of technologies and patents [4] leaves the two parties relatively independent. Both technology exchange agreements and research pacts [5] – which create more interdependence – can take a large number of organisational and legal forms. Production consortiums, cartels [6] and joint ventures [7] represent a considerable degree of interdependence. Often these agreements will be concluded for only one product area in which assemblers can agree on a formal (joint venture) or more informal (cartel, consortium) alliance. If assemblers decide to combine their efforts in all products, they will merge their business and become even more interdependent. International production consortiums will most likely occur between complexes that already experience a high degree of interdependence in their home market. Consequently the biggest international production consortia have appeared in the defence industry (where second sourcing is also a common phenomenon), public utilities (for instance the French-UK consortium between CGE and GEC), the construction industry, or in civil aircraft production (the Airbus consortium). Many of these industries developed under what comes closest to an 'industrial democracy' or macro-Fordist concept of control at home.

Direct investments [8] introduce a degree of dependence into a relationship. This increases in case of an acquisition [9]. The control over the acquired firm becomes more direct than in the case of a minority share. The core firm that is acquired loses its status of a core firm and will be a subsidiary. However, because the latter core firm itself is part of a complex, its relative autonomy in developing an own strategy *vis-à-vis* its new parent company might remain relatively large. This will lower the ability of the core firm to exercise direct control over its newly acquired subsidiary. Depending on the degree of integration envisaged by the parent company, the influence of the acquired firm – as well as its relative autonomy – might remain quite substantial. The ideal type micro-Fordist firm, therefore, would abstain as much as possible from international acquisitions, and rather choose to set up subsidiaries over which direct control can be exercised. The same holds even stronger for the ideal type Toyotist firm that will try to create internally induced growth.

The degree of dependency will increase if an end producer A allows another firm B to assemble A's product as an 'original equipment manufacturer' (OEM) [10]. An OEM agreement can mean that firm B assembles A's end product on the basis of readily delivered components or design. However, an OEM agreement may also refer to a situation in which A puts

---

[3] Simply stated, a common standard for car engines creates considerably more interdependence than for ashtrays. In the electronics industry, a joint standard of a new generation of microprocessors is of much more strategic importance than a joint standard in the design of a computer keyboard.

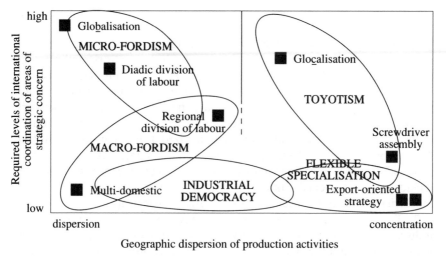

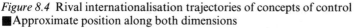

Geographic dispersion of production activities

Figure 8.4 Rival internationalisation trajectories of concepts of control
■Approximate position along both dimensions

its own label on an end product completely made by B. If B does not get
access to A's technology and know-how, B will be dependent, but with
some influence. If an assembler primarily functions as the distribution
channel [11] for another assembler it could become structurally dependent.
However, the actual interpretation of a distribution agreement should be
done with great care, since it depends on the relative openness of both
industrial complexes (or systems). Within a closed complex, an outside end
producer may have no alternative but to market its products through by a
competitor from within that complex. In such a situation, the two partners
will be much more interdependent. In the case where the core firm acts as
only one of many possible distribution channels, its status will be more like
a third-tier distributor (see section 4.6).

8.4 DOMINANT INTERNATIONALISATION PATTERNS AND CONCEPTS OF CONTROL

A core firm's realised internationalisation strategy can be read in two ways.
Firstly, it reflects the company's bargaining relations in its *domestic* industrial complex. Secondly, and equally important, it reflects the core firm's
actual control over its bargaining partners in its *host* industrial complex.
Figure 8.4 shows the internationalisation logic ensuing from each concept
of control. The spheres indicated in this figure present domestic and
international bargaining strategies that will not change overnight. However,
it should be born in mind that a concept of control is an ideal type that
refers to the *entire* set of *desired* bargaining relations. In many cases, a core
firm is embedded in a domestic arena where one or two bargaining relations

are dissimilar from the rest. Such lower levels of cohesion distort the hypothesised links.

1. The export-oriented strategy acts as the starting-point for many diverse internationalisation strategies. In this sense, the export-oriented strategy could be linked to all five concepts of control. However, internationalisation often proceeds beyond the point of mere exports, to some kind of production abroad. Only to firms operating in a flexible specialisation network will an export-oriented strategy often be the final objective of internationalisation. Many of these small and medium-sized firms may never capture large enough market shares abroad to justify an internationalisation of production, for lack of financial strength or marketing expertise. Examples include the often-cited Italian examples of the clothing and textiles industries, but also the specialised Dutch greenhouse firms.

2. The logical internationalisation strategy of a core firm subject to industrial democracy is an export-oriented strategy, possibly combined with a limited multi-domestic strategy. This core firm is confronted with bargaining partners which may be strong enough to contain it to its home industrial complex. If it does set up production abroad, it will limit itself to a few countries at most. It will select industrial systems with an advanced workforce which are not controlled by other strong core firms belonging to the same industry. For instance, Volvo's domestic bargaining arena conforms in at least three respects to the industrial democracy prototype.[4] As a result, Volvo has adopted a limited multi-domestic strategy, establishing production sites in two small foreign economies – the Netherlands and Belgium – where it can still acquire core firm status (Ruigrok and van Tulder, 1991). Volvo's largest foreign markets (the United States and the United Kingdom) are still served via an export strategy.

Other firms with a multi-domestic strategy include ABB and Electrolux. ABB has received ample attention above. Its decentralisation and its cutting of corporate staff from 4000 to 200 in the early 1990s indicates that ABB's headquarters were perceived to add little value by coordinating worldwide activities. Electrolux has shown a rapid acquisition-based growth over the late 1980s and early 1990s, following its take-over of, for instance, Zanussi and AEG Hausgeräte. It realises some economies of scale in production, but the three brand names mainly serve different national markets in the European Union (Electrolux in Scandinavia, AEG in Germany and some neighbouring countries, and Zanussi in Southern Europe: *FT*, 13 December 1993). A final example may be found with pharmaceutical companies, which are confronted with highly regulated bargaining arenas at home and abroad. The different health specifications and insurance requirements may

---

[4] Volvo has to take a relatively compliant attitude in its financial, government and supply relations. In its labour relations, it has seen its relative influence rise, leading to a coalition type of relationship, while it still lacks sufficient control over its own distribution (Ruigrok and van Tulder, 1991).

drive them into a compliant attitude to governments and local insurance companies, and into a partial multi-domestic strategy.

3. Fordist firms aim for vertical integration and an intra-firm division of labour. Macro-Fordism is based on a relative balance of power within the industrial complex, and relatively centralised bargaining. The most logical internationalisation strategy for a macro-Fordist firm is either a multi-domestic or a regional division of labour strategy. In both strategies, the core firm is confronted with relatively strong foreign bargaining partners, although the RDL strategy offers better possibilities to play off governments and trade unions. Macro-Fordist firms have been a main force behind the creation of regional trading blocs in North America and Europe. Corporations such as Fiat, Chrysler, Siemens and Olivetti are, each in their own way, aiming to establish a regional division of labour – although none has accomplished one as yet.

4. Core firms operating in a micro-Fordist industrial complex are facing relatively weaker bargaining partners. Consequently, they have more freedom of their own. Of all concepts of control, micro-Fordism perhaps allows a core firm the best chance to escape from, and later still retreat to, its domestic bargaining arena. Ideally, a micro-Fordist core producer exploits comparative advantages worldwide via a globalisation strategy. Micro-Fordism originated in the USA, although many US core manufacturers have been unable to sustain a micro-Fordist concept of control. The example of Ford's world car strategy has already been mentioned (section 6.3.1). Interestingly, Honda has also been thinking of launching a world car strategy in 1986. Compared to its Japanese competitors, Honda has had much weaker control over its domestic car complex (both over its supply, distribution and local government relations). This has forced Honda to escape to the USA which has become its largest market and which is soon to become its largest production base. Also in view of its faltering relationship with British car producer Rover (then a subsidiary of British Aerospace, but taken over by BMW in 1994), Honda may end up with a diadic division of labour strategy, alongside for instance US car maker General Motors.

In the oil industry, Exxon and Royal Dutch/Shell can be considered global players: they are very much in control of the whole supply chain, of financiers, and often even of governments and workers. An interesting case is Bosch. In its car components business, Bosch may be classified as a global supplier, setting it apart from the rest of the car component industry in the world. Paradoxically, the direct control strategy of General Motors and Ford hindered the rise of many independent US global suppliers: the history of the US car system reads as one effort of the Big Three to oppose or take over large and successful independent suppliers. Bosch, originating from a macro-Fordist bargaining arena, could benefit from this. Bosch owes its unique position to a combination of size, its control over a range of technologies developed in-house, its partial access to end consumers and its relative independence from client core firms, both at home and abroad. The few US global parts suppliers include TRW, United Technologies, Allied Signal and Rockwell. All of these existed before the Big Three gained their dominant position, and they could survive the car makers' direct control drive thanks to big cost-plus contracts from the USA Department of Defense (see also Chapter 9).

The complementary strategy of direct investment in local production for micro-Fordist firms has been mergers and acquisitions (M&As). M&As represent a substantial part of foreign investment flows for industrialised countries. Sachwald (1993a) and Chesnais (1994) for instance, note that M&As make up the majority of foreign direct investment flows. Schenk (1993) quotes sources estimating that on average 30 per cent of all gross investment is dedicated to M&As. Whichever estimate is used, however, a clear lead is taken by British, American and Dutch companies. Japanese M&A activities are estimated to be less than one-fifth of the average amount. In the early 1990s, the number of Japanese international mergers and acquisitions has even started to decline from this already low level (ibid; cf. Kester, 1991).

5. Core firms adhering to a Toyotist concept of control will do their utmost to guard their domestic cohesion – and structural control levels – as long as possible. This will initially lead them to adopt a simple export-oriented strategy. A Toyotist core producer buys as many parts and services as possible from suppliers under structural control. Its control over its domestic distribution moreover effectively hinders foreign companies from invading the Toyotist core firm's home base. Toyotist industrial complexes therefore generate unbalanced trade patterns with foreign industrial systems, and are likely to be confronted with trade barriers abroad. The trajectory of glocalisation is the logical internationalisation of the Toyotist concept of control. However, along the glocalisation trajectory, a Toyotist core firm will try to limit its internationalisation as much as possible in order to preserve its domestic cohesion. This means that it will favour an export strategy over establishing screwdriver facilities, and it will favour screwdriver facilities over glocalisation. A Toyotist core producer will only adopt the glocalisation strategy if governments of other countries or trade blocs with substantial markets can credibly threaten to raise severe trade restrictions without a major and integrated local presence of this Toyotist core producer. In the mid-1980s, Japanese companies such as Toyota, Nissan and NEC were following a screwdriver assembly strategy, and only after stricter regulation from the host countries have they moved in the direction of a glocalisation strategy.

We have to underline that the linkages stated here are theoretical ones, based on companies that have managed to realise their 'ideal' type concept of control. In reality, therefore, it requires considerable knowledge of the core firm and its domestic and international bargaining arena, before one can justifiably identify its internationalisation strategy. The lower the core firm's domestic cohesion, the more ambivalent and the more volatile its internationalisation strategy will be in the longer term.

Two examples may illustrate this. The Philips electronics complex virtually overlaps the Dutch electronics system. Local dominance reinforced a vertical integration (direct control) strategy in its supply, distribution and financial relations, and a very international presence from the start. However, in its labour and government relations, Philips has been confronted with stronger and coalition-seeking bargaining partners. It has proved difficult to translate this bargaining context into an internationalisation strategy. In the 1970s, when the labour union and the Dutch government had a strong position, Philips became a multi-domestic firm – with all the problems of low coordination levels associated with a matrix structure of management. For instance, Philips marketed different radios in countries such as Germany, the United States or Argentina, based on local designs and few or no common parts. Since then, Philips has moved towards a DDL strategy in the 1990s (while maintaining global aspirations), also because labour unions and governments saw their bargaining position deteriorate in the Netherlands and abroad.

Likewise, binational (British/Dutch) Unilever has long pursued a multi-domestic strategy. The consumer products company continues to face divergent tastes in many countries and, for instance in its food business, specific national or regional regulations. In the late 1980s, Unilever enhanced international coordination levels by setting up regional production centres. Unilever is unlikely to establish a full-fledged division of labour at a global level, but it is active in all three large trading blocs, plus many countries outside these regions, and it is seeking ways to step up scale economies in production and distribution.

If the hypothesised linkages between a core firm's concept of control and internationalisation strategy are correct, then the dominance of a certain internationalisation strategy reveals the relative expansion of one concept of control versus another. The trend towards 'Triadisation' in the late 1980s and early 1990s (section 6.6) suggests that the RDL, the DDL and the glocalisation strategies have dominated this period. Consequently, the dominant concepts of control of the late twentieth century would be Toyotism, micro-Fordism and macro-Fordism.

The shift towards RDL and DDL strategies is primarily a defensive move and represents a reaction to the emerging glocalisation trajectory. The RDL and DDL strategies reflect the wish to rearrange the domestic and international bargaining arenas of the core companies concerned, and suggest that Toyotism at the time outperformed micro-Fordism and macro-Fordism. In fact, a DDL strategy more often constitutes a retreat from globalisation than an expansion strategy. This is what can be observed in the latest data collected by UNCTAD (1994) in its 1994 World Investment Report. Of UNCTAD's ranking of the one hundred largest core companies, at least thirty-one companies witnessed a decline of their foreign assets at the early 1990s. Amongst these firms are European giants like Philips,

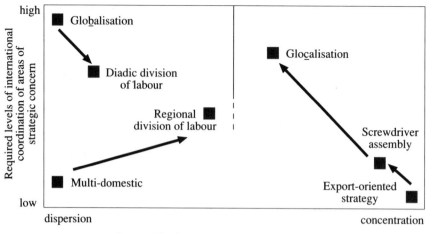

Figure 8.5 Rival internationalisation trajectories: dominant shifts by the early 1990s
■ Approximate position along both dimensions

Unilever, Akzo, Volvo, Fiat, ABB (!), Michelin and Thomson which are concentrating their production in one or two regions. Furthermore, an equally important group, including Shell, IBM, General Motors, Sony and Nissan, did not expand their foreign activities or their 'global posture'.

Paradoxically, the RDL and DDL strategies reinforce the glocalisation trajectory. The three strategies combined each contribute to the rise of trade blocs, although based on a different organisation of production and with quite different results for the regions concerned (see section 8.5). Figure 8.5 shows these dominant shifts.

8.5 IMPLICATIONS AT THE MACRO LEVEL

Combining the internationalisation trends of the late 1980s and early 1990s, and the dominant internationalisation strategies of large core firms over this period, we can better understand what a given firm actually means when it talks about globalisation or when it proclaims itself a 'global player'. Table 8.3 distinguishes five broad groups of firms, largely based on their national origins. Core companies in each group may speak about globalisation, yet on the basis of a different concept of control, mean something entirely different from companies in the other groups! There are four dominant meanings attributed to globalisation:

1 Globalisation as an advanced international division of labour, with sizeable reimportations back into the home industrial complex – ideally on a global scale, otherwise at a diadic level;

Table 8.3   Rival elaborations of 'globalisation'

Home base industrial complex	Elaboration of 'globalisation'
UNITED STATES, UNITED KINGDOM ♯ **THE NETHERLANDS** Examples: Ford, General Motors, IBM, BP, Exxon, British Telecom, GEC Royal Dutch/Shell, Unilever, Philips	1 Division of labour in world regions and between world regions (intended), between core firms and suppliers 2 Sizeable reimportations into home base from other regions 3 Primarily bi-regional (USA and EU); sometimes partly retreat strategy and/or regional reconfiguration 4 Shift of some decision-making centres (functional and product-line) to other Triad regions is possible 5 Inclined to international acquisitions and temporary alliances (in case of financial or technological weaknesses) 6 Considerable internationalisation of stock and capital provision over Triad regions 7 Expansion mostly via acquisitions and/or greenfield investment 8 Intended internationalisation of production and marketing: < 50% in home Triad region; > 15% in second and/or third Triad region; > 15% in developmental areas
LARGER EUROPEAN ECONOMIES Examples: Siemens, Daimler-Benz, Volkswagen, Fiat, Renault, Veba, Elf-Aquitaine, IRI, ENI, Olivetti, Alcatel-Alsthom	1 Regional division of labour within Europe; Eastern Europe as the low end market and production region 2 Reimportations within own region/industrial complex 3 Build-up of European stronghold: concentrated production for an integrated market; export strategy to other world regions, in particular to Triad markets 4 Shift of some decision-making centres within the European region 5 Inclined to enter into international strategic alliances (but as the strongest partner) 6 Regional concentration of stock and capital provision 7 FDI object: also via mergers and/or acquisitions 8 Intended internationalisation of production and marketing: < 80% domestic; > 80% in home Triad region, incl. developmental area
SMALL EUROPEAN ECONOMIES Examples: ABB, Volvo, Saab-Scania, Nokia, Electrolux, Ciba Geigy, Heineken	1 Multi-domestic presence 2 Limited international division of labour (though reimportations to home base can be sizeable) 3 Seeks local player status over the world 4 Shift of headquarters is possible 5 Less inclined, though sometimes forced into alliance (often as the weaker partner) 6 Sizeable internationalisation of stock and capital provision 7 Expansion also via mergers and/or acquisitions 8 Intended internationalisation of production and marketing: < 50% domestic; < 15% in developmental areas
SOUTH KOREA Examples: Samsung, Hyundai, Lucky Goldstar, Sunkyong	1 Triad: from screwdriver to glocalisation strategy 2 Limited international division of labour, limited reimportations into home country 3 *Pax Nipponica* succeeds *Pax Americana*: Pacific Asia under Japanese leadership; both market and low end production centre (for other Triad markets)

Table 8.3   Continued

Home base industrial complex	Elaboration of 'globalisation'
JAPAN Examples: Toyota, Nissan, NEC, Hitachi, Mitsubishi Matsushita	4 No shift of decision-making centres to other countries/ regions 5 Less inclined to strategic alliances or acquisitions: going-it-alone 6 Low internationalisation of stock and capital provision 7 FDI object: primarily greenfield investment 8 Intended internationalisation of production and marketing: < 50% in home Triad region; > 15% in second Triad region; > 10% in third Triad region; > 15% in developmental areas

2 Europeanisation and the establishment of a regional division of labour within Europe;
3 Glocalisation in the major trade blocs, with a limited international division of labour at most, and hardly any reimportations;
4 Multi-domestic presence, with a limited international division of labour.

In principle, three of these definitions present a worldwide strategic scope. The 'continental' European variant has a more limited focus to the (extended) European region. It is not by coincidence that the globalisation discussion has been the weakest in this part of the world. Core firms from small industrial systems are running the risk of finding their old multi-domestic strategy obsolete. The creation of large trading blocs and market liberalisations may not be to the full advantage of these firms skilled in manoeuvring and negotiating in complicated and small multi-party arenas.

One Dutch (Philips) plus two Dutch/British core firms (Royal Dutch/Shell and Unilever) display an internationalisation pattern similar to that of the large US plus some UK core firms. An interesting parallel is that the United Provinces were the hegemonic power through the seventeenth century, while the UK and the USA were the hegemonic economies of the nineteenth and twentieth centuries. As Chapter 9 indicates, hegemons and former hegemons share a relatively international outlook and a tradition of (relatively!) free trade. Moreover, the wealth accumulated by (former) hegemons has given rise to powerful and independent financial actors – which may drive production firms into a direct financial control strategy. Chapter 9 looks in more detail into the historical roots of the Fortune Top 100 firms.

Korean *chaebol* such as Samsung, Hyundai and Lucky Goldstar occupy an uneasy bargaining position. They have had to adopt a compliant attitude towards the Korean government, which has regulated the capital flows of even the largest Korean companies. The Korean giants furthermore lack a broad and well-developed domestic supply base. As a consequence, they have attempted to implement a direct control strategy in many strategic supply areas, but they are unable to produce all their essential inputs themselves, and are heavily dependent upon Japan. To bolster this dependence, the Japanese government in 1992 prohibited the transfer of two hundred high technologies to South Korea until 1995 (Bello, 1993: 35). By that time, it is thought that Japanese companies will have fully exploited these technologies. Japanese firms transfer only less advanced technologies to Korean firms, to integrate them into a regional division of labour led and controlled by Japanese firms.

Consequently, Korean conglomerates mainly serve the lower segments of the European and North American car and electronics markets. Just like US and European firms, they are facing huge barriers to entering the Japanese market to compete with Japanese producers. Unlike European and American governments, however, the Korean government lacks the bargaining power to persuade the Japanese government into at least some market opening concessions. Moreover, *chaebol* are denied every access to setting up facilities in the Japanese industrial system. The *chaebol* seriously risk staying in a compliant position and getting 'stuck in the middle' between a fragile multi-domestic strategy with low end production facilities in the margins of some trade blocs, and becoming the low end of a Japanese-led glocalisation strategy.

This interpretation adds up to a pattern of regional dependencies in which the Triad regions each have their 'developmental area' or 'sphere of influence'. These spheres are listed in Table 8.4, which shows that core firms from the United States in 1990 had a dominant investor status in most Latin American economies, while core firms from the European Union occupied a similar position in Eastern Europe and Africa, and Japan confirmed its orientation on the Asia-Pacific region.

The developmental areas linked to and dependent on Europe and North America are used as a production base primarily by firms originating from the core countries of these trade blocs. Core firms with a screwdriver or a glocalisation strategy entering a foreign trade bloc tend to eschew developmental areas. Governments in developmental areas usually lack the political power necessary to defend such entrant firms' interests *vis-à-vis* the core states of the region: the risk that the core states of a trade bloc suddenly target these entrant firms through trade barriers is too large to take. The inclusion of developmental areas into the North American and European trade blocs is simply a strategy to compete on low labour costs, prevent entrant competitors from following this strategy, and preserve these countries' dependent position. This also explains why Eastern European governments have found it difficult to gain rapid and full membership of the European Community. (Hence the word 'developmental area' should not be understood to incorporate any optimistic overtones.)

The *Pax Nipponica* may be considered the international equivalent of the hierarchical supply system as developed by car makers such as Toyota. In this grand design, Japanese firms aim for maximum control over lower-tier

Table 8.4   The formation of regional dependencies, 1990

Triad member	Domination of average inward FDI flow (1988–90)	Domination of inward FDI stock (1990)
UNITED STATES	**Latin America** Bolivia Chile Colombia Ecuador Mexico Panama Venezuela	**Latin America** Argentina Bolivia Chile Colombia Dominican Republic Ecuador El Salvador Honduras Mexico Panama Peru Venezuela
	Asia and the Pacific Bangladesh India Pakistan Philippines Taiwan Papua New Guinea	**Asia and the Pacific** Philippines Taiwan Papua New Guinea
	Africa and West Asia Nigeria Saudi Arabia	**Africa and West Asia** Ghana Saudi Arabia
EUROPEAN UNION	**Central and Eastern Europe** former Soviet Union former Czechoslovakia Hungary Poland Former Yugoslavia	**Central and Eastern Europe** Former Soviet Union Former Czechoslovakia Hungary Poland Former Yugoslavia
	Latin America Brazil Paraguay Uruguay	**Latin America** Brazil Paraguay Uruguay
	Africa and West Asia Ghana Kenya Morocco Tunisia Zambia	**Africa and West Asia** Kenya Morocoo Nigeria Jordan
	Asia and the Pacific Bangladesh	**Asia and the Pacific** Bangladesh India Sri Lanka

Table 8.4 Continued

Triad member	Domination of average inward FDI flow (1988–90)	Domination of inward FDI stock (1990)
JAPAN	**Asia and the Pacific** Hong Kong Malaysia South Korea Singapore Sri Lanka Taiwan Thailand Fiji	**Asia and the Pacific** South Korea

Source: United Nations Conference on Trade and Development, 1993: 167

producers in the newly industrialised economies (NIEs: South Korea, Taiwan, Hong Kong, Singapore) and the Association of South East Asian Nations (ASEAN: Thailand, Malaysia, Indonesia, the Philippines, Brunei and again Singapore). In the *Pax Nipponica* these economies, together with Australia and New Zealand, also have the task of supplying Japan with food and raw materials (see Chapter 10).

8.6 CONCLUSIONS

Looking back on the growth and spread of transnational corporations (TNCs), Peter Dicken argued that 'one of the most common features of much of the writing on TNCs [is] the tendency towards overstatement' (1986: 65). One of the gross overstatements of the 1980s has been the globalisation claim. This chapter therefore did not picture globalisation as an accomplished reality, but as a strategic concept. The framework developed here identified two distinct international expansion and retreat trajectories, culminating into two rival global strategies, i.e. globalisation, which aims at a worldwide intra-firm division of labour, and glocalisation, which is based on a geographically concentrated inter-firm division of labour. These strategies are based on differences in the organisation of production and on domestic and international dependency relations,. Hence, it is virtually impossible for a firm with an advanced internationalisation strategy along one trajectory to shift to the other trajectory. Because a core firm's bargaining patterns function as 'sunk costs', they also determine the margins of its internationalisation strategy. A core firm is *never* really footloose.

Finally, this chapter argued that globalisation tends to support the rise of international trade flows, while glocalisation leads to gradually declining international trade flows. The interplay between internationalisation strategies and international trade is further discussed in Chapter 9.

9 Rival trade policy strategies

9.1 INTRODUCTION

At a congressional hearing about the dragging US–Japan trade negotiations, Jeffrey Garten, US commerce undersecretary of the Clinton administration, once cried out: 'We do not seem to have even a common understanding of the problem, let alone consensus on the solutions' (*FT*, 4 February 1994). Garten's frustration is only too understandable. Many US core firms still aspire to micro-Fordism and an international division of labour. The US government's basic belief in free trade may at times appear halfhearted but still represents a programme for the world based on the interests and aspirations of leading US core firms. Many large Japanese exporters, on the other hand, aim for Toyotism and for vertical de-integration. Unlike their US counterparts, Toyotist core firms do not aim to exploit free trade but to circumvent or even exploit foreign trade barriers. Such diverging strategic outlooks effectively *do* hamper a common understanding of the US–Japanese trade 'problem'.

As a result of the competition between core firms adhering to different concepts of control, demand for industrial and trade policy measures has grown considerably in the United States and in Europe over the 1980s (Grilli, 1988). Since the second half of the 1970s, 'new' forms of trade barriers have come up by which importing countries have tried to circumvent rules agreed upon in the framework of the General Agreement on Tariffs and Trade (GATT). GATT rules restricted the erection of trade barriers such as tarrifs or quotas, but could do little to prevent deals between two states or trade blocs on the regulation of international trade (cf. Jones, 1989: 138). In many cases, these new trade barriers are not raised unilaterally but after negotiations with the exporting state. This rise of international managed trade consists of bilateral agreements on voluntary restraints of exports, floor prices for certain products and minimum or planned market shares in specific industries.

At the same time, a vivid debate dominated the second half of the 1980s on traditional and alternative theories of international trade. Various scholars criticised traditional thinking of international trade and the assumption that free trade would benefit all participating countries. Their arguments led to the rise of the strategic trade policy models which stated that a country, under certain circumstances, could appropriate wealth from other countries by increasing its domestic production. These models reacted in particular to the industrial and trade policies underlying the economic rise of Japan (Brander and Spencer, 1985; Krugman, 1986).

So far, surprisingly little of the arguments in the domain of international trade theory has entered the analysis of trade policy-making processes and the rise of trade barriers. Similarly, very few authors have assessed the effects of internationalisation strategies (such as discussed in Chapters 6, 7 and 8) on international trade policies. Helen Milner (1988) has been one of the exceptions with her work on the degree of a firm's internationalisation and its trade policy preferences. However, her work was not based on an analysis of corporate internationalisation strategies, but on an a priori established basic typology.

Since the early 1990s, many scholars have called for an alternative theory of international trade. According to John Odell (1990: 140), 'a better, unified theory – combining elements of economics, political science, and history – is gradually emerging in the arena of international trade policy'. This chapter aims to contribute to this emerging integrated theory. Extending the argument of the preceding chapters, it is argued here that there is a direct link between a core firm's domestic restructuring strategy, its internationalisation strategy and its trade policy strategy. In other words, the logic of a core firm's domestic industrial complex shapes not only its internationalisation strategy but also its vision of the organisation of world trade.

Section 9.2 considers the debate on international trade theory. Mainstream trade theorists have adopted a welfare-oriented, prescriptive, macro level and a-historical approach, yet were nevertheless able to lift free trade theory to a paradigmatic status. Section 9.2 also assesses the contributions of the strategic trade policy models and the dynamic technology perspective. Section 9.3 sets out to examine the historical dimension left out by mainstream trade theory. The question posed here is: did the leading industrial systems of today acquire their size and dominance on the basis of free trade government policies? And, if any, at what stage in the emergence of today's leading industrial systems did trade barriers occur? These questions all pertain to the *macro* (or state) level. Section 9.4 turns to the *micro* level of analysis, and examines to what extent the Fortune 100 core firms have arisen in free and open competition, or benefited from discriminatory trade policies. Section 9.5 addresses the *meso* level, identifying different types of trade barriers and exploring which types of barriers arise in which types of domestic (and international) bargaining arenas. Subsequently, section 9.6 establishes the link between a core firm's internationalisation strategy and its trade policy strategy. Section 9.7 presents some concluding remarks.

9.2 THE CRISIS OF FREE TRADE THEORY

Since the end of the eighteenth century, the dominant doctrine on international trade has stated that free trade is the best way to maximise national welfare and to make each country produce those goods in which it is best. After the Second World War, the GATT was to promote this objective. However, in spite of progress made in the reduction of tariffs and quotas, other trade barriers have emerged since the early 1980s which proved more difficult to oppose. This section tackles the 'discrepancy' between free trade theory and the reality of international managed trade.

9.2.1 Origins and argument of free trade theory

Free trade theory claims that free trade enables each country to make optimal use of its scarce resources if it specialises its production. Free trade would allow each country to reap maximum benefits from its economic potential. As a 'side-effect', free trade would also maximise wealth at a global level.

By the end of the eighteenth century, free trade theory emerged as a descriptive theory of how trade came about between states. According to Adam Smith, countries traded because they benefited from doing so. In 1815, at the onset of the second cycle of British hegemony, David Ricardo formulated his theory of comparative cost advantages. Looking at the existing case of British-produced cloth and Portuguese wine, Ricardo argued that two countries could still gain from trade if one country had an absolute disadvantage in the production of both goods. This thinking laid the foundations of British economic liberalism and the British campaign for international free trade in the nineteenth century.

Although the theory of comparative cost advantages has remained standard textbook knowledge since, even some contemporary authors had already criticised its logic. Around 1840, Friedrich List, the German 'grandfather' of economic development theory, argued that German infant industries would be unable to survive open competition with British producers (Senghaas, 1982). Reconstructing the effects of international trade based on comparative advantages, Sideri (1970) has indicated how the Portuguese 'specialisation' on wine severely hindered economic development. His findings led him to criticise classical economists for their tendency to 'put an alleged harmony of interests at the basis of their analysis' (1970: 71).

It took over a century before free trade theory reached a new milestone. The Heckscher–Ohlin theorem, developed in the interwar period, stated that international trade resulted from different factor endowments between countries. Thus a country with a relatively large amount of capital would export capital intensive goods, and a country with abundant labour would export labour intensive goods. The Heckscher–Ohlin theorem also derived rather simplistic trade policy orientations from this logic: in a country with abundant capital, capitalists would favour free trade (and labour would not), whereas in a labour abundant country, labour would be more in favour of free trade (and capital would not; Gill and Law, 1988: 236).

The Heckscher–Ohlin theorem performed essentially the same function for the new hegemon, the USA, as Ricardo's theory of comparative cost advantages did for the British. With the memory still fresh of declining world trade levels in the 1930s, the Heckscher–Ohlin theorem provided the perfect justification for a US-led campaign to liberalise international trade after the Second World War.

However, criticism arose almost immediately. Leontieff's input–output analysis of US 1947 trade showed that the capital intensity of US exports in that year was lower than of US imports, which was in direct contrast with the conclusions of the Heckscher–Ohlin theorem. None the less, mainstream economists at the time considered these findings a 'paradox' that had to be explained (or rather explained away), which is probably the best indication of the paradigmatic status that free trade theory had attained by then (cf. Dosi *et al.*, 1990: 8). By the 1950s, free trade theory had evolved from a descriptive into a primarily prescriptive theory which had lost much of its explanatory power. At the time, this was already argued by Gallagher and Robinson (1953).

Many other phenomena, such as the emergence and rapid growth of intra-industry trade (see section 9.3.3), could not be explained by free trade theorists at the time (Tharakan, 1983). Free trade theory's conception of international trade was essentially static: capital and labour were assumed to be perfectly mobile at the national level, but immobile at the international level. Consequently, international capital flows such as foreign direct investments could not be accounted for. It was assumed that identical production functions would exist across countries. In this way, differences between firms or industrial complexes were assumed to be irrelevant. The influence of a firm's institutional and regulatory environment received no attention in free trade theory, and technological development was supposed to be transparent and available to everybody, i.e. considered as exogeneously given rather than as specific to core firms and particular bargaining arenas. Until the late 1970s, so-called 'neo-factor' or 'neo-technology' trade theories continued to depart from many of the traditional assumptions (Hood and Young, 1979: 139ff.).

9.2.2 Critics of free trade theory

It was not until the second half of the 1980s that adherents of free trade theory acknowledged that their basic argument was seriously challenged. The strategic trade policy models started from traditional assumptions, such as imperfect competition and the importance of external economies, yet came to entirely different conclusions regarding international trade in industrial products.

The strategic trade policy models assumed that a given country, by stepping up its domestic production, could increase its share of potential monopoly rents or external economies (Krugman, 1986; Stegemann, 1989). According to these models, government intervention, either by means of trade barriers or by industrial targeting policies, could lead to profit-shifting from one country to another. If one country were to pursue such a strategy, free trade would no longer be beneficial to its trading partners. Under such circumstances, countries which continued to trade according to the 'old' rules of free trade would simply transfer wealth to their trading partner.

The strategic trade policy models implied that comparative advantages were not, by definition, the result of natural endowments, but could also be *created*. This argument reached down to the very foundations on which the free trade paradigm rested. Whereas previous criticism had particularly addressed 'unequal exchange' between North and South, the strategic trade policy models stated that trade among industrial countries could also lead to exploitation of one by the other. Thus these models strengthened the infant industry argument which held that temporary government support to products and/or industries in the early stages of the product life cycle (cf. Figure 6.1) could improve their competitive position in the world market.

The strategic trade policy models justified, in fact almost called for, government intervention in the national economy. Free trade theorists were quick to spell out that such intervention could give rise to mounting international trade conflicts. After all, if one state intervened, and others did not, the intervening state would reap extra profits. But if several governments intervened in the same industry, they could find themselves trapped in a prisoner's dilemma. In such a situation, strategic trade policies could lead to massive and subsidised investments in excess capacity, probably leading to mounting trade barriers, and to a global loss of wealth.

However, when proponents of the strategic trade policy models attempted to draw up general criteria for government intervention, they encountered major difficulties. Their assumptions appeared to be highly sensitive: the risks involved in identifying and targeting specific industries are high, and welfare benefits from profit-shifting can easily be outpaced by higher costs.[1] Moreover, governments tend to be susceptible to lobbying by large core companies, which will inevitably do their best to present their specific interests as strategic ones.

In the late 1980s, a number of authors criticised the rationale and the implications of the strategic trade policy models (Bhagwati, 1989; Kol and Mennes, 1989; de Grauwe, 1989). An OECD study evaluated the results of empirical research on the effects of trade liberalisation under the

---

[1] Domestic welfare effects of strategic trade policies depend for instance on the question of whether firms increase production (i.e. play a 'Cournot'-game) or prices (i.e. play a 'Bertrand'-game). Higher prices merely lead to higher costs for consumers and higher profits for domestic producers, but do not lead to a crowding-out of foreign producers (de Grauwe, 1989: 209).

assumptions of imperfect competition and economies of scale (Richardson, 1989). Taking the example of an economy that produces video casette recorders and tweed jackets, the study argued that even under the above-made assumptions, trade liberalisation still leads to significant welfare gains. These gains may even be two or three times larger than those estimated under perfect competition.

Thus all countries would still benefit if governments decided to 'cooperate' and remove their trade barriers. Some authors have therefore argued that free trade, though having lost its status as universal dogma, has retained its status as a set of practical policy norms (Stegemann, 1989; Kol and Mennes, 1989). According to these writers, it would be the task of economists to establish which are the truly strategic issues, and to identify lobbies which try to present their specific interests as 'strategic'.

The debate between free trade theorists and strategic trade policy theorists has been a debate between two schools of prescriptive thinking. Much of the criticism of the strategic trade policy models boiled down to the point that these models departed from too high a level of aggregation. Strategic trade policy models indeed tended to simplify the role of the state as a mere extension of domestic industrial interests. In reality, national governments are not confronted with anonymous interests or with firms stating essentially similar demands, but with stronger and weaker core firms and with more or less cohesive industrial complexes. Ironically, however, free trade theorists failed to apply their criticism to their own welfare reasoning. While strategic trade policy theorists did not claim objectivity and acknowledged the (political) implications of their approach, free trade theorists tended to keep a blind spot in this respect.

Many points raised and mechanisms identified by the strategic trade policy models are of great relevance to a better understanding of international trade policies. Core firms or states may, under certain conditions, try to step up production and create a 'crowding-out' effect of less competitive or financially vulnerable firms. Furthermore, the strategic trade policy models implied that national governments need better criteria to decide which demands for trade policies they should support, and how. In the trade policy-making process, governments have to take into account variables such as the size of a core firm's employment force, its value added, its contribution to the domestic diffusion of technology, the strength and shape of its entire domestic industrial complex, and even the potential dual (civil and military) use of its products. The latter reveals a fundamental flaw in the free trade doctrine. Contrary to its fundamental premise, the efficient allocation of scarce resources never has been, and never will be, the sole consideration in the choice of state policies. State policies are based on a mixture of political, social, economic and military considerations. National security and the prevention of domestic political and social disorder have been, and will remain, important government concerns, in addition to maximising efficiency (Strange, 1985; Rosecrance, 1986; Sen, 1984).

In 1991, a third stream of trade analysis has been put forward which *'starts* from differences of technological capabilities and innovativeness between countries and then focuses on the effects of such differences on international patterns of trade and growth' (Dosi *et al.*, 1990: 3, original italics). Dosi *et al.* (1990: 11) found that 'the international composition of trade by countries within each sector appears to be essentially explained by technology gaps, while comparative advantage gaps appear to be of lesser importance'. This dynamic technology perspective strongly criticises the neo-classical theory of international trade which by assumption ruled out the existence of international technological differences. At the same time, the strategic trade policy models are criticised for their 'simplicity of the way technological change is reduced to either "learning curves" or to the generation of new intermediate inputs under monopolistic competition' (Dosi *et al.*, 1990: 5–6).

Dosi, Pavitt and Soete are important contributors to the neo-Schumpeterian school of thought, discussed in section 2.2. Their attempt to explain international trade flows from a dynamic technology perspective has been an interesting contribution to the theory of international trade. However, their basic assumption that technological trajectories are largely given is challenged in this book. Technological trajectories are not given but depend on specific social, political and economic structures, i.e. on the nature of the industrial complex. Ultimately, competition between industrial complexes aspiring to different concepts of control is thought here to lead to the development of different technologies and to different trade patterns and trade policies. This implies that there is not one 'best-practice' technology trajectory but that potentially rival trajectories may coexist – at least for some time (see Chapter 2).

A final weakness, the dynamic technology perspective is unable to explain the demand for and the rise of trade barriers. Free trade theory also suffers from this failure as a *descriptive* tool. Macroeconomic hypotheses on the reasons for the rise of trade barriers abound. Variables such as the unemployment rate, inflation rate, state of the business cycle and real exchange rates have been proposed as key determinants of trade barriers. Empirical tests of these hypotheses have confirmed that macroeconomic variables significantly influence the *demand* for trade barriers. However, macroeconomic variables have only very little or no direct impact on the *actual rise* of trade barriers (cf. Takasc, 1981: 691). As Destler and Odell (1987: 96) conclude in their study of American trade politics since 1974, macroeconomic hypotheses are not very helpful in accounting for the rise of trade barriers. This does not imply that economic variables play no role at all in the formation of trade barriers. It only means that the mechanism explaining the rise of trade barriers is more complicated and that the macroeconomic level of analysis is not the appropriate level to trace such influence statistically.

An early contribution to the understanding of the formation of trade barriers was the simple distinction between strong, moderate, and weak states, and the significance of 'domestic policy networks' (Katzenstein, 1978). The concept of domestic policy networks refers to the specific type and intensity of organisational and ideological links between state and society (in particular the private sector). According to Katzenstein, weak patterns (as in the USA) would produce limited, *ad hoc* trade barriers. Strong patterns (as in France) would generate trade barriers, but only in exchange for domestic firms' adjustment to international market requirements. Although domestic policy networks obviously matter in the formation of trade barriers, the operationalisation of the concept was not self-evident. More importantly, Helen Milner (1988), in a comparative study even argued that the trade policy-making process does not differ very much between the USA and France. Firms' trade policy preferences have been deeply yet differently involved in the trade policy-making processes of both countries. She therefore concluded that knowledge of the trade policy-making process *and* of industry preferences are critical to an understanding of trade policy outcomes.

To sum up, the determinants of trade barriers cannot be traced sufficiently at a macro level of analysis, nor at the level of national governments *alone*. Trade barriers are the result of an interplay of core firms' trade policy preferences and the domestic trade policy-making process. Macro level analyses provide provocative arguments, but their explanatory capacity falls short of their ambitions. They systematically ignore domestic restructuring processes and the justifications associated with these, and they fail to link their structural argument with actual trade policy decisions. The challenges to free trade theory both regarding its descriptive and its prescriptive value have led to a paradigm crisis of international trade theory, but also paved the way for a more realistic approach to the analysis of international trade policies. The next sections will begin to work towards this more realistic approach by exploring the roots of industrialisation of today's leading industrial systems.

9.3 THE FORMATION OF LEADING INDUSTRIAL SYSTEMS: THE MACRO LEVEL

This section assesses the impact of trade barriers at the level of the industrial system, and considers the question whether and how trade barriers have played a role in the formative years of today's industrial systems. Section 9.3.1 addresses the international system level and proposes a cycle in the trade policy orientation of a (former) hegemonic industrial system. Section 9.3.2 moves to the historical backgrounds of the currently leading industrial systems, to find that virtually all leading US, German and Japanese companies have had trade support from their domestic government. Finally, section 9.3.3 looks at data on intra-industry trade between industrialised economies.

9.3.1 Hegemony, free trade orientation and international regimes

According to the eighteenth-century British philosopher John Locke, 'in a country not furnished with mines there are but two ways of growing rich, either conquest, or commerce' (quoted in Sideri, 1970: 69). Classical mercantilists regarded power as a means to achieve plenty, and international trade as a means to extract wealth from other countries (Rosecrance, 1986). Free trade theorists adopted an entirely different perspective, analysing international trade primarily in terms of welfare maximising without considering the longer-term effects of production specialisation on the industrial structure of both trading partners at all.

. Based on its economic superiority, a hegemonic state has an interest in dominating international trade, ensuring open trade routes and access to vital markets (at least for domestic producers and traders) and determining the 'rules of the game'. A state that is able to dictate the terms under which international trade is conducted can optimise its share of this transfer of wealth. Thus after the Second World War, when it was economically superior to other industrialised countries, the USA took the initiative to found international institutions that had to foster free trade (GATT) and coordinate economic (OEEC, later OECD) and monetary policies (IMF).

By the early 1990s, the USA had lost its productive edge in many industries (cf. Table 6.2). In general terms, firms in a formerly hegemonic state will increasingly be faced with more efficient producers from other countries, yet the government of the former hegemonic state is still likely to remain the most powerful government in the world for several more decades to come. The essential question then becomes whether the government of the old hegemonic state will stick to its liberal stand and uphold international free trade.

This question may appear as a non-question. One could argue that former hegemons such as the United Kingdom and the Netherlands only *temporarily* receded from liberalism to retake a free trade orientation after their hegemonic position had fully crumbled. Such a retreat into liberalism did not originate from a position of strength but rather resulted from weakness. Such a free trade revival had befallen the United Kingdom in the late 1980s.

There are several explanations for the paradoxical retreat into liberalism. Firstly, a post-hegemon's financial power lasts long after the actual productive and commercial power has passed. Amsterdam remained an important financial centre until late in the eighteenth century, second only to London. By the early 1990s, London has only been overtaken by New York and Tokyo and is still the largest financial centre in Europe, before Frankfurt and Paris, even if the German and French economies have become much stronger. Thus, slipping cohesion within an industrial system leads to a situation where financial interests outlive the core firms they once served. While large financiers in strong industrial systems tend to be more embedded – although the nature of this embeddedness depends on the specific concept of control – large financiers in weakened industrial systems may be among the few economic actors in the world to be footloose – not out of choice but out of necessity. This also produces a more international outlook. An indication of such financial dominance, a post-hegemon's main innovations tend to concentrate in the financial realm rather than in manufacturing. In the 1980s, the emergence of 'leveraged buy-outs', commercial paper and 'junk bonds' in the United States were the warning signals of such financial dominance.

A second explanation for a post-hegemon's retreat into free trade liberalism is that these industrial systems tend to conserve institutions, traditions and ideologies that helped to create wealth and power, and competition in the 'old days'. Domestic bargaining arenas are surprisingly static. Former hegemonic states long maintain a tradition of declared non-interference and tend to have a poor experience of how to organise industrial policies effectively. Anti-trust regulations may worsen problems of industrial restructuring, while competitiveness tends to be based on highly specialised and technology intensive industries. A large proportion of these, moreover, tend to be oriented to the military rather than the civilian sector. Firms depending on military-related projects may develop high-technology standards but often have major difficulties applying this technology in commercial products at a competitive price (cf. Kennedy, 1987: 463; Junne, 1984b). Ironically, both defence producers and governments consider it justified that defence producers are at least partly sheltered from international competition (see also sections 9.4.1 and 9.4.2).

Thus the hegemonic cycle (cf. Wallerstein, 1984) shows not only a sequential pattern of productive, commercial, financial and military superiority, but also a particular trade policy orientation. Figure 9.1 depicts this in a simplified manner. The intervals and amplitude are not absolute but only illustrate the argument. Articulate adherents of the 'infant industry' argument can be found particularly in nations contending against the leading industrial system of the time. Examples of this include Germany and the United States (acting against British hegemony) and Japan (against American hegemony). In these industrial systems, the infant industry argument appears to have had some validity – partly because they remained less exposed to inroads from the leading economy. In relatively closed industrial systems and complexes, it tends to be easier to create solid bargaining rules plus the accompanying institutions.

Adherents of free trade theory are most numerous among business people, academics and politicians in strong industrial systems (cf. section 6.2). Put differently, free trade is the protectionism of the strong (cf. Sideri, 1970: 69). Only the strongest governments have tended to introduce trade liberalisations unilaterally. Bargaining relations in leading and cohesive industrial systems are less vulnerable to, or affected by, inroads made by foreign firms. Once established and functioning over a longer period of

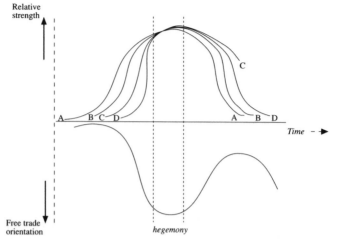

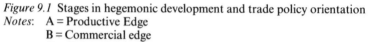

Figure 9.1 Stages in hegemonic development and trade policy orientation
Notes: A = Productive Edge
  B = Commercial edge
  C = Commercial edge
  D = Commercial edge

time, bargaining relations and institutions have shown remarkable continuity.[2] In the periphery of leading industrial systems, smaller industrial systems have tended to follow this free trade orientation, partly because they were unable to resist their stronger neighbour, partly in order to profit from the large neighbouring market. Finally, declining and formerly hegemonic industrial systems are most likely to generate articulate adherents of 'fair trade' arguments.

9.3.2 Emerging industrial systems and the significance of trade barriers

The former subsection argued that industrial systems in their formative years have tended to resort to large scale trade barriers. This subsection assesses this argument. The hegemonic power of the nineteenth century was Great Britain. From the 1820s onwards, Britain became the centre of the industrial revolution and accumulated massive riches. Its world economic dominance also led Britain to proclaim a free trade orientation – although

---

[2] The British weekly *The Economist* provides another illustration of the logic displayed in Figure 9.1. Founded in 1843 to resist trade protection in Britain, departing editor-in-chief Pennant-Rae declared 150 years later that *The Economist* still holds the view that 'everything should get out of the way of free markets' (quotation re-translated from Dutch into English, *Vk*, 13 March 1993). This remnant 'institution' of British hegemony is widely read among present-day decision-makers and opinion leaders, and continues to exert considerable influence.

it did not live up to this in every respect. For instance, British companies had the sole access to British colonies, enjoying monopoly trading rights. Furthermore, British tariffs after the 1870s tended to fluctuate rather than remain stable and low (cf. McKeown, 1983). The three largest UK core companies, plus the two Anglo/Dutch combinations in the Fortune 100 (see Table 9A, pp. 239–68) all date back to the nineteenth century.

Between the end of the American Civil War (1865) and the end of the Second World War (1945) the American micro-Fordist industrial system was moulded. At least twenty-eight out of the thirty US top 100 core companies in 1993 directly originated in this period. The social transformation towards micro-Fordism over these years cannot be understood without due reference to the role of the US government. At the time when Britain saw its hegemonic status gradually disintegrate, the US government raised high tariff barriers. Justification for raising these tariffs was provided by the 'infant industry' argument developed by Alexander Hamilton, the first American Secretary of the Treasury. In his 1791 *Report on the Subject of Manufactures*, Hamilton argued in favour of a national response to the supremacy of British manufacturing, either through subsidies or tariffs (cf. Reich, 1991: 19–21). Although other authors through the nineteenth century have put forward similar arguments (see below), the USA was most radical in using the 'infant industry' argument as the basis for practical policy. The reason for this is that the United States' economy at the time lagged further behind the British economy than most other contenders of UK hegemony.

Particularly after the end of the Civil War, US tariff barriers were significantly higher than the other major industrial countries. In 1897, US tariffs reached an average level of 57 per cent on all imports (tariffs on manufacturing imports were even higher); in 1902, average tariffs on imports of manufactured goods amounted to 73 per cent (Brown and Hogendorn, 1994: 190). At the same time, the involvement of the United States in international trade (import/export ratio) remained extremely low. Very few foreign producers exported to the United States (and even less located production in the USA), while US firms tended to focus on their large and growing domestic market. For decades, many US companies tended to see international markets and production sites as a second priority at most (for instance as an outlet for overcapacity created at home). Although the European continental states also contested British nineteenth-century hegemony by establishing tariff barriers, these were considerably lower than in the case of the United States: in 1902, average tariffs ranged from 23 per cent (Sweden), 25 per cent (Germany), 27 per cent (Italy) to 34 per cent (France) (Batra, 1993: 178).

In other respects, the *lack* of government intervention also helped US firms in their quest for direct control. Many firms enhanced vertical integration levels or grew via horizontal cartel agreements and mergers into major oligopolies – despite anti-trust regulations such as the 1890 Sherman Antitrust Act. Examples of such companies are American Telephone and

Telegraph, General United Fruit Company, General Electric or General Motors (cf. Fligstein, 1990: 38; Reich, 1983: 34). As a result of these and other government policies, industrial production in the United States quadrupled between 1870 and 1900. By the year 1900, manufacturing became the prime economic sector in the USA, accounting for 53 per cent of GNP and the USA became the leading producer in the world (Batra, 1993: 137). In these years and in the years that followed, sectoral trade unions grew up, and the US financial system took shape – two essential ingredients of micro-Fordism after the Second World War. In the first three decades of the twentieth century tariffs remained high. In 1931, average tariffs on imports measured 60 per cent, which in the postwar period, through several GATT Rounds, declined to 5.7 per cent in 1980.

Thus over a period of two centuries, tariffs raised by the US government on imports were rarely below 30 per cent (Batra, 1993: 36). Until 1970, according to Ravi Batra, America was practically a closed economy. The change in US trade policies only came about with the internationalisation of production by American core firms. The 'runaway' internationalisation of American micro-Fordism was even facilitated by the Federal government. After 1963, the US Tariff Schedules included substantial tariff breaks on offshore assembly operations, because 'imported articles assembled in whole or in part from US-fabricated components became dutiable only to the extent of the value abroad' (Tyson, 1992: 91). This 'hollowing out' of the US industrial system led to a breakup of previously existing micro-Fordist productivity coalitions. After the 'escape' of a large number of American core firms from the (closed) domestic bargaining arena (see Chapters 7 and 8), the link between wage and productivity growth ratios became disrupted for the first time in two centuries of American history and wages began to fall while productivity still rose (Batra, 1993: 47).

The formation of the German Customs Union in the early 1840s was supported by Friedrich List's argument (see section 9.2.1) that the newly formed union should adopt an inward-oriented policy (Senghaas, 1982). The ensuing German trade protection had an indisputable impact: all fifteen German core firms rated in Table 9.1 originate in the eighteenth, nineteenth or early twentieth century.

There are two interesting parallels between nineteenth-century German and US economic development: firstly, both the US Federal State and the German Customs Unions (which at the time was not a state as we know it today) had little internal cohesion, and secondly, cartels played an important role in both economies. The most renowned cartel in German history has been IG-Farben, the 1904 coalition of Bayer, BASF and Hoechst in chemicals. Even more than today, the chemical industry at the time was a very strategic industry, and one of the engines of economic growth. The creation of the strong IG-Farben cartel led to the formation (or consolidation) of rival complexes in rival states behind high trade barriers, such as

ICI in Britain, Du Pont in the USA, and Basle AG in Switzerland (consisting of Ciba, Geigy and Sandoz). This cartelisation contributed to international tensions at a political and even at a military level. Despite wars, divestitures and major restructuring schemes in the decades since, all original core firms are still at the heart of today's leading complexes in pharmaceuticals and chemicals.

In longer-established nation-states such as France, many industrial institutions were founded even earlier. In the seventeenth century, Jean-Baptiste Colbert, the famous Minister of Louis XIV, introduced an early type of industrial policy: a combination of direct intervention via subsidies, state ownership and managed trade policy. Many firms supported by the French state collapsed after Colbert's death, yet some survived. In 1665, for instance, Colbert founded glass producer Saint Gobain (no. 91 in the 1993 Fortune 100). Some 350 years later, Colbert's heritage is still very much alive in French industrial and trade politics.

Sometimes, however, early French trade barriers against British hegemony had unforeseen side-effects. Friedrich Krupp (no. 86), for instance, profited immensely from Napoleon's Continental System aimed at British exports (see also Chapter 3). This prevented, *inter alia*, the import of cast iron from England. Founded in 1811, Krupp focused on English cast iron and related products and gained a head-on start in continental Europe, since it did not have to face British competition. Krupp played a key role in pressing for a German custom's union (1834), in German political unification (1871) and in the efforts to unify large parts of Europe (under German rule, during the First and the Second World War). Thus for a century and a half, Krupp, a major defence contractor, has regarded war as 'trade policy by other means' (paraphrasing the expression by Von Clausewitz, the Prussian military adviser and strategist during and after the Napoleonic Wars).

Many Swedish, Swiss and Dutch industrial complexes were formed or consolidated around the same period as the German complexes, the second half of the nineteenth and the early twentieth century. Their smaller domestic markets and bigger dependence on foreign trade weakened the bargaining positions of these governments, leading to more favourable attitudes to open international trade. At the same time, however, they often adopted less visible trade barriers. The Dutch refusal in the 1869–1910 period to comply with international patenting law is a case in point (cf. Wennekes, 1993: 38). Dutch firms over these years copied foreign technologies without having to ask for permission or pay remunerations to the inventor. Companies now listed in the Fortune 100 ranking which 'illegally' copied technologies in this way include Anton Philips – who started his firm on copied light-bulb technology of Thomas Alvar Edison (General Electric) – and Simon Van den Bergh (one of the founders of Unilever) who together with seventy other Dutch margarine producers could freely copy the French margarine processing technology of Hippolyte Mège Mouriès. Both firms still count these activities among their core business.[3]

The first steps to transform the medieval Japanese society into a modern capitalist economy were taken in the 1870s (after the Meiji Restoration). At first, the government had organised an industrialisation programme itself, which however encouraged corruption and bureaucracy. From the 1880s onwards, the large *zaibatsu* that came to dominate much of Japan's economic life before the Second World War (such as Mitsubishi, Mitsui, Sumitomo, Yasuda, Furakawa and Asano) each received vital concessions from the Japanese government and were allowed to buy government-raised businesses at low prices: 'The government sold them its pilot plants, provided them with exclusive licences and other privileges, and often provided them with part of their capital funds' (Johnson, 1982: 85). After the government had been taken over by the military in the 1930s, so-called 'new *zaibatsu*' such as Nissan (which at the time also included Hitachi) were particularly favoured (Johnson, 1982: 131). These companies thrived on Japan's expansionism in the South East Asian region, and to date they still maintain close ties with the Japanese government. This expansionism and the takeover by a military government in the 1930s can partly be explained by Japan's lack of access to raw materials bases, which at the time were monopolised by the major colonial powers.

Chalmers Johnson (1982) has documented extensively how the Japanese government, and in particular the Ministry of International Trade and Industry (MITI), has facilitated Japanese economic recovery after the Second World War through a wide array of trade and industrial policies which went counter to mainstream economic theory of those days. As Mr Naohiro Amaya, one of MITI's most influential postwar bureaucrats, told Clyde Prestowitz, former US Commerce Department official and negotiator of the 1986 US–Japanese Semiconductor Agreement, '[w]e did the opposite of what American economists told us to do. We violated all the normal concepts' (Prestowitz, 1988: 128). In industries such as cars and electronics, the Japanese government maintained trade barriers until the 1980s. Only in the 1980s and 1990s did Japanese scholars and business people begin to join the ranks of supporters of an international free trade regime.

The South Korean industrial system in some ways followed the example set by the Japanese model – albeit with a time lag. Korea had been occupied by Japanese military forces from 1910. After the Second World War and the division with North Korea, the South Korean government received large financial and policy support from the US government (Cumings, 1984: 25). Due to the lack of large concentrated indigenous business,

---

[3] In the period that Philips could freely copy Edison's technology, Japanese firms like Toshiba and Hitachi were in a different regulatory setting from the Netherlands, and had to allow Edison's General Electric a considerable share in their companies. Toshiba and Hitachi could only reduce the influence of General Electric after the Second World War (see also Table 9A).

and the influence of US military forces, the Korean state could act relatively independent from established business interests. On the one hand, agricultural prices were kept artificially low, to bring about a migration of cheap workers to the cities and to be able to feed these workers with low-priced food (Hamilton, 1983). On the other hand, the *chaebol* were treated as 'infant industry' behind a variety of high tariffs and tight state control on capital allocation (Chang, 1994: 108ff; Scitovsky, 1985: 230). This tight credit policy continues to be a major instrument to force South Korean *chaebol* to comply with official state objectives. According to Chang '[South] Korea is not different from other countries in that industrial policy has created many inefficient firms. However what differentiates [South] Korea from other countries is that the [South] Korean state has been willing and able to withdraw support whenever performance . . . lagged' (Chang, 1994: 121). Nevertheless, the *chaebol* 'as a group . . . were certainly privileged in their access to various state-created rents' (Chang, 1994: 123).

9.3.3 International trade and the creation of dependencies

Despite widespread trade protection in the formative years of leading industrial systems, some national economies have nevertheless opened up their economies selectively to foreign competition via customs unions. Customs unions provide an interesting test of the effects of trade liberalisation. In the early 1960s, trade economists observed that integration of the Netherlands, Belgium and Luxemburg into the Benelux customs union had led to a pattern of intra-industry specialisation of these industrial systems *vis-à-vis* each other, rather than to inter-industry specialisation. This meant that companies active in a particular sector, being exposed to fiercer international competition due to the creation of the customs union, had specialised production to achieve economies of scale. Other studies indicated that the creation of the European Community also led to a pattern of intra-industry specialisation (Tharakan, 1983).

Thus open international competition can be associated with a high percentage of imports and exports of inputs and end products, and with high levels of intra-industry specialisation and intra-industry trade (Porter, 1986: 29). Intra-industry specialisation can be expressed as an index that measures the horizontal division of labour among countries. At an index of 1.0, an industry imports from its trading partners abroad exactly as much as it exports to them. An index of 1.0 therefore indicates a perfect horizontal division of labour. An index of 0.0 indicates that a particular industry only exports finished goods, without importing industrial inputs. An index of 0.0 would thus signify a completely vertical division of labour of one country versus its trading partners.

National systems such as France, Germany and the United States do exhibit a high degree of intra-industry specialisation. However, estimates indicate that Japanese intra-industry trade is one-third to two-fifths that of the other major industrial countries (Balassa and Noland, 1988: 69). An official Japanese study stated that the Japanese 1988 index of intra-industry trade amounted to 0.28, compared to 0.55 for the United States and 0.85 for what was then the European Community (Kato, 1990: 25). This suggests Japanese international trade does not promote a worldwide horizontal division of labour in which countries and firms specialise their activities in the *same* industries on the basis of comparative advantages. Chapter 8 puts forward the hypothesis that Toyotist core firms do not aim to establish an international division of labour. Although not every Japanese industrial firm strives towards Toyotism, this outcome suggests that Japanese international trade is nevertheless to a large extent shaped by the Toyotist concept of control.[4]

9.4 THE LACK OF A 'LEVEL PLAYING FIELD': THE MICRO LEVEL

Section 9.3 assessed whether and how trade barriers have played a role in the formative years of today's industrial systems. This section looks at the micro level of the individual core firm. Table 9A (see p. 239–68), which presents the same 1993 Fortune 100 companies as Table 7A, provides the starting-point of this exercise. The first column of Table 9A mentions the date of origin of the company, which makes it possible to see whether it arose and profited from a period of trade protection. The second column identifies major generic and specific strategic choices by the core firm, for instance with respect to particular product/market combinations (cf. Porter, 1980), with respect to the core firm's strategic areas of concern (see section 3.2) and its major bargaining partners, or with respect to its internationalisation strategy. The third column lists what can be regarded as 'salient' trade barriers that were helpful in the growth period of the core company concerned. 'Salient' trade barriers include both direct trade barriers (tariffs, quota, import/export cartels), non-tariff and managed trade barriers (such as voluntary export restraints), industrial policies (including subsidies, procurement and defence policies) and trade practices that deviated from other countries at the time in terms of size, impact or timing.

9.4.1 The striking continuity of core firms and core activities

The first conclusion from Table 9A is that almost all core firms continue to dominate the industry where they started in. Car makers are still primarily

---

[4] Large and competitive nations tend to have lower indices of intra-industry trade, and a trade surplus will further lower the index. However, even Germany, which during the second half of the 1980s had a trade surplus comparable to that of Japan, experienced high levels of intra-industry trade (Balassa and Noland, 1988: 66). Furthermore, Japan's index is lowered by its heavy dependence on the import of raw materials and food. Yet these remarks do not fundamentally alter the picture.

producing cars (and trucks), while food producers remained primarily food producers. Electrical firms moved down the technological path and became electronics firms, but electrical firms with a primary focus on consumers sustained their orientation (for instance electrical appliance firms progressed to consumer electronics), whereas firms serving public procurement markets (defence, utilities, transport, telecommunications) still have the bulk of their business in these segments.

Only four firms in Table 9A diversified into fundamentally different markets. Philip Morris (number 17) went from primarily tobacco products to food and healthcare, USX (number 74) shifted from steel production into oil and gas, Grand Metropolitan (number 94) switched from hotels to healthcare, while 3M (number 95) gradually proceeded from mineral exploitation to office and consumer products. More often, however, diversification has proven unsuccessful. Telling examples include Philips (in the 1980s retreating from telecom, computers, white goods), IBM (unsuccessful move into telecom, and robotics), Unilever (retreat from services), Shell (moved into the seed business and subsequently retreated), Chrysler and Ford (aerospace, insurance), Alcatel (consumer electronics), Daimler-Benz (AEG's white goods acquisition sold after less than a decade), and International Paper (moved into oil and gas, only to retreat later). This has brought many firms back to where they started from.

There is a large body of literature on the reasons why diversifications into new businesses and technologies may fail, which has given rise to concepts such as core technologies and core competencies (van Tulder and Junne, 1988; Prahalad and Hamel, 1990; Stalk *et al.*, 1992). An additional reason, in terms of the framework of this book, may be unfamiliarity with the bargaining dynamism of the new industrial complex, and difficulty in altering the rules of the game. This suggests that being among the first in a given national industry puts a firm in a position to shape dominant institutions, competition rules, and industrial and trade policies. Once solidly established, these rules help to discriminate against newcomers from the same industry and from totally unrelated industries.

We assess that at least twenty companies in the 1993 Fortune 100 would not have survived at all as independent companies, if they had not been saved by their respective governments. Some eighteen core firms have been nationalised, many of them during major restructuring periods, sometimes even facing immediate bankruptcy threats. The social costs for a nation as a result of the exit or demise of these core firms enabled them to demand that governments socialise their losses – albeit in return for temporary or long-term loss of autonomy. The formation of huge state-owned conglomerates such as IRI, INI and ENI (1920s–1940s) is a case in point.

Thus, companies in industries considered strategic or politically sensitive, such as steel, cars, shipbuilding, computers or microelectronics, have often exerted an influence way beyond the boundaries of their industrial complexes. In the postwar period, most large steel firms in Europe were allowed to create 'crisis cartels' behind considerable trade barriers, while French, Italian and British steel firms received state subsidies amounting to over 50 per cent of the value-added average in the first half of the 1980s (Commission of the European Communities, 1987). Between 1980 and 1985, state-owned Usinor Sacilor received subsidies of the equivalent of more than DM20 billion from the French government (Oberender and Rüter, 1993: 78). (For the critical role of military procurements policies, see section 9.4.2).

Among the many examples of 1993 Fortune 100 firms receiving large scale government support, including direct government bail-outs, the following may be mentioned:

- Chrysler (number 28): saved by the provision of government loans, early 1980s (Friedman, 1983: 383);
- McDonnell Douglas (number 69): indirect subsidy for its DC-10 production facilities sustained minimum scale of production to survive in the civilian market, 1980s (Tyson, 1992: 170);
- Renault (number 29): socialisation of billions of French francs in losses, 1980s;
- Daewoo (number 41): 1987 moratorium on heavy debt granted by South Korean government;
- Volkswagen (number 14): Seat subsidiary rescued by Spanish government, 1994.

There are also examples of government intervention through large banks. In the late 1940s, the Bank of Japan, the Japan Development Bank and the Industrial Bank of Japan, under the surveillance of the Japanese government, helped Toyota (number 5), Nissan (number 16) and Isuzu (number 110) to survive (Cusumano, 1985: 19). As recent as 1993, the Swedish government came to the support of the Skandinaviska Enskilda Banken (the Wallenberg consortium's family bank) and the Handelsbanken, Sweden's two major banks with large holdings in Swedish production companies such as Volvo (number 85), Electrolux (number 92), Ericsson (number 178), Asea (the Swedish half of ABB, number 33), Stora (number 183) and SKF (number 318). The Wallenberg consortium alone accounts for 40 per cent of the Stockholm Stock Exchange (*FT*, 2 September 1994). No government could ever ignore the demise of such a dominant economic force.

Despite the gradual deregulation of the world's major telecom markets, telecom producers have traditionally benefited from strict government regulations and purchasing. For decades, most national markets have been dominated by cartelised supply structures. An example of this has been the *Daini Denden* (or *Denden* family) in Japan, consisting of some forty companies. In 1982, five *Denden* family members – Hitachi (number 10 in 1993 Fortune 100; loosely affiliated to Fuyo, DKB and Sanwa), NEC (number 40; Sumitomo), Fujitsu (number 42; DKB), Iwasaki Electric (DKB), and Oki Electric (number 293; Fuyo) accounted for 95.2 per cent of all telephones sold in Japan (Gregory, 1986: 372). In the 1993 Fortune 100, at least six firms have more than 10 per cent of their activities in the telecommunications industry (Siemens, Alcatel Alsthom, Fujitsu, NEC, Philips, Bosch). Other firms such as Matsushita, IBM, Hitachi, IRI (Italtel) or Toshiba rank among the largest telecommunications equipment producers in the world, but due to their overall size only registered among 5 to 10 per cent in telecommunications. Section 7.2 has already indicated that the large telecom suppliers and operators have not been included in this list. Companies such as NTT and AT&T (ranking number 1 and 2 in the 1993 Business Week 1000) have long received exclusive treatment from their national governments.

Finally, at least ten leading core firms have modelled their internationalisation strategy partly on geo-political patterns of colonial rule (Royal Dutch/ Shell, British Petroleum, Unilever, Elf-Aquitaine, Alcatel-Alsthom, Total, ICI, British Aerospace, Petrofina, BTR). Many of these are oil companies exploiting sites established on the basis of concessions by colonial rule. Of all companies in the 1993 Fortune 100, at least twenty-three were directly engaged in the oil industry![5] Section 7.5 mentioned the Japanese government's attempts to reduce Japan's vulnerability to foreign oil supply disruptions, benefiting Nippon Oil (number 57) and Idemitsu Kosan (number 83). Likewise, the US government restricted the export of oil and refined petroleum from Alaska to limit the US dependence on foreign oil (Brown and Hogendorn, 1994: 144). In particular the industrial complex around Atlantic Richfield (number 67) has been affected by these 'export quotas'. As early as 1954, the US imposed quotas on imported oil, effectively keeping domestic oil prices one-third higher than international prices (ibid: 211).

Governments in all industrialised systems have regarded the steady supply of oil as of utmost strategic importance – as recently as January 1991, the Iraqi conquest of Kuwaiti oil fields even proved a *casus belli*. Both during and after colonial rule, the oil business has been extremely political. Many authors have attributed the two oil crises of the 1970s, and the ability of the Organization of Petroleum Exporting Countries (OPEC) to play a pivotal role during these periods, to the disintegration of US hegemonic power (cf. Keohane, 1984: 217ff). As one observer put it in the 1930s: 'operations in the oil business . . . are 90 per cent political and 10 per cent oil' (Yergin, 1991: 269).

9.4.2 Defence procurement and cross-subsidies

During their long formation periods, most leading core firms have survived one or two World Wars and/or major regional conflicts such as the Korean War (1950–3) and the Vietnam War (1960s–1970s). In the history of

---

[5] Exxon (ranked 2), Royal Dutch/Shell (4), British Petroleum (11), Mobil (13), ENI (21), Elf-Aquitaine (22), Chevron (24), Du Pont (26), Texaco (27), Total (45), Amoco (46), PDVSA (56), PEMEX (57), Nippon Oil (62), Repsol (64), Atlantic Richfield (67), Petrofina (70), USX (74), Idemitsu Kosan (83), Ssanyong (87), Petrobas (89), Sunkyong (90), Tenneco (99).

industrial capitalism, wars have had important direct and indirect effects. Mancur Olson (1982) argued that wars may break up social structures and thus pave the way for new bargaining constellations. Thus the Second World War gave rise in Germany and in the United States to varieties of 'war-Fordism'. Although wars sometimes led to subsidiaries from hostile nations being expropriated (such as German subsidiaries in the Second World War), at least seventy-five of today's 100 leading firms at some point in their history profited from a war. Many firms directly produced military equipment such as guns, aeroplanes, trucks, or gunpowder. Other companies benefited in sometimes surprising ways. Nestlé (number 23), for instance, over the 1941–5 period experienced booming sales to the US army of Nescafé and evaporated milk. Over the same years, Philip Morris (number 17) doubled its sales of cigarettes due to military orders. After the outbreak of the Korean War, the US army ordered US$23 million worth of trucks, military vehicles and other equipment with Japanese companies such as Toyota (number 5) and Nissan (number 16). These orders were inspired primarily by political reasons, and in retrospect have been decisive in the recovery of these companies and the Japanese economy as a whole (Cusumano, 1985: 19; Johnson, 1982: 200).[6]

Defence procurement may have an impact on the competitive position of companies in a number of ways. Firstly, it allows governments to discriminate in favour of 'national' producers. The 'Buy American Act' of 1933, for instance, allowed US firms to ask a 6 per cent higher price as compared to imported goods, 12 per cent higher prices in depressed regions, and more than 50 per cent higher prices in case of defence supplies. In 1982, this Act was extended to include public construction and steel production as well (Brown and Hogendorn, 1994: 159). Secondly, defence procurement is usually on the basis of so-called cost-plus contracts in which the buying agency pays the costs of developing the new product/technology plus an agreed profit margin. Both in the case of the Buy American Act and cost-plus contracts, companies are able to realise fat margins. This creates a basis for cross-subsidies in which the higher (or more secure) profits may be used to invest in other civil areas with more open competition. The time horizon of military contracts has usually been much longer than in civil markets. To many firms, military products thus created a stable basis to keep up competition in more cyclical or turbulent markets. This applies for instance to many combined truck/car producers, such as General Motors, Daimler-Benz and Nissan.

A cost-plus contract granted by a defence ministry often finances a large part of a company's R&D expenditures. For instance, over the 1950s and 1960s, the Pentagon paid more than one-third of IBM's (number 7) R&D budget. The Pentagon moreover acted as a 'lead user' to IBM, providing

---

[6] Moreover, they coincided with the 1949–50 dismissal of thousands of Japanese auto workers (the 'Red Purges'), and were probably instrumental in overcoming resistance against them.

the company with scale economies and vital feedback on how to improve its computers. In the 1950s, the Pentagon took care of half of IBM's revenues (Ferguson and Morris, 1993), enabling it to move abroad and flood foreign markets with competitively priced mainframe computers. Thus, IBM's defence contracts cross-subsidised its civilian activities at home and abroad, and helped it to establish a near monopoly position throughout most of the 1950s, 1960s and 1970s. Along similar lines, all formerly and/or currently leading US computers, semiconductors and electronics makers in the 1993 Fortune 100 have benefited tremendously from preferential defence contracts (GM – through its EDS subsidiary; number 1; IBM – number 7; General Electric – number 9; Hewlett-Packard – number 71; and Digital Equipment – number 93). During and long after the Second World War, Xerox (number 66) benefited from highly profitable contracts with the Pentagon. In this manner, Pentagon cost-plus contracts functioned as a *de facto* industrial policy (cf. Tyson, 1992; Junne, 1984b; Sandholz *et al.*, 1992).

The same mechanism can be observed in the aerospace industry (cf. Todd and Simpson, 1986). In the 1950s, for instance, Boeing (number 35) could make use of government-owned B-52 construction facilities to produce its B-707 model, providing the basis of its market dominance in large civilian aircrafts. The National Aeronautics and Space Administration (NASA) has often played a role comparable to the Pentagon. NASA facilitated cross-subsidisation to aerospace companies such as Hughes Aircraft (part of General Motors), Boeing, and McDonnell Douglas (number 69). A perhaps less obvious yet major beneficiary has been Eastman Kodak (number 61), developing advanced optical equipment for NASA.

Altogether, Table 9A shows that (supra)national government policies, in particular defence programmes, have been an overwhelming force in shaping the strategies and competitiveness of the world's largest firms. Even in 1994, without any major actual or imminent wars, ten to fourteen firms ranked in the 1993 Fortune 100 still register at least 10 per cent of their business in closed defence markets. On the basis of the data presented in Table 9.1, we can therefore draw the following conclusions:

Conclusion 1

Virtually all of the world's largest core firms have experienced a decisive influence from government policies and/or trade barriers on their strategy and competitive position. History matters! There never has been a 'level playing field' in international competition, and it is doubtful whether there ever will be one.

Conclusion 2

Neo-classical theorists have pointed out that 'picking the winners' and/or defining specific industries as being in their infant stage or of 'strategic' importance is virtually impossible and mainly incurs high costs. Nevertheless, government intervention has been the rule rather than the exception over the past two centuries. This intervention has taken the shape of all kinds of trade and industrial policies, and of a weak enforcement of competition or anti-trust regulations.

Conclusion 3

Government intervention has played a key role in the development and diffusion of many product and process innovations – particularly in aerospace, electronics, modern agriculture, materials technologies, energy and transportation technology.

9.5 TRADE BARRIERS AND DOMESTIC BARGAINING ARENAS: THE MESO LEVEL

The previous section concluded that governments have played a decisive role in shaping the world's major companies and businesses. However, this does not imply that governments have always been the initiating actor of these policies. On the contrary, governments often react to domestic pressures to defend domestic employment or to warrant the existence of particular strategic or intermediary good producers.

Neo-classical trade theory has difficulty in integrating the roots of trade barriers, other than by identifying pressures for trade protection and by rejecting distortions of the free flow of goods. It can explain that it may be beneficial for certain companies or industries to obtain protection from international trade, or that firms may construct cartels or other informal trade barriers, but it analyses these primarily in terms of the costs they incur for other groups. Free trade theory can explain why firms may, under certain circumstances, demand trade barriers, but it cannot explain why governments fail to reject these demands categorically.

The US government's attitude concerning *semiconductors* provides an interesting example. Semiconductors are not just a key input to a wide range of electronic goods, they are also a strategic component in many military products. According to a 1987 Pentagon report, twenty-one absolutely vital US military systems had become totally dependent on foreign (mainly Japanese) chip supplies (Prestowitz, 1988: 27). The vulnerability of these supplies became clear in the course of 1988. During a period of scarcity of chips on an international scale, Japanese producers chose to supply their domestic clients first, with only remainders going to their US clients. The US government therefore regards the semiconductor industry as strategic and essential to US military superiority. Consequently, the US government believes that the semiconductor industry should be subject to different trade principles than other industries (further illustrated below).

As stated earlier in this chapter, free trade theory emerged in the nineteenth century as a descriptive theory. It regarded the state as an independent, rather than as an embedded actor. While this assumption may have corresponded to nineteenth-century British capitalism, when social and production structures to some extent approached the flexible specialisation type, mature capitalism has produced bargaining constellations in which domestic governments perform markedly different roles (cf. section 5.3). Thus free trade theory's policy recommendations are based on a domestic bargaining constellation which is no longer the dominant type in international capitalism (if indeed it has ever been).

Based on the free trade paradigm, conventional trade theories have conceived of 'free trade' and 'protectionism' as diametrically opposed concepts. These theories assumed that domestic consumption would be negatively affected by trade barriers, and that foreign producers would oppose trade barriers if these barriers put them on an unequal footing with domestic producers. In this way, protectionism received its pejorative connotation (cf. Destler and Odell, 1987: 5). However, this traditional view of free trade and protectionism is not enough to analyse the rise of international *managed* trade. The word 'protectionism' is by no means clear and well-defined. Whereas free trade refers to a specific, 'ideal type' situation (i.e. the absence of any trade barrier), 'protectionism' denotes a wide range of trade and industrial policy measures (cf. Friman, 1988: 689–91).

A first step to operationalising the term 'protectionism' is to distinguish between unilateral trade barriers, indirect trade barriers and negotiated trade barriers. Unilateral trade barriers are raised by the importing state without any influence of, and often without consultation with, the trading partner(s) concerned. Indirect trade barriers are administrative measures, in the formal sense, that serve, for instance, industrial or competition policy ends. Negotiated trade barriers are only raised after (bilateral) negotiations between countries and/or trade blocs, which leaves the party concerned at least some influence on how it will be affected.

These three broad categories of trade barriers can be further subdivided into at least nine specific types of trade barriers, with notably different effects on domestic and foreign bargaining arenas. Thus it is possible to theorise on the rise of specific trade barriers in particular bargaining contexts and on the expected impact (see summary, Table 9.5). These nine barriers and their respective bargaining logic will be briefly discussed below.

The unilateral establishment of a tariff [1] will be of immediate advantage to the national state, because tariffs lead to extra government funds. (The numbers 1 to 9 within square brackets correspond to the numbers used in Tables 9.2, 9.3 and 9.5.) Tariffs have therefore been one of the oldest government instruments to raise extra funds. When Alexander Hamilton and Friedrich List argued that their respective national 'infant' industries could only catch up with low-priced British manufacturers if they received protection, they effectively argued in favour of tariffs (Brown and Hogendorn, 1994: 190). As with the British eighteenth-century 'Corn Laws' (also basically a tariff), US and German tariffs in the nineteenth century were originally aimed to support *agricultural* interests, as well as those of smaller manufacturers. By the late nineteenth and early twentieth century, these were the main modes of industrial activity.

Including the Uruguay Round, there have been eight GATT rounds on trade liberalisation. In 1947, before GATT was established, weighted average tariffs were around 35 per cent in nine major industrial country markets. In the 1980s, following the (seventh) Tokyo Round of negotiations, this had declined to less than 5 per cent, leaving average tariffs of the United States, Japan and the European Community at 3.9 per cent, 3.5 per cent and 4.2 per cent respectively (Low, 1993: 70,71). Thus GATT has been particularly successful in reducing tariffs.

Quotas [2] only date back to the beginning of the twentieth century and thus are a surprisingly recent invention. Quotas were first raised during the First World War, and more extensively during the 1930s Great Depression. In the latter period, the French government initiated quotas to shelter its farmers, quickly followed by other countries. By the end of the 1930s, the situation 'had grown so serious that the term *free trade* came temporarily to mean trade that was unhindered by quotas, even though the tariffs paid might be quite high' (Brown and Hogendorn, 1994: 126).

Governments do not have an inherent interest in establishing quotas, other than as support for ailing companies. However, it is simpler for a government to adjust a quota on a yearly basis than to adjust a tariff. To a domestic producer, inflexibility in adjusting a tariff is an advantage rather than a disadvantage. Moreover, tariffs have the effect of raising consumer prices, with the margin flowing to the government, whereas quotas usually lead to higher revenues for the foreign competitor (assuming that supply diminish while demand remains equal). To the foreign producer, the extra profits due to the establishment of a quota may, under certain conditions, even offset the short-term loss of market share.

The unilateral establishment of tariffs and quotas was officially prohibited under GATT rules. However, there have been three major exceptions to these rules. Firstly, countries with agricultural price support programmes are allowed to raise quotas in order to sustain these price levels. Looking at the national systems where agricultural quotas and subsidies have played a dominant role, there seems to be a relation between the size of the agricultural (core) firms and the nature of trade protection sought and provided.

The Japanese agricultural system is dominated by many small and inefficient farms, and has traditionally had lower self-sufficiency rates in agricultural products than other industrialised countries. Japanese farmers have relied heavily on strict quotas on the import of, for instance, foreign rice, beef, lamb, wheat, sugar and oranges (Balassa and Noland, 1988: 51ff). The weighted average producer price of seven important agricultural goods in Japan amounted to 2.54 times the world market price in the period 1980–2. As an illustration, Japanese consumers have had to pay six to nine times the world market price for their daily bowl of rice. Japanese farmers have succeeded in demanding quotas on the basis of their organisation in cooperatives and the peculiarities of the Japanese constituency system, which gave rural regions a disproportionably large vote in the Japanese Parliament (the *Diet*). In 1991, 66 per cent of the farmers' income was generated through trade protection and subsidies.

In the European Union, national agricultural systems have gradually become dominated by medium-sized companies, although cooperatives still play an important role. While the EU has also made extensive use of import quotas, these quotas have tended to be somewhat less distortive than in the case of Japan. The weighted average producer price of the same seven agricultural goods in the EC over the 1980–2 period amounted to 1.54 (Balassa and Noland, 1988: 52). In 1991, EC farmers received 49 per cent of their income from European Community programmes (Brown and Hogendorn, 1994: 147).

Farming complexes in the United States have been much more Fordist oriented, implying larger core firms and a generally lower interest in quota on agricultural imports. In 1988, the imports of agricultural commodities into the United States affected by direct trade barriers was very low (18 per cent, although growing, as opposed to 50 per cent in Japan). The US weighted average producer price of the seven agricultural goods over the 1980–2 period amounted to 1.16 (Balassa and Noland, 1988: 52). In 1991, 30 per cent of farmers' income came from trade protection measures (Brown and Hogendorn, 1994: 148).

Unlike other industries' trade policy campaigns, farmers' lobbying efforts have often been openly observable and (partly) directed against the public (French farmers throwing potatoes on the street, Dutch farmers blocking the highway to the capital). In Washington, the 12,600 US (small and medium-sized) sugar producers are paying amongst the highest sum per capita to have their lobby gain congressional support for sugar quotas (Brown and Hogendorn, 1994: 149). In 1988, these efforts led to a severe reduction of sugar imports, particularly from developing countries, leading to levels of sugar imports that were the lowest since 1875!

Agricultural income subsidies have also acted as a cross-subsidy to the suppliers of agro-chemical inputs and agricultural machinery. In most larger countries, agro-industrial complexes have tended to be relatively closed: agricultural cooperatives and banks have induced farmers to buy inputs and machinery from other firms linked to their agro-industrial complex. Agricultural trade protection and subsidies have thus contributed to the formation of such big agro-industrial conglomerates as Feruzzi (no. 75) in Italy or Conagra (no. 58) in the United States.

According to the Uruguay Round deal, December 1993, all agricultural import barriers will be converted to tariffs and cut by 36 per cent. Export subsidies are also to be cut by 36 per cent in value and 21 per cent in volume. Domestic farm support measures are to be trimmed by 20 per cent (*FT*, 16 December 1993). However, there is a long way between this agreement and its actual execution. At the time of writing this, for instance, it was far from certain that the US Congress would ratify the deal. Likewise, the mechanism to monitor whether member states are actually abiding the accord will have to be developed. Nevertheless, the deal was the first initiative in the GATT framework to try to curtail agricultural protection measures.

The second major exception to the GATT quota prohibitions can be found in the textiles and clothing industry. In 1956, the United States government persuaded its Japanese counterpart to restrict its textiles exports on a voluntary basis (Low, 1993: 107). In 1961, President Kennedy (a former senator of a major textile-producing US state, cf. Destler, 1992: 25) initiated a multilateral deal under GATT auspices. What started off in 1961 as a 'Short-Term Arrangement Regarding International Trade in Textiles' (STA) became a 'Long-Term Arrangement' (LTA) in 1962. The US government had explicitly sought GATT involvement to profess its otherwise still strong commitment to an international free trade regime. In the years that followed, the LTA was broadened to include wool and man-made fibres.

In 1974, the United States and the EC enforced the Multi-Fibre Arrangement (MFA), a higly discriminative and increasingly restrictive arrangement, aimed particularly at developing countries. As Patrick Low puts it: '(w)hile the STA involved sixteen countries and about sixty products, MFA IV encompasses forty-one signatories (counting the EC as one) and thousands of products' (1993: 108). Although formally restrictions are negotiated on a bilateral basis, taking the form of voluntary export restraints, they are better compared to quotas for lack of any bargaining power on the part of the developing countries. Despite long and bitter complaints from these countries, the MFA has been renewed several times over the 1970s, 1980s and 1990s. Under the 1993 Uruguay Round Agreement, MFA quotas are to be dismantled in ten years' time and tariffs are to be reduced.

A final major exception to GATT quota rules concerns closed procurement markets. Until the Uruguay Round, telecommunications (including public broadcasting), defence, public utilities and public transportation had been left out of the GATT jurisdiction. During the Uruguay Round talks, these industries and the issue of public procurement have been put on the international agenda, yet no major breakthroughs have been achieved (cf. Low, 1993: 159, 274).

Two major indirect trade barriers are state-induced production cartels/ consortiums [3] and subsidies [4]. Both measures are related to industrial and competition policy, and are the domain of national governments. Foreign producers have very limited possibilities for influencing the nature of state subsidies or state-led production cartels. Of these two, domestic producers tend to prefer subsidies over the establishment of a production cartel. A production cartel may be an *ultimum remedium*, through which a national government forces domestic producers to jointly reduce (excess) capacity, usually after providing them relief from foreign competition first. Examples include the steel and shipbuilding industries, which have been major employers and vital to the national security. Production cartels may also be created in strategic industries in a more offensive manner, as the UK-French-German-Spanish Airbus consortium indicates (cf. Voorzee, 1994). In the latter case, the constituting companies had the European national armies and government-controlled airline companies as their major buyers, providing the British, French, German and Spanish governments with considerable bargaining power.

Subsidies were covered by article XVI of the GATT, as supplemented by the 1979 Tokyo Round Code on Subsidies and Countervailing Duties. This Code officially outlawed export subsidies on manufactured products, but only stated that they should be avoided in the case of primary products. In the latter case, the Code has not proved enforceable for obvious reasons, but also in the case of production subsidies GATT has proved impotent on enforcing the Code (Low, 1993: 153/4). As a result, subsidies remained an integral part of national trade and industrial policies in a range of infant, defence-related and mature industries. The 1993 Uruguay Round deal did not succeed in defining which subsidies are legal or not. No deal was reached on civil aircraft subsidies.

Another popular indirect or administrative trade barrier is the anti-dumping measure [5]. Dumping refers to price discrimination between national markets. According to classical trade theory, dumping would lead to lower prices in the targeted country and thus increase this country's welfare. Although classical trade theorists acknowledged that dumping could cause problems to domestic industries, they did not consider the possibility of dumping as an integral part of a firm's market approach. GATT's anti-dumping code only came into force in 1968. Article 6 of this code stipulated that:

> dumping, by which products of one country are introduced into the commerce of another country at less than the normal value of the products, is to be condemned if it causes or threatens material injury to an established industry in the territory of a contracting party or materi-ally retards the establishment of a domestic industry.
>
> (quoted in Dale, 1980: 4)

Anti-dumping practices have been widely criticised for the vague definition

Table 9.1   Anti-dumping cases initiated (July to June)

Year Country	83–84	84–85	85–86	86–87	87–88	88–89	89–90	90–91	91–92	92–93	Total
USA	46	61	63	41	31	25	24	52	62	78	483
EC/EU	33	34	23	17	30	29	15	15	23	33	252
Canada	26	35	27	24	20	14	15	12	16	36	225
Australia	70	63	54	40	20	19	23	46	76	61	472
Other developed countries	01	00	02	05	09	12	05	09	21	08	72
Developing countries	00	00	03	04	13	14	14	41	39	38	166
Total	176	193	172	131	123	113	96	175	237	254	1,670

Source: *Financial Times*, 25 November 1993, based on GATT data.

of dumping – centring around the concept of normal value – and for the unclear procedures and their arbitrary use (cf. van Bael and Bellis, 1985). Foreign producers are also opposed to anti-dumping measures, because the revenues raised – if the dumping complaint is granted – will disappear into the pockets of the importing state.

First introduced in 1904 (Canada), dumping charges made up 77 per cent of all trade actions monitored by GATT between 1979–88 (Brown and Hogendorn, 1994: 238). Over the second half of the 1980s, the use of anti-dumping measures temporarily receded, both in the USA and in the EC, to pick up again in the early 1990s. As Table 9.1 shows, anti-dumping cases have been popular in smaller Anglo-Saxon economies such as Australia and Canada. Since the early 1990s, developing (including Eastern European) countries have increased the number of anti-dumping investigations. Since it often takes years before anti-dumping cases are concluded, it is possible that US and EC governments have initiated anti-dumping cases as a bargaining tool against the Japanese government to gain a better negotiated trade deal, or as a kind of 'last-resort' trade restriction after such negotiations have failed. In the 1993 deal signed after the Uruguay Round, it was agreed to develop clearer rules for the conduct of investigations, and criteria for determining whether dumping occurred and whether this created injury to the domestic industry. Effectively, this means that these rules and definitions could not be reached during the Uruguay Round.

By local content regulations [6], a government stipulates what percentage of the value-added of a product should originate from that country in order to be recognised as a 'domestic' product free of duty, and/or which parts of a foreign firm's production process should be performed in the host country. Local content regulations usually aim to encourage foreign producers to invest in the country concerned. If a firm fails to meet the required local content levels, it may face similar sanctions as under anti-dumping law. Although not allowed under GATT, domestic content rules have a long tradition. Until the 1980s, they could be found mostly in developing countries as part of some wider import substitution programmes. Over the

1980s, however, both the United States and the European Community also installed local content requirements to avert the establishment of Japanese screwdriver facilities in the car, electronics and integrated circuit (semiconductor) industries. However, because local content requirements have proved both difficult to measure and difficult to enforce, they have lost some of their popularity.

In the sphere of negotiated trade barriers, voluntary export restraints (VERs) [7] may be regarded as more refined import quotas. The financial impact of VERs is comparable to that of quotas. The history of VERs is closely related to the rise of Japan as a major exporter of cars, steel and electronics to the United States and Europe. The first VER, dating back to 1935–6, was a negotiated restriction on Japan's exports of cotton textiles to the United States (Brown and Hogendorn, 1994: 133). However, until the 1970s, VERs were scarcely negotiated (with the notable exception of textiles, see above). From then onwards, the USA started several initiatives to establish a VER. In 1981, the USA and Japan agreed upon a Japanese VER on cars, which was followed by the European Community one year later. In 1982, the USA and Japan agreed upon a VER on steel, which also was followed by the European Community.

By the early 1990s, VERs affected 15 per cent of world trade (Brown and Hogendorn, 1994: 132). More than 33 per cent of Japanese exports to both the European Union and the United States were subject to VERs (particularly of cars, steel, television sets and VCRs, machine tools and semiconductors) (OECD, 1993: 9). Nevertheless, no case involving a VER has ever been taken to the GATT, indicating that Japan has favoured VERs over other trade barriers. One reason for this is that VERs are monitored by the exporting industrial system itself, rendering core firms more strategic room for manoeuvre. For instance, a producer may decide to temporarily focus attention on a third market which has a sudden increase of demand, and meet the agreed quotas later in the year. Furthermore, an exporting country participates directly in the VER negotiating process. This provides it at least with some influence – such as the threat to withhold agreement and create a serious international trade row.

Richard Pomfrett has presented another, less conventional argument on the effect of VERs that helps to explain Japan's bargaining strategy. According to Pomfrett, certain trade barriers not only fail to act as an obstacle, but even turn out to be of benefit to what he referred to as 'global' firms (Pomfret, 1989). Under conditions of one domestic producer (or a small group of united domestic producers), high barriers to entry, and oligopolistic market structures, domestic and 'global' producers have a joint interest in replacing free trade by voluntary export restraints. Under these conditions, 'global' producers approach monopoly rents in the national market concerned, and the domestic producer benefits from a trade barrier that ensures its short-term market share and profit margin, and may enable it to restructure its production process. In such a situation, trade barriers do not manifest international rivalry, but mutual understanding.

There are of course factors that may destabilise this *modus vivendi* between domestic and 'global' producers. If domestic firms campaign for lower quotas, monopoly rents may no longer be attained by the foreign producers. In spite of high barriers to entry, producers from third countries which do not restrain their exports may enter the scene (Pomfret, 1989: 67). Nevertheless, the hypothesis of the existence of common interests of domestic and foreign producers is not purely academic. The GATT secretariat has even argued that the Japanese government itself encouraged the use of voluntary export restraints at a time when the US government no longer pursued such trade barriers (*FT*, 14 October 1992). In 1992, for instance, MITI voluntarily lowered the Japanese VER on cars to 1.65 million units, although neither General Motors, Ford nor the US government had pressed for a continuation of the VER at all. The extra profits generated by the VER may have been used to move upmarket, and to establish subsidiaries in the USA and the EU, in order to ensure future market shares. The 1993 Uruguay Round deal prohibited the use of what it referred to as 'safeguard measures', although it is doubtful how effective this ban will be. During the Uruguay Round, the car industry as such was not on the agenda.

Floor prices [8] may be raised unilaterally but more often will be established after talks with the government of the main exporters of a given product. Under certain conditions, floor prices may be preferred by domestic and foreign producers. Domestic producers will favour floor prices over voluntary export restraints only if they are competing directly with foreign producers but are unable to meet domestic demand, which is generally an indication of a rather weak structural position. Floor prices in fact represent a 'subsidy' by client industries or consumers to domestic or foreign producers. To legitimise this 'subsidy' *vis-à-vis* these clients, the industry concerned will need strong arguments, for instance on the 'strategic nature' of the product supplied. Floor prices have been established by the European Commission in the field of semiconductors, and previously, for instance, in the steel industry. To foreign producers, floor prices mean higher margins.

The trade policy instrument of a guaranteed or minimum market share [9] is of an entirely different nature from voluntary export restraints and floor prices. Although minimum market shares are the outcome of trade negotiations, they can hardly be considered a trade barrier. A minimum market share is demanded in an attempt to formulate an offensive trade policy strategy, since it is not raised by the state demanding market share, but permitted by a state with a domestic economy that is perceived to be difficult to penetrate by foreign companies. Thus, a national state campaigns to have its domestic producers acquire a minimum market share in another country. Domestic producers demanding a minimum market share wish to have this share in another country, whereas the 'foreign' producers will be confronted with increased competition in their domestic market and will be negatively affected by a minimum market share. The 1986 US-Japanese Semiconductor Trade Pact for instance contained a targeted 20 per cent market share in Japan to be attained by US chip makers at the end of the duration of the agreement, i.e. by 1991. In reality, it may be difficult to reach such market shares, since the demanding government always depends on the other government's willingness and ability to enforce the deal.

Table 9.2 lists the main elements of the deal reached by December 1993, at the end of the Uruguay Round talks. Table 9.3 summarises the discussion on the nine trade barriers (plus the situation of free trade) in terms of the domestic bargaining arena and the apparent internationalisation strategies of the companies campaigning for each trade barrier. The fourth column of Table 9.3, on internationalisation strategies, has not been discussed explicitly yet, but this will be the focus of the next section.

9.6 THE LINK BETWEEN INTERNATIONALISATION STRATEGIES AND TRADE POLICY ORIENTATION

In earlier sections, we have argued that at many instances in time, and by various trade and industrial policies, governments have played a decisive role in protecting major core firms from international competition or even from an all-out bankruptcy. Furthermore, we have suggested that there is a relationship between a core firm's domestic bargaining arena and its trade policy preferences. In this section, we shall further develop this argument by looking at the relationship between a core firm's internationalisation strategy and its trade policy orientation.

In the introduction to this chapter, reference was made to a number of authors arguing in favour of an alternative and broader theory of international trade (Cohen, 1990; Odell, 1990; Odell and Willett, 1993; Evans *et al.*, 1993). An important contribution to this has been made by Helen Milner (1988). In a comparative study, Milner tried to establish a relationship between a firm's degree of internationalisation and its trade policy preferences, when faced with a sudden rise of severe import competition. She argued that over the 1970s, the US and French trade policy-making processes did not differ much, because firms' trade policy preferences have been deeply – yet differently – involved in the trade policy-making processes of both countries. She therefore concluded that knowledge of the trade policy-making process and of industry preferences are critical to an understanding of trade policy outcomes. Table 9.4 summarises her main hypotheses.

Milner's work can be the starting-point of a less prescriptive and more analytical approach to the process of international trade policy-making. The central argument throughout this book is that large and internationally operating core firms have different yet generally increasing levels of influence on the organisation of domestic industrial complexes and systems, and

Table 9.2   Summary of results: GATT Uruguay Round (1986–93)

Trade barrier	Contents of GATT-deal plus industries concerned
1 Tariff	OECD countries cut tariffs by more than a third, over 40% of imports enter duty-free. Pertains to all industrial goods, in particular: pharmaceuticals, construction equipment, medical equipment, steel, beer, furniture, farm equipment, spirits, wood, paper, toys
2 Quota	*Agriculture*: all import barriers converted to tariffs and cut by 36%, gradual opening-up of Japanese and South Korean rice markets; *Textiles*: MFA quotas gradually dismantled over ten years and tariffs reduced; *Government procurement*: enlarged procurement code to include services, public works, procurement by local/national governments and public utilities, separate telecom talks; *Services*: market-opening pledge in wide range of service sectors (no sanctions), acknowledgement that services are subject to GATT rules (non-discrimination)
3 Production consortium/cartel	New provisions on state-owned enterprises (no deal on aircraft subsidies)
4 Subsidy	*Agriculture*: subsidised exports cut by 36% in value and by 21% in volume
5 Anti-dumping measure	Clearer rules for conduct of investigations and criteria for determining dumping
6 Local content	No provisions
7 Voluntary export restraint	'Safeguard actions' (to protect domestic industry against sudden import surge) subject to 'rules for conduct of investigation'; no provisions for industries that often use VERs, such as cars and consumer electronics
8 Floor price	No provisions
9 Minimum market share	No provisions
Other barriers	*Technical barriers* (such as standardisation) subject to better rules and to harmonisation around international standards; *Intellectual property rights*: recognised on patents, copyright, trademarks, industrial designs, etc., including provision of effective enforcement

Sources: *FT*, 16 December 1993, *NRC Handelsblad*, 15 December 1993

on the organisation of the world economy. This argument also holds for the area of international trade. From 1982 to 1990, for instance, US 'multinational companies' accounted for roughly two-thirds of US manufactured exports (ECAT, 1993: 17). While this pertained to trade in which the 'multinational' was only one of the parties, the OECD has estimated that as early as 1982, 32.9 per cent of US exports and 40.8 per cent of US imports were made up of flows between units controlled by one 'multinational group' (OECD, 1992: 220). In Japan, the 1983 data were 23.7 per cent for company-internal exports and 27.7 per cent for company-internal imports. The latter percentages only represented the company-internal trade subject to direct control, which is not the dominant strategy in Japan, and tell nothing of the percentage of trade subject to structural control.

Table 9.3 Trade barriers and campaigning core firm's domestic bargaining context and internationalisation strategy

Trade barrier	Category	Domestic bargaining context	Internationalisation strategy	Examples
1 Tariff	Unilateral	Domestic firms unable to compete at world market prices (domestic price hike benefits government)	No internationalisation, at most minor exports	On the decline after eight GATT rounds
2 Quota	Unilateral	Domestic firms unable to compete at world market prices, face choice to step up prices and/or output	Little or no internationalisation; if domestic firms increase output: may be beginning of internationalisation	Sugar, rice, oil seeds, dairy products; textiles (MFA); public procurement (incl. broadcasting)
3 Production cartel/ consortium	Indirect	Several domestic producers face structural surplus capacity: coordinating role for government	Export-oriented or multi-domestic; domestic industrial base of prevalent importance, may lead to retreat	Steel, shipbuilding, aeroplanes (Airbus)
4 Subsidy	Indirect	(a) Defence: firms compliant to government; (b) Non-defence, infant industries: may strengthen SME competitiveness in erratic markets; (c) Non-defence, mature industries: relative balance of power/ interests between firms and government, may precede formation of production cartel	(a) Export-oriented or multi-domestic; (b) Domestic or export-oriented; (c) Primarily multi-domestic and regional division of labour	(a) Computers, ICs, telecommunications (b) Biotechnology (c) Steel, shipbuilding
5 Anti-dumping measure	Indirect	Abstruse administrative procedure helps to exclude foreign entrants from domestic market	Regional or diadic division of labour	Consumer and office electronics, steel
6 Local content	Indirect	Attempt to stem invasion of domestic system by foreign producers, or integrate them into domestic bargaining structures	Regional or diadic division of labour	Cars, consumer electronics, ICs
7 Voluntary export restraint	Negotiated	Inability to stem invasion of foreign producers	Regional or diadic division of labour	Cars, consumer electronics
8 Floor price	Negotiated	Inability to produce sufficient volumes at home; balancing act between producers and client firms at home	Regional or diadic division of labour (not present in region of origin of imported goods)	ICs (EU)
9 Minimum market share	Negotiated	Insufficient control over home market to halt foreign entrants, attempt to break up cohesion of foreign complexes	Diadic division of labour (striving towards globalisation)	ICs (USA), car parts (USA)
10 Free trade	No barrier	Large vertically integrated companies have sufficient control over domestic arena to pursue international division of labour	Globalisation; screwdriver facilities	Not industry-based but (partially) firm-dependent

Table 9.4   Helen Milner's hypotheses on internationalisation degree and trade policy preference

	Low export dependence	*High export dependence*
High multinationality	'Type IV' Mixed interests; less protectionist than Type I; selective protectionist	'Type III' Least protectionist; most free trade
Low multinationality	'Type I' Most protectionist; for global protection; intensity of demand varies with economic difficulty	'Type II' Less protectionist than Type I; most favored is open markets abroad

Source: Milner, 1988: 25

On the basis of the preceding sections, we argue (a) that all large internationally operating core firms tend to develop and articulate implicit or explicit trade policy orientations towards their home government, and (b) that a core firm's trade policy orientation is an integral part of its internationalisation strategy. This means that, *ceteris paribus*, trade policy orientations depend on a company's internationalisation strategy. Table 9.5 presents a first approximation of the theoretical link between the seven internationalisation strategies (see Chapter 8) and the nine trade policy barriers (discussed above) plus free trade. An ultimate interpretation of these attitudes requires an analysis of the industry concerned and the core firm's domestic bargaining arena.

The first group of firms consists of small and medium-sized enterprises employing a domestic strategy with most of their production and their main market in their home base. If faced with severe foreign competition, such firms will be most vulnerable. Since retaliatory measures by foreign governments will only affect them marginally, they have little to fear from voicing a clear preference for strict trade barriers.

As Milner indicated, firms with an export-based strategy generally do not resist domestic trade barriers at all costs, but they will wish to prevent impediments that lead to extra profits to competitors, in order to maintain their competitive edge. Their basic interest is to secure open markets abroad, hence they often prefer a multilateral negotiating forum.

A multi-domestic strategy can be seen as a series of national strategies with low levels of coordination of production and marketing. The combination of dispersion and low levels of coordination may pose a problem in international competition and may induce a firm to move upwards along the dimension of coordination. Its relatively close relations with a series of national governments lead to a pattern of trade policy preferences close to that of domestic firms. However, its more international orientation still leads it to support bilateral or even multilateral negotiating bodies.

Table 9.5 Theoretical link between a core firm's internationalisation strategy and trade policy orientation

Category of trade barrier	Trade policy instrument	Domestic strategy	Export-based strategy	Multi-domestic strategy	Regional division of labour	Diadic division of labour	Globalisation	Screwdriver assembly	Glocalisation
Unilateral trade barrier	1 Tariff	+ +	± / –	+	+	+	– –	– –	+
	2 Quota	+	–	±	+	+	– –	– –	±
Indirect barrier	3 Production cartel/ consortium	–	–	+	–	±	± / –	– –	– –
	4 Subsidy	+ +	+	+	+	+		–	+ / –
	5 Anti-dumping	+	±	+	+ +	+	–	–	– –
	6 Local content	+ +	±	+	+	+	–	– –	– –
Negotiated trade barrier	7 Voluntary export restraint	+	–	+	+ +	+ +	–	– –	+
	8 Floor prices	+	–	+ +	+ +	+ +	± / +	± / +	+ +
	9 Minimum market share (*)	±	– –	– –	+	+ +	± / +	+ + (**)	+ + (**)
No barrier	10 Free trade	– –	+	± / –	–	+ / ±	+ +	+ +	–
	Preferred level of bargaining	Unilateral	Multilateral	Bilateral/multi-lateral	Bilateral	Multilateral/ bilateral	Multilateral	Multilateral	Bilateral

Note: Trade policy orientation

(+) + = (very) positive
± = neither positive nor negative
(–) – = (very) negative

(*) = concerns foreign market
(**) = unlikely combination

Producers with a strategy towards a regional division of labour have most of their production and markets in one trade bloc. This strategy may represent an expansion beyond a domestic base, but it can also represent a retreat from an earlier multi-domestic or diadic division of labour strategy. A firm with a regional division of labour strategy may be caught between its ambition to produce and compete on an international scale and its inability to expand to a diadic division of labour or globalisation strategy. In international trade negotiations, these firms tend to prefer bilateralism over multilateralism.

The strategy of a diadic division of labour will often reflect a firm's inability to employ a fully-fledged globalisation strategy, meaning that the company aims to benefit from the shelter provided by trade barriers. Faced with severe competition, a firm with a diadic division of labour strategy may support various types of trade policy instruments. However, its basic philosophy remains to expand to a strategy of globalisation as soon as the opportunity is there. Moreover, its presence in more than one trade bloc is likely to prevent it from radical campaigns for trade barriers that exert a lot of influence with governments, such as anti-dumping measures. A producer with a diadic division of labour strategy will tend to favour multilateral bargaining over international trade.

Globalisation involves a dispersion of in-house activities yet high levels of coordination of both production and marketing. This makes the firm highly dependent on international trade. In most cases, therefore, a firm aspiring to globalisation will be negatively affected by trade barriers, and will resist such barriers most fervently. It will always favour multilateral over bilateral trade bargaining.

From Table 9.5, it appears as if the strategy of establishing screwdriver facilities in another trade bloc fosters a strong 'free trade' orientation. A firm with this type of strategy is operating in a potentially unfriendly environment that may try to curb its activities through various kinds of trade restrictions. It therefore supports a multilateral bargaining arena. However, a screwdriver facility strategy may also serve as a transition from an export-based strategy towards a strategy of glocalisation.

Glocalisation implies a geographically concentrated division of labour and high levels of coordination of both production and marketing. In terms of trade policy-making, glocalisation is important mainly in connection with foreign markets, but not so much with domestic markets. A firm adopting a strategy of glocalisation will try to become an 'insider' in each of the three major trade blocs, buy most of its parts locally and diminish its export dependence. However, before evolving into an insider, this firm will have done its utmost to make the host government more dependent on it than vice versa. As a result of these attempts, a firm striving for glocalisation will be less vulnerable to certain trade barriers. It may even benefit from certain trade policy instruments which lead to extra profits, provided that the company is allowed to continue to develop into a 'local' producer.

Table 9.5 shows that the balance of forces for and against managed trade is very delicate. Under certain circumstances – depending on the composition of national bargaining arenas and on the barriers to entry to firms from other industries or countries – some types of managed trade are more likely to emerge than free trade. Such an international trade regime may not be governed by GATT or WTO rules, but can still be relatively stable in the case of a limited number of firms and a mutual understanding of the potential gains of the negotiated trade arrangement.

In Chapter 8, the dominant shifts in the two rival internationalisation trajectories were observed towards a regional and diadic division of labour, and towards glocalisation. As Table 9.6 suggests, the trade policy orientations of firms with the currently dominant strategies towards a regional division of labour, a diadic division of labour and towards glocalisation, tend to converge around negotiated trade barriers. Therefore, if these shifts continue to dominate the 1990s, a further rise of international managed trade may be envisaged.

Only firms adopting the strategy of globalisation truly favour a multi-lateral negotiating forum on issues of international trade. Globalising firms will be damaged most seriously by trade barriers and will almost always resist protectionist demands. The strategy of glocalisation, however, is to become invulnerable to trade barriers by establishing production facilities within trade blocs. In certain cases, they could even benefit from these barriers. The example of glocalisation also shows that highly efficient firms need not always favour free trade over certain types of managed trade. Glocalisation is motivated to an even larger extent than globalisation by political objectives, and in this way reinforces bilateralism rather than multilateralism.

9.7 CONCLUDING REMARKS

This chapter discussed the role of national governments and large core firms in the formation of international trade policies. It was concluded that the crisis of free trade theory has paved the way for a more realistic analysis of international trade policies. Free trade theory's welfare argument is valid in its own right, but it attributes a rationality to governments that is not realistic, and it ignores the trade-related implications of the strategies of large core firms to both national and supranational governments.

Adopting the bargaining perspective of this chapter, the dynamism in postwar international trade can be interpreted as a race between national or supranational governments responding to domestic trade preferences by introducing new non-tariff barriers, and international core firms from abroad trying to circumvent these barriers. Thus, from the 1950s onwards, large core firms established themselves on a multi-domestic basis to become

238 The logic of international restructuring

insiders in all major industrialised systems and reduce their vulnerability to tariffs and other trade barriers. By the 1970s, the multi-domestic strategy had become the dominant internationalisation strategy and thus undermined the use of the established trade barriers. The GATT Tokyo Round in the 1970s had the objective of eliminating those barriers which had become obsolete and had lost their 'function' to firms demanding protection. However, only four years after the Tokyo Round had been concluded, the OECD (1983) reported the rise of what it referred to as the new protectionism: a combination of industrial policies and indirect and negotiated trade barriers. These barriers facilitated both the re-runaway of many US and European production companies to the North American and European regions, as well as the internationalisation of leading Japanese core firms to these regions. The Uruguay Round can be seen as a response to the new protectionism, but the fact that, under certain not altogether hypothetical circumstances, managed trade barriers may be beneficial to both US, European and Japanese producers, explains why the 1993 Uruguay Round deal has not succeeded in removing these newly arisen trade barriers.

Some may argue that the explanatory power of our framework is limited because the number of independent variables is so high. Incessantly, this argument in favour of parsimony pops up in literature on international trade. Obviously, any model explaining international trade policies will have to identify the essential actors and processes, and will have to specify which patterns of interaction and which strategies produce particular outcomes. Yet some students of international trade policies appear to be obsessed with parsimony, which can lead to absurd claims that two or three supposedly 'independent' variables would suffice to explain processes as complicated as the direction of international trade or the formation of international trade policies.

In the analysis of international trade (policies), no variable is truly independent. Scholars analysing international trade and international trade policies who regard parsimony as the ultimate form of 'science' create a false precision. We think it is better to acknowledge the complexity of international trade policies, and to develop a framework that helps to tackle this complexity.

In Chapter 8, we developed the linkages between a company's concept of control and its internationalisation strategy. In this chapter, we went on at a more empirical level to develop the linkage between a core firm's domestic bargaining arena and its trade policy orientation, and the linkages between a core company's internationalisation strategy and its trade policy orientation. In section 10.2, these three linkages are combined to depict the logic of international restructuring of each of the five basic concepts of control.

Table 9A Fortune 100 companies (1993): key strategic features, related trade barriers

Rank Company Founded (Incorporated)	Historic strategic feature	Salient trade barrier
1 **GM** c.1892 (1916)	• 1910s: Olds, Buick, Cadillac realigned into GM; • 1920s and 1930s: rapid domestic growth; • 1930s: start of internationalisation through acquisitions; • Rapid growth in WWII and during Korean war (war production: 19% of capacity); • 1970s: diversification strategy into defence/aerospace; • 1980s: unsuccessful major investment programme ($80 bn) in increased efficiency through automation; • 1990s: record losses of GM ($4 bn in 1991) necessitate further restructuring	• Early 20th century: highest tariffs (45%) of all car producing countries in USA provided stable environment for realignment; • 1920s: flexible – but still high – tariff regime facilitated rapid growth in home market; • WWII, 1950s, 1970s: cross-subsidisation via military procurement; • 1980s: VER imposed on shipment of Japanese cars
2 **Exxon** c.1859 (1882)	• Rockefeller started with oil refining (Standard Oil Company); thrived on booming oil business; moved up downstream: first to aim at vertical integration; • Dominated US refining capacity in 1878; spurred antitrust laws (Sherman Antitrust Act, 1890); • No foreign oil production before 1900; by 1914 only some limited activities in Mexico and Romania; • Rapid internationalisation only after WWI; • 1972: name change into Exxon	• Start: dominance of the company over refining in the USA was silently condoned by the Federal government; • *Interbellum*: Open Door policy to break open the protected British, Dutch and French colonies in favour of US oil majors (continued more rigorously after WWII); US and UK Navy rivalry; • 1928: cartel with Shell and Anglo-Persian (BP); government involvement in quest for control over oil sources abroad; • 1930s: prime interest of US government on domestic oil market in support of own oil industry: controls on domestic oil production by state governments and controlled importation of foreign oil; • 1940s and 1950s: no antitrust cases against dominant US oil majors, because of national security reasons (Cold War); • Since 1948 US became a net importer of oil: domestic oil and coal industry successfully lobbied for mandatory oil quota, tariffs (from 1959–1970s) and voluntary restraints on oil imports; US government maintains Strategic Petroleum Reserves and prohibits exports of crude petroleum unless explicitly approved

Table 9A Continued

Rank Company Founded (Incorporated)	Historic strategic feature	Salient trade barrier
3 **Ford Motor** c.1903 (1919)	• 1910s/1920s: vertical integration and rapid growth initiated behind high trade barriers; • 1930s: threat of bankruptcy; • Postwar: continued internationalisation via subsidiaries; • 1970s: diversification (see GM); • 1980s: efforts to regroup foreign affilitates; acquisition of luxury cars (like GM and Chrysler); • 1990s: record losses, restructuring continues	• see GM (1); control over dealer structure in USA as well as in Europe can be treated as non-tariff barrier; • Saved from bankruptcy in 1940s by defence procurement; • 1970s and 1980s: company restructuring strategy included direct plea for VER towards Japanese producers (which was granted)
4 **Royal Dutch/Shell** 1830 (Shell); 1890 (Royal Dutch)	• Foundation of Royal Dutch: oil drilling in Dutch colonies (Sumatra); refineries only later founded, first in home countries serving national markets; merger (1907); • 1920s: start of diversification; • 1928: CEO Detering initiated cartel with Standard Oil and Anglo-Persian oil; • 1950s–1960s: rapid growth; • 1970s: diversification efforts (some terminated in 1980s)	• Production sites primarily in Dutch and British colonies were initially protected from 'foreign' competition; • First enterprise helped by Dutch King William III's granting of 'Royal' in the name of the enterprise: resulted in 4.5 times oversubscribed first stock flotation in 1890; • Company is still the prime concessionary in Dutch offshore oil and gas fields
5 **Toyota** c.1935	• Grew as a major war producer (trucks); • 1950s: Growth due to Korean war procurement; • 1950s–1960s: growth primarily in domestic market, resulting in a dominant national position; vertical deintegration and concentration of production in one region; • 1970s–1980s: export orientation from dominated national market; production strategy: high productivity, high quality, product differentiation at the same time	• 1936: Automobile Manufacturing Industry Law required vehicle makers to be licensed. Only Toyota and Nissan were licensed; • War effort closed state procurement markets (e.g. trucks); • Postwar trade measures daunted US firms keeping sites in Japan; • 1948: saved from bankruptcy by Bank of Japan (guided by state); • Barriers lowered: from 30% in 1950s to zero in 1978; • Until 1971 government control on inward FDI (including cars); • 1970: strong emission regulation in Japan supports production strategy of Toyota and creates entry barriers especially for US firms • Until 1983: strict inspection of each imported car

Table 9A Continued

Rank Company Founded (Incorporated)	Historic strategic feature	Salient trade barrier
6 **IRI** 1933	• Istituto per la Riconstruzione Industriale founded to save companies from bankruptcy; Diversified into military, telecom, iron, steel, electrical utilities, broadcasting, airlines; • Since 1948: (again) instrument in restructuring of Italian industry: building highways; taking over industry in Southern Italy; • 1970s: difficult period for many subsidiaries	• Majority state-owned conglomerate since 1933; • Primarily in government procurement markets, implying cost-plus contracts and from time to time direct financial aid (for instance in iron and steel), crisis cartel allowed; • 1970s crisis: government acquired stocks to forestall decapitalisation; of the 400 companies, 18 are listed on the Milan stock exchange
7 **IBM** 1910	• 1910–1930s: rapid growth of large tabulating systems (under lease) with governments and private customers; • World War II: IBM helped build the world's first computer (Mark I) for the military; • Postwar period: rapid internationalisation and growth of mainframe business especially since 1955 (705 computer generation); primarily lease strategy to 'lock-in' customers; international division of labour sought; • 1980s: major problems with PC-based technologies: decentralisation of company; recentralisation; major restructuring programme leads to mass dismissals; nevertheless: 1993 saw a record loss of $8.1 bn	• 1930s: vast need for IBM's machines with governmental offices; 'lock-in' strategy kept IBM dominating public procurement market; • In 1940s and 1950s lead-user of first IBM mainframe 'computers': Pentagon and other governmental agencies; 1950s: Pentagon provided half of IBM's revenues; 1960: defence paid 35% of IBM's R&D budget; lease often implied cost-plus contract; • Cross-subsidies from military supplies enabled rapid internationalisation of civilian business; • 1968–1981: third antitrust suit against IBM terminated partly due to (trade) political considerations; • 1960s onwards: DARPA (defence) continued as major source of funding for latest technologies and in support of IBM standards
8 **Daimler-Benz** c.1880 (1926)	• 1900: Daimler builds plant in Austria; • 1926: Daimler and Benz merged, saved from bankruptcy; • 1930s–1940s: rapid growth of business; 1940s: nationalised; • Truck division has been most stable part of portfolio; • 1960s: plants located in Argentina, Brazil, India, Belgium, Ireland, Mexico and South Africa; • 1985–1986 acquisitions: second largest defence contractor; • Sizeable efforts to gain technological synergies; • 1990: historic strategic alliance with Mitsubishi Conglomerate (never before did Mitsubishi as a *keiretsu* strike an alliance with a western firm); • 1993: obtained historical loss (DM 3.3 bn)	• 1930s: government procurement (mainly trucks); • Cross-subsidisation from trucks to cars; • Government procurement: one-sixth of employees work for DASA (primarily military); 47% of sales of MBB in 1989 were in military aircraft; • Deutsche Bank owns 28% of stock; Baden Württemberg government provides subsidies, training facilities and the like; Kuwaiti government owns 14% of stock

Table 9A   Continued

Rank Company Founded (Incorporated)	Historic strategic feature	Salient trade barrier
9 **General Electric (USA)** 1878 (Edison) (1892)	• G.E. Corp. was created when Edison and Thomson-Houton merged; concentration on electricity and railway market; later: diversified into steam turbines and utilities; • Rapid growth in WWII: GE's revenues quadrupled; • Post WWII: further diversification into jet aircraft, turboprop engines, aerospace, nuclear power; • 1980s: further growth through acquisitions (for instance RCA, broadcasting, later sold again)	• Start-up phase: primarily (local) government procurement markets; • 1913: US Navy bought first turbine motors and thus acted as lead user; • Government/military procurement (cost-plus) contracts as solid basis for profits and cross-subsidies for civilian business
10 **Hitachi** c.1910	• Since its inception diversified into government dominated markets, comparable to General Electric (9): power supplies, locomotives, telecommunications, etc.; • Rapid growth periods during two wars; • Tied up with GEC and RCA (USA); gradually withdrawn from these alliances; • Preferential supplier to NTT in telecommunications; • Diversified, grew rapidly in electronics and computers; • With Matsushita, Toshiba and Mitsubishi Electric, Hitachi has a long history of cartelisation in consumer electronics	• First important customer due to WWI (power company); • Part of *Denden* family (prime telecom contractors to Nippon Telegraph and Telephone, NTT, the telecommunications monopoly); this implies cost-plus contracts, the use of NTTs laboratories, which strongly facilitates cross-subsidies towards other business; • Exemption of the computer and semiconductor industry from national Anti-Monopoly Act. • Since 1960s: part of most government subsidised 'high-tech' consortia (computers, integrated circuits, telecommunications)
11 **British Petroleum** (1909)	• Started as the Anglo Persian Oil Company (APOC); • With the help of the British government APOC could break into the oligopoly of the big oil companies; • Postwar period: struggling to keep its oil resources secured; invested also in Alaskan and North Sea oilfields; • 1970s: BP lost most of its direct access to crude oil supplies in Middle Eastern countries, on which it still heavily depended (some subsidiaries were nationalised); • 1970s and 1980s: diversification into chemicals, mining and coal; partly on the basis of acquisitions (Monsanto, Union Carbide); • Diversification into coal and mining were not very successful: divestments appeared in the early 1990s	• 1899–1914: very active involvement of government – the Navy recognises the strategic importance of oil as ship fuel – in support of William Knox D'Arcy's (founder of APOC) ventures in oil exploration abroad. APOC became 'national champion' and foreign policy in oil – including military action – mirrored the firm's interests (more than in the case of the US firms); • acquisitions in Bahrain, Qatar, Iraq with strong government involvement; • 1914: British government buys control into APOC; • *Interbellum*: protected exploration and markets in colonies; • Prime concessionary in offshore oil fields in British territorial waters (close consultation with own government); • 1987: BP privatised; but, after it became clear that Kuwait had acquired a 21.6% stake in BP, the government intervened to reduce this stake to less than 10%

Rank Company Founded (Incorporated)	Historic strategic feature	Salient trade barrier
12 **Matsushita** 1917 (1935)	• Started as an electronic plugs manufacturing company; • Prewar period: rapid growth of the firm in radios, batteries, electric motors; • Since 1950s joint venture with Philips; • Rapid growth through differentiation; • Created *de facto* standard in VCR (VHS system); • 1990: $6.9 bn acquisition of Universal/MCA (software)	• Prewar period: firm operated as a *zaibatsu* (with close links to the ruling elite); • 1950s: international alliances stimulated by Japanese government to get access to foreign technology; • Prime beneficiary of trade barriers in electronics and government support programmes (See also Hitachi, **10**)
13 **Mobil** c.1866 (1931)	• Offshoot of Standard Oil: Socony Vacuum Corp (SVO); • Took most foreign activities of Standard Oil; • Suffered much from the German occupation of Europe (14 refineries alone in Europe); • Postwar: SVO has the highest dependence on Arabic oil of all US oil firms (in 1966: 43% of its production); • 1960s: diversification into chemicals; • 1966: name change into Mobil Oil Corporation; • 1980s: search for additional sources outside Saudi Arabia; acquired Superior Oil Company (1984; $5.7 bn); • Financial difficulties prompted Mobil to decrease its level of vertical integration and move out of many retail chains, while closing down some refineries	• See Standard Oil/Exxon (**2**); • WWI loss was compensated for by considerable supplies to the military; • Mobil has one of the closest links with the Saudi leaders (supported by the oil diplomacy of the US government), implying more secure supplies than other firms; • Mobil – like many of the American oil multinationals – has been a major supporter of the American involvement in the 1991 Gulf War: in return the company will probably get improved concessions from both Kuwait and Saudi Arabia
14 **Volkswagen** 1937	• 1930s: Porsche's quest for financiers for its move into car production succeeded only under Hitler; • WWII: military production; • End 1940s: 'people's car' (beetle) introduced; • 1960s: set up of production in USA (retreated in 1980s); • 1960s–1990s: growth and internationalisation through acquisitions (Audi, SEAT, Skoda, Trabant); • 1990s: sizeable restructuring of factories; productivity coalition with IG-Metal, layoffs abroad	• Until 1960: wholly state-owned; • 1950s: Beetle was built under postwar British administrators; • After 1960s: declining state ownership; 1990: 20% owned by Federal government, 20% owned by Lower Saxony state government; provides subsidies and training facilities; • Acquisitions involved state subsidies and other trade barriers (by host governments); SEAT acquisition in 1994 saved from bankruptcy amongst others by Spanish government subsidies

Table 9.4 Continued

Rank Company Founded (Incorporated)	Historic strategic feature	Salient trade barrier
15 Siemens c.1847 (1897)	• Start-up: booming telegraph business, very international (for instance in British empire); • Since 1877 produced also telephones, dynamos and electricity and electric power equipment, even explosives; • Problems after outbreak of WWI continued until 1935; • Postwar: continued diversification into (see below); • 1980s: growth through acquisition; • 1990: extremely diversified firm, but primarily in public procurement: military (4–10%), power plants (17%); medical techn. (10%), telecom (22%)	• WWI increased orders for particular equipment, but in general hurt Siemens' business due to assets abroad that were seized; • 1935: strong revival of firm due to Nazi procurement; • 1980s: two-thirds of business in (semi-) restricted government procurement markets; cross-subsidy for 'civil' business; • Increasing direct subsidies for core technologies (chips/computers/production equipment) by German government and European Commission; various EC trade barriers in electronics
16 Nissan 1911 (1933)	• Very difficult start-up (Kwaishishu Motor/Datsun); • 1930s–1940s: Growth through sales boom in trucks; • Postwar production based on licences (e.g. Austin, 1952); • 1960s: unsuccessful effort to enter the US market; • 1966 take-over of Prince; focus remains cars/trucks; • 1970s onwards: renewed internationalisation via exports; • 1980s: set up of production facilities in USA and Europe; • 1990s: runs into difficulties (1993: loss of $844m)	• Government procurement for trucks helped Nissan to go through difficult start-up phase; • Active government support of technology licensing; • Active government intervention in take-over of other Japanese car manufacturer (Prince); • Nissan and Toyota have been benifiaries of MITI strategies; see also Toyota (**5**)
17 Philip Morris c.1847 (1919)	• Started as tobacco firm (introduction of Turkish style cigarettes: remnant of involvement in Crimean War); • *Interbellum*: focused on innovative marketing and increased control over distribution; • 1939–1942: rapid growth (doubling of sales); • 1970s: diversification in beverages through acquisitions (brewing, Seven Up in 1978) was not successful; • 1960s–1990s: duopoly on the US cigarette market (Morris and Reynolds) created high profits; • 1970s: rapid internationalisation (escape declining US market) made Marlboro world's best selling cigarette; • 1980s: successful acquisitions into foods: Gen. Foods ($5.75 bn); Kraft Inc. (1988 $13 bn); Jacobs Suard (1990 $4 bn; more than 50% of PM's business became non-tobacco	• US market: until 1911 fully dominated by the American Tobacco Trust Monopoly (condoned by non-implementation of antitrust regulation); • WWII increased the consumption of cigarettes produced in the USA enormously (closed market, partly defence); • Postwar: American market has been difficult to enter due to high marketing costs, the condoned oligopoly of a few firms (Philip Morris and Reynolds primarily) and a 75% 'local content' on American cigarettes (still in existence in the 1990s); • The extraordinary postwar cash flow enabled rapid internationalisation in the 1960s and 1970s and a rapid acquisition/diversification strategy in the 1980s, at the time the cigarette market in the USA started to decline

Table 9A Continued

Rank Company Founded (Incorporated)	Historic strategic feature	Salient trade barrier
18 **Samsung** 1938	• Start: operated under Japanese colonial rule; as a general trading company (*chaebol*) experienced strong growth during the war; • 1950s: diversified into transportation, real estate, banking, milling; rapid growth (e.g. 1700% in 1951); • 1990s: Samsung has become the largest of Korean *chaebol*; which are all producing in: shipbuilding, semiconductors, financial services and textiles; Samsung is also in: electronics, machinery and chemicals	• 1950s: major gain from supplies to United Nations' forces; • Postwar perod: *chaebol* received most (1) export subsidies, (2) loans, (3) investment licences, (4) could take over state-owned firms on favourable terms; continued active government intervention in company strategy; • Samsung not allowed to diversify into car manufacturing (1981 and 1986 laws allowed only two producers) nor to enter into an alliance with Chrysler; • 1993: important restructuring, again spurred by government
19 **Fiat** 1899	• Started as producer of automobiles and engine parts; • Expansion and diversification in WWI; became conglomerate of various manufacturing enterprises; • Rapid growth in 1930s; • Postwar: Marshall loans from US government; • 1950s: growth via lucrative NATO contracts; • 1960s problems due to EC membership, Italian tax policies; • In 1980s: major restructuring continues (for instance sell-off telecommunications subsidiary); still around 5% of turnover remains for military	• High tariff protection initially; result: 80% of all cars in Italy were from Italy in *interbellum*; growth aided by Mussolini's modernisation programme; Cross-subsidies from military markets; • 1950s: France and Italy highest tariff (c. 30%) in cars; • Strict and low quota (maximum of 1,800 cars) for imports of Japanese cars until 1992; • Fiat major beneficiary of location subsidies (in Southern Italy); • Especially Italian government favours strict 'local content' rules in the EC
20 **Unilever** late 19th century (1929)	• V.d. Bergh (one of the Dutch founders) could 'copy' French margarine processing technology; • 1880s: Lever expansion of soap sales in Commonwealth (North America, Australia and South America); 1915: Lever diversified into margarine; • Tradition of extreme vertical integration of both companies to produce raw components in-house; • 1929: merger of Lever and Margarine Union; • Postwar period: internationalisation of production, marketing and R&D; EEC creation triggered strategy change; • 1980s: massive restructuring: selling of most services and non-core business, while acquiring smaller companies all around the world in detergents, foods, cosmetics and perfume, specialty chemicals and agribusiness; non-core product accounted in 1982 for 29%, and in 1993 only for 3% of turnover	• 1869–1910 policy of Dutch government to deny international patenting law made copying of products possible; • 1914: UK government asked Lever to produce margarine in order to safeguard food imports (threatened by the Germans); • Both companies had exclusive colonial supply base as well as markets for considerable time; • In particular the food industry remains strongly regulated and open to manifold trade restriction between world regions; large parts of the food industry, however, are also object of subsidy policies for farmers, and technology policy in particular in support of developments in biotechnology

Table 9A Continued

Rank Company Founded (Incorporated)	Historic strategic feature	Salient trade barrier
21 **ENI** c.1920 (1953)	• Origins in AGIP: Azienda Generale Italiana Petroli; • Ente Nazionale Idrocarburi received monopoly exploitation rights in Po Valley, Italy; • Later on company tried to diversify in (petro)chemical and metallurgy, sometimes through direct investments, often through acquisitions, mostly in Italy; • 1989: merger of Montedison and Enichem to create one of the largest chemical companies in the world	• AGIP was created by government to pursue oil and gas exploration in Italy; later – asked for by the government – other trailing energy companies were acquired by ENI; • ENI has been state owned since its foundation and heavily supported in various ways by the Italian government; for instance in 1973/4 Shell and BP left the Italian market (complaining the government did not allow them sufficient profit margins) in favour of ENI
22 **Elf-Aquitaine** 1939 (1976)	• 1939: gas exploration in France; • 1950s: gas and oil in France and Algerian Sahara; forward (vertical) integration; • 1970s: start of efforts to diversify (in pharmaceuticals)	• State owned since its foundation; WWII: Vichy government started oil and gas production in Aquitaine region; • Postwar: de Gaulle strongly supported oil exploration by the company in France, its colonies and French protectorates
23 **Nestlé** (1866)	• Started as Anglo-Swiss Condensed Milk Company in Switzerland; quickly became the leading producer of condensed milk in Europe based on an export strategy; • Due to import duties company expanded after 1900 in Europe; WWI prompted Nestlé to move to other product sites around the world as well; multi-domestic internationalisation process gained pace in the 1930s; • Postwar period: expansion through many acquisitions; • Diversified to non-food business only in 1974; • 1990s: largest food company in the world with factories in 60 countries	• Food industry has always been heavily regulated, including in Switzerland; company always adopted a very low-profile public strategy internationally partly because of this circumstance; • Nescafé and evaporated and powdered milk products were in heavy demand from American military; biggest increase in booming sales in 1941–5 period appeared in the United States
24 **Chevron** (1906)	• Originated from the Pacific Coast Oil Company (1879) amongst other firms; • Incorporated as Standard Oil Company of California (Socal); gained almost monopoly on US West Coast; • Postwar: Kept strong US production basis and wide net of gas stations adding to low transportation costs and high profit margins; dependence on Saudi Arabian oil became more than three-quarters of Socal's proven reserves; • 1984: name change, Chevron Corporation; undertook a record $13.2 bn acquisition of Gulf corporation, making it the leading domestic retailer in the USA	• See also Mobil/Exxon (**2/13**); • Allied powers won the World Wars due to ample supply of oil from domestic basis of which Socal was the national production leader in the United States by the 1920s; • Saudi Arabic interests of Socal have always been heavily backed by the US government

Table 9A Continued

Rank Company Founded (Incorporated)	Historic strategic feature	Salient trade barrier
25 Toshiba c.1875 (1939)	• Original company (Shibaura Seisakusho) focused on (steam) engines, electric lighting and broadcast equipment; • Was partly owned by General Electric (USA): 30% in 1939; share lowered later on; • *Interbellum*: continued solid growth; • 1960s: ran into troubles; major restructuring took place; merger with shipbuilding and engineering firms; • 1970s: further diversification and internationalisation into computers, consumer and medical electronics, chips; • 1980s: entered into increasing number of alliances with IBM, Motorola, AT&T (aimed at entering the Japanese market, partners are considered stronger); or with firms like Siemens in chips (partner is considered weaker)	• The firm was one of the first 'products' of the newly formed (1870) Japanese Ministry of Industry that aimed at integrating foreign technology with Japanese business; • Government self-sufficiency policies supported firm in first half of 20th century in many ways; • Part of *Denden* family (see also Hitachi/**10**); • Fifth largest defence contractor in Japan (1990: 2% of total sales); cross-subsidisation possibilities due to sizeable protected procurement markets (e.g. also train systems)
26 Du Pont 1802 (1915)	• Prime product in 19th century: gunpowder, explosives; in 1905: 75% of US market, resulted in antitrust suit in 1912; • 1930: discovery of nylon by Du Pont; • 1980s: growth through acquisitions: took over Comoco oil; other acquisitions made it world's largest chemical firm	• Closed defence procurement markets: explosives, etc. • In 1952: 30,000 patents and trade secrets of IG-Farben cartel (see e.g. Hoechst) were acquired by allied forces and given to firms like Du Pont; • Protected – 'strategic' – markets in fibres (nylon, polyamide, etc.); cost-plus development contracts
27 Texaco c.1901 (1926)	• Founded in early boom years of Texas oil industry; • 1930: expansion abroad in Columbia and Venezuela; • 1950s and 1960s: internationalisation (partly) through acquisitions; • 1970s: selling of part of the business	• WWII: 30% of production for defence; • Made use of federally sponsored pipelines; • Start of Butadiene for synthetic rubber gave Texaco a start in petrochemical industry (helped also by gradual acquisition of government owned butane plant)
28 Chrysler 1925	• 1920s and 1930s: Rapid growth especially in USA; • 1940s: growth through war production; • 1950s–1960s: military production continued (for instance Saturn booster rocket); minority share in Mitsubishi; • Threat of bankruptcy in 1970s; rapid retreat to the Northern America region: selling of foreign subsidiaries (e.g. Talbot); once recovered acquired American Motors; • 1980s: continued restructuring (incl. major losses and layoffs; gradual withdrawal from Mitsubishi Motors)	• Flexible trade regime in 1920s implied big trade barriers; • Military procurement (cost-plus contracts) made cross-subsidisation possible, stabilised business in vital periods of the company; • Postwar: gradual decline of tariffs: 10% in 1950, 2.8% in 1983; • 1979: guaranteed loans from Federal government saved company from bankruptcy; • Since 1981: VER of 1.8 million cars a year with Japan settled especially upon request of Chrysler

Table 9A Continued

Rank Company Founded (Incorporated)	Historic strategic feature	Salient trade barrier
29 **Renault** 1899	• WWI: produced aviation engines and light tanks; • Penalty for Nazi collaboration: nationalisation; • Postwar period: rapid growth; regional localisation of production (in Belgium and Spain); internationalisation to USA through acquisition of American Motors; • 1980s: firm ran into serious difficulties; divestiture of American Motors, collaboration talks with Volvo; • 1992-3: merger with Volvo announced/denounced	• Pre-WWII: major business in defence markets; • Since WWII: state-owned firm; received substantial subsidies; • 1950s: growth behind high tariff walls (up to 30%); • 1980s: 3% import quota on Japanese cars; restructuring under government tutelage (several *plans de filières* aimed at the whole industrial complex, *Contracts de Plan* aimed at state enterprises; • 1993: merger with Volvo denounced amongst others due to continued state involvement in Renault
30 **Honda** 1938 (1948)	• Started as supplier of piston rings to Toyota; • 1950: first motor cycle produced; • 1964: shift of control obtained from dealers to Honda; • 1967: first cars and trucks produced; early internationalisation in particular towards USA; • 1980s: minority share in Rover, terminated in 1994 (due to BMW acquisition of Rover)	• Cross-subsidisation of motor to car business (mid-1970s); • See other Japanese car manufacturers for particular trade barriers in cars; Honda remained a relatively marginal player in Japan (influencing for instance its position in quota allocation)
31 **Philips** c.1891 (1912)	• Anton Philips could copy (without remunerations) the light bulb technology of Edison; • Post WWII: diversification into telecom, etc.; • Internationalisation on the basis of multi-domestic strategy made Philips a 'national champion' in many countries; strategy of extreme vertical integration; technology push oriented company; • 1980s: back to core business in light and consumer electronics: CD, HDTV, etc.; retreat from many closed markets (telecom, defence); struck very large number of strategic alliances; efforts towards vertical deintegration; major layoffs in 'Centurion-operation', initiator of many EC cooperation programmes (e.g ESPRIT and EC1992)	• 1869-1910 policy of Dutch government to deny international patenting law enabled Philips's strategy; • favourable treatment in many countries; subsidies because of strategic nature of industry (chip projects); • telecom and defence contracts (1980s: around 25%) create ample possibilities for cross-subsidisation; • 1980s: EC tariff policies and local content regulation in consumer electronics and chips

Table 9A Continued

Rank / Company / Founded / (Incorporated)	Historic strategic feature	Salient trade barrier
32 **Sony** (1946)	• Started as Tokyo Tsuhin Kogyo (TTK); quickly moved from home appliances to electronic consumer goods: tape recorders, radios, television, videos, etc.; • TTK had difficulty in doing business via the traditional Japanese trading houses; required an own internationalisation strategy and a strong brand name (Sony, first invented for TTK's radios, since 1958 the whole company's name); • Lost battle for standard in videos, but won that in walkmans; CD-technology developed in collaboration with Philips (to get the standard worldwide adopted); • End of 1980s further move downstream: costly acquisition strategy in US 'software' for consumer electronics (1987 CBS records; 1989: $3.4 bn acquisition of Columbia Pictures); in most other sectors, the company still adopted a 'going alone' strategy	• Both founders of Sony (Morita and Ibuka) started in the defence industry; • In many respects Sony has been left out of many collaborative ventures in Japan, but has also profited from the relatively closed nature of the postwar Japanese market; • Since the 1980s Sony has been heavily involved in High-Definition Television (HDTV), an area that is very much influenced by government regulation and open to major trade policy disputes between the USA, Japan and Europe
33 **ABB** 1883 (ASEA); 1891 (BBC)	• 1933: ASEA's cartel with Ericsson created control over electrical equipment in Sweden; • Production of both companies primarily aimed at closed procurement markets: electricity, locomotives, (nuclear) power equipment; • 1988: ASEA BBC (Brown Boverie Co.) merger; • 1989: acquisition of Westinghouse (USA)	• Dependence on government procurement: more than 30%; in many countries ASEA and Brown Boverie were treated like (semi) 'national champions'; • likelihood of cost-plus contracts and cross-subsidisation to 'civilian business' is considerable; • In 1991, the Industrial Bank and largest shareholder of ASEA (Enskilda Banken) was sheltered from bankruptcy by the Swedish government
34 **Alcatel Alsthom** 1898 (CGE)	• Firm was part of Compagnie General d'Electricité, a large and diversified electricity conglomerate; • 1980s: major restructuring product portfolio; • Specialisation: 80–90% in railway, power plants (Alsthom) and telecommunications (Alcatel)	• 1938 nationalised; 1981 renationalised; 1987 denationalised again; • Various periods, but especially in the 1980s: restructuring under direct tutelage of French government (e.g. take over of telecom from and divestiture of defence electronics to Thomson-CSF); • Heavily influenced by government procurement policies in many countries; relatively closed markets; cost-plus contracts

Table 9A Continued

Rank Company Founded (Incorporated)	Historic strategic feature	Salient trade barrier
35 **Boeing** 1916 (1934)	• 1934: government investigation led to divestiture; • Until 1953 primarily focused on military production; • 1953: major success achieved in the production of new civilian/military jet (B-707); highly profitable, major source of internationalisation; • 1950s–1960s: expanding aerospace business (NASA); • In 1989: 23% of sales to the military, rapidly declined to 10% of sales in 1994	• Military and NASA procurement on the basis of cost-plus contracts has meant cross-subsidies for Boeing's civilian aspirations; • For B-707 (civilian) firm could make use of the government owned B-52 construction facilities; • Export orders (especially to authoritarian countries) were never achieved without direct government involvement; • American Eximbank – giving export credits at low tariffs – is popularly labelled the 'Boeing Bank' (after its largest client)
36 **Procter & Gamble** 1837 (1890)	• 1850s: rapid growth as a soap and candle company; • 1860s: shortage of rosins due to civil war made P&G experiment with silicate of soda which later became a key ingredients in modern soaps and detergents; • Until end of WWII hardly any international operations; rapid expansion in home market; • Since 1953: continued growth in detergents, personal care, over-the-counter drugs, cosmetics (like Unilever); • Since 1950s: acquisition strategy; prime aim: get a sufficient share of the market and profits will follow	• 1860s (Civil War) until 1940s: often high trade barriers in most relevant products; • WWII: limited influence; 'Procter and Gamble Defense' remained small part of P&G business
37 **Hoechst** 1863	• First 40 years primarily dye production; • After 19th century: concentration on pharmacology; diversification after WWII; • 1924–52: rapid growth in cartel (IG-Farben with Bayer and BASF), world's strongest chemical cluster; • Post-WWII: thrived on growth of German industry; • 1980s: aims towards innovative 'high-chem' image	• IG-Farben was one of the staunchest supporters of Hitler and vice versa; this was a very profitable relationship (firms could make use of slave labour, reinforce innovative potential); • Pharmaceutical firms often operate in relatively closed markets with very specific national regulations and government-owned procurement agencies
38 **Peugeot** c.1891 (1896)	• Started with the purchase of Daimler engine; • WWI created rapid growth market; • 1929: introduction of 201 model; • Production almost halted during WWII; • Postwar period: take over of Citroën, Talbot; • 1980s–1990s: withdrawal on internationalisation track, major restructuring (layoffs) undertaken	• Profited from military procurement in the early decades of its existence; • Increasing trade barriers in the 1930s by French government; • Acquisition of Talbot under tutelage of government; • Beneficiary of a variety of subsidies, credits and the like; • 1980s: restructuring behind a 3% import quota on Japanese cars

Table 9A Continued

Rank Company Founded (Incorporated)	Historic strategic feature	Salient trade barrier
39 **BASF** 1861 (1952)	• 1904 cartel in German chemical industry; In WWI and WWII considered most critical industry to defence; • 1930: growth through domestic and foreign acquisitions; • After WWII: growth and major acquisitions; • 1952: split-up of IG-Farben in BASF, Hoechst, Bayer and nine smaller companies; • 1960s: diversification into oil business; 1968: acquired Whithersall (half of German potash, quarter of natural gas market); internationalisation by acquisitions and alliances in the USA; • 1980s: diversification strategy (e.g. in main frames)	• Member of IG-Färben cartel and beneficiary of many trade policy barriers: see also Hoechst (**37**)
40 **NEC** 1898 (1899)	• Started as a 54% subsidiary of Western Electric (USA); joined the Sumitomo group in 1930s; • Government sales were a major source of expansion over first 50 years; • 1960s–1970s: moved into computers with Toshiba; established foreign offices (Asia, USA) for computer business; • Like Hitachi, Fujitsu, Toshiba, Mitsubishi Electric and Oki, NEC has been in all major government sponsored research projects since the mid-1970s; • 1990: 2% of turnover in defence business	• Since 1931: gradual withdrawal of US interests under Japanese 'natural monopoly' over cable communications in imperialist Japan; • Postwar interest by US investors in NEC was gradually reduced to zero by 1978 (aided by government intervention and regulation); • Member of *Denden* family: cross-subsidy in telecommunications; NEC and Fujitsu have also been the main beneficiaries of preferential procurement policies of NTT in computers; • Joint venture with Toshiba backed up by Japanese government
41 **Daewoo** (1967)	• In 1967, created out of 25 firms of earlier origin; • Very diversified firm (*chaebol*): shipbuilding, semiconductors, financial services and textiles; • 1980s: slight and temporary relaxation of government patronage resulted in a number of joint ventures with US and European firms (for instance Sikorsky and GM); • Acquisition strategy at home continued abroad, as prime bearer of internationalisation; As a result: debt increased considerably; • 1989: increasing labour unrest (with unrecognised labour unions) prompted management to increase wages	• 1975: licensed as a general trading company by the government; • See Samsung (**18**): restructuring under government tutelage and a wealth of imposed trade barriers (since 1962); firm had to take over ailing companies (comparable to IRI, INI and ENI); • Like other *chaebol* Daewoo is a prime defence contractor with around 10% of its business in this protected market implying considerable cross-subsidisation possibilities; • 1987: seven-year moratorium granted on Daewoo's debt to the Korean Development Bank (as well as further loans and subsidies) bailed out debt-ridden Daewoo

Table 9A Continued

Rank Company Founded (Incorporated)	Historic strategic feature	Salient trade barrier
42 **Fujitsu** 1935	• Firm was created as spin-off of Fuji Electric (which still is a major shareholder); • Go-it-alone strategy where most other Japanese computer firms had alliances with US firms; • Biggest computer company in Japan; • 1970s: take over of Amdahl (IBM offspring) spurred own computer technology; • 1980s: Suffered major penalties for illegal copying of American computer technology; • Important defence contractor (1989: 4% of turnover); • Take over of ICL in 1991	• Part of *Denden* family in telecom procurement markets; • 1960s: Buy-Japan policies, tariffs, import controls; creation of JECC institute provided financial assistance to computer industry; encouraged by MITI, IBM licensed patents especially to Fujitsu; • 1970s: 60% of R&D in computer industry provided by the government; • Restructuring of computer industry under tutelage of government: Fujitsu–Hitachi alliance, but also: Oki, Toshiba and Mitsubishi left computer production; • 1980s: VLSI and other government coordinated projects helped Fujitsu increase its capabilities in core technologies; acquisition of ICL: indirect subisidies of UK government
43 **Bayer** 1865	• Organised/headed IG-Farben cartel (see also BASF and Hoechst); • 1930s: internationalisation through exports and foreign acquisitions; • 1952: dismantling of cartel, but most important segment of firm remains pharmacology (for instance aspirin)	• Cartel created *de facto* quota, protected profit margins; • Early 20th century: Bayer tried to exchange patents for colonies with the British (which did not succeed and contributed to the outbreak of WWI); • Postwar success of Bayer: partly because the Allied Forces allowed Bayer to keep the aspirin formula
44 **Mitsubishi Electric** 1868 (1921)	• Spin-off of Mitsubishi trading (*zaibatsu*) • *Interbellum:* 1923 alliance with Westinghouse (hydraulic generators); slowly moved out of this alliance; • rapid growth in 1930s; export orientation; • Postwar: diversification into all parts of electronics; • 1960s: production facilities in Thailand and Europe, close relations remain with both Westinghouse and General Electric; • 1990: third largest defence contractor (4% of sales)	• 1930s: radio plus other military projects as primary source of growth; • Postwar period saw a wealth of trade measures to help the 'infant' Japanese electronics industry: see Hitachi, NEC
45 **Total** 1924	• Compagnie Française des Pétroles was founded to control the exploitation of French oil rights in Mesopotamia; • Continuously aimed at forward (vertical) integration	• From its inception: close government tutelage and related trade barriers; • Since 1931: state owns 35% of shares (40% of voting rights); • Acivities primarily in France and French colonies (see Elf/**22**)

Table 9A Continued

Rank Company Founded (Incorporated)	Historic strategic feature	Salient trade barrier
46 **Amoco** 1911	• Former Standard Oil (Indiana); firm created after 1892 divestiture, primarily as oil refining company; • 1920s: downstream investments to secure oil supply; upstream investments in transport (primarily in USA); • 1930s: difficulties, sold important foreign interests, retreated on foreward integration (leasing gas stations); • 1940s: major investments in pipelines and technology; • 1950s: largest US oil company, (re)internationalisation; • 1970s: move into chemicals and new materials; closing of Iranian facilities dropped foreign oil interests by one-third; • 1980s: expansion in oil and gas through acquisitions (Dome Petroleum, $4.2 bn) and joint ventures in fibres; • Name change to Amoco (1985) as ultimate consequence of brand name strategy, started in 1960s	• See Exxon (**2**); • Firm grew rapidly in national market behind considerable trade barriers; • Wartime state support for infrastructure (pipelines, Texas–East Coast) and new technologies (such as wax coatings, synthetic rubber, or high octane fuels) meant a head start for the firm's postwar civil activities; the margins earned in these areas in the national market facilitated Amoco's internationalisation strategy in the 1950s
47 **Mitsubishi Motors** c.1917 (1970)	• 1917: Mitsubishi Shipbuilding produced first car; • 1970: subsidiary of Mitsubishi Heavy Industry (**49**); • 1971: Chrysler bought 15% stake in the firm; in the course of the 1970s and 1980s stake slowly declined; • 1970s and 1980s: internationalisation in Asian region independently, in Europe and USA through alliances (with Daimler-Benz, Volvo, Chrysler)	• See Toyota and Nissan for relevant trade barriers in cars; • Enforcement of Foreign Capital Law (1950, abolished only in 1980) prohibited foreign firms to take a controlling interest in Japanese firms, including the car industry; • Part take-over of Volvo Car (Netherlands) makes Mitsubishi Motors the only 'national' car producer in the Netherlands and thus more open for government support (loans, subsidies, tax relief)
48 **Nippon Steel** 1857	• 1934: integrated the Japanese iron and steel industry; • Postwar: industry split up, partly remerged in 1970; • Rapid growth due to booming Japanese industry; • 1980s: erosion of Japanese steel market; started to diversify (also new materials, computers, biotechnology); modest internationalisation: joint-ventures with US steel companies	• 1930s: iron and steel restructuring under government auspices; • 1950s and 1960s: steel industry has been one of the major 'targeted' industries in Japan (buy Japanese, government supported restructuring, cartels, etc.)
49 **Mitsubishi Heavy Ind.** 1880 (1964)	• Leading shipbuilder throughout most of its history; • Since mid-1970s: rapid diversification into heavy machinery, power plants, construction equipment, aircraft, rocket design; 1989: shipbuilding constitutes only 11% of sales; • 1990: MHI is by far the largest defence contractor in Japan (19% of its turnover)	• Since early 20th century, shipbuilding in Japan thrived on government (defence-oriented) contracts and was restructured several times under state tutelage (e.g. Shipbuilding Promotion Law); • Aiming at defence procurement and other public procurement markets (utilities) implies cost-plus contracts, cross-subsidisation to other businesses and similar trade barriers

Table 9A Continued

Rank Company Founded (Incorporated)	Historic strategic feature	Salient trade barrier
50 **Thyssen** 1891 (1953)	• Started by purchasing coal mines; • 1889: upstream integration; start of steel production; • Rapid expansion abroad; • Confiscation of foreign sites after WWI: • 1926: cartel with four German coal and steel firms; • 1930s–1940s: war production (not wholeheartedly); • Only in 1953: restart as a public company; Allianz insurance holds more than 25% of stock; • 1950s–1960s: booming steel demand, acquisition strategy; • 1970s: diversification efforts; • 1980s: move into high-tech transport sector	• End 19th, early 20th century military procurement helped expansion; • 1951: start of European Coal and Steel Community in order to restructure European industry; support of existing national champions, quasi-cartel arrangements, etc.; • Move into government procurement markets (e.g. rapid rail transport), but with difficulties in internationalisation; • 1988: end of quota system of European Commission, and more critical stance against direct subsidies accelerated restructuring of steel producers (motivated many mergers, for instance, between Thyssen, Krupp and Metallgesellschaft)
51 **Pepsico** c.1890 (1919)	• Dependent upon international price/supply of sugar; • Bankruptcy in 1923 due to supply problems; • WWII: acquisition of sugar plantation in Cuba; • 1960: diversification and back in food industry; 1970s and 1980s: growth through acquisition; • 1970s: major marketing successes in the (former) Soviet Union	• History of company is closely related to US trade policies on sugar; extremely strong quota regulation towards sugar imports (assessed at a tariff equivalent of more than 200%) also includes products containing sugar; for non-US software drink producers this barrier has the effect of very strict local content regulation; • US patent laws created barriers for new entrants; this left high profit margins open to established brands like Pepsi and Coca-Cola, and enabled Pepsico's diversification and acquisition strategy; • Foreign policy of Nixon administration supported Pepsi; foreign policy of Carter administration supported Coca-Cola (China)
52 **Robert Bosch** 1886	• Leader in ignition systems; in 1914: Bosch had 70% of its business in the USA (much more than in the 1990s); • WWI: forced retreat out of USA; • 1930s: strong growth at home; • Postwar period: rapid growth first at home, later internationally; diversification strategy into white goods, telecommunications (26% of 1985 sales), professional electronics	• Loss of American business meant a 'subsidy' to US ignition suppliers (contributed to their technological sophistication); • 1930s: military procurement spurred sales and technology; • Postwar: growth of Bosch car business helped by state-owned Volkswagen; cross-subsidies from closed markets (e.g. telecommunications) to other civilian business

Table 9A Continued

Rank Company Founded (Incorporated)	Historic strategic feature	Salient trade barrier
53 **United Technologies** 1934	• Growth through acquisition created a diversified firm; • UT has successfully focused on becoming one of the largest members of the 'military industrial complex'; • Pratt and Witney supplies half of all aircraft engines	• Military cross-subsidisation of (international) civilian business; • Periods of rapid growth linked to intensified military activities (WWII, Korean War, etc.); • 1989: still 30% of turnover reaped in military sector; • 'Buy America Act' very relevant for United Technology's business
54 **INI** 1941	• The Instituto Nacional de Industria was founded by government decree and modelled after Italian IRI (6); • Merged a number of already existing companies that specialised in mining, fertilizers and electricity; • Experienced an enormous growth in the 1940s; • 1950s: alliances with foreign firms (e.g SEAT-Fiat); • 1980s–1990s: major restructuring, discussion on privatisation and divestiture, e.g. led to SEAT sale to VW (1984)	• 1939–59 has been Spain's period of autarky (based on the 1939 Law of Protection): implying nationalisations and government-led industrialisation; • INI has remained a state-controlled holding company; even companies that were sold (like the SEAT subsidiary) have remained state-sponsored in many ways into the 1990s
55 **ICI** c.1871	• Started as a dynamite producer (Nobel); • WWI: thrived on German dye embargo; 1926: British cartel formed; • Coordinated chemical production of the British throughout two world wars; not dismantled like Du Pont or IG-Farben (in different periods); • Since 1984: growth through acquisition	• Started with near monopoly over chemical markets in Britain and Commonwealth colonies (UK response to German dye embargo); • First part of 20th century: government-supported strategy: state paid for the construction of plants and ICI managed these plants; • Big cash reserves of the firm (earned in relatively protected markets) facilitated acquisition strategy
56 **PDVSA** c.1878 (1976)	• Primarily focused on oil, since 1978 also diversified to coal; • Tries to move downstream into refineries abroad (in particular the USA and Europe)	• Since 1943 Venezuelan government has gradually been taking control of the own oil industry; • 1959: no further concessions to foreign-owned companies; • 1976: full nationalisation of industry
57 **PEMEX** (1938)	• State monopoly; aimed at national vertical integration; • Since 1959 the firm has been in basic petrochemicals; concentrates on domestic refineries	• Firm was created due to expropriation of US and British oil interests; major state involvement, a wide variety of trade barriers exist

Table 9A Continued

Rank Company Founded (Incorporated)	Historic strategic feature	Salient trade barrier
58 **Conagra** (1919)	• Started as Nebraska Consolidated Mills Company; • First 25 years: milling boomed due to war efforts; • Gained foothold in prepared foods market; divested again in 1956 to concentrate on basic commodities: grains and feeds; supplemented by acquisition strategy; • Limited internationalisation; 1965: expansion into EC; • Listed on NY Stock exchange as Conagra in 1973; • 1975: bad acquisitions almost caused bankruptcy; • Continued internationalisation, acquisition and diversification into food throughout the 1980s	• Started production in relatively closed US food market (gained sizeable economies of scale and an oligopolistic position); • Growth first appeared behind various trade barriers, only much later did internationalisation appear; • The grain and animal feed markets in the United States have always been extremely regulated, and are still object of international trade debate (and partly exempt from GATT regulation); in 1980s the share of US agricultural imports covered by quota-like barriers increased from 6% to 18%
59 **Mazda** 1920	• Start: machine tools, motorcycles and light trucks; • Only after WWII, the firm started to produce cars; • 1970s and early 1980s: saved from bankruptcy by Sumitomo bank and by Ford (minority shareholder); • Since 1970s limited internationalisation, mainly in South East Asian region and the United States; internationalisation of production capacity towards Europe hampered by difficulties with Ford Europe	• Early (prewar) growth was very much spurred by war procurement efforts and developed in relatively closed market(s); • Full take-over of the firm by its alliance partner (Ford) was blocked by government regulation; • See also Toyota (**5**) and Mitsubishi (**47**)
60 **BMW** 1913 (1917)	• Original product were aircraft engines for Austria; • Built its first car in 1929; • Since 1960s renewed growth of (sports) car business; • 1990: stepped up internationalisation, decision to locate production in the United States; acquisition of majority share in Rover (1993)	• WWI defence procurement supported the start of BMW; • Further growth in the 1930s due to Luftwaffe supplies; merger under government tutelage; • Postwar period: close collaboration with state government of Bayern; training facilities, (indirect) subsidies; internationalisation implies a wealth of funding and support by local host governments

Table 9A Continued

Rank Company Founded (Incorporated)	Historic strategic feature	Salient trade barrier
61 **Eastman** **Kodak** c.1881 (1901)	• Main focus on films and cameras since foundation; • Since 1900: internationalisation (plants and distribution centres) started in the UK; • 1920s: steady vertical integration and diversification; • 1963: introduction of 'Instamatic camera'; • 1970s: major restructuring: diversification into copiers; reduction of workforce (meeting Japanese competition); • 1980s: move into videotapes and (consumer) electronics; decentralisation into business units; • 1976–1990s: dispute with Polaroid (instant cameras); Kodak had to pay about $1bn in charges; • 1990s: sell of non-core (e.g. household) business	• In particular Kodak has been defence contractor in sophisticated optical components; implied cost-plus contracts, the defence market as test-bed for new technologies and cross-subsidisation towards civil business (Eastman had been explicitly civil-oriented); During WWI: aerial cameras, aeroplane wing-coating materials and lenses for gas masks were developed; WWII spurred the development and production of equipment and film; • Since 1960s: military contracts became supplemented by cost-plus contracts with NASA, a leading user of advanced optical equipment
62 **Nippon** **Oil** 1888 (1893)	• Company was founded as result of Meiji restoration: create independent production base; • Focus on domestic market and Middle East supplies; • 1950s: joint venture with Caltex (USA); • 1960s: sustained growth interrupted by 1970s oil crisis; • 1980s–1990s: sharing of marketing and transport of Nippon Oil and Mitsubishi Oil; actively tried to reduce dependence on Middle East supplies by spreading sources (1991 already 37% of supplies from South East Asia); joint deals with Texaco, Chevron in US exploration	• 1900–WWII: Japanese government closed national oil market; only one refinery with foreign interests existed; • Postwar: Allied Forces initially tied Japanese oil industry to five oil majors (Shell, Mobil, Exxon, Texaco, Chevron); • 1950s onwards: Japanese government actively tried to reduce its dependence on foreign oil companies; 1962: Petroleum Industry Law increased regulation on foreigners; 1967: creation of the Japan Petroleum Development Corporation and active encouragement of smaller companies into one big company, called Kyodo Sekiyu; • 1980s: MITI actively pursued rationalisation of own oil industry
63 **Dow** **Chemical** c.1890	• 1900–20: rapid growth in bromide production; • WWI: went into manufacturing of phenol and magnesium which later played an important role for the growth of Dow Chemical: phenol was instrumental in the development of plastics, whereas magnesium became an important input in aviation; • WWII: profitable supplies to the British economy; • Postwar period: prime supplier to Defence Department (produced e.g. Napalm during Vietnam War)	• US and German chemical cartel fought an international 'bromide war' (also contributing to WWI); • WWI: Dow was more or less pressed into the production of phenol and magnesium by the US government; • After WWI: large number of measures taken by the US government to safeguard an independent American chemical industry (because of its strategic relevance in times of military conflict); continued after WWII: created cross-subsidies for civilian business and other trade barriers to foreign chemical firms

Table 9A Continued

Rank Company Founded (Incorporated)	Historic strategic feature	Salient trade barrier
64 **Repsol** 18th century (1987)	• Collection of over two hundred state-controlled oil, gas and chemical companies; • Merged to become Repsol in 1987; dominates Spanish oil production and almost completely controls distribution; • Late 1980s: internationalisation and acquisition strategy to tackle the threat posed by increasing inroads made on the Spanish domestic market	• 1927: decree by Spanish government to expropriate all foreign and domestic oil companies; • All restructuring developed under close government tutelage; • 1986: Spain joins the EC; start of a continued struggle with the EC Commission over liberalisation of the Spanish oil market; • Spanish government sold part of its shares; remains two-thirds owner; • International acquisitions by Repsol are paid for by past monopoly profits in Spanish market
65 **Mannesmann** 1890	• Started as an international company: Deutsche-Österreichische Mannesmann Röhren-Werke; established backward integration from the production of pipes into full-scale steel production; • 1960s: major diversification effort into machinery and electronics through acquisitions; • Continued in 1980s: Kraus-Maffei acquisition (1989); • End 1980s: Thyssen, Krupp and Mannesmann bring some of their steel operations together	• See Krupp/Thyssen for German steel policies in 20th century; • Mannesmann has also been restructuring under the auspices of the European Community (crisis cartel in coal and steel industry); subsidies of German government have been relatively limited; influence on formation of clusters of firms (end of 1980s), however, considerable; • 1980s: efforts to move further into military production in order to profit from relatively closed markets; possibilities of cross-subsidisation increase
66 **Xerox** (1906)	• Started as Haloid Co. producing photographic paper; • 1946: received important patents in optic technology from Batelle Institute (Ohio); made itself the worldwide holder for these patents (in 1955); struck major alliances abroad with Rank (UK) and Fuji (Japan); • 1980s: diversification into services (insurances); • 1989/1990s: start of major downsizing operation	• Booming business during WWII: army needed Xerox's high-quality photographic paper; • Cost-plus contracts due to relations with Pentagon, could also make use of xerography knowledge of the Batelle Institute which proved very important bargaining chip in international alliances with strong partners

Table 9A Continued

Rank Company Founded (Incorporated)	Historic strategic feature	Salient trade barrier
67 Atlantic Richfield, ARCO (1870)	• Rio Grande Oil Co, predecessor of Richfield, initially experienced rapid growth in Texas/Mexico region; • Early 20th century: Atlantic focused primarily on refineries, moved downstream into oil exploration; • 1930s: major consolidation and restructuring; • 1938: oil discovery in California led to rapid growth; • 1950s: exploration abroad, most importantly in Alaska (1968: biggest discovery in western hemisphere); • 1966: merger of Atlantic and Richfield into ARCO; • 1970s: Alaska pipeline granted by US government (decision spurred also by Arab oil embargo of 1973); • 1980s–1990s: major restructuring, decentralisation and diversification into petrochemicals, coal, transportation	• Army procurement in Texas and Mexico spurred initial growth of Richfield; • WWII: regulated demand for Californian oil; • Postwar period: see Exxon (**2**); • US government has treated American companies like ARCO favourably in allotting oil exploration areas in most states, including Alaska (important additional bargaining actor in this arena: the environment movement)
68 British Aerospace 1910–1928 (1978)	• From start of company: focused on defence markets; • 1960s: 'rationalisation' of British aircraft industry; large number of British firms merged; • 1979: BA got a 20% share in Airbus consortium; • 1980s: diversification into autos (acquisition of Rover, sold to BMW in 1994); • 1989: 54% sales to military. 1993: still more than one-third in defence	• Defence procurement as cross-subsidy for other civilian business; • 1960s and 1970s: restructuring under tutelage of Royal Air Force and UK government; 1975: nationalisation of two constituting firms; • 1980s: Rover acquisition with considerable government backing; Airbus consortium backed by state subsidies and preferential procurement strategies; • 1993: 90% of profits are in defence
69 McDonnell-Douglas 1920/ 1938	• Rapid growth in 1930s–1950s period; • McDonnell and Douglas merged in 1967; • Growth in civilian aircraft in 1970s and 1980s: DC-9 and DC-10 most successful versions; suffered severely from 1980s depression in commercial airlines; • Early 1990s: still three-quarters of business is defence-related; • 1990–4: employees cut from 120,000 to 70,000	• Pentagon aircraft orders provided stability in civilian market; • 1980s: US Air Force procurement of 60 KC-10cs (almost identical military version of the DC-10 production line open until late 1980s, providing the breathing space for the development of its MD-11

Table 9.4 Continued

Rank Company Founded (Incorporated)	Historic strategic feature	Salient trade barrier
70 **Petrofina** (1920)	• 4 German oil companies in Romania were taken over by the Bank of Antwerp after their expropriation (WWI); • Lost assets during WWII; aim: vertical integration; • Postwar: acquisitions and alliances (e.g. with BP); • Consequently: spread of activities in particular over Europe (refineries in 26 different European locations)	• Strategy of firm always closely tutored by Belgian government; first production and exploration bases were in Belgium, France, UK and Belgian Congo (Zaire); • Late 1940s: Belgian government actively supported the upgrading of the country's refinery capacity, i.e. of Petrofina
71 **Hewlett Packard** 1939	• Rapid growth only in test products and instruments: • 1960s: internationalisation through acquisitions; • 1974: move into business computing; decentralisation; • 1980s: many new products (printers, ICs); takeovers (Apollo, 1989) and alliances (e.g. Hitachi, Canon); • Continued restructuring (downsizing and innovation)	• Cross-subsidisation from military procurement (see also IBM/7); engaged in microwave signal generators in World War II; growth of the firm closely linked to growth of defence electronics; • Personal ties with military: 1969–72, David Packard was deputy Secretary of Defense, after which he returned to HP
72 **Usinor** (1836) **-Sacilor** (1704) (1986)	• Company roots: French tradition of mergers of mining and steel companies, often on government initiative; • 1986 merger of two remaining French mining firms; • Chose to remain primarily in the iron and steel business; vertical forward integration through acquisitions abroad; 30% control level of distribution	• State-owned company: creates by definition a number of non-trade barriers; • French government supported firm in various manners; for the 1980–5 period the firm received an assessed amount of more than DM 20 bn in subsidies; • European trade barriers: see Thyssen (**50**)
73 **Metall-gesellschaft** c.1730 (1883)	• Started in banking; moved into materials and services; • Early internationalisation (finding resources abroad); since 1870 thrived on industrialisation of Germany; • Hit hard by WWI (subsidiaries abroad expropriated); • 1930s: hit particularly hard by the recession; • Postwar: diversification and new internationalisation; • 1980s: major restructuring activities, divestments; • 1993/4 major problems (bad financial management)	• End of 19th century: expansion in Germany enabled due to German customs union; • Nazi armaments programme saved company in 1930s; • EC coal and steel policy: see Thyssen (**50**); • 1993/4: German state government helped the firm to recover from a major crisis

Table 9A Continued

Rank Company Founded (Incorporated)	Historic strategic feature	Salient trade barrier
74 **USX** (1901)	• USX is the continuation of Carnegie Steel (1864); • Acquisition strategy, booming business in world wars; • 1980s–1990s: further diversification; acquisition of Marathon Oil (1982); 50/50 joint venture with Kobe Steel (for USX's bar and pipe-making works in Ohio); • Created a very diversified energy and steel company, that has 65% of turnover in oil and gas business	• Growth triggered several times by (preferential) war procurement; • 1969: VERs installed by USA on EC steel exports • 1980s: various trade barriers of US government saved USX from immediate bankruptcy and gave USX breathing space to restructure; • 1982: VERs imposed on Japanese steel industry (spurred the willingness of large Japanese steel firms to strike alliances abroad); • 1990s: steel continues to be object of US–EU 'fair trade' disputes
75 **Feruzzi** **Finanziaria** c.1944	• Started as a forest company; quick move into seed and grain business; • 1960s–1970s: internationalisation to Americas (North Carolina and Amazon) for production of grain; • 1962: vertical integration into: building (grainsilos), distribution (over sea); related diversification (e.g. soya); • 1980: substantial expansion of soya area; • 1980s–1990s: acquisition and alliance strategy to become the world's third largest agro-industrial group; reduction of commitment to chemicals and pharmaceutics; 1986: hostile takeover of Montedison (chemical industry); • 1989: realignment of chemical business in a joint venture with state-owned Enichem (Enimont); after intense power struggle with the state, CEO Gardini acquires 51% majority in Enimont; 1990: resale of majority in Enimont to Italian state (artificially high share prices); • 1990s: firm becomes loss-making (1993: $1.5 bn loss)	• Agricultural policies of Italy and Common Agricultural Policy of the European Union created high barriers for foreign producers; • Substantial wage subsidies to farmers from government created effective demand for sophisticated inputs; • 1980s: Soya policy of European Community: subsidies for production and trade policy protection (soya wars with USA are notorious); • Takeover of Montedison and formation of Enimont involved indirect subsidies of Italian government; resale of shares of Enimont to Italian government involved high prices and thus can be counted as a substantial cross-subsidy

Table 9A Continued

Rank Company Founded (Incorporated)	Historic strategic feature	Salient trade barrier
76 **Ciba** (1884) **Geigy** (1758)	• Geigy started as dyestuff manufacturer; Ciba moderately diversified from dyestuff into pharmaceuticals and speciality chemicals; early internationalisation to Germany (evade labour shortage and pollution control); • 1918–51: Ciba, Sandoz and Geigy formed a cartel (Basle AG) sharing profits, technology; this facilitated product differentiation; in order not to provoke the German cartel (producing bulk dyes) Swiss cartel moved into specialty dyes; this created various forms of German-Swiss labour division; • Basle AG dissolved to evade US antitrust allegations; • 1950s onwards: diversification in speciality chemicals and pharmaceuticals (core technology: biotechnology) • 1970: merger of Ciba and Geigy; part of business sold to escape from antitrust lawsuits in the USA	• Cartel of three largest Swiss companies (facilitating cross-subsidies to other businesses and internationalisation) allowed by Swiss government; the resulting product differentiation and niche orientation are still prime strategic aim of the firms; • Early 20th century: preferential access gained to British market (see also ICI/ **55**) to provide alternatives for IG-Farben; consequently during WWI: profits of the Swiss cartel increased fivefold
77 **Rhône-Poulenc** c.1858 (1938)	• Early days of the company are characterised by a series of mergers and an active interest in diversification; • 1960s: rapid growth (other firms joined the group); • 1982: nationalisation; • Since 1986: internationalisation through acquisitions; • 1993: <u>de</u>nationalisation	• 1960s: government-led restructuring of chemical industry in France; • Acquisitions abroad developed under tutelage of French government
78 **Viag** 1923	• Holding company to consolidate German government interests in electricity production, distribution and aluminium (Viag most important maker); • 1980s: Viag entered natural gas market; • 1986: privatisation of 40% (remaining 60% in 1988); • 1980s–1990s: diversification through acquisition into trading and glass production (around one-third of turnover)	• During large parts of its history, the firm has been government owned; • 1980s: 30–40% in energy business and public utilities, i.e. very often public procurement markets; 50% in aluminium which is affected by EC steel policies

Table 9A Continued

Rank Company Founded (Incorporated)	Historic strategic feature	Salient trade barrier
79 **RJR** **Nabisco** (1898)	• Started as merger of many biscuit firms (NBC); • Modest/late internationalisation primarily in the region (Nabisco's first foreign subsidiary in Canada in 1926); • 1960s and 1970s: stepped up internationalisation through acquisitions in Europe and alliances in Asia; • 1981: merger with Standard Brands, a food company; • 1985 R.J. Reynolds (tobacco) acquired Nabisco: created the largest US consumer products company; • Since 1988: financial troubles due to a leveraged buyout procedure (gigantic $24 bn debt in 1994)	• Army food rations in the wars were especially provided by NBC; preferential procurement created basis for growth and profit; • Food industry and agriculture at the time of NBC's start was very protected (and still is heavily regulated); basic ingredient of biscuits for instance is American flour, a product that has been subject to agricultural policy and international trade negotiations; • In tobacco (Reynolds): local content regulation, see Philip Morris (**17**), earned the company monopoly profits in a largely protected home market, which created ample capital reserves for its 1980s acquisitions
80 **BTR** (1864)	• Started in rubber and tyres, diversified into construction, engineering, and industrial supplies; • 1850s onwards: established a telegraph/cable firm; • 1934: British Tyre and Rubber established; • 1956–1960s: major reorganisations (1956 left tyres); • 1970–1990s: growth and diversification through acquisitions at home and abroad, creating a holding with eight divisions in widely varying businesses	• Telegraph market and construction have been relatively closed markets in which governments play a very strong regulating role • Rubber and other (plastics) products of BTR were/are in high demand by the military (in particularly the Air Force), implying protected markets and often preferential (cost-plus) contracts
81 **Ruhrkohle** 19th century (1968)	• 1968: 19 Ruhr area companies merged to face the rationalisation of the German mining industry; • They created the largest coal-producing company in Germany, producing 70% of all German coal	• 1968 merger ensued under strong government pressure; • Subject to EC steel and coal policy: see Thyssen (**50**)
82 **Preussag** 1923	• Origin as state-owned steel and mining company; • 1959: became a public company; • 1960s: diversification through acquisitions; • 1970s: entry and exit of aluminium market; • 1990: merger with Saltzgitter	• Company was founded by the government of Prussia; • Prone to government-led procurement (*interbellum*, world war) and restructuring (1960s and 1970s); subject to EC steel and coal policy; see Thyssen (50)

Table 9A Continued

Rank Company Founded (Incorporated)	Historic strategic feature	Salient trade barrier
83 **Idemitsu Kosan** (1911)	• Start: trading company in fuel and lubricants; 1914: internationalised (Manchuria, China, Taiwan and Korea); • 1949: included in ten petroleum suppliers in Japan; • 1950s onwards: search for oil resources, transport (buying tankers), set-up of refining capacity in Japan; • 1960s: opposes MITI's efforts to restrict production and organise the industry in a national federation (became member again in 1966); • 1980s: acquisition of foreign concession (oil, uranium, coal mining, e.g. in Australia) in order to spread exploration activities; active search for energy alternatives; • Since 1985: oil price slump terminated some alternative energy ventures	• *Interbellum*: internationalisation of the firm followed (was facilitated by) Japan's imperialistic plans in the region; drawback: military rule also implied tight control of the firm; • See also Nippon Oil (**62**); • MITI installed import restrictions on oil (Oil Industry Law), reduced the number of foreign suppliers and facilitated Idemitsu's strategy of backward integration at various moments
84 **Canon** 1937	• Start: producer of cameras; a technology-driven firm; • 1950s: period of growth; established one of the first overseas Japanese branches in the United States (1955); • 1960s: diversification into business machines and calculators (together with Texas Instruments); • 1960s–1970s: diversification into copiers; licensed technologies to competitors, because of weak marketing organisation; this created financial problems in 1975; • 1980s: diversification (PCs, facsimiles, typewriters, ICs); collaboration agreements (e.g. with Apple, later minority share in Next, Steve Job's spin-off from Apple)	• Profited from government procurement in optical technology; and from trade barriers and targeting practices in electronics; • However, the firm has often remained a relatively marginal player with a weak control over its Japanese dealers (contributing to its financial difficulties) and a weak bargaining position towards MITI, which prompted the firm to internationalise earlier (1950s) than most other Japanese firms
85 **Volvo** c.1915 (1926)	• Origins in ball-bearing industry (SKF); became a producer of trucks, buses and tractors in 1935; • Postwar: regionalisation of production in Europe (Belgium, Netherlands); specialisation in luxury market; • 1980s: profits primarily from US market; • Acquisition and diversification strategy in Sweden, invested for instance in food and services; • 1990s: merger with Renault announced and denounced	• Initial growth in protected markets, cross-subsidies to other business from government procurement; • Prime defence contractor to the Swedish forces; end of 1980s: defence contracts still account for 5–10% of Volvo's business; • In early 1990s the Handelsbanken and the Enskilda Banken (industrial banks to Volvo) were guarded from bankruptcy by the Swedish government (indirect subsidies to Volvo)

Table 9A Continued

Rank Company Founded (Incorporated)	Historic strategic feature	Salient trade barrier
86 **Friedrich Krupp** 1811 (1861)	• Focused first on English cast iron and products; • 1830s–1850s: rapid growth (railways were big market); • 1873: firm almost collapsed; since then rapid growth, also in shipbuilding; • WWI: booming sales; crisis after lost war; since 1933: renewed growth; • Postwar: Allies made firm lose its raw materials base; • 1967: financial crisis initiated major restructuring; • 1994: company split-up in 4 separate units announced	• Ready market in Europe due to Napoleon's Continental blockade (preventing imports of cast iron from England); • Growth spurred by Germany's customs union; • Government procurement (gunnery division and the fleet) saved company from collapse around 1870s; • Nazi procurement triggered growth in *interbellum*; • 1967 crisis: firm received security from banks, federal and state government (required to seize family ownership); consequently, the Iranian government could acquire a 25% stake in Krupp (1976)
87 **Ssangyong** c.1939	• Diversified conglomerate (*chaebol*) in engineering, construction, autos, oil refining, securities, heavy industries, machinery, paper, insurance, computers	• Postwar targeting policy by South Korean government has helped this industry in various ways; see also Samsung (**18**)
88 **NKK** 1912	• Firms focused on steel and pipes (Nippon Kohan KK); experienced rapid growth during WWI • 1950s: expansion and vertical integration; internationalisation (partly) through acquisitions; • 1980s: move towards new materials and supercomputers; joint venture with National Steel (USA)	• Government-led steel restructuring in the 1950s–1960s; • MITI has supported strategies in computers and new materials through a variety of subsidy measures and more direct trade policies
89 **Petrobras** 1953	• Firm focuses on exploration, refining and transportation of oil and oil derivatives; • Since 1972 internationalisation through joint ventures in 16 (primarily developing countries)	• State monopoly with active involvement of central Brazilian government
90 **Sunkyong** c.1953	• Started as a textiles company; • 1970s and 1980s: start of diversification strategy; making it Korea's fifth largest *chaebol*; specialised in refinery (more than 40% of 1993 sales), trading, chemicals, fabrics; • In 1980s move vertically upstream (acquisition of Gulf Oil Korea) and downstream (petrochemicals, largest domestic refiner); low profit margins nevertheless; • 1990s: diversification into cellular phones (acquisition of Korea Mobile Telecom) in 1994	• See other first-tier *chaebol* (Daewoo, Huyndai, Samsung, Lucky Goldstar); • Very protected market (oil and oil refineries); new move into equally closed market (telecommunications)

Table 9A Continued

Rank Company Founded (Incorporated)	Historic strategic feature	Salient trade barrier
91 **Saint Gobain** c.1665 (1830)	• Founded as glass-producing company under minister Colbert; • Expanded often through acquisitions; • Postwar: diversification into other materials than glass continuous until today	• *Colbertisme* is considered to be the forerunner of French 20th-century industrial policy; • 1982 nationalised, 1986 privatised again
92 **Electrolux** 1910	• Started as distributor of vacuum cleaners, later integrated backwards; pioneered marketing techniques (door-to-door sales and advertising campaigns); • 1920s: rapid internationalisation; diversification (especially refrigerators) through acquisition; • 1950s: continued diversification (e.g. washing machines); stepped-up involvement of the Enskilda Banken; • 1970s–1990s: aggressive acquisition strategy; more than 200 firms acquired, e.g. Zanussi (1984), AEG (1994); • 1990s: consolidation/restructuring: recentralisation, plant modernisations, disposing 'non-strategic' assets	• Defence supplier in WWII: munition and air cleaners; • Electrolux's industrial bank (Enskilda Banken) saved from bankruptcy by the Swedish government in 1993/94
93 **Digital Equipment** 1957	• Founded by Kenneth Olson as spin-off of IBM; • 1950s–1970s: niche production for academic and sophisticated industrial market users; rapid growth in minicomputers; rapid internationalisation; • 1990s: major acquisitions of sizeable computer subsidiaries of Mannessmann and Philips; strikes an increasing number of international alliances; continued restructuring: asset sales, vertical deintegration (halving employment from 126,000 in 1989 to 65,000 employees in 1995)	• Founder Olson was former IBM employee and could build on the same knowledge basis acquired in defence contracts as IBM itself (see IBM/7); • Large parts of academic markets are government procurement markets (especially abroad)
94 **Grand Metropolitan** c.1926 (1934)	• Growth through acquisition (in particular hotels); • Efforts to integrate vertically; • 1970s–1980s: problems with Mergers and Monopolies Commission spurred internationalisation and diversification; • Since 1985: diversification and entry into healthcare	• Vertical integration strategy hampered by government regulation that did not allow liquor producers to own retail outlets; • Move into healthcare business implies focus on government procurement markets that are under heavy government regulation in most countries

Table 9A Continued

Rank Company Founded (Incorporated)	Historic strategic feature	Salient trade barrier
95 **Minnesota** **Mining (3M)** 1902 (1929)	• Mineral exploitation company, moved quickly into industrial wares (e.g. sandpaper), developed aggressive sales techniques directly to retailers; • Early focus on innovation (very high share of sales dedicated to **R&D**), led to invention of e.g. Scotch Tape, gave 3M sources of profits during the 1930s depression; • WWII: 3M did not shift to military production; • 1960s: first dry-printing photocopying developed; • 1970s: faced fierce competition from Japan (in media such as tapes); • 1980s: restructuring, centralisation; move further into consumer products such as optical disks	• American patenting system and adjoining foreign policy were very supportive of 3M's innovation oriented strategy
96 **Bridgestone** 1931	• Manufacturer of aircraft tyres; had a number of plants in Japanese colonies that were lost after WWII; • 1950s–1979: technical link with Goodyear (the latter providing technical assistance to the Japanese company) gradually changed into a 'mutual assistance' contract; • Firm dominates 50% of the Japanese tyre market; • 1980s: internationalisation, following car assemblers; • 1988: won take-over battle with Pirelli over Firestone	• Aircraft procurement, primarily military (closed) markets; • Subcontractor to car industry, profiting from trade barriers to western car producers and subcontractors on the import of components and car parts
97 **Johnson &** **Johnson** (1887)	• Started in healthcare business, very innovative; • 1910s–1920s: rapid growth and internationalisation through the set-up of foreign affiliations; • 1930s: decentralisation, move into pharmaceuticals and textiles; firm was in favour of raising minimum wages; • 1950s: acquisition strategy; spread of portfolio (aim: single items should not represent more than 5% of sales)	• WWII: Robert Johnson (CEO and former military) became vice-chairman of War Production Board; • pharmaceutical and healthcare market is heavily regulated in most countries

Table 9A Continued

Rank Company Founded (Incorporated)	Historic strategic feature	Salient trade barrier
98 **Sumitomo Metal Ind.** c.1590	• Result of several mergers of steel and copper producers (1935, 1953, 1963); • 1930s: heavy dependence on military industry (copper as strategic input); • Prime markets of the company are aircraft and railways	• 1930s: sizeable government subsidies to copper industry; • 1950s–1960s: mergers often under government tutelage (Japan Development Bank, Fiscal Investment and Loan Programme, mostly aimed at basic industries like shipyards, energy sector and steel); • End-product markets have been prime government procurement markets ('Buy Japanese' tradition)
99 **Tenneco** c.1940 (1947)	• Tennessee Gas and Transmission Company: first operated a pipeline as part of the war effort; • Late 1940s: Henry Symonds (founder of Tenneco) established business in oil and gas exploration; • 1950s: growth by acquisitions primarily in USA, but since 1970s also abroad; • 1981: Newport News (shipbuilding) restructured; • End of 1980s: diversified, but 75% still in oil and gas	• Profits from pipeline (government dominated procurement) has been important source of investment of Symonds in oil and gas; • Allegations of undue deals with Federal Power Commission (if true: this created non-tariff trade barriers); • 1980s: restructuring of company's commercial shipbuilding in the direction of defence contracts
100 **International Paper** 1898	• Result of a 1989 merger of 18 paper and power companies; specialised in paper production and distribution (1900: supplied c.60% of US newsprint); • 1920s: investment in power plants; rapid expansion; • WWII: important defence supplier, start of stepped-up R&D efforts, entering competition based on innovation; • 1960s onwards: late internationalisation (excl. Canada) through acquisitons, primarily in Latin America; diversification in leaps, not always very successful, created high debts, ultimately also necessitated factory closures; • 1974: step into oil and gas through acquisitions (and back again, ultimate focus primarily on paper and pulp); • Since 1988: started to step up its presence in Europe	• Focus on power plants: closed procurement markets, was terminated in 1935 with Public Utility Holding Act prohibiting to be both an industrial and a power company; • WWII: spurred innovation with the firm on the basis of cost-plus contracts and defence as lead-user; developed capabilities of the firm to compete on the basis of innovations

Sources: Annual Reports, press clippings, Derdak (1988), Ferguson, Morris (1993: 6,221), Glimstedt (1993), Hast *et al.* (1991, 1992), Jacoby (1974), Mirabile *et al.* (1990), Office of Technology Assessment (1991: 37), Turner (1978), Yergin (1991), International Metalworkers' Federation (1992a,b,c), US Department of Commerce (1987), Vogel (1992: 73), Molle (1993: 77ff.), Sobel (1983), Tyson (1992: 170ff.), van Tulder and Junne (1988: 192ff.), Wennekes (1993: 38), *The Economist*, 12 March 1994, Bartlett, Doz and Hedlund (1990), *Business Week*, 21 February 1994, Keller (1993), Brown, Hogendorn (1994: 147ff.), Stopford (1992), Chang (1994: 115ff.)

10 The management of international dependencies

10.1 INTRODUCTION: RIVAL PERSPECTIVES TO RESTRUCTURING

According to the Flemish novelist Oskar van der Hallen, he 'who has struggled for a long time trying to find solutions to problems, has done nothing but enrich his vocabulary' (1965). Although we do not subscribe to this pessimistic view, it is undeniable that the study of international restructuring has produced a glut of elusive and often unrelated concepts. In this book, we have argued that this conceptual jungle is the gloomy outcome of different types of analytical perspectives:

- Different levels of analysis:
  both restructuring, internationalisation and international trade have been analysed at the micro, meso and macro levels, producing rival conclusions on strategies or policies to implement;
- Different objects of research (stakeholders) and different stakes:
  theories on restructuring, internationalisation and international trade have tended to focus on companies and/or governments only. Often, the choice for a level of analysis depends solely on the scientific discipline from which a scholar originates, fostering one-dimensional approaches and isolated concepts, and hindering an interdisciplinary study of what is truly a multi-faceted object of research;
- Different time horizons:
  strategies or configurations which appear as self-evident today are the product of historical formation processes. Companies, governments and industrial networks cannot be seen as a *tabula rasa*, but carry with them established bargaining practices and mind-sets;
- Different national backgrounds:
  interpretations of corporate strategies or international affairs often originate from specific national settings, creating divisions in audiences along rival national lines.

These different perspectives have been at the basis of rival interpretations of the international restructuring race in which scholars often used identical concepts to which they however attributed different meanings. Table 10.1 summarises our discussion on the concepts of post-Fordism (Chapter 2), globalisation (Chapter 6) and free trade (Chapter 9). In our view, leading champions of these concepts have tended to confuse their analysis of 'reality' (*sein*) with what they believe the future should look like (*sollen*). Whether by intention or not, such juggling with concepts and evidence has a distinct ideological bias.[1] Table 10.1 also summarises the findings of our analyses of post-Fordism, globalisation and free trade, plus an alternative approach.

As the final row of Table 10.1 indicates, we think that at the basis of this confusion of facts and concepts there is often an unfounded belief that the world is progressing towards a state of increasing inter-dependence. Many authors have postulated rather than substantiated that post-Fordism, globalisation and free trade would promote growing interdependence between managers and workers, between companies, or between nations (cf. Ohmae, 1990; Reich, 1991; Bhagwati, 1988; Womack *et al.*, 1990; Coriat, 1990).[2]

A scan of the Anglo-Saxon management literature confirms this 'uncon-scious' increase of the word interdependence. Whereas one could only read the word interdependence ten times in the abstracts of leading business periodicals in 1972, this had increased to sixty-six times in 1991. (Interest-ingly, the use of the word dependence slightly decreased from 213 to 210. The search is based on the Abi/Infor database, Louisville, KY).

In international relations literature, the concept of interdependence has played a key role, although scholars have tended to define it differently and have usually disagreed on whether or not 'interdependence' between coun-tries and companies was actually increasing or decreasing. For instance, Robert Gilpin, in his standard work, *The Political Economy of International Relations*, stated that: '[t]he postwar international economic order is gradu-ally disintegrating. The Bretton Woods system of trade liberalization, stable currencies, and *expanding global economic interdependence no longer exists*. Spreading protectionism, upheavals in monetary and financial markets, and

---

[1] Ideologies can be defined as 'enclosed belief-systems that cannot be affected by evidence which contradicts them' (Hollis and Smith, 1991: 84). By its very nature, any definition of 'ideology' can be rejected as an ideology in itself. Other definitions include Heilbronner's, who defines ideology as 'systems of thought and belief by which [individuals and groups] explain . . . how their social system operates and what principles it exemplifies' (quoted in Gilpin, 1987: 25). Lodge defines ideology as 'the collection of ideas that a community uses to make values explicit in some relevant context' (1987: 3), while Therborn sees ideology as 'that aspect of the human condition under which human beings live their lives as conscious actors in a world that makes sense to them to varying degrees' and 'the medium through which this consciousness and meaningfulness operates' (1980: 1–2).

[2] Since the beginning of the 1990s, leading protagonists of post-Fordism like Martin Kenney and John Mathews (mentioned in Chapter 2) have gradually come to underscore the relevance of the criticism put forward against the ideological and/or elusive use of the concept. They consequently declined to use the concept of post-Fordism as their basis for analysis or prescription.

Table 10.1 Claims, critics and conclusions in the analysis of international restructuring processes

	Appeal to what should be (sollen)	Claim on what is (sein)	'Champions'	A closer look suggests	Alternative approach
Ideology of post-Fordism	Promises cooperative restructuring without major losers; improving management–worker relations, inter-firm network relations, use of new technologies	A second industrial divide has evolved; Japanese firms *do* present a case of post-Fordism; new technologies *do* open avenues for evolutionary growth	Scholars that look at industries facing huge restructuring efforts (especially USA, UK, France)	1 Post-Fordism is weak and contradictory analytical concept; 2 Overlooks side-effects at different levels of analysis (e.g. good labour relations within core firms at expense of supply pyramid; consequences technological change for other groups in society)	1 Re-define restructuring strategies and post-Fordism in terms of relations within industrial complex; 2 'Post-Fordism' refers to flexible specialisation or to Toyotism
Ideology of globalisation	Promises a better world: no confrontation but integration, cooperation (the global village; implicitly also appeals to awareness of global environmental crisis)	Competition *is* becoming more global; large firms *are* developing global strategies	1 Advisers of Japanese firms on internationalisation strategy; 2 Advisers of American firms (world markets and economies of scale)	1 National borders still relevant; 2 Triadisation (regionalisation) in terms of trade and FDI, and in terms of investment decisions; 3 Illusion of HQ control	1 Globalisation is no reality but a possible strategy; 2 Define globalisation as strategy and as trajectory; include retreat as an option; 3 Link to restructuring and trade policy strategies
Ideology of free trade	Promises that free trade leads to optimisation of global economic wealth (although never universally shared by all states)	Trade barriers *do* impede optimisation of worldwide economic wealth	Scholars from formerly, current or potentially hegemonic industrial systems	1 Strategic trade policy models undermined rationale free trade theory; 2 Free trade has been exception, trade protection the rule of international competition; 3 Firms/industrial complexes, not states, produce trade barriers	1 Specify how certain firms and/or strategies are affected by given trade barriers; 2 Link core firm's trade policy orientation to its domestic bargaining arena and its internationalisation strategy
Ideology of interdependence	Promises harmony and more cooperation within/between states, firms, workers – who could ever object?	States, firms, workers *are* becoming more interdependent	Various theorists of restructuring, internationalisation and trade policies	1 Word interdependence obscures potential conflicts; 2 Usually only case evidence: (a) best-practice; (b) partial evidence, no link to other analytical levels	1 Define interdependence vs. other dependency relations; 2 Assess dependency relations within industrial complexes and industrial systems

divergent national economic policies have eroded the foundations of the international system' (Robert Gilpin, 1987: 3, our emphasis).[3]

The question whether or not the world is becoming more 'interdependent' is debated mostly by nationals from the industrial systems with the previously hegemonic concept of control, i.e. micro-Fordism, and nationals from the industrial system with a rival concept of control, i.e. Toyotism. Europeans or nationals from developing economies have far less reason to conceive of the world economy as an interdependent playground.

At the time when the USA still occupied a hegemonic position in the world (although nearing its end), Kenneth Waltz had already proved an eloquent critic stating that '[t]he American rhetoric of interdependence has taken on some of the qualities of an ideology. The word "interdependence" subtly obscures the inequalities of national capability, pleasingly points to a reciprocal dependence, and strongly suggests that all states are playing the same game' (Waltz, quoted in Schlupp et al., 1973: 298).[4]

It seems hardly an overstatement to suggest that any author from whichever national, ethnic, professional, religious or political background promising a better future should be read with utmost suspicion. Such authors tend to postulate their claim or to build it on one or two cases only. A prime motivation of this study, therefore, has been to develop a framework to assess (inter)dependence relations, to apply this framework to a variety of concepts in the literature on international restructuring, and where possible to try and operationalise these concepts in order to diminish the conceptual confusion and disorder. The results of this exercise are presented in the next section.

10.2 THE LOGIC OF INTERNATIONAL RESTRUCTURING

In an excellent comparative study of industrial policies in Western Europe, Francois Duchêne and Geoffrey Shepherd argued that governments do not confront their domestic firms nor the working of the market in a neutral

---

[3] The notion of international *economic* interdependence has been developed particularly by American scholars faced with declining US hegemony in the 1970s. Robert Keohane and Joseph Nye's *Power and Interdependence* contributed to a more sophisticated view on interdependence, allowing for the possibility of asymmetrical interdependency relations, and for the *rise* of international conflicts as a result of increasing 'interdependencies' (for a different approach, see Bryant, 1980). Others have introduced the term 'lopsided' interdependencies, arguing that 'mutual dependence need not mean mutual reward' (Russett and Starr, 1992: 440). These and other critical remarks have motivated us to develop the dependency scale in Chapter 4. Another body of interdependence literature deals with the growing concerns over the world's environment and the inability to share costs and rewards between nations (cf. OECD, 1981; MacNeill et al., 1991).

[4] In the wake of dependency theorists working in peripheral countries such as Andre Gunder Frank (1969), Celso Furtado (1970) and Raul Prebisch (1964), a large number of European and only some US authors in this period rejected the concept of interdependence as a myth or even as an ideology (cf. Russett, 1970: 143; Waltz, 1970; Schlupp et al., 1973; Junne and Nour, 1974).

manner, but that they have increasingly become 'strands in the fabric' (1987: 12). This book has shown how different the fabric can be from one economy to the other.

The framework developed in this book regards industrial complexes as the centres of gravity of the international restructuring race. This implies that, although national economies and individual firms are important actors in the international restructuring race, international competition is best studied as a race between industrial complexes adhering to rival concepts of control. In the preceding chapters, numerous strategies and bargaining agreements which are in some way related have been discussed and elaborated upon. In strategic terms, a concept of control is at the basis of these interrelationships: a concept of control represents an agenda for the management of dependencies within an industrial complex, an industrial system, a world region, and ultimately the world. The scale of dependencies shows the logic of these interrelationships: Figure 10.1 positions the rival concepts of control, internationalisation strategies and trade policy orientations along this scale. Below, we discuss the logic of international restructuring along each of the five concepts of control (cf. Chapters 4, 5, 8 and 9).

Flexible specialisation: the logic of export orientation

Firms aiming for a flexible specialisation concept of control may serve primarily domestic markets, and have no internationalisation strategy [1] at all (the numbers within square brackets correspond to the numbers in Table 10.1). When threatened with severe import competition, such firms have an interest in protecting their domestic market – regardless of the effects this could have abroad ('autarky') [9]. Flexible specialisation firms that do internationalise have always opted for a 'simple' export orientation strategy [2]. The primary interest of these firms is to see foreign markets opened, but if faced with fierce import competition and if the likelihood or consequences of foreign retaliation are limited, they will not hesitate to campaign for domestic trade barriers such as tariffs [10] or quotas [11].

Individual producers functioning in a regime of flexible specialisation have an interest in sustaining a balanced domestic bargaining pattern and in preventing foreign or large competitors from invading and taking control. Since these firms do not have direct power over their domestic government – and hence can never be sure that the trade barriers sought will be granted – another defence mechanism has been to establish cooperatives and maintain very strong political links as a group. Examples of firms adhering to a flexible specialisation concept of control can be found in the textiles and clothing industries, shoes and leather, and certain agricultural segments. Not every agricultural or textiles producer is necessarily embedded in a flexible specialisation type of network: it may either have outgrown its network or it may have been unable to create one in the first place. A

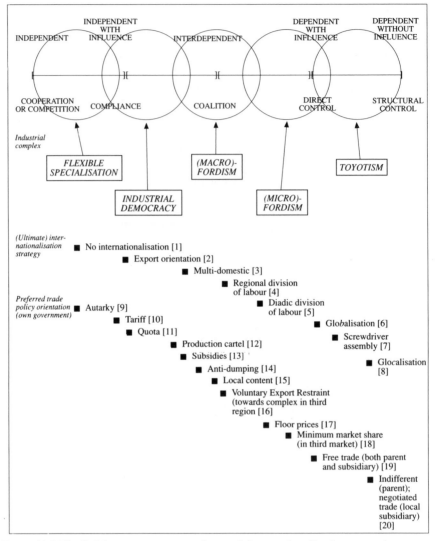

Figure 10.1 The link between concepts of control, internationalisation strategies and trade policy

concept of control refers to a core firm's strategic orientation, not to the accomplished reality.

Firms in flexible specialisation networks have usually been unable to bargain with their home government for more indirect – let alone negotiated – trade barriers, and have often found it difficult to gain sizeable government subsidies [13].[5] Excess capacity in networks of smaller domestic firms

---

[5] The agricultural sector would appear to be an exception to this. However, import quota and tariffs have been the basis of agricultural protection in the EU and Japan. Agricultural

is usually eliminated by direct bankruptcies. Production cartels [12] appeared primarily in industries dominated by large firms, and imply government influence to an extent that is unacceptable to firms with a 'pure' flexible specialisation concept of control. The concept of flexible specialisation, therefore, coincides with a preference for a unilateral trade regime: a combination of domestic trade barriers (if necessary) and foreign expansionist trade policy strategies. Thus the industrialised countries have enforced exceptions from standard GATT rules in the agriculture and textiles sectors (Multi Fibre Arrangement). Chapter 9 illustrated that European and Japanese support for unilateral agriculture trade policies has been more pronounced than American support, due to the smaller size of the firms that belong to the agricultural complexes in Europe and Japan.

Under certain conditions, core firms operating on the basis of a concept of control other than flexible specialisation, but confronted with a weakening industrial complex due to inroads by foreign complexes, have also favoured unilateral trade policies to defend their position. Such inroads have diminished the core firms' control over domestic actors and decreased the cohesion of their domestic complex. If they had widespread international operations, these firms tended to combine a preference for unilateral trade barriers with a retreat strategy to increase their domestic cohesion. Depending on these firms' concept of control and on the international context, they also favoured indirect trade barriers (such as subsidies [13] or local content regulation [15]).

Industrial democracy: a limited multi-domestic logic

Firms operating under a regime of industrial democracy are confronted with a government that favours an export orientation over direct production abroad, since the latter diminishes the influence of the national government (and of the other bargaining partners) on that company. Companies that have internationalised parts of their production have tended to do so on a limited scale. If faced with severe import competition, domestic governments are most inclined to establish production cartels [12], provide subsidies [13] or perhaps consider anti-dumping measures [14], i.e. indirect trade barriers in which the core firm remains to some extent dependent on the national government. Exporting firms in a regime of industrial democracy contribute substantially to a country's trade balance, but at a world level they tend to be vulnerable to (potential) retaliation. Indirect trade barriers therefore have to increase the industry's competitiveness without provoking direct retaliation from other countries.

Industries subject to an industrial democracy regime have generally not been the object of multilateral trade negotiations. Government procurement

---

subsidies have tended to be trade-related (export subsidies) or to facilitate immediate and tangible restructuring.

policies in telecommunications have long been excluded from GATT negotiations, and the defence industry still is. The initiative to put telecom procurement on the Uruguay Round agenda primarily originated from national systems in which the telecommunications industry has been liberalised, such as the United States and the United Kingdom. Greater strategic freedom and lower dependence on national governments represented a changing concept of control and hence a change of trade policy orientations at leading core firms in these systems. More closed industrial systems have tried to withstand these efforts in the Uruguay Round with some success.

The division of labour entailed in international Fordism

Fordist firms aim for an international intra-firm division of labour. The internationalisation of production has constituted an integral part of Fordism, and the globalisation trajectory (see Figure 8.4) represents the most logical extension of the Fordist concept of control on an international scale. If the Fordist firm aims at a worldwide division of labour (globalisation [6]), it has had a direct interest in free trade enforced under a multilateral trade regime [19] to make an optimal use of geographical advantages.

However, as noted in Chapter 8, the globalisation trajectory also includes several other strategies, plus a retreat option. Fordist complexes seeking a regional or diadic division of labour [4, 5] have generally favoured negotiated trade barriers such as voluntary export restraints [16], floor prices [17] or minimum market shares in third markets [18]. Micro-Fordist core firms in the United States appear to have been better able to bargain for negotiated trade barriers than their macro-Fordist equivalents in Europe, probably because they are better able to coordinate the strategies of other actors. European macro-Fordist firms internationalised primarily into other European countries. Those firms internationalising from a macro-Fordist context facing a weakening domestic industrial complex, tended to bargain more for indirect trade barriers, such as subsidies [13], anti-dumping measures [14] or local content regulations [15], and only tended to follow trade barriers negotiated by the United States. In the 1980s, the United States and later the European countries (individually or through the European Commission) initiated negotiations with Japan and have struck semiconductor pacts and voluntary export restraint agreements for Japanese cars and steel exports. A shift away from a liberal trade policy orientation has generally been accompanied and rationalised by a rhetoric favouring 'fair trade'.

The glocal logic of Toyotism

Core firms doing business on the basis of a Toyotist concept of control have done their utmost to guard their level of domestic cohesion – and structural control – as long as possible. Considering the fact that Japan ranks amongst the countries with the lowest share of inward foreign direct investment, Toyotist core firms have thus far been very skilful in achieving cohesion. The efforts to sustain a high level of domestic cohesion have initially led Toyotist core firms to adopt a simple export-oriented strategy [2] (see Figure 8.4) and, if confronted with severe import competition, to favour unilateral or technical trade barriers. The structural control of Toyotist end producers over their domestic complex also explains the low levels of Japanese intra-industry trade: Toyotist core producers have bought as many of the parts and services they needed from suppliers under their control, and these suppliers were also driven to purchase their parts from other industrial 'group' members (cf. Chapter 7). Unlike the premises of free trade theory, Toyotist international trade prevented rather than supported the rise of a pattern of international intra-industry specialisation.

The structural control of Toyotist core firms over their domestic industrial complex created unbalanced trade patterns with foreign countries, and produced foreign trade barriers in the car, electronics and steel industries. This invoked retaliation from trading partners, and the trajectory of glocalisation has been the unavoidable extension of the Toyotist concept of control on an international scale, aimed to circumvent these barriers. However, along this trajectory, Toyotist core firms have tried to limit their degree of internationalisation as much as possible in order to preserve their domestic cohesion – the basis of their competitiveness on international markets. This meant that Toyotist core firms favoured an export orientation over the establishment of screwdriver facilities [7], and favoured screwdriver facilities over a strategy of glocalisation [8]. Toyotist core producers only seriously considered a strategy of glocalisation if governments of other countries or trade blocs with substantial domestic markets installed trade restrictions and have shown resolution in maintaining or even making these restrictions harsher without a major and integrated local presence of Toyotist core producers.

Internationalisation along the trajectory of glocalisation has led core firms to formulate fundamentally different trade policy orientations from firms along the globalisation trajectory. The ultimate objective of glocalisation has been to sustain domestic cohesion and reduce the core firm's vulnerability to trade barriers [20], *not* to benefit from free trade. Only in the early stage of setting up 'local' screwdriver assembly plants has the glocalising firm had a strong yet transient interest in 'free trade' [19]. However, if the Toyotist firm reckons it can appease resistance by limiting its foreign presence to screwdriver facilities, it will be tempted to do this in order to preserve its domestic cohesion. Thus, paradoxically, a government which is seeking to attract large investments from a glocalising Toyotist firm undermines its bargaining position by actively campaigning for free trade (unless it is part of a wider legal unit, such as the UK which is a member of the EU).

Although the internationalisation of Toyotist firms is of relatively recent date, there are many indications which suggest that, as soon as the glocalising core firm has started to transform its screwdriver plants into more integrated facilities and attracted suppliers from its domestic industrial complex to set up operations abroad, its free trade orientation has given way to a more pragmatic orientation.[6] This orientation, which can be understood as a 'prelude' to the status of glocalisation, allows the core firm to bargain over the establishment of negotiated trade barriers [20]. Since Toyotist core firms do not depend on an international division of labour and therefore not on the liberalisation of international trade as such, they will never conceive of 'free trade' as the 'natural' state of international relations. Ultimately, the internationalisation of Toyotism, therefore, reinforces bilateralism rather than multilateralism, and negotiated trade rather than free trade.

Figure 10.1 suggests that if a core firm is confronted with fierce import competition at home, its trade policy preference can be derived from the organisation of its domestic industrial complex. On the dependency scale, unilateral barriers are clustered at the left-hand side, indirect trade barriers are more in line with the concepts of industrial democracy and macro-Fordism, while negotiated trade barriers are favoured by complexes organised along the concepts of micro-Fordism (pertaining to domestic barriers) and Toyotism (faced with demands for trade barriers abroad).

10.3 THE COHESION OF INDUSTRIAL COMPLEXES AND SYSTEMS

Several factors may lead to a deviation from the 'ideal linear' linkages pictured above (Figure 10.1). Most of these factors, however, follow logically from the framework presented here. We shall discuss two interesting cases. In the first case, an industrial complex is embedded in an industrial system with other industrial complexes adhering to different concepts of control. The bargaining dynamism ensuing from this is discussed in section 10.3.1. Section 10.3.2 discusses the bargaining dynamism which results from the internationalisation of a core firm from its domestic system, and the dynamism ensuing after penetrating a foreign industrial system.

---

[6] Early in 1985, the European Commission announced a regulation which granted the European car makers a ten-year general exemption from open competition. This exemption, which was granted *en bloc* and which has therefore been known as the 'block exemption', allowed car makers to maintain a selective distribution system within the EC. At the time, Japanese producers such as Toyota and Nissan, were vehemently opposed to the block exemption. In 1994, the European Commission extended the block exemption until the year 2005. Toyota and Nissan, which had invested in large scale exclusive dealerships throughout Europe, no longer resisted but even supported this continuation. Smaller car makers such as Honda, Mitsubishi and particularly Mazda (which in 1994 had no production facilities in Europe), were far behind the former two in setting up a European distribution structure, and still opposed the block exemption.

10.3.1 The dynamism of strong and weak industrial complexes and industrial systems

A high degree of cohesion refers to a situation in which the core firm's bargaining relations are all positioned at one specific point of the dependency scale.[7] However, while individual core firms have often been unable to establish and maintain high levels of cohesion, this is even more the case for national industrial systems. If a national industrial system contains more than one industrial complex, different types of bargaining (i.e. different concepts of control) may coexist and compete for a transient period. However, within national industrial systems, bargaining patterns have tended to converge gradually between complexes along the lines of the bargaining rules set by the most cohesive complex, and at the expense of the weaker complex(es).

In some cases, particular complexes have even come to dominate the entire industrial system. Such an overlap may be found in the defence industry and in telecommunications, which are highly dependent on government procurement (cf. Chapter 5). Generally, the smaller the country, the higher the chance that a national industrial system is made up of just one complex. If one complex makes up a national industrial system, the bargaining scene between industry and government is likely to be less open: the core firm does not have to compete with rival core firms to gain support, and is therefore less likely to articulate bargaining preferences in public.

From the discussion in Chapter 9 we can infer that a strong national industrial system is usually characterised by (1) a sizeable number of core firms, (2) a strong supplier structure, and (3) relatively stable relations between core firms and government (which is not the same as interventionism). A weak national industrial system often contains (1) a limited number of core firms, (2) a weak or eroded supplier structure, and (3) possibly disturbed bargaining relations between the national government and the leading core firm(s).

The interaction between weak and strong industrial complexes and weak and strong national systems is shown in Table 10.2, illustrated by four exemplary industries from various national industrial systems: (1) cars (as the 'engine' of the Fordist regime), (2) consumer electronics, and (3) computers as sectors in which the postwar electronics revolution evolved, and (4) telecommunications as the provider of the information technology infrastructure of the past, the present and (possibly) the future.

As Table 10.2 indicates, weak complexes operating in weak national industrial systems have risked being taken over or run over by another complex. Governments have run into high costs supporting a weak

---

[7] In the past it has been proved possible to create or increase cohesion in an artifical manner and at a moment when bargaining relations are still susceptible to change. Chapter 9 discussed how the German, US and Japanese governments established trade barriers which helped to create cohesion and a leading position.

Table 10.2   Relationship between the strength of industrial complexes and industrial systems: some examples

	Strong industrial complex	*Weak industrial complex*
Strong national system	Mutually reinforcing relationship (yet danger of rising costs)	Weak complex may benefit from know-how of suppliers and from established bargaining practices which it could not attain itself; possible risk of being taken over or overpowered by stronger complex
	Cars: Toyota/Japan Consumer electronics: Matsushita/Japan Telecommunications: AT&T/USA Computers: Fujitsu/Japan	Cars: Suzuki/Japan Consumer electronics: Pioneer/Japan Telecommunications: MCI/USA Computers: start-ups/USA
Weak national system	Gradual domination of strong complex over national system; risk of rigidity and clientism	Candidate for erosion, invasion or take-over by foreign complex(es)
	Cars: Fiat/Italy Consumer electronics: B&O/Denmark Telecommunications: Nokia/Finland Computers: Olivetti/Italy	Cars: Rover/UK Consumer electronics: Grundig/GER Telecommunicatons: Plessey/UK Computers: ICL/UK

industrial complex in a weak industrial system. By contrast, it has been much easier for governments to spur competition between strong industrial complexes and to enhance the dynamism of a strong national industrial system. It was this type of national industrial system that Michael Porter championed in his 1990 book *The Competitive Advantage of Nations*. In a strong national industrial system, 'success stories' abound. For instance, in the US information technology industry, start-up firms such as Compaq and Microsoft emerged which developed into strong players themselves and which even entered the Fortune 500 within a few years. If only one strong complex dominated an otherwise weak national system, core firms have tended to gradually gain control over state policies, which in many instances has led to rigidity and clientism. This bargaining logic is further discussed in Appendix I.

10.3.2 Internationalisation and the bargaining pendulum

The link between restructuring, internationalisation and trade, as presented in Figure 10.1 does not operate only one way: the core firm's internationalisation strategy also influences its domestic bargaining relations. Any internationalisation strategy beyond a mere export orientation potentially undermines the cohesion of the core firm's domestic complex. If it substitutes domestic production by production abroad, the core firm inevitably cuts down orders with domestic suppliers and reduces domestic employment, affecting its domestic labour relations. The domestic government also loses influence on the core firm and finds it more difficult to support it through industrial policies or to represent it in international trade negotiations.

A bargaining analysis of international restructuring processes produces an interpretation of the internationalisation of firms which is very different from mainstream approaches, which analyse internationalisation in terms of evolutionary and consecutive stages or in terms of the 'internalisation' of markets (cf. section 6.3). It also produces a different periodisation of the postwar internationalisation of US core companies, based on a historical bargaining pendulum rather than on a narrow view of the firm as a single unit. Table 10.3 illustrates this pendulum.

After forging their domestic bargaining arena along micro-Fordist lines over the 1930s, 1940s and 1950s, US core firms through the late 1950s became confronted with increasingly adversarial bargaining relations and with stronger bargaining partners. The latter was partly attributable to the success of micro-Fordism and the ensuing shortage of, for instance, labour and supplies. Thus the dominant motive of internationalisation over the 1960s was to escape from a constricting bargaining arena and export the accustomed and preferred bargaining practices abroad. Gradually, however, an additional motive emerged: by threatening to leave, or by actually deciding to run away, US core firms, paradoxically, also hoped to influence their domestic bargaining arena. By stepping up their international presence, US core firms had found that they could also end up entangled in foreign bargaining constellations with which they were even less familiar. The third stage, since the early 1980s, has been aimed at creating a truly international division of labour. In such a globalisation strategy, a firm may even re-import semi-finished or end products to undermine a domestic actor's bargaining power. Just like the first stage, however, this strategy to become footloose and hence invulnerable to the domestic bargaining arena, has at most been only partially successful.

As Chapter 7 showed, a similar bargaining pendulum could be observed in the case of the internationalisation strategies of large micro-Fordist complexes from the UK and the Netherlands (see also Table 8.4). However, the escape motive has been much less dominant in the case of core firms from the major continental European industrial systems. These core firms have tended to seek and foster longer-term relationships with their national and supranational bargaining partners. Major European core firms have often limited their internationalisation to an export or a multi-domestic strategy, or to a regional division of labour. To some extent, even the regional division of labour strategy did not represent a proactive escape

Table 10.3 The internationalisation of US firms: the bargaining pendulum

Stage, period	International focus	Strategy to domestic bargaining partners	Strategy to foreign bargaining partners	Results: swing of the bargaining pendulum
1 1960s: rise of US multinationals	Europe, Canada	Escape	Unprepared attempt to export domestic bargaining relations	Core firms faced with declining control over domestic bargaining arena: relative increase of bargaining power by bargaining partners
2 1970s: international division of labour	Latin America, South East Asia	Enforce domestic concessions by continued internationalisation	Control or acquire foreign actors; attempt to forge regional coordination	Core firms unable to regain control
3 1980s: international/ 'global' division of labour	Pacific Basin, Europe	Combined attempt to coordinate domestic and foreign bargaining relations; partial retreat ('re-runaway')	Combined attempt to coordinate domestic and foreign bargaining relations	Declining cohesion of domestic bargaining arena, aggravated by inroads of foreign producers (with foreign concept of control)
4 1990s: retreat towards regional/diadic division of labour	North America (including Mexico); Europe (including Eastern Europe)	'Regional escape' yet at the same time attempt to gain domestic concessions	Attempt to gain exclusive exploitation of foreign labour in 'development annex'; attempt to scare non-US producers off because of inequality in bargaining power	Possible outcome: 1 Further reduction of domestic cohesion (foreign inroads); 2 Inability to reverse adversarial bargaining relations; 3 In some sectors loss of domestic producers

strategy but a reactive strategy adopted only after the major European states had been convinced of the benefits of a single European market. Similarly, the expansion of European car makers such as Volkswagen, Fiat and Renault to Eastern Europe has been backed by the German, Italian and French governments.

To most Japanese core firms, internationalisation has not been inspired by the escape motive. On the contrary, they have tended to foster their domestic cohesion with utmost care and to use an export strategy to maintain constant pressure on their bargaining partners. As Chapter 7 indicated, Honda and Sony are among the few exceptions in this respect: their runaway has been driven by insufficient control over their domestic supply and distribution structure. This situation was virtually impossible to change exactly *because* competitors such as Toyota, Nissan and Matsushita maintained such structural control over their own complexes and the Japanese industrial system.

The example of the US bargaining pendulum also shows how the cohesion of a national system can be affected if it is penetrated by core firms from another industrial system. The success of a penetration is higher and the effects are more serious if the new entrants strive for a different concept of control than the domestic complexes. A national system consisting of two (or more) industrial complexes striving for different concepts of control suffers from low levels of cohesion. In this situation, a domestic core firm's bargaining partners are facing different bargaining practices and outcomes. For instance, American suppliers have had to meet stricter requirements regarding quality and frequency of delivery with new Toyotist car makers, while old bargaining practices continued to govern their relations with the domestic (micro-Fordist) US end producers. Likewise, existing social arrangements have been undermined on a national scale. To the US government, it has become increasingly difficult to support their domestic complexes through industrial and trade policies.

Ironically, the problem of two or more industrial complexes striving for different concepts of control may only turn out to be a transitory dilemma to many host governments: if faced with low levels of cohesion and a weak national system, a government has always tended to give preference in its industrial and trade policies to the complex aiming for a concept of control at the right-hand side of the dependency scale (which will only enhance its dependence on this complex). Thus, if the penetrating firm came from a complex with a high level of cohesion and if it operated on the basis of a concept of control positioned further to the right-hand side of the dependency scale, the firm gradually started to dominate the host industrial system. Eventually, the host government may be manoeuvred into the role of a *compradore* government, championing the interests of the penetrating firm. The British government, which has seen its national car and electronics industry gradually come under domination of Toyotist producers such as Toyota, Nissan and Fujitsu, provides a case in point. Another example is the Dutch government, which came to the support of Fuji's Dutch-based production facilities and bargained over trade barriers with the United States in 1994.

10.4 THE MANAGEMENT OF DEPENDENCIES IN INDUSTRIAL SYSTEMS: SHIFTING COHESION, SHIFTING CONCEPTS OF CONTROL

Over the history of industrial capitalism, one may observe a gradual shift of the leading concept of control from the left to the right-hand side on the dependency scale. Attention for a rival concept of control grows when dominant core firms appear to be unable to sustain their bargaining practices on the basis of their established concept of control: increased attention for a rival concept of control often stems from weakness. Managers, academics and decision-makers functioning in the context of a declining concept of control tend to be preoccupied with those bargaining relations that appear to function better in complexes pursuing a rival concept of control. Such narrow interest in a rival concept of control, however, may easily lead one to overlook that different bargaining relations only function well because they are embedded in a broader set of (different but consistent) bargaining and power relations.[8]

Over the 1980s and 1990s, the international restructuring race triggered major changes in most national bargaining arenas. These changes were associated with the internationalisation of domestic and foreign firms and thus represented the 'clash' of rival concepts of control on an international scale. Table 10.4 appraises the shifting concepts of control and levels of cohesion in eight industrial systems: Germany, France, the UK, Italy, Sweden, the Netherlands, the USA and Japan. These systems have been the home base of most leading core firms in the world. They are briefly discussed below.

At the beginning of the 1980s, the United Kingdom was the only industrial system facing a weak cohesion. Bargaining relations between core firms on the one hand, and workers and bankers on the other had created a disturbed domestic setting. Furthermore, the UK had a high number of foreign investors in the national economy. By 1988, the relative importance of foreign direct investment stock in the UK economy was between 15 and 20 per cent (UNCTAD, 1992: 63), a figure only surpassed by the Dutch economy.[9] Although American firms had been the prime investors in the

---

[8] The regulation school (cf. Chapter 2) tends to underestimate the significance of the Japanese institutional arrangements as an integral part of the Toyotist concept of control. Dankbaar (1993: 227) for instance correctly indicates that the crisis of Fordism cannot be solved by introducing one or two Toyotist control resolutions, but does not really take into account that Toyotism is a rival concept of control in itself.

[9] Over the 1975–88/89 period, the ratio of foreign-direct-investment inward stock to gross domestic product, according to UN estimates (UNCTAD, 1992: 326) had remained stable and extremely low in Japan (from 0.3 per cent in 1975 to 0.6 per cent in 1989), stable and

Table 10.4 Diverging bargaining arenas and shifting concepts of control in Europe, the USA and Japan

Industrial system	Dominant concept of control (± 1980)* / cohesion (indic.)	Trends in domestic bargaining arena (1990s)	Government's bargaining position (re industrial/trade policies)
Germany	• Macro-Fordism • Strong cohesion	Cohesion still considerable; East Germany offers new chances: towards renewed macro-Fordism?	Sustained, partly due to need for coordination in East Germany
France	• Macro-Fordism (sometimes leaning towards industrial democracy) • Strong cohesion	Gradual opening-up to foreign competition may undermine cohesion (e.g. increasingly weak supply base)	Privatisations reflect gradual decline of government power; government may opt for further concentration (e.g. in cars)
UK	• Micro-Fordism • Weak cohesion	Independence of major core firms lost, increasingly becoming extension of Toyotist core firms	Increasingly operating in line with Japanese and/or Toyotist interests
Italy	• Flexible specialisation/macro-Fordism • Strong regional cohesion	Gradual opening-up to foreign competition will undermine cohesion	Business response is to seize even more control over government
Sweden	• Industrial democracy (leaning towards macro-Fordism) • Strong cohesion	Slipping domestic cohesion; independence of core firms under siege (cf. Volvo, Saab), may end up as extension of foreign micro-/macro-Fordist firms	Government faced with inability of banks to play traditional role as financiers; government power also negatively affected by declining bargaining power of labour
Netherlands	• Macro-Fordism • Medium cohesion	Dominance distribution interests undermines position of core firms; Toyotism on the rise	Relatively weak government will further undermine manufacturing base and thus promote Toyotism
USA	• Micro-Fordism • Medium cohesion	Slipping cohesion due to runaway US firms (1960s to 1990s) escaping from domestic bargaining arena; cohesion further undermined by massive inroads of Toyotist producers	Caught between free market ideology and declining cohesion/competitiveness: relaxes antitrust regulations, champions 'fair trade'; perhaps rehabilitation defence policy as disguise for industrial policy
Japan	• Toyotism • Strong cohesion	Cohesion relatively high yet under stress from 'bubble' economy, temporary increase in workers' bargaining power (due to labour shortage) and internationalisation; current restructuring aimed at reviving Toyotism appears successful	National government supports core firms' restructuring agenda: to facilitate restructuring banking system; maintains pressure to save (also to discipline workers) and to reduce pace of internationalisation

Note: The dominant concept of control in this table serves as a point of orientation at the state level. However, a dominant concept of control may not be accomplished by all or even by the majority of core firms in a given industrial system.

UK economy, and although these shared a micro-Fordist concept of control, US firms regarded their UK activities as an extention of their US home base, and the centre of decision-making processes remained firmly in the United States.

Through the 1980s, the United States became confronted with an eroded domestic micro-Fordist regime, due to a combinaton of events such as inroads by foreign firms with a different concept of control, the US core firm's runaway from their own bargaining arena (section 10.3.2), and the priority that consecutive American governments have given to military expenditures over productive investments. Of all OECD countries, the United Kingdom and the United States' industrial systems have been most adaptive to the Japanese concept of control. This is attributable to the weakened cohesion, but also to the fact that on the dependency scale, micro-Fordist bargaining based on direct control is least remote from Toyotist bargaining on the basis of structural control.

In continental Europe, the dominant postwar concepts of control have been macro-Fordism and in some instances industrial democracy. These concepts of control have crystallised at relatively high levels of cohesion. Over 1980s and 1990s, Dutch companies and financiers have been among the leading sources of foreign direct investments in the United States – even outpacing Japanese investors. This enormous investment 'leakage' contributed to a gradual de-industrialisation, to lower cohesion and to a downward pressure on wages and purchasing power. Moreover, a rapid decline of trade union membership (from 35 per cent in 1980 to around 20 per cent in 1994) undermined the traditional tripartite corporatist bargaining practice. The Dutch government also actively stimulated inward-oriented FDI, and the Dutch economy became a major target of Japanese distribution centres, accelerating the demise of macro-Fordism and creating a gradual shift towards Toyotism.

Over the 1980s, Sweden faced only limited inflows of foreign direct investments (below 5 per cent).[10] However, the Swedish cohesion was undermined by the internationalisation of Swedish multinationals to the European continent, stimulated by the industrial banks (see section 7.4). To some extent, this 'hollowed out' the corporatist bargaining institutions and stimulated the Swedish government to apply for full membership of the

---

relatively low in Sweden (4.4 per cent in 1988) and Italy (5.0 per cent in 1975, 5.3 per cent in 1989), while the penetration was low, but rising in France (1.5 per cent in 1975 to 4.9 per cent in 1989) and the United States (1.3 per cent in 1975 and 7.3 per cent in 1989). The foreign owned stock in Germany in 1989 was assessed to be of comparable size to the stock in the United States. The ratio for the Dutch economy had moved most rapidly to an extremely high level of foreign involvement in the national economy from 12 per cent in 1975 to 22.2 per cent in 1989.

[10] Germany, Switzerland, France, Italy and Japan also experienced less than five per cent investment inflows as a percentage of gross domestic capital formation over the 1986–9 period. For the US, this amounted to 5.1 to 10 per cent, and for the Netherlands and the UK even 10 to 15 per cent (UNCTAD, 1992: 61).

European Union. However, while trade union membership declined in all other major industrial systems, membership increased in Sweden from 80 per cent in 1980 to 85.3 per cent in 1985 (OECD, 1993: 49).[11] This created a counter-movement from trade unions and large parts of the Swedish population. In this respect, the Swedish 1993 application for membership of the European Union reflected a declining domestic cohesion and posed a test case of the relative bargaining strength of the Swedish trade unions.[12]

By 1980, the Italian industrial system was based on a mixture of flexible specialisation and macro-Fordist institutions. These institutions had materialised in a sub-national, i.e. regional context, complemented by weak central state regulation. Over the 1970s, this setting had spurred economic growth, but it also created an extremely closed system in which two rival concepts of control coexisted. This unstable balance of power was undermined by two forces. Firstly, the continued rivalry between regions and related concepts of control could not be resolved for lack of a strong central government. Secondly, the Single European Act forced the Italian government to gradually open up the Italian economy. On the one hand, traditional core firms such as Fiat, Olivetti, IRI, Feruzzi and ENI became confronted with increasing international competition. On the other hand, new business moguls such as Carlo de Benedetti, Silvio Berlusconi and the Benetton family skilfully profited from the (chaotic) remains of the regionally organised clientist system. With a moderate capital involvement, these family-owned holding companies seized control over a considerable part of the Italian industrial and service economy. In the case of Benetton, the family holding company gradually supplanted networks of flexible specialisation into Toyotist networks of informal hierarchical control. Thus a third concept of control joined the battle for dominance in Italy. The ascendance of Berlusconi, a prime minister in 1994 coming from a non-core part of the industrial system (the media), suggests that the battle for control over the state is likely to continue.

In spite of considerable pressure over the 1980s and 1990s, French bargaining institutions have shown remarkable adaptability to the international restructuring race. The French industrial system has long protected itself from inroads of industrial complexes representing alternative concepts of control, while those foreign core firms that did establish themselves in France have been forced to adapt to French bargaining institutions. The

---

[11] Over the same period, union density declined in all other important industrial systems in the following manner: USA (23 per cent to 16 per cent), Japan (31 per cent to 27 per cent), Germany (37 per cent to 34 per cent), France (19 per cent to 12 per cent), Italy (49 per cent to 40 per cent), UK (51 per cent to 42 per cent), Netherlands (35 per cent to 25 per cent) (OECD, 1993: 49).

[12] In the preparations of the September 1994 Swedish elections, four core players (Volvo, Ericsson, Stora and ABB) publicly threatened to stall investment projects of more than 4 billion ECUs and further move abroad in case of a victory of the Social Democratic party, the architect of Swedish corporatism. The Wallenberg family issued similar warnings (*Vk*, 13 September 1994).

spirit of Colbert has lived on in France: in particular, industries with a high public procurement content (defence, aerospace, public utilities, banking and telecommunications) have been able – in close consultation with state agencies – to restructure and remain amongst Europe's most competitive industries. In the car and computer industries, however, it has proved difficult to complement a weak supply base by big national investment projects, aimed at creating a *filière* (chain) of supply activities. Another French government strategy to defend macro-Fordism has been to strengthen bilateral bonds with Germany (home of the renowned *Mittel-stand* of small and medium-sized enterprises). At the same time, it has taken a more active (although still ambivalent) approach to promoting European integration: over the 1980s, French government and industry bureaucrats have flooded the European bureaucracy.

The cohesion of the German industrial system over the 1960s and 1970s was extremely high. The economic success and international competitiveness of its most important core players retained most investments for the national system, fostering the stability of the corporatist bargaining institutions (cf. Grabher, 1993). Cohesion started to slip after the late 1970s. Inroads by foreign core firms only played a minor role in this. More important was that the German institutional setting proved ill-adapted to the challenges of the microelectronics revolution (see Appendix). Furthermore, over the 1970s and 1980s many German firms began to search for a regional division of labour within Europe in a modest effort to profit from regional scale economies and in an equally modest effort to escape from domestic bargaining arrangements. After reunification, German firms suddenly faced a potential market of almost 80 million people, representing a growth of potential domestic purchasing power of around 30 per cent. The importance of this new market can hardly be overstated: it could absorb the bulk of German exports, and it could re-focus attention on domestic expansion and bargaining. In the period from October 1990 to the end of 1994, the German federal government funnelled 514 billion Deutschmarks to the five East German states, as much as the complete federal budget for one year (*Vk*, 17 February 1995). German core and medium-sized players set up large scale investment programmes, often aimed at creating a division of labour within Germany instead of within the European region. Consequently, Germany's international trade dependence is likely to come more into line with the US and Japanese industrial system (both dedicated around 8 per cent of their GDP to trade in 1993) (*The Economist*, 1994: 28). There appear to be reasonable chances for a renewed macro-Fordist growth regime within Germany.

During and particularly after the end of the 'bubble economy', the cohesion of the Japanese industrial system has been under strain from factors such as road congestion (hindering just-in-time deliveries), pressure on exports (due to an appreciating yen and to trade protection in the USA and Europe) and labour shortages. Despite these pressures, however, the cohesion of the Japanese industrial system has remained remarkably high. The costs of adjustments, however, have been distributed very unevenly over society. While Japanese core firms have been faced with sharply declining profits and occassional losses, many lower-tier suppliers did not survive the post-bubble recession and went bankrupt. The Japanese government has remained relatively weak. It has been interesting to note that under these circumstances, Toyota, which has traditionally maintained a low political profile, has deemed it necessary to strengthen its hold over the Japanese bargaining institutions. In the early 1990s, Toyota took over the chairmanship of the Keidanren, the Japanese employers' federation. At almost the same time, the chair of the Autoworkers Union went from Nissan – that suffered much more from the recession due to a lower degree of cohesion – to Toyota. While this might indicate that Toyota is sustaining its structural control over the Japanese car industry and its domestic bargaining arena in general, another interpretation could be that even Toyota is finding it increasingly difficult to sustain its structural control strategy and that it is resorting to a more direct control strategy.

10.5 WHITHER THE RIVALRY BETWEEN CONCEPTS OF CONTROL? THE MANAGEMENT OF REGIONAL DEPENDENCIES

Over the 1980s, the international restructuring race led to a 'regionalisation' within the Triad regions (Europe, Japan plus the Asia-Pacific, and the United States), rather than the alleged 'globalisation' (see Chapter 6). However, the question remains whether and to what extent this regionalisation should be seen as a step towards increasing global integration or global rivalry. This concluding section discusses the nature of these regional trade regimes, in particular the question to what extent they will be able to create or sustain cohesion.

European Union: battleground of four rival concepts of control

The six European industrial systems which were at the cradle of the European Coal and Steel Community (1951) and the European Economic Community (1957) (France, Italy, Germany, Belgium, the Netherlands and Luxemburg) each shared a macro-Fordist oriented regulatory environment.[13] The European Community provided its member states with both scale economies and the possibilty to build up their own domestic bargaining institutions. Thus the original cohesion of the European Community was relatively high. Between 1973 and 1986, six additional member countries were admitted to the EEC: Britian, Ireland, Denmark, Spain, Portugal and

---

[13] This even holds for the Grand Duchy of Luxemburg, which has been heavily influenced by bordering France, Germany and Belgium. With the latter, it maintains an economic union (BLEU).

Greece (following a variety of political and economic motives which are beyond the scope of this study). However, in none of these industrial systems, did macro-Fordism represent the dominant concept of control. The late 1970s and early 1980s, which became known as the period of 'Eurosclerosis', manifested this declining cohesion at the level of the European Community. Problems were reinforced by Toyotist competition in two carriers of European macro-Fordism, i.e. the electronics and the car industries. Next to coal and steel, the electronics and car industries had been well represented in the six original member states of the European Community, but had been non-existent, poorly developed or virtually disappeared in the new member states. Thus, while political consensus on steel could still be achieved, the car and electronics industries faced a scattered bargaining arena at the European Community level.

In response to the declining cohesion of their complexes, leading core firms over the 1980s took initiatives to break the apathy of Eurosclerosis and to step up integration. Table 10.5 shows some of the most active core firms in Europe (participating in at least two important initiatives at the same time) and the institutions they helped shape. Section 5.3.3 has already mentioned the 1983 ESPRIT initiative, which facilitated many pre-competitive collaborative research projects in Europe. Complementary and subsidiary projects often received sweeping acronyms to indicate a renewed dynamism in European integration and in increasing cohesion and competitiveness such as RACE, AMICE, START or BRITE. The year 1983 also saw the birth of the European Round Table of Industrialists (ERT), providing European core companies with a European discussion forum as well as a sounding board for the European Commission.[14]

Parallel to the creation of the ESPRIT committee and the ERT, Philips president Dekker presented a plan called 'Europe-1990, An Agenda for Action' in which he introduced a design for further integration (e.g. via harmonisation of standards and procurement policies) and the breakdown of customs procedures. Many elements reappeared in the June 1985 White Paper 'Completing the Internal Market' by Commissioner Lord Cockfield – although the target year became 1992 instead of 1990. Other 'spin-off' initiatives included the 1984 Euroventures (coming from ten of the original ERT members, aimed at providing venture capital to smaller European companies), the 1985 Standard Promotion and Application Group (SPAG, initiated by eight of the twelve ESPRIT founders) and the 1988 European Foundation for Quality Management (initiated by Philips) to stimulate the creation of European Quality Standards. In computers and telecommunications, eight large European firms joined forces in the X/Open consortium in

---

[14] While Pehr Gyllenhammer (then CEO of Volvo) has often been described as the driving force behind the ERT in its first six years, it was in fact the European Commission's former industry commissioner, Etienne Davignon, who recruited most of its members (cf. van Tulder and Junne, 1988: 215).

Table 10.5 A sequence of core companies most active in forging European cohesion

Company	Country	1	2	3	4	5	6	7
Philips	Netherlands	×	×	×	×	×	×	×
Olivetti	Italy	×	×	×	×	×		×
Siemens/Nixdorf	Germany	×	–	×	×	–		×
Daimler/AEG	Germany	×	–	×	×	–		×
Robert Bosch	Germany	×	×	–	–	×	×	–
Fiat	Italy	×	×	–	–	×	×	–
Bull	France	–	–	×	×	×		×
Saint Gobain	France	×	×	–	–	–	×	–
CGE/ALCATEL	France	–	–	×	×	–	×	–
Thomson	France	×	–	×	×	–		–
Renault	France	×	–	–	–	×	×	–
Volvo	Sweden	×	×	–	–	–	×	–
Plessey	UK	×	–	×	×	–	–	–
STC/ICL	UK	–	–	× /-	×	–		×
GEC	UK	–	–	×	×	–		–
STET (IRI)	Italy	–	–	×	×	–		–
Nestlé	Switzerland	×	–	–	–	×	–	–
ASEA/BBC	Sweden/Switzerland	×	×	–	–	–		–
Ciba/Geigy	Switzerland	×	–	–	–	×	–	–
Volkswagen	Germany	–	–	–	–	×	×	–
Telefónica	Spain	×	–	–	–	–	×	–
Other companies		> 20	2	–	–	5	> 20	11*

Notes:
1 Important member of Round Table of European Industrialists over most of its history
2 Euroventures
3 ESPRIT/Round Table (x/-: ICL was ousted after being taken over by Fujitsu)
4 SPAG
5 Founders of European Foundation for Quality Management
6 ODETTE
7 X/Open group
* Includes US founders, DEC, AT&T, Sun, Unisys, HP

order to break the power of IBM.[15] In the area of component supply, European companies active as assemblers or suppliers in the car industry, created the ODETTE consortium (Organisation for Data Exchange by Tele Transmission in Europe). Finally, in 1987, 150 large European core companies (including Philips and Fiat) established the Foundation for European Montary Union, to support the creation of a single European currency.

The most active firms supporting these programmes were those car, electronics and computer companies which were trying to reorient their

[15] Other large American computer firms, Japanese computer firms like Hitachi and NEC, as well as strong user companies such as Shell, joined this campaign in favour of open standards. It also received support from the European Commission.

domestic or multi-domestic strategies into a regional division of labour, with larger and more integrated production sites within Europe. Both in the ESPRIT programme and in the ERT, Philips (through its CEO Wisse Dekker) and Olivetti (through its CEO Carlo de Benedetti) played a leading role. Philips, facing severe Japanese competition, hoped these projects would help its international restructuring process from a multi-domestic production organisation towards a regional division of labour. (By allying with European partners, Philips also hoped to modify its weak bargaining position in some partnerships with American and Japanese firms.) To Olivetti, the European cooperation programmes offered an opportunity to gradually diminish its dependence on its Italian home market.[16]

Due to these combined initiatives, European integration got a new impetus. Reduced customs procedures and the harmonisation of standards and procurement stimulated intra-EC trade from an already high level of 52 per cent in 1981 to 61 per cent in 1990. EFTA (the European Free Trade Association, consisting of Sweden, Norway, Finland, Iceland, Liechtenstein, Austria and Switzerland) also saw its share of trade with EC countries increase from 51 per cent in 1981 to 58 per cent in 1990 (UNCTAD, 1992: 68–9). Likewise, intra-European foreign direct investments was boosted. In 1992, European Community member countries such as France (US$22 billion), Britain (US$18 billion), Belgium/Luxemburg (US$11 billion), Spain (US$8 billion), Germany (US$7 billion) and the Netherlands (US$5 billion) were the largest recipients of inward foreign direct investments of all developed economies (*Fortune*, 25 July 1994). By comparison, the 1992 foreign direct investment inflow in the United States had amounted to a meagre US$2.4 billion, lower even than the investments inflows into some of the smaller European countries (ibid). These growing intra-European investment flows point at a growing mutual penetration of the European economies, although in 1995 it was still unclear whether they will actually strengthen or undermine cohesion at a European level.

Increasing European integration inevitably led to a shift of bargaining power in favour of the European Commission. However, the shape of major European bargaining institutions has tended to reflect those of the strongest and (relatively) most cohesive industrial system, i.e. the German

---

[16] One will only find a few European (petro)chemical or pharmaceutical core firms among the most active players striving for further European integration. In the mid-1980s, core firms in these industries tended to be competitive, leading relatively cohesive complexes. Thus, when Commissioner Davignon attempted to organise the European chemical and pharmaceutical industry into a biotechnology consortium modelled after the way the electronics industry had organised itself in ESPRIT, this initiative badly failed due to unwillingness of the industry to collaborate. The envisaged 'Roundtable' was to include such firms as Rhône-Poulenc, Hoechst, Vyoril, ICI, Novo, Celltech, Montedison, Gist Brocades, Akzo, Solvay, Wellcome, Elf-Aquitaine and Amylum.

[17] In September 1994, DG-III Commissioner Bangemann (former German minister of Economic Affairs) presented the outline for a renewed industrial policy for the European Union. One of its main components were the extension of intra-European collaboration forms for which competition policy should be adjusted. Research of Neven *et al.* (1993) on the

one and to a lesser extent the French industrial system. This holds particularly for the areas of competition policy[17] and the creation of a relatively independent European Central Bank,[18] while the establishment of a European system of company councils can be read as a more moderate version of the German *Betriebsrat*.[19]

The most important challenge facing the European Union is the large variety of competing concepts of control *within* the European trade bloc. On many occasions, the UK government has blocked or frustrated European decision-making,[20] while it bargained for three provisos in important parts of the 1991 Maastricht Treaty: an exemption from the social charter on workers' rights, a clause preventing more power to be given to the European Commission, and an opt-out provision on the membership of the Monetary Union (cf. Milner, 1994: 29). The September 1994 foundation of European Company Councils, for instance, will not apply to the United Kingdom. In most of these cases, the British government supported the interests of Japanese core firms internationalising on the basis of a Toyotist concept of control. As a result, cohesion in the European Union has been further undermined, making the European Union the battleground of all five rival concepts of control. The discussion on a 'multi-speed Europe' (with the core industrial systems of Germany, France, the Netherlands, Belgium and Luxemburg proceeding more rapidly with monetary and political integration than the other member states) thus represents an attempt to sustain the cohesion of the old macro-Fordist European industrial systems, and to limit potentially disruptive competition from hostile concepts of control (see Table 10.6).

---

practice of European competition policy revealed that of the two hundred cases submitted for review in the 1990–4 period, only one case (the merger between three aircraft manufacturers) had been rejected, while about ten projected mergers or acquisitions had to meet additional requirements.

[18] Helen Milner (1994: 27) notes that the German Bundesbank had insisted that the ECB would be politically independent and would have the maintenance of price stability as its main objective. Other countries such as France, with different banking institutions and a much more dependent central bank (see also section 5.2.2) had to accommodate to these demands, knowing that the German government's support for EMU largely depended on support of the (independent) Bundesbank.

[19] In September 1994 (after twenty years of negotiations, for instance on the Vredeling Directive, which was never adopted), the European Commission decided to require companies with more than one thousand employees (of whom at least 150 work in at least two member states of the European Union) to establish a European Company Union.

[20] On behalf of Honda, Nissan and Toyota, the UK government prevented Japanese transplants being included in the EC–Japan car trade agreement (1991) (cf. Ruigrok and van Tulder, 1991: 197ff). On behalf of ICL (taken over by Fujitsu), it successfully bargained for ICL's admission to EU collaboration programmes, and pressured the European Commission to open up EU collaborative programmes to companies from non-EU member states. (In the United States, by comparison, participation to pre-competitive R&D programmes is restricted to companies that are at least 51 per cent American-owned, while *de facto* restrictions in Japan are even more restrictive (ATB, 25 August 1994). On behalf of Japanese television makers with UK facilities such as Sony, Matsushita and Sharp, the UK government frustrated the adoption of a European High Definition TV standard.

Regional integration as the expression of slipping cohesion: NAFTA

The bargaining pendulum in the internationalisation of US core firms, fierce rivalry among US core companies (inevitably associated with a regime of direct control), and the inroads by Japanese car and electronics producers have seriously undermined the cohesion of the US industrial system. Since the early 1960s, US trade policy came to facilitate the rise of US multinationals. The USA–Canada Auto Pact in 1965, for instance, was to provide free car trade between the two countries - with only little progress towards a North American division of labour.[21] A series of negotiated trade barriers, primarily with Japan, could not halt a trend of cohesion slipping further, even leading to the disappearance of major independent US car and consumer electronics firms. Often, only firms with substantial government procurement, plus a group of small and medium-sized information technology companies, managed to survive. To many US core firms, the creation of NAFTA represented at least a partial retreat from the globalisation ideal type – which they never accomplished in the first place.

It has been estimated that the economic gains of NAFTA for the US economy as a whole will be relatively small, whereas the gains for Mexico would be much greater (*NYT*, 14 November 1993). While the USA accounted for 71 per cent of Mexico's exports and 76 per cent of Canada's exports in 1990, they only accounted for respectively 9 and 20 per cent of US exports in 1991 (*The Economist*, 1994). During the NAFTA negotiations, special attention was given to textiles, agriculture and petrochemicals where mostly domestic US players felt endangered by the influx of cheap imports from Mexico. The electronics industry was not thought of as a sensitive sector, largely because American producers had not located many production sites in Mexico (Milner, 1994: 21). Thus the US government paid most attention in the NAFTA negotiations to industries where Toyotist competition and the prospects of a North American division of labour are limited. The only (formerly) micro-Fordist stronghold interested in creating a regional division of labour, which was discussed extensively during the NAFTA negotiations was the car industry.

Moreover, when the administration tried to get NAFTA ratified by Congress, trade unions – led by the United Auto Workers – successfully pressed the US government to restart negotiations over labour-related issues. Hence, it seems uncertain that NAFTA will facilitate a North American division of labour. NAFTA does not seem to impose any barriers

---

[21] At the time, the Canadian government stipulated that the US car makers had to produce as many cars as they sold in Canada - to ensure sufficient production volumes in Canada – plus a 50 per cent local content requirement. In retrospect, the major result of the USA–Canada Auto Pact was to facilitate the Big Three in developing an essentially multi-domestic strategy towards Canada, rather than promoting a North American division of labour.

for glocalising firms, and could even make it more difficult to formulate a coherent trade policy. In 1990, for instance, the United States Trade Representative, in a trade dispute with the EU, ruled that cars produced at Honda's US plant and exported to the EU had to be treated as 'American' products. At almost the same time, the 'American content' of Honda cars became severely questioned by the US customs. Partly because of the inability to formulate a coherent trade policy at home, the US response to Toyotist competition has been to bargain over Japanese 'structural impediments' and to demand market openings from, for instance Japanese car, (micro)electronics and glass producers, plus improved access to the Japanese distribution system. The deals concluded as a result of these campaigns were always reached just before a US deadline expired, always after tough negotiations, and still rendered only minor results. It seems implausible that the creation of NAFTA will do anything to change this pattern. In conclusion, therefore, it seems improbable that NAFTA will prove able to bring an end to the gradual decline of US cohesion.[22]

The Pax Nipponica: the strength of weak ties[23]

Many authors have speculated about the rise of a Japanese-led regional division of labour in the Asia-Pacific region. In many industries, Japan's huge labour shortages, its rising wages, and the continuing need to innovate production and technology at home would all contribute to a regional division of labour, since core firms and component suppliers would increasingly look for South East Asia as a cheap production base. Many have also argued that the political vision of the Japanese government does not seem to match the economic strength of Japanese complexes in the region. These observers searched for Japanese government initiatives towards political and economic integration comparable to that of the European and Northern American industrial systems – and did not find them. Likewise, analysts of companies' internationalisation strategies have tended to search for an explanation for the shape of Japanese foreign direct investments (hardly any acquisitions and often direct investments or minority shareholdings) in the Pacific-Asia Region by pointing at the relative inexperience of Japanese firms in foreign direct investments (Lipsey, 1993: 216). All three types of observers, in our view, have failed to grasp the essence of Toyotism and its complementary logic of glocalisation. According to the framework of this book, the logic of a regional division of labour headed by Japanese core firms would differ from the international division of labour that would emerge through US or European complexes' strategies. If many Japanese

[22] For a study of the prospects of North American integration from a Quebec perspective, see Latouche, 1992.
[23] The notion of 'strength through weak ties' was already used by Granovetter (1973) and taken up further for instance, by Grabner (1993) in his analysis of regional network structures.

core firms do strive for glocalisation, as the evidence of this book suggests, these firms' and their suppliers' internationalisation to the Asia-Pacific region will be relatively limited.

Toyotism in Japan emerged not only in the context of high domestic vulnerability of core firms (see section 3.4) but also in the context of extreme international and regional vulnerabilities. The dependence of the Japanese industrial system on the import of food and raw materials has forced the Japanese government firstly, to aim for the unhindered supply of raw materials and food products. Secondly, the Japanese government has maintained an absolute control over Japan's foreign trade and currency rate.

Because of Japan's dependence on importing food and raw materials, exerting structural control over the South East Asian region may be even more critical to Japanese core firms than securing access to the US and EU markets. The attraction of the Asian region to Japan is not only based on the region's wealth of mineral fuels waiting to be explored and exploited (such as in Siberia and the South Chinese Sea). Equally important is the fact that none of the region's economies matches the Japanese industrial strength and technological sophistication, putting Japanese firms in an ideal bargaining position versus South East Asian governments eager to attract Japanese investors. Often, the investment strategy of Japanese firms is backed by official Japanese development aid funds. The prime focus of Japan's development funds therefore has been the South East Asian region: Japanese foreign aid to the region is twice as high for instance as US foreign aid to the region. Japanese assistance is partly aimed at infrastructural and industrial projects that facilitate Japanese internationalisation strategies, or that help the large construction companies to find business in the region. While Japanese companies focused their investment strategies in the region on factories and distribution, more than half of the US investment has been in the exploration of petroleum (*BW*, 12 September 1994).

Depending on the bargaining strength of the local government and industry, Japanese core firms have relied on direct investments or on indirect measures to enforce structural control in the South East Asian region. In South Korea, for instance, Japanese firms were faced with strong local conglomerates. As a result, 'knowledge-based assets obtained from licensing technical services contracts, turnkey plants, and machinery imports were more important than foreign direct investment' (Doner, 1993: 184). In Taiwan, direct Japanese investments were freely allowed. By the mid-1980s, Japanese trading companies controlled some 50 per cent of Taiwan's trade (Doner, 1993: 193) and frustrated the creation of indigenous Japanese-like trading institutions – despite considerable government efforts.

The NIEs and the ASEAN economies, known in Western Europe and the USA for their export orientation, have suffered for many years from a trade *deficit* with Japan. The 1992 bilateral trade deficit of Singapore and Hong Kong with Japan reached a level of 20 per cent of GDP, while the ratio was around 5 per cent for both Taiwan and Malaysia (*FT*, 29 August

1994). Most of the goods the NIEs are importing from Japan are industrial and capital goods. Japanese firms have been careful not to transfer any technology not yet fully commercialised. The Japanese government has even prohibited the transfer of two hundred high technologies to South Korea until 1995 (Bello, 1993: 35). By that time, Japanese companies should have fully exploited the possibilities of these technologies. Japanese firms only transfer less advanced technologies to Korean and Taiwanese firms. Consequently, Korean conglomerates such as Samsung, Hyundai and Lucky Goldstar can only serve the lower segments of the European and North American car and electronics markets. Just like US and European firms, they are facing huge barriers to entering the Japanese market to compete with Japanese producers. However, whereas European and US public authorities have pressed Japanese firms to develop into full-fledged 'insiders', none of the national governments in the South East Asian region can even hope to pose similar conditions on Japanese investors.[24]

South East Asian operations enable Japanese companies to export manufactured goods or semi-finished inputs to the other Triad markets, which has lowered the Japanese trade surplus of manufactured goods with the United States and Europe while retaining control over the import of manufactured goods. As Richard Doner (1993: 207) puts it: 'In broad terms Japan sells capital goods to the rest of East Asia, the rest of East Asia sells finished goods to the United States, and the United States sells raw materials to Japan. Japan is a critical contributor to each of these developments'.[25] As a result, East Asian intra-regional trade over the 1980s increased only marginally, from 33 per cent to 37 per cent (*BW*, 10 January 1994). As indicated above, intra-EC trade in 1990 amounted to 61 per cent of total EC trade. At the same time, exports to the Triad regions (in particular the United States) increased from 32.8 per cent of total exports in 1960, via 30.3 per cent in 1976 to 38.3 per cent in 1990 (UN Handbook, quoted in Jones, 1994: 35).

Within a slowly developing intra-regional trade regime, Japanese exports rose from 22 per cent in 1970 to 29 per cent in 1990 of all intra-regional trade (ibid). US exports to the South East Asian region also increased, but at a lower level: from 9 per cent of total exports in 1970 to 14 per cent in 1990 (Keizai Koho Center, 1994: 54). Between 1989 and 1994, Japanese foreign direct investments in the region jumped from 12 to 20 per cent of total Japanese FDI. The stock of Japanese investments in the Asian region, however, trailed this figure: over the 1951–92 period, accumulated investments in Asia were around 15 per cent of total Japanese foreign investments worldwide. This reflects the glocalisation investment surge to North

---

[24] Richard Doner (1993: 191) mentions an interesting example of US firms trying to interest Thai firms in American machinery. The Thai firms refused because they had already adopted Japanese specifications.
[25] In 1993, Japan became a net importer of colour televisions, assembled by Japanese companies in South East Asian economies (*FT*, 15 July 1994).

America (43 per cent of 1992 flows, 44 per cent of stocks) and Europe (21 per cent of 1992 flows, 20 per cent of stocks), which disturbed the long-term Japanese orientation to the Asian region.

These particular regional dynamics create favourable political and economic circumstances for the Japanese industrial system. In times of a domestic recession or of mounting energy prices, Japanese producers will be better able to control the prices and/or if necessary reduce the volumes of these manufactured imports to ensure that oil and food imports can proceed. Generally, Japanese core firms in the region have opted for a going-it-alone strategy or for minority shareholdings. However, an important distinction here should be made between horizontal and vertical *keiretsu*. In the car industry, we found that Mazda and Mitsubishi Motors had been much more interested in investing in a regional division of labour than Toyota, Honda or Nissan (Ruigrok and van Tulder, 1991: 90ff; Doner, 1991). In a detailed study of the internationalisation strategies of Japanese electronics firms, René Belderbos (1994) finds confirmation for this distinction.

Certain electronics companies as well as textiles and apparel producers belonging to large horizontal conglomerates such as Mitsubishi, have made steps towards a regional division of labour that even led to some re-importations of (semi-)finished products into Japan. In this way, Mitsubishi responded to pressures from MITI which aimed to calm down anti-Japanese sentiments in the region and reduce USA–Japan and EU–Japan trade tensions by locating some export-oriented production in other Asian countries. Horizontal conglomerates have tended to be more receptive to these pressures than vertical *keiretsu*, because they are also involved in other activities in the region for which they require government support and development assistance, such as the exploitation and trade of minerals and foods, and local building activities. The regional strategies of Japanese suppliers mirror those of their core companies.

Japan's moderate expression of a political vision for the region mirrors the weak position of the Japanese government at home, as well as the dominant position of the Japanese industrial system in the region. While many Japanese core firms share a clear interest in gradually extending their ties with the Asia-Pacific region, they do not have a strong interest in forging a formal regional organisation at a political level. The Japanese government has not been a catalyst in promoting the Asia-Pacific Economic Cooperation forum (APEC) but instead has tried to follow these developments and play a diplomatic role. It is not in the Japanese interest that Asian and Pacific economies delegate sovereignty to an organisation in which Japan is confronted with strong bargaining partners such as the United States, China and Australia (which has actively campaigned for Asia-Pacific integration). Development of APEC as an official bargaining institution rather than as a loose federation might moreover accelerate the integration process of the Association of South East Asian Nations

(ASEAN) and improve the bargaining position of its member states versus Japan and other regional powers.

Thus, Japan's dominant interest is to keep the Asia-Pacific region fragmented, and to increase control over the region by supporting only loose political ties. At the same time, the Japanese government has stated its support to reducing trade barriers throughout the region. This is in line with the objective to reduce its international vulnerabilities. A liberalisation of regional trade could boost Japan's regional exports, could enhance its strategic room of manoeuvring in the imports of minerals and foods, and could give it greater freedom in locating and relocating production facilities in the region. As long as Toyotism remains the dominant concept of control in Japan, and as long as cohesion is maintained, the danger of a substantial and uncontrolled penetration of leading consumer or capital goods markets in Japan by non-Japanese producers remains virtually hypothetical.[26]

The dynamism of the international restructuring race, then, seems to point at a continuing, though not necessarily growing, rivalry between the three Triad regions. Europe is struggling with five different concepts of control, North America seems incapable of reversing the trend of a gradually declining cohesion, and Japan has refocused attention on the Asia-Pacific region in order to stimulate freer regional trade and to advance its grip on the region. In a gloomy scenario, this dynamism could promote rivalry and an inward orientation in the Triad regions. In a more optimistic scenario, however, one could envisage the rise of a bigemony between the United States and Japan, leading to new international bargaining institutions, in an effort to avert an escalation of international conflicts.

---

[26] For a different view on Asian regional integration, see Institute for Economic Planning for Peace, 1992.

Table 10.6   Rival regional regimes

	Europe	North America	(South) East Asia
Dominant concepts of control	Flexible specialisation; industrial democracy; macro-, micro-Fordism; Toyotism (UK)	Micro-Fordism; Toyotism (in some states)	Flexible specialisation and Toyotism
Nature of internationalisation	Intra-regional; relatively open; sizeable flows of inward and outward FDI	Retreat strategy; relatively closed; declining flows of inward FDI	Regional consolidation; low flows of inward FDI, decreasing flows of FDI to Triad; increasing FDI to region
Regional cohesion?	Medium, mixed	Weakening	Strong
Trade regime	EU, EES	NAFTA	APEC
Supranational political control?	Yes (partly): supra-national executive body, including a parliament	Some: by international (trilateral) organisations, without supranational authorities	Hardly: no multilateral governing agencies yet, nation-state remains sovereign unit
Political relations with countries/ peripheral countries in region?	Rising pressure to include (esp. Eastern European) perhipheral countries in regional regime, which may become lower end of European division of labour	Loose political relations; peripheral countries kept out of NAFTA; subregional trade blocs (Andes Pact, Mercosur)	Very loose political relations; rival core states try to influence the same region
Nature of bargaining in the region	Coalition-oriented: relative balance of power between political entities and industrial complexes, despite German dominance. Aim: integrate the region, but sustain national differences	Dominance of the US industrial complexes: NAFTA as effort to gain direct control over the region. Aim: economic integration, only minor labour and environmental harmonisation	Dominance of Japanese industrial system: efforts to gain structural control over the region (e.g. via FDI, development aid, APEC); interested in keeping region fragmented, but to spur free trade (Japanese structural barriers to foreign imports remain)
Trade consequences	Continued regionalisation of trade	(Moderate) globalisation of trade	Increasing regional trade, declining global trade

Appendix

The bargaining dynamism of industrial complexes and industrial systems

THE BARGAINING LOGIC OF WEAK INSTITUTIONS WITHIN A DEGENERATING HEGEMON

Table 10.2 illustrated that it is relatively easy to find British examples of a combination of a weak national system *and* weak industrial complexes. This underlines the sustained impact of institutional arrangements stemming from the era in which the British industrial system had gained hegemonic status and which were re-established time and again. When these arrangements proved to be superfluous at the time the American institutions had shown their superior qualities, it proved prohibitively difficult to change the agreed-upon rules of the game (the institutions). The continuation of old institutional arrangements in postwar Britain – including a free trade orientation – thus also created the condition for a sustained weakness of industrial complexes, notwithstanding major restructuring schemes of subsequent British governments.

With a declining competitiveness of the national industrial system, it became also more likely that interests between various groups in society started to diverge. This represents the declining 'edge' of particular interests in the economy, as specified in Figure 9.1. In case of a declining hegemon like the United Kingdom we expected that first the interests of manufacturing core firms would become more difficult to represent since they got trapped in a vicious circle of sustained weakness illustrated in particular by low levels of productivity growth. At the same time other interests, in particular those of services (banks, i.e. the City) and the military, remained relatively unscathed in the national bargaining arena as a legacy of the hegemonic past. Schumpeter had already hinted at the existence of anachronistic practices in an economy that could prevent firms and sectors jumping on a consecutive upward swing in a long wave. The continuation of 'old' bargaining rules in declining economic powers could thus be called an institutional anachronism. Under these circumstances it proves difficult to start fundamental restructuring processes (to put it fashionably, the capacity to 're-engineer' society remains limited) and the weakness of industrial complexes continues in a vicious bargaining dynamism.

The bargaining setting only changes when confronted with direct inroads from (often foreign) core firms which represent fundamentally different concepts of control. This is what happened with the British economy in the course of the 1970s and 1980s. Initially, foreign firms only entered and were welcomed as partners from the expectation that they might provide a complement to the weakened production base of British industrial complexes. But this strategy hardly took the strategic intent of the partners into account, nor was the domestic bargaining arena restructured to facilitate maximum benefit from the partnership. The partnerships proved not to have the (desired) effects on the cohesion of the endogenous complexes. On the contrary, the British core firms experienced sustained weakness and consequently, the alliances were often the first phase in a take-over strategy. This mechanism represents the bargaining logic over the direction of restructuring within a declining hegemon. The remarkable parallels in logic will be illustrated by the postwar experience of three different British core firms in the example industries, each the outcome of strong government involvement: Rover in cars, ICL in computers and Plessey in telecommunications.

Over the postwar years the Rover Group was forged as the result of numerous realignments of the British car industry under the pressure of consecutive British governments. Governments of various political credentials merged the remnants of former independent and renowned producers like Austin, Morris and Leyland. The cohesion of the British car system nevertheless remained weak, partly due to the slipping strength of the British supply industry (cf. Amin and Smith, 1990: 209ff). The British government tried to link the car complexes with stronger industrial complexes, first with British Leyland and later with British Aerospace. This put Rover in a different bargaining context (aimed at different concepts of control) in which the interests of the larger groups prevailed and the firm was confronted with internationalisation plans like the plan for a 'car for Europe' (cf. Clark and deBresson, 1990) that had no relation to its domestic production base. Moreover with the takeover in the 1980s by one of the last really strong British firms, British Aerospace (BAe), Rover with its micro-Fordist orientation became drawn into the military industrial complex where BAe operated with its logic of industrial democracy. BAe was aided by considerable government subsidies but could not (or did not want to) really create synergies between Rover and the rest of its complex. The effect of the alliance with BAe and previous realignments was that the cohesion of the British car system was further eroded, but now with only one indigenous core producer left (next to Ford-UK and Vauxhall, a GM subsidiary).[1]

---

[1] Another example from a different business underlines the same bargaining dynamics. The Dutch construction conglomerate Ballast-Nedam was acquired by BAe in 1987. Its cohesion remained weak partly because of the non-core nature of the Ballast-Nedam activities in BAe's portfolio. In 1993 the firm regained 'independence' after considerable losses, but this was only feasible on the basis of a stronger partner in the same sector (German building conglomerate Hochtief AG took a 48 per cent minority share) and strong banking involvement (Dutch ING group took a 49.9 per cent share).

At the end of the 1980s Rover had to allow Honda a minority shareholding and thus got partly entailed in a moderate globalisation strategy, on the basis of a weak Toyotist concept of control. This alliance gave the company new bargaining momentum towards subcontractors, dealers, financiers, trade unions and even towards the British government. But despite important internal restructuring efforts Rover remained confronted with a relatively weak British industrial system. Honda did not want to take a majority share in the firm. Because of its concept of control a firm like Honda prefers an international 'going alone' strategy over an acquisition (see Chapter 8). Consequently, the relative weakness of the firm continued. The misconstrued internationalisation strategy of the firm played an important role in this sustained weakness. In the end in 1993 Rover became easy takeover prey for German car producer BMW, a strong core firm from a strong national car system, with a strong export orientation, and a macro-Fordist concept of control. BMW's take-over of Rover was much to the disdain of Honda, who were thus frustrated in any efforts at sustaining structural control over Rover – without the burden of a majority ownership contained in the direct control strategy of BMW. But, at the same time it also reveals the weakness of Honda's internationalisation efforts and also, indirectly, the weakness of Honda in the Japanese car system.

Plessey, a major British telecommunications producer had been thriving on closed procurement practices of British Telecom and the Ministry of Defence. As the core of an industrial complex, however, Plessey remained relatively small and weak, witnessing its difficulties in investing sufficient resources in a new generation of public digital switching equipment (System X, for which it allied with GEC, the other British Telecom supplier). When in 1982 the British government decided to privatise British Telecom and grant a licence to a rival telecommunications operator (Mercury) the cohesion of the national industrial system started to erode as well.[2] Confronted with this double weakness, and after unsuccessful efforts to find international outlets for its products, Plessey first allied and subsequently was taken over by Siemens and GEC, both multi-domestic but much more diversified conglomerates than Plessey. Interestingly enough GEC had originally been the only contender for Plessey. In 1985 GEC launched a direct take-over bid for Plessey. GEC was encouraged by the Department of Trade and Industry (DTI) which saw possibilities of strengthening the cohesion of the telecommunications and military industrial complexes in the country and thus withstanding a further erosion of their competitiveness. However, in the development phase of the British national system as a declining hegemon, financial and military interests indeed started to dominate productive interests. The bargaining consequence of this distorted

---

[2] This happened despite numerous efforts even of the British conservative government to keep the slipping cohesion of the British telecommunications system under control, for instance by ruling against alliances of British Telecom with American IBM.

cohesion in the national British system was that the interests of the Ministry of Defence (MoD) predominated over the interests of the DTI. According to Cawson *et al.* (1990: 104ff.) the MoD was 'horrified at the combined lobying power of a company which would have nearly 25 per cent of its £7.8 billion equipment budget'. The national merger was thus opposed due to the particular bargaining arenas the two firms had to operate in, which gave opportunities to a firm from a strong foreign industrial complex (Siemens) to first ally with GEC and then take part of the prey.

A comparable restructuring logic can be delineated for the last remaining British computer maker ICL. In the postwar period, ICL also emerged as the result of a number of mergers of small and relatively weak British computer manufacturers under the tutelage of the British government. ICL tried to escape its national bargaining arena by moving abroad in particular into Europe. But instead of strengthening the company's competitiveness, ICL's internationalisation strategy spread its resources thinly over too many countries, thereby contributing to a sustained weak level of cohesion at home. ICL had been created partly because of military interests which necessitated a domestic knowledge base in computer technology. As a consequence it can be assumed – although further research is necessary to substantiate this claim – that ICL aimed at a wider product portfolio than was feasible. Because of the military interests in mainframe computers, ICL was probably asked to include mainframe computers in its portfolio as well as its smaller systems for which it has become best known. The wide product portfolio contributed to a sustained weakness of the UK computer complex, because ICL had to rely on a large number of subcontractors from various sections of the electronics industry. It is our impression that, if the firm could have been more focused on a more limited product line, the cohesion of the computer industry in the UK could have been enhanced. Mastering the whole range of computers clearly meant overstretching the capabilities of an already weak complex in a weakening national system. In order to achieve the desired portfolio, ICL first became an OEM producer for Fujitsu mainframe computers and later was taken over by this strong core firm from the highly cohesive Japanese system. ICL thus got absorbed into a Toyotist concept of control aimed at and included in a glocalisation strategy.

All three British cases thus reveal a weak–strong dynamism at the meso and macro level of analysis that we also detected with weak–strong international strategic alliances at the micro level of analysis (see section 8.3). The alliance was the first step in a take-over strategy. The weaker partner remained weak in terms of bargaining power *exactly because* it allied with a strong partner. In the case of the British industrial system the sustained weakness of the industry has been due as much to structural and institutional factors as to failing strategic choices of individual companies. In all three examples the foreign industrial complexes had a high degree of cohesion, which made it more easy for them to bargain and get a better deal from the less cohesive partner. The latter either had been deprived of a clear concept of control and/or had come under the influence of financial and/or military interests often representing a different concept of control.

Other examples of a comparable 'weak–weak' bargaining logic can be found in a number of peripheral states in the USA, in most of the smaller industrial countries, in peripheral European countries, and in most of the newly industrialising countries like Taiwan or Singapore. Within the OECD region, these location sites have been the prime focus of the Toyotist glocalisation strategy. None of the one hundred largest core firms as identified in Chapters 7 and 9, however, can be qualified as part of a 'weak complex' (which does not mean that they have to be profitable). Their relative cohesion has created the preconditions for influencing the institutional setting at home (with implications for many other firms as well) and to become and remain big and influential for a prolonged period of time.

THE LOGIC OF WEAK COMPLEX COHESION ENCOUNTERING STRONG BARGAINING INSTITUTIONS

The weakening of a particular industrial complex can also take place while other industrial complexes sustain their strength. The history of the German consumer electronics industry provides an example of the bargaining logic developing under these circumstances. The German industrial system has traditionally been very strong in mechanical engineering, but not in electronics. In the terms of this book's framework, the institutional arrangements of the German system did not create a favourable bargaining setting to develop a strong electronics industry. Institutional arrangements in the German national system were dominated by the interests of core firms in the machine-tool industry, cars, chemicals and steel in particular. Owing to these unfavourable institutions, hardly any start-up firms in semiconductors or computers (with the exception of Nixdorf) developed. Likewise, a consumer electronics industry did not mature either, although firms like Grundig, Blaupunkt, AEG, Telefunken, Nordmende, Saba and the consumer electronics division of Standard Elektrik Lorenz (SEL) had been potent players in this industry at a time the appliances produced for consumers (televisions, home appliances, etc.) were largely built on a combination of electrical and mechanical engineering capabilities.

In the postwar boom German consumer electronics firms had flourished (Cawson *et al.*, 1990: 289). The Telefunken laboratories had pioneered the PAL colour TV, and Grundig brought many innovative products in the European market. Most of the industrial complexes built around these firms, however, remained relatively weak, because they could not profit from a well-developed (strong) national industrial system as with American start-ups in computers, software and biotechnology. Neither did they belong to the complexes organised around long-established German core films like Siemens, Bosch, Daimler-Benz, Krupp and Thyssen, or Bayer and BASF. This deprived them as with most postwar German start-ups (like Nixdorf in computers), of solid institutional arrangements in which their interests would be served. The latter, for instance, made them among the smaller players in the allocation of Federal and state subsidies. Their weak representation in the meso and macro bargaining arena made it also very difficult for consumer electronics firms to have their interests represented in trade policy issues. The German state, for instance, did not adopt an 'infant industry' argument in the case of consumer electronics. Grundig, Blaupunkt, AEG and other consumer electronics firms remained relatively weak complexes which were confronted by large inroads of foreign firms in an early period of their formation. Consequently, they could become a target for alliances as the first step in a takeover strategy.

As in the British case, the nature of government involvement in the restructuring strategy of the trailing firms has been important for the outcome of the bargaining process. But unlike in the case of a declining hegemon, Germany represented a booming economic power in the postwar period (which in the prewar period had not been able to become a hegemon on its own terms). This means that the influence of the military industrial complex is relatively limited as compared to that of the institutions of industrial policy like the Ministry of R&D and of industry at both federal and state level. The Bavarian Economics Minister tried to save Grundig from being taken over by French consumer and military electronics firm Thomson. Siemens and Bosch were stimulated to acquire shareholdings in the firms, but none of them did. In the end Thomson did not take over Grundig, but the firm first allied with Philips when Philips still represented a very strong complex and had no major military interests. Philips took a majority share in Grundig by the end of the 1980s. Its majority shareholding mirrors Philips's Fordist orientation in which it aims at directly controlling its subsidiaries.

Blaupunkt became jointly owned by Siemens and Bosch, while Nixdorf was ultimately taken over by Siemens. AEG was acquired by Daimler-Benz partly because of its defence electronics activities, after which Daimler further dissolved AEG's consumer products department. In 1988 SEL sold its consumer electronics division to Nokia of Finland when firms like Nordmende, Saba and Telefunken had already been acquired by Thomson. Most of these developments coincide and show remarkably comparable bargaining patterns.[3] In not more than fifteen years, large parts of the German consumer electronics industry were taken over by (foreign) complexes with a considerably stronger cohesion. The German government

---

[3] An excellent and detailed account of the bargaining dynamism of German consumer electronics core firms and governments, banks, trade unions, and industry associations is given by Cawson *et al.*, 1990: 289ff.

proved not very able to influence the outcome of this process, firstly, because of the relative bargaining strength and independence of the stronger German complexes which were not willing to comply with the 'German solution' proposed by the government in the case of Grundig for instance. The second reason was the relative weakness and low international competitiveness of the German consumer electronics firms. Thirdly, the German government had been unwilling/unable to unilaterally raise tariffs or quota in consumer electronics (like the French government had done), because this did not represent the trade interests of the complexes around Siemens and Bosch which had a stronger cohesion, but also a stronger commitment to a (regional) free trade regime.

LINKING THE COHESION OF INDUSTRIAL SYSTEMS AND GOVERNMENT TRADE POLICIES

Section 10.4.2 advanced the expectations that (1) in the case of a strong cohesion of the national system, trade policy preferences of the national government tend to mirror the trade policy stance of most individual complexes; and (2) in the case of lower degrees of cohesion in the national industrial system, governments' actual policies tend to follow the trade policy preferences of the industrial complex with the highest degree of cohesion and/or the complex that operates on the basis of a concept of control positioned further to the right-hand side of the dependency scale.

In both the United States and Japan, the breeding ground for the two most comprehensive, but at the same time fundamentally rival contemporary concepts of control (micro-Fordism and Toyotism) evidence supports this 'double logic'. As already stated, the late nineteenth and early twentieth century represents the constituting phase of the US industrial system. At that time, the cohesion of most industrial systems (oil, cars, electricity, food) was relatively high. Many firms were still embedded in networks of flexible specialisation and had not yet internationalised. The Federal government followed the policy preferences shared by most industrial complexes (although often implicitly) and instituted quota and tariff barriers. The temporary unilateral trade regime adopted by the US government enabled many American firms to restructure and shift from flexible specialisation to the right on the scale towards (micro- or macro-) Fordism. Shifting along the dependency scale always implies a drastic change of *all* bargaining relations, and it might have been impossible to make such a shift in a more or less controlled manner if the American market had been left without barriers to foreign entry. In the case of many US industries this shift had already appeared at the end of the nineteenth century. In the case of the American car industry this shift appeared later, in the 1910s and 1920s. A firm like General Motors thus could become realigned from the remnants of many smaller firms like Olds, Buick and Chevrolet behind contemporary tariff walls that were the highest in the industrialised world.

The same logic applies to the trade policy stance of the Japanese government in the course of the 1950s and 1960s. In those years, most of today's
leading complexes in cars, steel, computers and electronics were relatively
small and at times assemblers had to comply with the wishes of either
financial actors or their national government. It is in this period that the
Ministry of International Trade and Industry (MITI) performed its function
of a 'developmental state' (cf. Johnson, 1982). Through these decades, most
core firms preferred unilateral trade barriers. Sheltered from international
competition, many core firms – notably of course Toyota – forced their
bargaining partners towards the right end of the dependency scale into a
position of structural control. Ultimately this process led to the emergence
of a truly rival concept of control, challenging Fordism.

The reversed logic also applies. In the 1980s, the US government was
confronted with a declining degree of cohesion in many industries that had
been among world leaders, for instance in cars, computers, steel, or consumer electronics. Nevertheless for a relatively long period, the Federal
government largely followed the trade policy preferences voiced by the
core firms that had controlled their complex with the highest degree of
cohesion and had manoeuvred their bargaining partners furthest to the right
of the dependency scale. These core firms in any case include GM in the car
system, IBM in computers, Exxon and Mobil in oil, Philip Morris and
Procter and Gamble in food, Du Pont in new materials, and AT&T in
telecommunications. The American government maintained a (moderated)
free trade policy, despite (or due to?) widely diverging trade policy preferences among major core firms and other interest groups embedded in the
weakening US industrial system. Only after the cohesion of some of these
leading companies' complexes (in particular General Motors, IBM, AT&T)
themselves became undermined, the US trade policy stance gradually shifted
somewhat to the left of the dependency scale. This made it even conceivable that in the 1990s an industrial policy was formulated under the
Clinton Administration (but *de facto* already under the Bush Administration) to support trailing US industrial systems. The effectiveness of
such a late shift in a situation of declining cohesion may be questioned,
however.

Within the Japanese industrial system, the same logic has been found as
in the case of the US industrial system in the 1980s: the Japanese government most closely followed the trade policy preferences of the strongest and
most cohesive Japanese complexes, i.e. Toyota and Nissan in cars, Fujitsu
in computers, NEC and Hitachi in chips and telecommunications, Nippon
Oil and Idemitsu Kosan in oil, Kao in food, Matsushita in consumer
electronics. These firms are the core of complexes that we would position at
the far right-hand side of the dependency scale. These firms either represent
vertical *keiretsu* or can be considered strong members of a horizontal
keiretsu with a relatively weak cohesion (implying a limited influence
of the industrial bank; see Chapter 5). In the early 1980s, the Japanese

government agreed to restrain exports to the USA and the EC in voluntary export restraint agreements in chips, cars, telecommunications and steel, granting leading firms the highest quota. In the early 1990s, MITI even extended the Japanese voluntary export restraint in cars to the USA - without the US government demanding such an extension – in an attempt to appease US fears for a Japanese domination of the US car market, while at the same time making it more difficult for other Japanese car assemblers (in particular Honda, but also Mitsubishi and Mazda) to expand abroad. Comparable policies were adopted in electronics. The Japanese government clearly favoured VERs over other measures of managed trade as proposed by the American government, such as minumum market shares and floor prices (cf. Tyson, 1992).

The Japanese government has tended to give preference to the interests of the most cohesive complexes, not only because of the relatively high degree of structural control of the core firms within these complexes, but also because the *effectiveness* of government policies ultimately critically depended on the willingness of these core firms in particular to accept the policies fostered. The government – as a consequence of the dominance of the Toyotist concept of control – is in a relatively weak bargaining position. An unfavourable allocation of voluntary export restraint quota to Toyota for instance might have provoked Toyota to move much more of its production abroad than it actually did over the 1980s and 1990s. For a long time Toyota represented more than half of the Japanese car production volume. So in the case of Toyota deciding to frustrate governmental policies this would really have had an impact. It should not come as a surprise that the VER with the USA and the European Union did not seriously affect Toyota's internationalisation strategy; some say it even has been supported by Toyota. Honda's car complex, however, has been positioned a bit more to the left on the dependency scale and had started to internationalise much earlier. It has been hurt much more by the VER. Honda therefore had a strong and relatively early incentive to move beyond the national bargaining arena, which made it the only Japanese car assembler to expand along the globalisation trajectory.

In their internationalisation strategy towards host governments, important Japanese industrial complexes have made use of the same logic. Most Japanese car firms *systematically* chose regions or countries where they could be the strongest and most cohesive complex (cf. Sachwald, 1993b for further details on the Japanese strategies towards Europe). Host governments (local as well as national) also tend to give preference to complexes that are either the most cohesive and/or located furthest on the right-hand side of the scale of dependencies, even if this discriminates against the interest of traditional local complexes. Following this logic, it should not come as a surprise that the UK government, which had faced rapidly declining levels of cohesion in its domestic industrial systems in cars, consumer electronics, semiconductors, computers from the 1960s to the 1980s, began to support the interests of the Japanese transplants by the late 1980s even within the trade deliberations of the European Union.

Bibliography

Abegglen, J. C. and Stalk jr, G. (1985) *Kaisha, The Japanese Corporation: How Marketing, Money, and Manpower Strategy, Not Management Style, Make the Japanese World Pace Setters*, New York: Basic Books.

Aglietta, M. (1979) *A Theory of Capitalist Regulation: The US Experience*, London: New Left Books.

Amin, A. and Robins, K. (1990) 'The re-emergence of regional economies? The mythical geography of flexible accumulation', *Environment and Planning D: Society and Space* 8: 7–34.

Amin, A. and Smith, I. (1990) 'Decline and restructuring in the UK motor vehicle components industry', *Scottish Journal of Political Economy* 37, 3 August: 209–41.

Andersen Consulting, A. (1989) *Eurotechnologie: Strategie voor Ondernemend Nederland*, The Hague: Bureau EG Liaison.

Andersen, E. Slot and Lundvall, B.Å. (1988) 'Small national systems of innovation facing technological revolutions: an analytical framework', in: Freeman, C. and Lundvall, B. (eds) *Small Countries Facing the Technological Revolution*, London/New York: Pinter Publishers.

Ansoff, H.I. (1968) *Corporate Strategy: An Analytic Approach to Business Policy for Growth and Expansion*, Harmondsworth: Penguin Books.

—— (1969) 'Toward a strategic theory of the firm', in Ansoff, H.I. *Business Strategy: Selected Readings*, Harmondsworth: Penguin, pp. 11–40.

Aoki, M., Gustafsson, B. and Williamson, O. (eds) (1990) *The Firm as a Nexus of Treaties*, London: Sage Publications.

Archibugi, D. and Michie, J. (1993) *The Globalisation of Technology, Myths and Realities*, Cambridge: Cambridge University Press, Judge Institute of Management Studies, no.18.

Axelrod, R. (1984) *The Evolution of Cooperation*, New York: Basic Books.

Bachrach, P. and Baratz, M. (1969) 'Decisions and non-decisions: an analytical framework', in: Bell, R., Edwards, D. and Harrison Wagner, R. (eds) *Political Power: A Reader in Theory and Research*, New York: Free Press.

Badham, R. and Mathews, J. (1989) 'The new production systems debate', *Labour and Industry*, 2, 2, June: 194–246.

Bael, I. van and Bellis, J.F. (1985) *International Trade Law and Practice of the European Community: EEC Anti-Dumping and Other Trade Protection Law*, Bicester: CCH Editions.

Balassa, B. and Noland, M. (1988) *Japan in the World Economy*, Washington DC: Institute for International Economics.

Banville, E. de and Chanaron, J.J. (1991) *Vers un système automobile Européen*, Paris: CPE-Economica.

Barker, J. (1993) 'Tightening the iron cage: coercive control in self-managing teams', *Administrative Science Quarterly* 38: 408–37.

Bartlett, C. and Goshal, S. (1987) 'Managing across borders: new organizational responses', *Sloan Management Review*,Fall: 43–53.

—— (1989, 1992) *Managing Across Borders: The Transnational Solution*, London: Century Business.

Bartlett, C.A., Doz, Y. and Hedlund, G. (1990) *Managing the Global Firm*, London: Routledge.

Batra, R. (1993) *The Myth of Free Trade; A Plan for America's Economic Revival*, New York: Charles Scribner's sons.

Belderbos, R. (1994) *Strategic Trade Policy and Multinational Enterprises*, Amsterdam: Thesis Publishers.

Bell, D. (1973) *The Coming of Post-Industrial Society: A Venture in Social Forecasting*, New York: Basic Books.

Bello, W. (1993) 'Trouble in paradise: the tension of economic integration in the Asia-Pacific', *World Policy Journal* 10(2), Summer: 33–39.

Belussi, F. (1986) *New Technologies in a Traditional Sector: The Benetton Case*, BRIE Working Paper no.19, October, Berkeley Roundtable on the International Economy, University of California.

Beniger, J.R. (1986) *The Control Revolution. Technological and Economic Origins of the Information Society*, London/Cambridge, MA: Harvard University Press.

Bergsten, F. and Noland, M. (1993) *Reconcilable Differences? United States–Japan Economic Conflict*, Washington DC: Institute for International Economics.

Bessant, J. (1991) *Managing Advanced Manufacturing Technology: The Challenge of the Fifth Wave*, Oxford: Blackwell.

Best, M. (1990) *The New Competition: Institutions of Industrial Restructuring*, Cambridge: Polity Press.

Bhagwati, J. (1988) *Protectionism*, Cambridge, MA: MIT Press.

—— (1989) 'Is free trade passé after all?', *Weltwirtschaftliches Archiv* 125 (1): 17–44.

Bianchi, P. and Gualtieri, G. (1990) 'Emilia-Romagna and its industrial districts: the evolution of a model', in: Leonardi, R. and Nanetti, R. (eds) *The Regions and European Integration: The Case of Emilia-Romagna*, London: Pinter Publishers.

Blinder, A.S. (ed.) (1992) *Paying for Productivity: A look at the Evidence*, Washington DC: Brookings Institution.

Bonefeld, W. (1991) 'The reformulation of state theory', in: Bonefeld, W. and Holloway, J. (eds) *Post-Fordism and Social Form: A Marxist Debate on the Post-Fordist State*, Basingstoke: Macmillan: 35.

Bongardt, A. (1990) 'Coordination between customers and suppliers in intermediate goods markets and associated patterns of R&D collaboration: market power and efficiency', PhD thesis, European University Institute, Florence.

Bosch, F. van den (1989) *Boundaries of Organizations*, Rotterdam School of Management, Delft: Eburon.

Boyer, R. (1989) *New Directions in Management Practices and Work Organisation: General Principles and National Trajectories*, Paris: OECD.

—— (1993) 'Comment emerge un nouveau système productif?', in: Boyer, R. and Durand, J.P. *L'après-fordisme*, Paris: Syros, pp. 8–81.

Brander, J. and Spencer, B. (1985) 'Export subsidies and international market share rivalry', *Journal of International Economics* 18: 83–100.

Braun, D. (1988) *Der Niederländische Weg in die Massenarbeitslosigkeit (1973–1981); Ein politisch-institutionelle Analyse*, PhD thesis, University of Amsterdam.

Braverman, H. (1974) *Labor and Monopoly Capital*, New York: Monthly Review Press.

Brenner, R. and Glick, M. (1991) 'The regulation approach: theory and history', *New Left Review* 188: 45–120.

Brödner, P. (1987) *Fabrik 2000: Alternative Entwicklungspfade in die Zukunft der Fabrik*, Berlin: Edition Sigma, Wissenschaftszentrum Berlin.

Bröker, G. (1989) *Competition in Banking: Trends in Banking Structure and Regulation in OECD Countries*, Paris: OECD.

Brouthers, L.E. and Werner, S. (1990) 'Are the Japanese good global competitors?', *Columbia Journal of World Business* Fall: 5–11.

Brouwer, M. and Does de Willebois, L. van der (1990) *Innoveren en Concurreren*, Schoonhoven: Academic Service, Bedrijfskundige Signalementen.

Brown, W. and Hogendorn, J. (1994) *International Economics; Theory and Context*, Reading, MA: Addison-Wesley.

Bryant, R. (1980) *Money and Monetary Policy in Interdependent Nations*, Washington DC: Brookings Institution.

Buckley, P. and Casson, M. (1976) *The Future of the Multinational Enterprise*, London: Macmillan.

—— 1988) 'A theory of cooperation in international business', in: Contractor, F. and Lorange, P. (eds) *Cooperative Strategies in International Business*, Lexington, MA: Lexington Books.

—— (1991) *The Future of the Multinational Enterprise*, Basingstoke/London: Macmillan.

Buitelaar, W. and Vreeman, R. (1985) *Vakbondswerk en Kwaliteit van de Arbeid*, Nijmegen: Sun.

Burawoy, M. (1985) *The Politics of Production*, London: Verso.

Butaney, G. and Wortzel, L. (1988) 'Distributor power versus manufacturer power: the customer role', *Journal of Marketing* 52, January: 52–63.

Cameron, D. (1978) 'The expansion of the public economy: a comparative analysis', *American Political Science Review* LXXII (3) December: 1234–61.

Caporaso, J. and Levine, D. (1992) *Theories of Political Economy*, Cambridge: Cambridge University Press.

Cawson, A. (ed.) (1985) *Organized Interests and the State: Studies in Meso-Corporatism*, London: Sage Publications.

Cawson, A., Morgan, K., Webber, D., Holmes, P. and Stevens, A. (1990) *Hostile Brothers: Competition and Closure in the European Electronics Industry*, Oxford: Clarendon Press.

Chandler, A. (1962) *Strategy and Structure: Chapters in the History of the Industrial Enterprise*, Cambridge, MA: MIT Press.

—— (1990) *Scale and Scope: The Dynamics of Industrial Capitalism*, Cambridge, MA: Belknap Press.

Chang, H.J. (1994) *The Political Economy of Industrial Policy*, New York: St Martin's Press.

Chesnais, F. (1988) 'Technical co-operation agreements between firms', *STI Review* 4, December: 52–119.

—— (1993) 'Globalisation, world oligopoly and some of their implications', in: Humbert, M. (ed.) *The Impact of Globalisation on Europe's Firms and Industries*, London: Pinter Publishers.

—— (1994) *La Mondialisation du Capital*, Paris: Syros, Alternatives Economiques.

Clark, P. and deBresson, C. (1990) 'Sector evolvement and strategic courses: the case of Rover in the 20s and 60s', UMIST 1990 conference, 'Firm Strategy and Technical Change: Micro Economics or Micro Sociology'.

Clarke, S. (1990) 'The crisis of Fordism or the crisis of social democracy?', *Telos* 83, Spring: 71–98.

Clegg, S. (1989) 'Postmodern organizations?', mimeo, Brisbane: Queensland University of Technology.

Coase, R. (1937) 'The nature of the firm', *Economica* 4: 386–405.

—— (1960) 'The problem of social cost', *The Journal of Law and Economics* October: 1–45.

Cohen, B. (1990) 'The political economy of international trade', *International Organization* 44 (2), Spring: 261–81.

Cohen, R. and Zysman, J. (1987) *Manufacturing Matters: The Myth of the Post-Industrial Economy*, New York: Basic Books.

Cohen, S. (1991) *Globalization and Production*, University of California, Berkeley Roundtable on the International Economy, BRIE, Working Paper 45. Berkeley Roundtable on the International Economy, University of California.

Commission of the European Communities (1987) *Report on State Aid*, Brussels: DG-IV.

—— (1988) *FAST-II Programme: Results and Recommendations*, Brussels.

Contractor, F. and Lorange, P. (1988) 'Why should firms cooperate? The strategy and economics basis for cooperative ventures', in Contractor, F. and Lorange, P. (eds) *Cooperative Strategies in International Business*, Lexington, MA: Lexington Books, pp. 3–30.

Cooke, P. and Morgan, K. (1991) 'The network paradigm: new departures in corporate and regional development', *Regional Industrial Research Report* no. 8.

Cooke, P., Moulaert, F., Swyngedouw, E., Weinstein, O. and Wells, P. (1992) *Towards Global Localisation: The Computing and Telecommunications Industries in Britain and France*, London: University College of London Press.

Coriat, B. (1990) *L'Atelier et le Robot*, Paris: Editions C. Bourgois.

Cox, R. (1987) *Production, Power, and World Order: Social Forces in the Making of History*, New York: Columbia University Press.

Cukierman, A. (1992) *Central Bank Strategy, Credibility and Independence*, Cambridge, MA/London: MIT Press.

Cumings, B. (1984) 'The origins and development of the Northeast Asian political economy: industrial sectors, product cycles, and political consequences', *International Organization* 38 (1): 1–40.

Cusumano, M. (1985) *The Japanese Automobile Industry*, Cambridge, MA: Harvard University Press.

Dahl, R. (1957) 'The concept of power', *Behavioral Science*, 2: 201–5.

Dale, R. (1980) *Anti-dumping Law in a Liberal Trade Order*, London: Macmillan.

Damme, E. van (1993) 'De kunst van het onderhandelen', *Economisch Statistische Berichten*, 24 February: 186–9.

Daniel, W.W. (1987) *Workplace Industrial Relations and Technical Change*, London: Frances Pinter in association with Policy Studies Institute.

Daniels, J. and Radebaugh, L. (1993) *International Business; Environments and Operations*, Reading, MA: Addison-Wesley.

Dankbaar, B. (1989) 'Sectoral governance in the automobile industries of West Germany, Great Britain and France', University of Maastricht, MERIT paper, 89–008.

—— (1993) 'Economic crisis and institutional change: the crisis of Fordism from the perspective of the automibile industry', PhD thesis, Universitaire Pers Maastricht.

Dankbaar, B. and Tulder, R. van (1989) 'The construction of an open standard: process and implications of defining the manufacturing automation protocol (MAP), The Hague: State Publishing Co.

Davidson, W.H. (1984) *The Amazing Race: Winning the Technorivalry with Japan*, New York/Chichester: John Wiley.

De Meyer, A. and Ferdows, K. (1991) *Removing the Barriers in Manufacturing: Report on the 1990 European Manufacturing Survey*, paper, Fontainebleau: INSEAD.

Dekker, W. (1991) 'De trek naar het Oosten', speech at symposium on Malaysia,

24 October, Rotterdam: Erasmus University, Philips Corporate External Relations.

Derdak, T. (ed.) (1988) *International Directory of Company Histories*, Volume I, Chicago, London: St James Press.

Destler, I.M. (1992) *American Trade Politics*, Washington, DC: Institute for International Economics.

Destler, I.M. and Odell, J. (1987) *Anti-protection: Changing Forces in the United States Trade Politics*, Washington DC: Institute for International Economics.

Deutschmann, C. (1987) 'Economic restructuring and company unionism, the Japanese model', IIMV-Arbeitsmarktpolitik, October, Berlin: Wissenschaftzentrum Berlin.

Dicken, P. (1986) *Global Shift: Industrial Change in a Turbulent World*, London: Paul Chapman Publishing.

—— (1992) *Global Shift; The Internationalization of Economic Activity*, 2nd edn, London: Paul Chapman Publishing.

Dodgson, M. (1993) *Technological Collaboration in Industry: Strategy, Policy and Internationalization in Innovation*, London: Routledge.

Dodwell Marketing Consultants (1990) *Industrial Groupings in Japan 1990/91*, Tokyo: Dodwell Marketing Consultants.

Dohse, K., Jürgens, U. and Malsch, T. (1984) *Vom 'Fordismus' zum 'Toyotismus'? Die Japan-Diskussion in der Automobilindustrie*, Berlin: Wissenschaftszentrum Berlin, Publications series of the International Institute for Comparative Research/Labour Policy, no. IIVG/pre84–212.

Doner, R. (1991) *Driving a Bargain: Automobile Industrialization and Japanese Firms in Southeast Asia*, Berkeley: University of California Press.

—— (1993) 'Japanese foreign investment and the creation of a Pacific Asian region', in: Frankel, J. and Kahler, M. (eds) *Regionalism and Rivalry; Japan and the United States in Pacific Asia*, Chicago/London: University of Chicago Press.

Dore, R. (1987) *Flexible Rigidities: Industrial Policy and Industrial Adjustment in the Japanese Economy, 1970–1980*, London: Athlone Press.

Dorman, L. (1991) 'De Handelspreferenties van de Europese Halfgeleiderproducenten', MA thesis, University of Amsterdam, Department of International Relations and Public International Law.

Dosi, G., Freeman, C., Nelson, R., Silverberg, G. and Soete, L. (eds) (1988) *Technical Change and Economic Theory*, London: Pinter Publishers.

Dosi, G., Pavitt, K. and Soete, L. (1990) *The Economics of Technical Change and International Trade*, Hemel Hempstead: Harvester/Wheatsheaf.

Doz, Y., Hamel, G. and Prahalad, C.K. (1987) 'Strategic partnerships: success or surrender? the challenge of competitive collaboration', INSEAD paper (mimeo), revised version.

Duchêne, F. and Shepherd, G. (1987) *Managing Industrial Change in Western Europe*, London: Pinter.

Dunning, J. (1991) 'The competitive advantage of countries and TNC activity: a review article', University of Reading, Discussion Papers in International Investment and Business Studies, Series B, Vol IV: No 45.

—— (1993) *Multinational Enterprises and the Global Economy*, Wokingham: Addison-Wesley.

Durand, J.P. (ed.) (1993) *Vers un nouveau modèle productif?*, Paris: Syros/Alternatives.

ECAT (Emergency Committee for American Trade) (1993) *A New Account of the Critical Role of U.S. Multinational Companies in the U.S. Economy*, Washington: ECAT.

Economist, The (1994) *Pocket World in Figures*, London: Penguin and Economist Books.

Edquist, C. and Jacobson, S. (1988) *Flexible Automation – The Global Diffusion of new Technologies in the Engineering Industry*, Oxford: Basil Blackwell.

Egan, C. and McKiernan, P. (1994) *Inside Fortress Europe; Strategies for the Single Market*, The Economist Intelligence Unit Series, Wokingham: Addison-Wesley.

Eisenhardt, K. (1989) 'Agency theory: an assessment and review', *Academy of Management Review* 14(1): 57–74.

El-Ansary, A. and Stern, L. (1972) 'Power measurement in the distribution channel', *Journal of Marketing Research* 9, February: 47–52.

Elam, M.J. (1988) *A Critical Introduction to the Post-Fordist Debate: Technology, Markets and Institutions*, paper prepared for the EASST/4S Conference, Amsterdam, November.

Emerson, R. (1962) 'Power-dependence relations', *American Sociological Review* 27, February: 31–41.

Ergas, H. (1984) *Why Do Some Countries Innovate More than Others?*, CEPS-Papers, no. 29, Brussels: Centre for European Policy Studies.

Ernst, D. (1990) 'Globalisation of competition, LDCs and MNCs', paper presented on 'Technology and Competitiveness', Paris, 24–27 June.

Evans, P., Jacobson, H. and Putnam, R. (eds) (1993) *Double-edged Diplomacy: International Bargaining and Domestic Politics*, Berkeley: University of California Press.

Fennema, M. (1982) *International Networks of Banks and Industry*, Studies in Industrial Organization, vol. 2. The Hague: Martinus Nijhoff Publishers.

Ferguson, C. and Morris, C. (1993) *Computer Wars; The Fall of IBM and the Future of Global Technology*, New York: Random House, Times Books.

Fisher, R. and Ury, W. (1981) *Getting to Yes: Negotiating Agreement without Giving in*, Boston, MA: Houghton Mifflin.

Fleenor, D. (1993) 'The coming and going of the global corporation', *Columbia Journal of World Business*, Winter: 7–16.

Fligstein, N. (1990) *The Transformation of Corporate Control*, Cambridge, MA: Harvard University Press.

Frank, A. Gunder (1969) *Capitalism and Underdevelopment in Latin America*, New York: Monthly Review Press (also published by Penguin, London: 1971).

Fransman, M. (1990) *The Market and Beyond: Cooperation and Competition in Information Technology Development in the Japanese System*, Cambridge: Cambridge University Press.

Frazier, G. and Rody, R. (1991) 'The use of influence strategies in interfirm relationships in industrial product channels', *Journal of Marketing* 55, January: 52–69.

Freeman, C. (1982) *The Economics of Industrial Innovation*, 2nd Edn, London: Frances Pinter.

—— (1988a) 'Japan: a new national system of innovation?', in: Dosi, G., Freeman, C., Nelson, R., Silverberg, G. and Soete, L. (eds) *Technical Change and Economic Theory*, London: Pinter Publishers.

—— (1988b) 'Technology gaps, international trade and the problems of smaller and less-developed economies', in Freeman, C. and Lundvall, B-A. (eds) *Small Countries Facing the Technological Revolution*, London/New York: Pinter Publishers.

Freeman, C. and Lundvall, B-A. (eds) (1988) *Small Countries Facing the Technological Revolution*, London/New York: Pinter Publishers.

Friedman, D. (1983) 'Beyond the age of Ford: the strategic basis of the Japanese success in automobiles', in: Zysman, J. and Tyson, L. (eds) *American Industry in International Competition: Government Policies and Corporate Strategies*, Ithaca, NY/London: Cornell University Press.

—— (1988) *The Misunderstood Miracle: Industrial Development and Political Change in Japan*, Ithaca, NY/London: Cornell University Press.

Friedrich, W. and Rönning, G. (1985) *Arbeitsmarktwirkungen moderner Technologien*, Cologne: Institut für Sozialforschung und Gesellschaftspolitik.

Friman, H.R. (1988) 'Rocks, hard place, and the new protectionism: textile trade policy choices in the United States and Japan', *International Organization* 42(4), Autumn: 689–723.

Fröbel, F., Heinrichs, J. and Kreye, O. (1977) *Die neue internationale Arbeitsteilung*, Reinbek bei Hamburg: Rowohlt Taschenbuch Verlag.

—— (1986) *Umbruch in der Weltwirtschaft*, Reinbek bei Hamburg: Rowohlt Taschenbuch Verlag.

Furtado, C. (1970) *Economic Development of Latin America*, London/New York: Cambridge University Press.

Gallagher, J. and Robinson, R. (1953) 'The imperialism of free trade', *Economic History Review*, 2nd series, 6(1), August: 1–15.

Gallarotti, M. (1985) 'Towards a business-cycle model of tariffs', *International Organization* 39(1), Winter: 155–87.

Galtung, J. (1964) 'A structural theory of aggression', *Journal of Peace Research* 2: 95–119.

—— (1971) 'A structural theory of imperialism', *Journal of Peace Research* VIII/2: 437–82.

Gaski, J. (1984) 'The theory of power and conflict in channels of distribution', *Journal of Marketing* 48, Summer: 9–29.

Gerlach, M. (1992) *Alliance Capitalism: The Social Organization of Japanese Business*, Berkeley: University of California Press.

Gill, S. and Law, D. (1988) *The Global Political Economy: Perspectives, Problems and Policies*, New York: Harvester Wheatsheaf.

Gilpin, R. with the assistance of Gilpin, J. (1987) *The Political Economy of International Relations*, Princeton, NJ: Princeton University Press.

Glimstedt, H. (1993) 'Restructuring the transformer industry – limits to national development strategies, recent international mergers and the emerging forms of industrial relations', Copenhagen: Nordic Seminar and Labour Reports.

Godfroij, A. (1981) 'Netwerken van Organisaties: Strategieën, Spelen, Structuren', PhD thesis, VUGA Uitgeverij, The Hague.

Goldstein, J.S. (1988) *Long Cycles: Prosperity and War in the Modern Age*, New Haven, CT and London: Yale University Press.

Gordon, D. (1988) 'The global economy: new edifice or crumbling foundations?', *New Left Review* 168, March/April: 24–64.

Grabher, G. (ed.) (1993) *The Embedded Firm*, London: Routledge.

Gramsci, A. (1980) *Selections from the Prison Notebooks*, edited by Q. Hoare and G. Nowell Smith, New York/London: Lawrence and Wishart.

Granovetter, M. (1973) 'The strength of weak ties', *American Journal of Sociology* 78: 1360–80.

Grauwe, P. de (1989) 'Nieuwe handelstheorie en industriebeleid', *Economisch Statistische Berichten*, March: 208–12.

Gregory, G. (1986) *Japanese Electronics Technology: Enterprise and Innovation*, Chichester: John Wiley.

Grilli, E. (1988) 'Macro-economic determinants of trade protection', *World-Economy* 11(3): 313–27.

Groenewegen, J. (1989) 'Planning in een Markteconomie: Indicatieve Planning, Industrie-beleid en de Rol van de Publieke Onderneming in Frankrijk in de Periode 1981–1986', PhD thesis: Maastricht.

Grou, P. (1990) *L'espace des multinationales*, Paris: Reclus-La Documentation Française.

Hagedoorn, J. (1990) 'Organizational modes of inter-firm co-operation and technology transfer', *Technovation* 10(1): 17–28.

Hagedoorn, J. and Schakenraad, J. (1991) 'Technology cooperation, strategic alliances and their motives: brother, can you spare a dime, or do you have a light?', Interim Report, Fast Workshop, February, Brussels: Commission of the European Communities.

Håkanson, H. (1989) *Corporate Technological Behavior: Cooperation and Networks*, London: Routledge.

Hall, P. (1986) *Governing the Economy: The Politics of State Intervention in Britain and France*, Cambridge: Polity Press.

Hallen, O. van der (1965) *Aphorisms of the Last Hour* (in Dutch)

Hamel, G. and Prahalad, C.K. (1994) *Competing for the Future*, Boston, MA: Harvard Business School Press.

Hamilton, C. (1983) 'Capitalist industrialisation in East Asia's Four Little Tigers', *Journal of Contemporary Asia* 13(1): 35–73.

Harrigan, K.R. (1988) 'Joint ventures and competitive strategy', *Strategic Management Journal* 9: 141–58.

Harrop, J. (1992) *The Political Economy of Integration in the European Community*, 2nd edn, Cheltenham, Glos: Edward Elgar.

Hashimoto, M. (1990) 'Employment and wage systems in Japan and their implications for productivity', in: Blinder, A.S. (ed.) *Paying for Productivity: A Look at the Evidence*, Washington DC: Brookings Institution.

Hast, A. *et al.* (eds) (1991) *International Directory of Company Histories*, Volumes III and IV, Chicago, London: St James Press.

Hast, A. *et al.* (eds) (1992) *International Directory of Company Histories*, Volume V, Chicago, London: St James Press.

Helling, J. (1991) *Världsmästarna: En ny Generation av Tillverkningsföretag*, Stockholm: Sellin & Partner Förlag.

Helper, S. (1990) *Supplier Relations and Investment in Automation: Results of Survey Research in the US Auto Industry*, Preliminary draft of paper, April.

Hergert, M. and Morris, D. (1988) 'Trends in international collaborative agreements', in: Contractor, F. and Lorange, P. (eds) *Cooperative Strategies in International Business*, Lexington, MA: Lexington Books, pp. 99–109.

Hesselman, L. (1983) 'Trends in European industrial intervention', *Cambridge Journal of Economics* 7: 197–208.

Hilferding, R. (1910, 1968) *Das Finanzkapital: Eine Studie über die jungste Entwicklung des Kapitalismus*, Frankfurt am Main: Europäische Verlagsanstalt.

Hills, J. (1984) *Information Technology and Industrial Policy*, London: Croom Helm.

Hirschman, A.O. (1970) *Exit, Voice and Loyalty*, Cambridge, MA: Harvard University Press.

Hirst, P. and Zeitlin, J. (eds) (1989) *Reversing Industrial Decline?*, Oxford: Berg.

Hodgson, G. (1988) *Economics and Institutions: A Manifesto for a Modern Institutional Economics*, Cambridge: Polity Press.

Hollis, M. and Smith, S. (1991) *Explaining and Understanding International Relations*, Oxford: Clarendon Paperbacks.

Hood, N. and Young, S. (1979) *The Economics of Multinational Enterprise*, London: Longman.

Houweling, H. (1987) 'Samenwerking en Conflict tussen Staten', in: Soetendorp, R. and Staden, A. van (eds) *International Betrekkingen in Perspectief*, Utrecht: Aula Pocket, pp. 132–63.

Howells, J. and Wood, M. (1993) *The Globalisation of Production and Technology*, London: Belhaven Press.

Hu, Y.S. (1992) 'Global or stateless corporations are national firms with international operations', *California Management Review* 34(2), Winter: 107–26.

Hübner, K. and Mahnkopf, B. (1988) *Ecole de la Regulation: Eine kommentierende Literaturstudie*, Berlin: Wissenschatszentrum Berlin, Internationales Institut für Management und Verwaltung.

Hufbauer, G.C., Berliner, D. and Elliot, K.A. (1986) *Trade Protection in the United States: 31 Case Studies*, Washington DC: Institute for International Economics.

Imai, K., Nonaka, I. and Takeuchi, H. (1988) 'Managing the new product development process: how Japanese companies learn and unlearn', in: Tushman, M. and Moore, W.L. (eds) *Readings in the Management of Innovation*, 2nd edn, Cambridge, MA: Ballinger Publishing Company.

Institute for Economic Planning for Peace (1992) *Economic Development and Regional Integration in Asian Regions: Current Status Analysis and Scenarios for Regional Cooperation*, Brussels: Commission of the European Communities/Monitor-Fast, FOP 313.

International Metalworkers' Federation (IMF) (1991) *The IMF and the Multinationals. The Role of the IMF World Company Councils*, Lisbon, 23–24 May.

International Metalworkers' Federation (IMF) (1992) *Electrolux; Confronting the Challenges of the 1990s*, Geneva.

International Metalworkers' Federation (IMF) (1992) *A Profile of General Electric; Development and Performance 1986–1990*, Geneva.

International Metalworkers' Federation (IMF) (1992) *Europe 1992 and the Steel Industry Worldwide*, Geneva.

Itoh, M. (1990) *The World Economic Crisis and Japanese Capitalism*, London: Macmillan Press.

Israelewicz, E. (1989) 'La révolution financière', in: Cassen, B. and Saussay, P. de la (eds) *Le Monde vu de l'Europe*, Paris: Economica.

Jackson, M. (1991) *An Introduction to Industrial Relations*, London: Routledge.

Jacoby, N. (1974) *Multinational Oil*, New York: Macmillan.

Jessop, B. (1991) 'Regulation theory, post-Fordism and the state: more than a reply to Werner Bonefeld', in: Bonefeld, W. and Holloway, J. (eds) *Post-Fordism and Social Form: A Marxist Debate on the Post-Fordist State*, Basingstoke: Macmillan.

Johnson, C. (1982) *MITI and the Japanese Miracle: The Growth of Industrial Policy, 1925–1975*, Tokyo: Tuttle.

Jones, B. (1994) 'Globalisation, regionalisation and the political economy of the European Community: empirical and theoretical issues', paper prepared for the 22nd annual ECPR Conference on: 'The Single Market and Global Economic Integration', 18–22 April, Madrid.

Jones, D. (1989) 'A second look at the European motor industry', paper presented to the International Motor Vehicle Program, International Policy Forum, May, Acapulco.

Jong, H.W. de (1985) 'Industriepolitiek: een lege doos', *Economisch Statistische Berichten* 27 February: 192–7.

—— (ed.) (1993) *The Structure of European Industry*, Dordrecht: 3rd revised edn, Kluwer Academic Publishers.

Julius, D.A. (1990) *Global Companies and Public Policies: The Growing Challenge of Foreign Direct Investment*, London: The Royal Institute of International Affairs/Pinter Publishers.

Junne, G. (1984a) *Der strukturpolitische Wettlauf zwischen den kapitalistischen Industrieländern*, Politische Vierteljahresschrift, XXV: 134–55.

—— (1984b) 'Het Amerikaanse defensiebeleid: een substituut voor industriepolitiek?', *Internationale Spectator* July, xxxviii–7: 419–27.

—— (1987) 'Automation in the north: consequences for developing countries' exports', in: Caporaso, J. (ed.) *A Changing International Division of Labour*, London: Francis Pinter.

—— (1990a) 'Managementstrategien und Standortwahl', in: Welzmüller, R. (hrsg)

Marktaufteilung und Standortpoker in Europa, Köln: Bund Verlag, Europahandbuch für Arbeitnehmer, Band III, pp. 84–99.

—— (1990b) 'Theorien über Konflikte und Kooperation zwischen Kapitalistischen Industrieländern', in: Rittberger, V. (ed.) *Theorien der Internationalen Beziehungen, Bestandsaufnahme und Forschungsperspektiven*, Opladen: Westdeutscher Verlag, pp. 353–71.

Junne, G. and Nour, S. (1974) *Internationale Abhängigkeiten, Fremdbestimmung und Ausbeutung als Regelfall internationaler Beziehungen*, Frankfurt am Main: Fischer Athenäum Taschenbücher.

Kaplinsky, R. (1985) 'Electronic-based automation technologies and the onset of systemofacture: implications for Third World manufacturing', *World Development* 13(3): 423–40.

—— (1990) 'Is, and What is, Post-Fordism?', in: Schulze, P. and Willman, J. (eds) *Post-Fordism*, London: Friedrich Ebert Foundation, Occasional Papers, 1.

Kato, Y. (1990) 'Trends in trade at the outset of the 1990s', *Economic Eye*, Winter: 24–6.

Katzenstein, P. (ed.) (1978) *Between Power and Plenty: Foreign Economic Policies of Advanced Industrial States*, Madison: University of Wisconsin Press.

—— (1985) *Small States in World Markets: Industrial Policy in Europe*, Ithaca, NY / London: Cornell University Press.

Keizai Koho Center (1990, 1991, 1994) *Japan: An International Comparison*, Tokyo: Japan Institute for Social and Economic Affairs.

Keller, M. (1993) *Collision; GM, Toyota, Volkswagen and the Race to Own the 21st Century*, New York: Currency Doubleday.

Kennedy, P. (1987) *The Rise and Fall of the Great Powers: Economic Change and Military Conflict from 1500 to 2000*, New York: Random House.

Kenney, M. and Florida, R. (1988) 'Beyond mass production: production and the Labor Process in Japan', *Politics and Society* 16(1): 121–58.

—— (1993) *Beyond Mass Production. The Japanese System and its Transfer to the U.S.*, New York: Oxford University Press.

Keohane, R. (1984) *After Hegemony*, Princeton, NJ: Princeton University Press.

Keohane, R. and Nye, J. (1977) *Power and Interdependence: World Politics in Transition*, Boston: Little, Brown and Company.

Kern, H. and Schumann, M. (1984) *Das Ende der Arbeitsteilung Rationalisieuring in der industriellen Produktion*, Munich: C.H. Beck Verlag.

Kester, W.C. (1991) *Japanese Takeovers: The Global Contest for Corporate Control*, Boston, MA: Harvard Business School.

Kitschelt, H. (1991) 'Industrial governance structures, innovation strategies, and the case of Japan: sectoral or cross-national comparative analysis?' *International Organization* 45, Autumn: 453–93.

Kleinknecht, A. and Reijnen, J. (1991) 'More evidence on the undercounting of small firms in R&D', *Research Policy* 20: 579–87.

Kobayashi, N. (1985) 'The patterns of management style developing in Japanese multinationals in the 1990s', in: Takamiya, S. and Thurley, K. (eds) *Japan's Emerging Multinationals: An International Comparison of Policies and Practices*, Tokyo: University of Tokyo Press, pp. 229–64.

Kogut, B., Shan, W. and Walker, G. (1990) *The Structure of an Industry: Cooperative Agreements in the Biotechnology Industry*, Paper for the Workshop 'On the Socio-Economics of Inter-Firm Cooperation', University of Berlin, 11–13 June.

Kohler-Koch, B. (1994) *Regionalization and the Future of International Governance*, Paper prepared for presentation at the symposium on 'European Integration-South Asian Cooperation', Colombo, 22–23 January.

Kol, J. and Mennes, L. (1989) 'Moderne Handelstheorieën en Implicaties voor de

Handelspolitiek', in: *Export: Preadviezen van de Koninklijke Vereniging voor de Staathuishoudkunde 1989*, Leiden: Stenfert Kroese, pp. 1–20.

Kolko, J. (1990) *Restructuring the World Economy*, New York: Pantheon Books.

Krasner, S. (1978) *Defending the National Interest*, Princeton, NJ: Princeton University Press.

Krugman, P. (ed.) (1986) *Strategic Trade Policy and the New International Economics*, Cambridge, MA: MIT Press.

Lafeber, W. (1980) *America, Russia and the Cold War*, 4th edn, New York/Chichester: John Wiley.

Lambooy, J. (1991) 'Company and environment: a strategic relation', (in Dutch) in: Jagers, H. and Limvers, P. (eds) *The Tension between Strategy, Structure and Culture* (in Dutch), proceedings of symposium held on 6 June, Amsterdam: Stichting Instituut voor Bedrijfseconomie.

Lang, T. and Hines, C. (1993) *The New Protectionism: Protecting the Future Against Free Trade*, New York: New Press.

Latouche, D. (1992) *The New Continentalism: Prospects for Regional Intergration in North America*, Brussels: Commission of the European Communities/Monitor-Fast, FOP 314.

Lehner, F. (1991), *Synthesis Report on Anthropocentric Production Systems*, report, Brussels: FAST.

Levitt, T. (1983) 'The globalization of markets', *Harvard Business Review* May/June: 92–102.

Lipietz, A. (1982) 'Towards global Fordism?', *New Left Review* 133, May/June: 33–47.

—— (1987) *Mirages and Miracles: The Global Crisis of Fordism*, London: Verso.

—— (1992) *Towards a New Economic Order. Postfordism, Ecology and Democracy*, New York: Oxford University Press.

Lipsey, R. (1993), 'Comments to Richard Doner', in: Frankel, J. and Kahler, M. (eds) *Regionalism and Rivalry; Japan and the United States in Pacific Asia*, Chicago/London: University of Chicago Press.

Lodge, G. (1987) 'Introduction: ideology and country analysis', in: Lodge, G.C. and Vogel, E.F. (eds) *Ideology and National Competitiveness: An Analysis of Nine Countries*, Boston, MA: Harvard Business School Press.

Lorange, P. and Roos, J. (1992) *Strategic Alliances: Formation, Implementation and Evolution*, Cambridge, MA: Blackwell.

Low, P. (1993) *Trading Free: The GATT and the US Trade Policy*, New York: Twentieth Century Fund Press.

Lukes, S. (1974) *Power: A Radical View*, London: Macmillan Press.

Lundvall, B.Å. (1988) 'Innovation as an interactive process: from user-producer interaction to the national system of innovation', in: Dosi, G., Freeman, C., Nelson, R., Silverberg, G. and Soete, L. (eds) *Technical Change and Economic Theory*, London: Pinter Publishers.

—— (ed.) (1992) *National Systems of Innovation: Toward a Theory of Innovation and Interactive Learning*, London: Pinter Publishers.

McGrew, A.G. (1992) 'Conceptualizing global politics', in McGrew, A.G., Lewis, P.G. *et al.* (eds) *Global Politics: Globalization and the Nation-State*, Cambridge: Polity Press.

McGrew, A.G., Lewis, P.G. *et al.* (eds) (1992) *Global Politics: Globalization and the Nation-State*, Cambridge: Polity Press.

McKeown, T. (1983) 'Hegemonic stability theory and the 19th century tariff levels in Europe', *International Organization* 37, Winter.

Macmillan, D. (1984) *The Japanese Industrial System*, Berlin: De Gruyter.

MacNeill, J., Winsemius, P. and Yakushiji, T. (1991) *Beyond Interdependence*, Oxford: Oxford University Press.

Madura, J. (1989) *Financial Markets and Institutions*, Saint Paul/New York: West Publishing Company.

Marion, M.F. van (1992) 'Liberal trade in Japan: the incompatibility issue', unpublished PhD thesis, University of Groningen.

Marshall, A. (1961) *Principles of Economics*, 9th edn, London: Macmillan.

Martijn, J.K. (1989) 'Real exchange rates and protectionism', *De Economist* 137(3): 328–50.

Mathews, J. (1989) *Age of Democracy: The Politics of Post-Fordism*, Melbourne: Oxford University Press.

Michalet, C.A. (1989) *Global Competition and its Implications for Firms*, Paris: Organization for Economic Cooperation and Development, DSTI/SPRI/89.7.

Milner, H. (1988) *Resisting Protectionism: Global Industries and the Politics of International Trade*, Princeton, NJ: Princeton University Press.

—— (1994) *The Domestic Political Economy of International Economic Cooperation: A Comparison of the NAFTA Accord and the Maastricht Treaty*, paper prepared for the 22nd annual ECPR Conference, 18–22 April, Madrid, Spain.

Mirabile, L. *et al.* (eds) (1990) *International Directory of Company Histories*, Volume II, Chicago, London: St James Press.

Miyashita, K. and Russell, D. (1994) *Keiretsu: Inside the Hidden Japanese Conglomerates*, New York: McGraw-Hill.

Mjøset, L. (1987) 'Nordic economies in the 1970s and 1980s', *International Organization* 41(3), Summer: 403–56.

—— (1990) *Comparing British and U.S. Hegemony: A Summary*, Contribution to the Conference 'After the Crisis', University of Amsterdam, 18–20 April.

—— (1992) *The Irish Economy in a Comparative Institutional Perspective*, Report No. 93, Dublin: National Economic and Social Council.

Modelski, G. (1972) *Principles of World Politics*, New York: Free Press.

—— (1978) 'The long cycle of global politics and the nation state', *Comparative Studies in Society and History* 20: 214–35.

Molle, W. (1993) 'Oil refineries and petrochemical industries: coping with the midlife crisis', in: de Jong, Henk (ed.) *The Structure of European Industry*, 3rd revised edn, Dordrecht: Kluwer Academic Publishers.

Morris, D. and Hergert, M. (1987) 'Strategic partnerships: a triad perspective', *Euro-Asia Business Review* 6(3), July: 16–19.

Morrison, A.J. Ricks, D.A. and Roth, K. (1992) 'Globalization versus regionalization: which way for the multinational?', *Organizational Dynamics* 19(3), Winter: 17–30.

Muldur, U. and Colombo, M. (1991) *La Globalisation: Mythe ou Réalité?*, Brussels: Commission of the European Communities/Monitor-FAST, FOP 273.

Mytelka, L. (ed.) (1991) *Strategic Partnerships: States, Firms and International Competition*, London: Pinter Publishers.

Naruse, T. (1991) 'Taylorism and Fordism in Japan', in: Morioka, K. (ed.) *Japanese Capitalism Today: Economic Structure and the Organization of Work*, International Journal of Political Economy, New York, Fall, 21, 3: 32–49.

National Research Council (1983) *The Race for the New Frontier: International Competition in Advances Technology*, New York: National Academy Press, Simon & Schuster.

Nelson, R. (1984) *High-Technology Policies: A Five Nation Comparison*, Washington/London: American Enterprise Institute, Studies in Economic Policy.

—— (1993) *National Systems of Innovation*, Oxford: Oxford University Press.

Nelson, R. and Winter, S. (1982) *An Evolutionary Theory of Economic Change*, Cambridge, MA: Belknap Press of Harvard University Press.

Neven, D., Nuttall, R. and Seabright, P. (1993) *Merger in Daylight: The Economics and Politics of European Merger Control*, London: Centre for Economic Policy Research.

Niehans, J. (1977) 'Benefits of multinational firms for a small parent economy: the case of Switzerland', in: Agmon, T. and Kindleberger, C. (eds) *Multinationals from Small Countries*, Cambridge, MA: MIT Press.

Nishigushi, T. (1989a) 'Strategic dualism: an alternative in industrial societies', PhD thesis, Nuffield College.

—— (1989b), 'Is JIT really JIT?', paper for the IMVP, International Policy Forum, Acapulco, 7–10 May.

Nonaka, I. (1990) 'Managing globalization as a self-renewing process: experiences of Japanese MNCs', in: Bartlett, C., Doz, Y. and Hedlund, G. (eds) *Managing the Global Firm*, London: Routledge.

Oberender, P. and Rüter, G. (1993) 'The steel industry: a crisis of adaptation', in: de Jong, H. (ed.) *The Structure of European Industry*, 3rd revised edn, Dordrecht: Kluwer Academic Publishers.

Odell, J. (1990) 'Understanding international trade policies: an emerging synthesis', *World Politics* October: 139–67.

Odell, J. and Willett, T. (eds) (1993) *International Trade Policies: Gains from Exchange between Economics and Political Science*, Ann Arbor: University of Michigan Press.

OECD (Organisation for Economic Cooperation and Development) (1981) *Economic and Ecological Interdependence*, Paris: OECD.

—— (1983) *Positive Adjustment Policies: Managing Structural Change*, Report, February, Paris: OECD.

—— (1985) *Structural Adjustment and Multinational Enterprises*, Report, November, Paris: OECD.

—— (1988) *Structural Adjustment and Economic Performance*, Report, March, Paris: OECD.

—— (1991) *Strategic Industries in a Global Economy: Policy Issues for the 1990s*, Report, Paris: OECD.

—— (1992) *Technology and the Economy: The Key Relationships*, Technology/ Economy Programme (TEP), Paris: OECD.

—— (1993) *Obstacles to Trade and Competition*, Paris: OECD.

Office of Technology Assessment (1991) *Global Arms Trade*, Washington DC: Congress of the United States.

Ohmae, K. (1985) *Triad Power: The Coming Shape of Global Competition*, New York: Free Press.

—— (1987) *Beyond National Borders: Reflections on Japan and the World*, Homewood, Illinois: Dow Jones-Irwin.

—— (1990) *The Borderless World: Power and Strategy in the Interlinked Economy*, London: Fontana.

Oliver, N. and Wilkinson, B. (1988) *The Japanization of British Industry*, London: Basil Blackwell.

Olson, M. (1982) *The Rise and Decline of Nations*, New Haven, CT: Princeton University Press.

O'Siochrú, S. (1993) *Global Sustainability, Telecommunications and Science and Technology Policy*, Brussels: Commission of the European Communities/ Monitor-Fast, FOP 329.

Overbeek, H. (1990) *Global Capitalism and National Decline: The Thatcher Decade in Perspective*, London/New York: Unwin Hyman.

Parsons, T. (1957) 'The distribution of power in American society', *World Politics* 10, October: 123–43.

Patel, P. and Pavitt, K. (1991) 'Large firms in the production of the world's technology: an important case of "non-globalisation"', *Journal of International Business Studies* 1: 1–21.

—— (1994) 'The nature and economic importance of the national innovation systems', *STI Review* (OECD) no. 14: 9–32.

Pateman, C. (1979) *Participation and Democratic Theory*, Cambridge: Cambridge University Press.

Pavitt, K. (1992) 'Internationalisation of technological innovation', *Science and Public Policy* 19(2).

Peláez, E. and Holloway, J. (1991) 'Learning to bow: post-Fordism and techno-logical determinism', in: Bonefeld, W. and Holloway, J. (eds) *Post-Fordism and Social Form: A Marxist Debate on the Post-Fordist State*, Basingstoke: Macmillan, pp. 135–45.

Perez, C. (1983) 'Structural change and the assimilation of new technologies in the economic and social system', *Futures*, October: 357–75.

—— (1985) 'Microelectronics and world structural change: new perspectives for developing countries', *World Development* 13, March: 441–63.

Perez, C. and Soete, L. (1988) 'Catching up in technology: entry barriers and windows of opportunity', in: Dosi, G., Freeman, C., Nelson, R., Silverberg, G. and Soete, L. (eds) *Technical Change and Economic Theory*, London: Pinter Publishers.

Peters, T. (1992) *Liberation Management: Necessary Disorganization for the Nanosec-ond Nineties*, New York: Fawcett Columbine.

Petrella, R. (1989) 'La Mondialisation de la Technologie et de l'Economie', *Futuribles*, September: 3–25.

Pfeffer, J. (1988) 'The institutional function of management', reprint with deletions from original 1976 publication, in: Quinn, J.B. and Mintzberg, H. (eds) *The Strategy Process*, London: Prentice Hall International.

—— (1992) *Managing with Power: Politics and Influence in Organizations*, Boston, MA: Harvard Business School Press.

Pfeffer, J. and Salancik, G. (1978) *The External Control of Organizations: A Resource Dependence Perspective*, New York: Harper and Row.

Pijl, K. van der (1984) *The Making of an Atlantic Ruling Class*, London: Verso.

—— (1992) *Wereldorde en Machtspolitiek: Visies of de Internationale Betrekkingen van Dante tot Fukuyama*, Amsterdam: Het Spinhuis.

Piore, M. and Sabel, C. (1984) *The Second Industrial Divide: Possibilities for Prosperity*, New York: Basic Books.

Pomfret, R. (1989) 'Voluntary export restraints in the presence of a monopoly power', *Kyklos* 42(1): 61–72.

Porter, M. (1980) *Competitive Strategy*, New York: Free Press.

—— (1985) *Competitive Advantage: Creating and Sustaining Superior Performance*, New York: Free Press.

—— (1986) 'Competition in global industries, a conceptual framework', in Porter, M.E. (ed.) *Competition in Global Industries*, Boston, MA: Harvard Business School Press, pp. 15–60.

—— (1990) *The Competitive Advantage of Nations*, New York: Free Press.

Porter, M. and Fuller, M. (1986) 'Coalitions and global strategy', in: Porter, M. (ed.) *Competition in Global Industries*, Boston, MA: Harvard Business School Press.

Pot, F. (1988) *Payment Systems Bargaining in the Netherlands 1850–1987* (in Dutch), Leiden: NIPG/TNO.

Poulantzas, N. (1978) *L'Etat, le Pouvoir, le Socialisme*, Paris: Presses Universitaires de France.

Powell, W. (1990) 'Neither market nor hierarchy: network forms of organization', *Research in Organizational Behavior* 12: 295–336.

Prahalad, C.K. and Doz, Y. (1987) *The Multinational Mission: Balancing Local Demands and Global Vision*, New York: Free Press.

Prahalad, C.K. and Hamel, G. (1990) 'The core competence of the corporation', *Harvard Business Review*, May/June, 68(3): 79–91.

Prebisch, R. (1964) *Towards a New Trade Policy for Development*, report by the Secretary General of UNCTAD, New York: United Nations.

Prestowitz, C. (1988) *Trading Places: How We Are Giving Our Future to Japan and How to Reclaim It*, New York: Basic Books.

Raiffa, H. (1982) *The Art and Science of Negotiation*, Cambridge, MA: Harvard University Press.

Reich, R. (1983) *The Next American Frontier*, New York: Times Books.

——(1991) *The Work of Nations: Preparing Ourselves for 21st Century Capitalism*, New York: Alfred Knopf.

Richardson, J.D. (1989) 'Empirical research on trade liberalisation with imperfect competition: a survey', *OECD Economic Studies* 12: 7–50.

Rittberger, V. (ed.) (1990) *International Regimes in East-West Politics*, London/New York: Pinter Publishers.

Rockart, J.F. and Short, J.E. (1989) 'IT in the 1990s: managing organizational interdependence', *Sloan Management Review*, Winter:7–17.

Roobeek, A. (1987) *De Rol van Technologie in de Ekonomische theorievorming*, Amsterdam: Scheltema, Holkema en Vermeulen.

——(1989) '*Een race zonder finish*', PhD thesis, Amsterdam: Free University.

—— (1990) *Beyond the Technology Race: An Analysis of Technology Policy in Seven Industrial Countries*, Amsterdam: Elsevier Science Publishers.

Root, F. (1988) 'Some taxonomies of international cooperative arrangements', in: Contractor, F. and Lorange, P. (eds) *Cooperative Strategy and International Business*, Lexington, MA: Lexington Books.

Rosecrance, R. (1986) *The Rise of the Trading State: Commerce and Conquest in the Modern World*, New York: Basic Books.

Rosenberg, N. (1982) *Inside the Black Box: Technology and Economics*, Cambridge: Cambridge University Press.

Rothschild, K. (1971) 'Introduction' in: Rothschild, K. (ed.) *Power in Economics: Selected Readings*, Harmondsworth: Penguin.

Rothwell, R. and Zegveld, W. (1985) *Reindustrialisation and Technology*, London: Longman.

Rugman, A., Lecraw, D. and Booth, L. (1986) *International Business: Firm and Environment*, New York: McGraw-Hill International Editions.

Ruigrok, W. (1990) 'De beperkte mondialisering van de Europese industrie: handelspolitieke consequenties', *Internationale Spectator*, 44(5), May: 304–11.

Ruigrok, W. and Tulder, R. van, with the assistance of Geert Baven (1991) *Cars and Complexes: Globalisation versus Global Localisation Strategies in the World Car Industry*, Brussels: Commission of the European Communities/Monitor-FAST, FOP 285.

Ruivenkamp, G. (1989) '*De invoering van biotechnologie in de agro-industriële productie-keten: de overgang naar een nieuwe arbeidsorganisatie*', PhD thesis, Utrecht: Van Arkel.

Russett, B. (1970) 'Interdependence and capabilities for European cooperation', *Journal of Common Market Studies* IX (2): 143–50.

Russett, B. and Starr, H. (1992) *World Politics, The Menu for Choice*, 4th edn, New York: W.H. Freeman and Company.

Sabel, C., Kern, H. and Herrigel, G. (1989) 'Collaborative manufacturing: new supplier relations in the automobile industry and the redefinition of the industrial corporation', paper presented at International Motor Vehicle Program, International Policy Forum, May, Acapulco.

Sachwald, F. (ed.) (1993a) *L'Europe et la Globalisation; Acquisitions et Accords dans L'industrie*, Paris: Masson, Institut Français des Relations Internationales.

——(ed.) (1993b) *Les Entreprises Japonaises en Europe. Motivations et stratégies*, Paris: Masson, Institut Français des Relations Internationales.

——(ed.) (1994) *Les Défis de la Mondialisation. Innovation et Concurrence*, Paris: Masson, Institut Français des Relations Internationales.

Saeki, M. (1992) 'New Forces in Global Strategies: The Ecology of Competition for Japanese Corporations', London: Strategic Management Society, Annual Conference.

Samuels, R. (1989) 'Consuming for production: Japanese national security, nuclear fuel procurement, and the domestic economy', *International Organization* 43(4), Autumn: 625–46.

Sandholz, W., Borrus, M., Zysman, J., Conca, K., Stowsky, J., Vogel, S. and Weber, S. (1992) *The Highest Stakes, The Economic Foundations of the Next Security System*, A BRIE Project, New York: Oxford University Press.

Sassen, S. (1992) 'The cost of growth: in Japan, telltale signs of social distress', *International Herald Tribune* 11 January.

Sayer, A. and Walker, R. (1992) *The New Social Economy: Reworking the Division of Labor*, Cambridge, MA/Oxford: Blackwell.

Schelling, T. (1956) 'An essay on bargaining', *American Economic Review* 46: 281–306.

Schenk, H. (ed.) (1987) *Industrie- en Technologiebeleid*, Groningen: Wolters-Noordhoff.

——(1993) *Mergers: Size, Scope and Trends. An International Inventorisation* (in Dutch), Management Report series, no. 127, Rotterdam: Rotterdam School of Management, Erasmus University.

Schenk, H., Renirie, M., Koene, R. and Chan, C.W. (1994) 'Leading manufacturers in the Common Market', mimeo, Rotterdam: GRASP, Erasmus University, Rotterdam.

Scherer, F.M. (1992) *International High-Technology Competition*, Cambridge, MA: Harvard University Press.

Schlupp, F., Nour, S. and Junne, G. (1973) 'Zur theorie und ideologie internationaler interdependenz', *Politische Vierteljahresschrift*, Sonderheft 5: Internationale Beziehungen als System, Opladen: Westdeutscher Verlag: 246–307.

Schonberger, R. (1982) *Japanese Manufacturing Techniques: Nine Hidden Lessons in Simplicity*, New York: Free Press.

Scitovsky, T. (1985) 'Economic development in Taiwan and South Korea', *Food Research Institute Studies* 19(3): 214–64.

Scott, J. (1979) *Corporations, Classes and Capitalism*, London: Hutchinson.

Sen, G. (1984) *The Military Origins of Industrialisation and International Trade Rivalry*, London: Frances Pinter.

Senghaas, D. (1982) *Von Europa lernen: Entwicklungsgeschichtliche Betrachtungen*, Frankfurt/Main: Edition Suhrkamp.

Servan-Schreiber (1967) *Le Défi Americain*, Paris: Denoël.

Shepherd, W. (1989) *The Economics of Industrial Organization*, 2nd edn, Englewood Cliffs, NY: Prentice-Hall International.

Sideri, S. (1970) *Trade and Power: Informal Colonialism in Anglo-Portuguese Relations*, Rotterdam: Rotterdam University Press.

Singer, D. (1961) 'The level-of-analysis problem in international relations', in: Knorr, K. and Verba, S. (eds), *The International System*, Princeton NJ: Princeton University Press.

Smith, A. (1983) *The Wealth of Nations*, London: Penguin (with an Introduction by Andrew Skinner).

Smith, M. (1992) 'Modernization, globalization and the nation-state', in: McGrew,

A.G. and Lewis, P. *et al. Globalization and the Nation-State*, Cambridge: Polity Press.

Sobel, R. (1983) *IBM, Colossus in Transition*, Toronto: Bantam Books.

Soete, L. (1991) *Technology in a Changing World: Policy Synthesis of the OECD Technology Economy Programme*, MERIT/TEP mimeo, Maastricht.

Sölvell, Ö., Zander, I. and Porter, M. (1991) *Advantage Sweden*, Stockholm: Norstedt Juridikförlag.

Stalk, G., Evans, P. and Shulman, L. (1992) 'Competing on capabilities', *Harvard Business Review*, March/April: 57–69.

Stegemann, K. (1989) 'Policy rivalry among industrial states: what can we learn from models of strategic trade policy?', *International Organization* 43(1), Winter: 73–100.

Stern, L. and El-Ansary, A. (1988) *Marketing Channels*, 3rd edn, Englewood Cliffs, NY: Prentice-Hall International.

Stoop, S. (1992) *De Sociale Fabriek: Sociale Politiek bij Philips Eindhoven, Bayer Leverkussen en Hoogovens IJmuiden*, Utrecht: Stenfert Kroese.

Stopford, J. and Strange, S. with Henley, J. (1991) *Rival States, Rival Firms: Competition for World Market Shares*, Cambridge: Cambridge University Press.

Storper, M. and Walker, R. (1989) *The Capitalist Imperative: Territory, Technology, and Industrial Growth*, Oxford: Basil Blackwell.

Strange, S. (1985) 'Protectionism and world politics', *International Organization* 39(2), Spring: 233–59.

——(1986) *Casino Capitalism*, Oxford: Basil Blackwell.

Stranger, S. (1990) *Satisfaction Guaranteed: The Making of the American Mass Market*, New York: Pantheon.

Streeck, W. (1988) *Kollektive Arbeitsbeziehungen und Industrieller Wandel: das Beispiel der Automobilindustrie*, Berlin: Wissenschaftzentrum.

Sweezy, P. (1953), 'Interest groups in the American economy', in: *The Present as History: Essays and Reviews on Capitalism and Socialism*, New York/London: Monthly Review Press.

Takasc, W. (1981) 'Pressures for Protectionism: an empirical analysis', *Economic Inquiry* 19, October: 687–93.

Taylor, M. and Thrift, N. (1982) *The Geography of Multinationals: Studies in the Spatial Development and Economic Consequences of Multinational Corporations*, London: Croom Helm.

Teece, D. (1985) 'Multinational enterprise, internal governance and industrial organization', *American Economic Review* 75(2): 233–8.

——(1988) 'Technological change and the nature of the firm', in: Dosi, G., Freeman, C., Nelson, R. and Soete, L. (eds) *Technical Change and Economic Theory*, London: Pinter Publishers.

Tharakan, P.K.M. (ed.) (1983) *Intra-industry Trade: Empirical and Methodological Aspects*, Amsterdam: North-Holland.

Therborn, G. (1980) *The Ideology of Power and the Power of Ideology*, London: Verso.

Thurow, L. (1980) *The Zero-Sum Society: Distribution and the Possibilities for Economic Change*, New York: Basic Books.

Todd, D. and Simpson, J. (1986) *The World Aircraft Industry*, Dover, MA: Auburn House Publ. Co.

Tsurumi, Y. with Tsurumi, R.R. (1984) *Sogoshosha, Engines of Export-Based Growth*, revised edn, Boston, MA: Institute for Research on Public Policy.

Tudyka, K. (ed.) (1974) *Multinationale Konzerne und Gewerkschaftsstrategie*, Hamburg: Hoffmann und Campe Verlag.

Tulder, R. van, with the assistance of Eric van Empel (1984) *European Multinationals in the Semiconductor Industry: Their Position in Microprocessors*, pilot study for the Institute for Research on Multinationals, Geneva, October.

Tulder, R. van (1987) 'Bigger business and the state: European high-tech multi-nationals and national innovation policies', *Public Policy and Administration* 2(2), July: 192–228.

——(1989) 'Studies of small industrial countries and economic and technological development', in: Tulder, R. van (ed.) *Small Industrial Countries and Economic and Technological Development*, The Hague: Staatsuitgeverij, Small Industrial Countries Research Association (SICRA), Netherlands Organisation for Technology Assessment (NOTA), pp. 9–33.

——(1990) 'Dutch dilemmas: the Netherlands and European technology programmes', in: Schregardus, P. and Telkamp, G. (eds), *Autonomy and Interdependence: International Affairs through a Dutch Prism*, special issues of *Internationale Spectator*, 44, 11, November: 671–9.

——(1992) 'The misleading concept of a meta-paradigm shift', *Issues in Strategic Management: Strategic Grammar, Management Report Series*, no. 116, Rotterdam: Erasmus University Rotterdam.

——(1993) *Skill Sheets*, 3rd revised edn, Rotterdam: Erasmus University.

Tulder, R. van and Junne, G. (1988) *European Multinationals and Core Technologies*, Chichester/London: Wiley & Sons.

Turner, L. (1978) *Oil Companies in the International System*, London: George Allen & Unwin, The Royal Institute of International Affairs.

Tyson, L. (1992) *Who's Bashing Whom? Trade Conflict in High-Technology Industries*, Washington DC: Institute for International Economics.

UNCTAD (United Nations Conference on Trade and Development) (1992) *Handbook of International Trade and Development Statistics*, New York: UNCTAD

——(1993) *World Investment Report 1993: Transnational Corporations and Integrated International Production*, New York: UNCTAD, Programme on Transnational Corporations.

——(1994) *World Investment Report 1994: Transnational Corporations, Employment and the Workplace*, Geneva: UN Publications.

UNCTC (United Nations Centre on Transnational Corporations) (1991) *World Investment Report 1991: The Triad in Foreign Direct Investment*, New York: United Nations.

UNIDO (United Nations Industrial Development Organisation) (1979) *Structural Changes in Industry*, Vienna.

United Nations (1993) *World Investment Report 1993: Transnational Corporations and Integrated International Production*, New York: United Nations Conference on Trade and Development, Programme on Transnational Corporations.

United States International Trade Commission (1985) *Foreign Industrial Targeting and its effects on U.S. Industries; Phase III: Brazil, Canada, The Republic of Korea, Mexico, and Taiwan*, Washington DC: USITC Publication 1632.

Vandermerwe, S. and Rada, J. (1988) 'Servitization of business: adding value by adding services', *European Management Journal* 6, Autumn: 314–24.

Vernon, R. (1971) *Sovereignty at Bay: The Multinational Spread of US Enterprises*, New York: Basic Books.

——(ed.) (1974) *Big Business and the State: Changing Relations in Western Europe*, Cambridge, MA: Harvard University Press.

Viner, A. (1988) *The Financial Samurai: The Emerging Power of Japanese Money*, London: Kogan Page.

Vogel, D. (1987) 'Government–industry relations in the United States: an overview', in: Wilks, S. and Wright, M. (eds) *Comparative Government–Industry Relations: Western Europe, the United States and Japan*, Oxford: Clarendon Press, pp. 91–117.

Vogel, S. (1992) 'The power behind 'spin-ons': the military implications of Japan's commercial technology', in: Sandholz, W. *et al.* *The Highest Stakes, The Economic*

Foundations of the Next Security System, A Brie Project, New York: Oxford University Press, pp. 55–81.

Voorzee, J. (1994) '*Internationale samenwerking en conflict in de civiele vliegtuigindustrie*', MA thesis, University of Amsterdam, Department of International Relations and Public International Law.

Vroey, M. de (1984) 'A regulation approach interpretation of contemporary crisis', *Capital and Class* 23.

Walker, R. (1989) *Regulation, Flexible Specialisation and Capitalist Development: The Forces of Production in the Dynamics of Industrial Change*, Paper for Cardiff Symposium on Regulation, Innovation and Spatial Development, University of Wales, 13–15 September.

Wallensteen, P. (1973) *Structure and War: On International Relations 1920–1968*, Uppsala: Political Sciences Association.

Wallerstein, I. (1980) *The Modern World System II: Mercantilism and the Consolidation of the European World-Economy, 1600–1750*, New York: Academic Press.

——(1984) *The Politics of the World-Economy: The States, The Movements and The Civilizations*, Cambridge: Cambridge University Press/Paris: Editions de la Maison des Sciences de l'Homme.

Walton, R. and McKersie, R. (1965) *A Behavioral Theory of Labor Negotiations: An Analysis of a Social Interaction System*, New York: McGraw Hill.

Waltz, K. (1970) 'The myth of national interdependence', in: Kindleberger, C. (ed.) *The International Corporation – A Symposium*, Cambridge, MA: MIT Press.

Wassenberg, A. (1990) 'Strategic collaboration: mixed motives, mixed blessing' (in Dutch), in special issue of *International Marketing Magazine*, pp. 5–10.

——(1994) *Strategische Allianties: Feiten en Ficties*, Erasmus University Rotterdam, ERASM Management Report Series, 168.

——(forthcoming) *Industrial Diplomacy: The Unfolding of Power in Industrial Networks*, Erasmus University Rotterdam: GRASP.

Watanabe, S. (1993) 'Searching for a global management model: the case of Japanese multinationals', in: Humbert, M. (ed.) *The Impact of Globalisation on Europe's Firms and Industries*, London: Pinter Publishers, pp. 229–38.

Webber, D., Moon, J. and Richardson, J. (1984) *State Promotion of Information Technology in France, Britain and West Germany*, Glasgow: Strathclyde Papers on Government and Politics, no. 33.

Weiss, L. (1988) *Creating Capitalism: The State and Small Business since 1945*, Oxford: Basil Blackwell.

——(1992) 'The politics of industrial organisation: a comparative view', in: Marceau, J. (ed.) *Reworking the World: Organizations, Technologies and Cultures in Comparative Perspective*, Berlin: Walter de Gruyter.

Wennekes, W. (1993) *De Aartsvaders. Grondleggers van het Nederlandse Bedrijfsleven*, Amsterdam/Antwerp: Uitgeverij Atlas.

Wilks, S. (1989) 'Corporate strategy and state support in the European motor industry', in: Hancher, L. and Moran, M. (eds) *Capitalism, Culture and Economic Regulation*, Oxford: Clarendon Press.

Wilks, S. and Wright, M. (eds) (1987) *Comparative Government–Industry Relations: Western Europe, the United States, and Japan*, Oxford: Clarendon Press.

Williamson, O. (1975) *Markets and Hierarchies: Analysis and Antitrust Implications*, New York: Free Press.

——(1979) 'Transaction cost economics: the governance of contractual relations', *Journal of Law and Economics* 22: 233–61.

——(1990) 'The firm as a nexus of treaties: an introduction', in: Aoki, M., Gustafsson, B. and Williamson, O. (eds) *The Firm as a Nexus of Treaties*, London: Sage Publications.

Williamson, O. and Ouchi, W. (1981) 'The markets and hierarchies perspective:

origins, implications, prospects', in: Francis, A., Turk, J. and Willman, P. (eds) (1983), *Power, Efficiency and Institutions: A Critical Appraisal of the 'Markets and Hierarchies Paradigm'*, London: Heinemann.

Wolfe, D. (1987) *Socio-political Contexts of Technological Change: Some Conceptual Models*, paper presented to the Conference 'Understanding Technological Change', University of Edinburgh, revised version.

Wolferen, K. van (1989) *The Enigma of Japanese Power*, London: Macmillan.

Womack, J.P., Jones, D.T. and Roos, D. (1990) *The Machine that Changed the World*, New York: Rawson Associates.

Woolcock, S., Hart, J. and Ven, H. van der (1985) *Interdependence in the Post-Multilateral era: Trends in U.S.–European Trade Relations*, Center for International Affairs, Boston, MA: Harvard University, University Press of America.

De Woot, P., Doz, Y., Haspeslagh, P. and Lorenzoni, G. (1990) *Les Enjeux de la Croissance Externe*, Brussels: Commission of the European Communities, FAST programme.

World Bank (1989, 1990) *World Development Report*, New York: Oxford University Press.

World Commission on Environment and Development (1987) *Our Common Future*, Oxford/New York: Oxford University Press.

Wurff, R. van der (1992) 'Neo-Liberalism in Germany? *The "Wende" in Perspective*', unpublished manuscript, University of Amsterdam, Department of International Relations.

Yergin, D. (1991) *The Prize; The Epic Quest for Oil, Money and Power*, New York: Simon and Schuster/Pocket Books.

Young, M. (1992) 'A Framework for Successful Adoption and Performance of Japenese Manufacturing Practices in the United States', *Academy of Management Review* 17 (4): 677–700.

Zysman, J. (1983) *Governments, Markets and Growth: Financial Systems and the Politics of Industrial Change*, Ithaca, N Y: Cornell University Press.

Index